Penguin Education

Aggregate Investment

Edited by J. F. Helliwell

Penguin Modern Economics Readings

General Editor

B. J. McCormick

Aggregate Investment

Selected Readings

Edited by J. F. Helliwell

Penguin Education

Penguin Education
A Division of Penguin Books Ltd,
Harmondsworth, Middlesex, England
Penguin Books Inc, 7110 Ambassador Road,
Baltimore, Maryland 21207, USA
Penguin Books Australia Ltd,
Ringwood, Victoria, Australia
Penguin Books Canada Ltd,
41 Steelcase Road West,
Markham, Ontario, Canada
Penguin Books (N.Z.) Ltd, 182-190 Wairau Road,
Auckland 10, New Zealand

First published 1976
This selection copyright © J. F. Helliwell, 1976
Introduction and notes copyright © J. F. Helliwell, 1976
Copyright acknowledgements for items in this volume
will be found on page 333

Made and printed in Great Britain by
Richard Clay (The Chaucer Press) Ltd,
Bungay, Suffolk
Set in Monotype Times

Contents

Introduction

These readings are selected from the large number of quantitative studies of aggregate business fixed-investment published between 1962 and 1972. The volume is intended for undergraduates requiring specialized reading in investment behaviour, while we hope it will also be of some use to post-graduates and researchers. The potential value of the book to those concerned with aggregate investment behaviour needs no explanation. For specialists in other subject areas, the selection may be helpful in illustrating a number of basic issues that arise generally in applied econometrics. Investment has been perhaps the most active subject area for applied econometrics over the past decade, so that we can expect some of the methods and models discussed in this volume to find further application in other subject areas.

The first selection is a survey of issues written especially for this volume. It removes the need for any introductory discussion of trends in the theory and estimation of investment equations. This introduction is therefore merely a reader's guide to the volume. The survey of issues may be read either at the beginning, to get the lay of the land, or at the end, to help place the issues in perspective. A compromise between these two extremes is probably preferable, the more detailed parts of the survey being left until the reader has some familiarity with several of the readings.

The survey of issues comprises Part One of the volume. The twelve selections that follow the survey are divided into five further parts, each of which has a brief introduction. The order of the parts, and of the papers within each part, is more or less the chronological order in which the studies were undertaken. The volume concludes with some suggestions for further reading and indexes by author and by subject.

Part Two uses a single paper by de Leeuw to represent the eclectic approach to investment equations that was common prior to the mid-1960s. This approach emphasizes the multiplicity of factors impinging on investment decisions, and does not use a precisely defined maximizing framework to derive the algebraic form of the estimating equation. Similarly, there are few theoretical constraints placed on the shape of lag distributions, and the shapes are generally assumed to be fixed by technical factors.

By contrast, Part Three contains two papers devoted to theoretical derivation of lag distributions that depend explicitly on the costs of adjusting the capital stock to a newly desired level. These papers are the only ones not embodying empirical work. The complexity of the issues raised in these, and other theoretical papers dealing with adjustment costs, helps to explain the lack of empirical studies that make more than casual use of adjustment cost conditions when explaining investment expenditure.

One of the hallmarks of investment studies during the 1960s has been the increasing use of explicit theoretical models to provide many constraints on the form and content of investment equations. Very prominent among such studies have been the many papers by Jorgenson and several collaborators based on a particular model of neoclassical profit-maximizing behaviour and a two-factor aggregate Cobb–Douglas production function. The two papers in this part, especially the one by Bischoff, emphasize the value of testing the various aspects of an investment theory separately, and incidentally reveal that substantial variations in results can frequently be due to supposedly inconsequential differences in data definitions or estimation periods. The relations between the reprinted papers and those of Jorgenson (who chose not to have any work reprinted in this volume) are discussed more fully in the survey of issues.

Part Five contains four papers in which aggregate investment equations are used to assess the direct impacts of tax policies intended to encourage investment spending. The first two papers, by Bischoff and by Coen, relate to investment and tax policy in the United States, while the second pair, by Feldstein and Flemming, and by King, apply to Britain.

Part Six (Further Developments) provides three examples of developments underway at the end of the decade under study. To complete this general introduction, it might be appropriate to include an editor's forecast of further developments over the next decade. The list is not in any special order:

1 Aggregate investment equations will be increasingly evaluated within the context of macroeconomic models. This will lead to less attention being paid to microeconomic theories based on perfect markets with instantaneous adjustment. The corresponding increase in emphasis will lie in the derivation of explicit non-price links between aggregate supply conditions and investment behaviour, and in the role of investment equations in the generation of macroeconomic fluctuations.

2 There will be further efforts to broaden the assumed aggregate technology to include a wider range of inputs, e.g. Reading 11; and outputs, e.g. Hall (1973).

3 The consideration of more factors and products will require the use of more flexible functional forms in which different pairs of factors can differ in the extent to which they are substitutable for one another. For examples, see Berndt and Christensen (1973), Christensen *et al.* (1973), and Diewert (1971).

4 Concentration on the substitutability of factors leads quite naturally to vintage models (e.g. Readings 7 and 10) in which factor substitution is assumed to be easier at the blueprint stage than thereafter. More developments may be expected here, especially as disaggregation by vintage helps to bypass the worst of the problems involved in treating capital as a homogeneous factor.

5 The productive roles of land and other natural resources will be taken more seriously, with many data complications and important consequences for equations explaining investment expenditure.

6 Investment studies in the past decade have concentrated on business investment, to the unfortunate exclusion of investment by governments and other non-commercial institutions. This is sure to be rectified, although it will be some time before there are explicit theories appropriately rich in behavioural and institutional detail.

7 Increasing complexity and detail of theoretical models will require more sophisticated and flexible estimation techniques, which will be rendered more efficient by systematic use of prior information about parameter values and lag shapes.

8 More attention may be paid to the expectations processes governing investment decisions (e.g. Reading 13). More accurate separation of expectations and expenditure lags will permit more appropriate estimation of the timing of the impacts of temporary and permanent changes in monetary and fiscal policies.

9 More attention will be paid to the economic determinants of scrapping and replacement decisions. Feldstein and Rothschild (1974) explain some of the consequences of specifying depreciation rates and replacement expenditures as economic variables. The end result may be gross investment equations that abandon any distinction between expansion and replacement (as in Reading 13) or include separately the determinants of replacement and expansion expenditure, e.g. Driehuis (1972).

The foregoing list obviously reflects only an individual viewpoint, but even so suggests that there is a substantial body of work to be done. If we also make allowance for the undoubted diversity of views amongst researchers, and the possibilities for substantial improvements in the range and quality of data, there is every chance that the rest of the 1970s will see many new results coming forth. I hope that the present collection may be of use to students of investment behaviour, and may persuade some to contribute to the great leap forward.

References

BERNDT, E. R., and CHRISTENSEN, L. R. (1973), 'The translog function and the substitution of equipment, structures, and labor in US manufacturing 1929–68', *J. Econometrics*, vol. 1, pp. 81–114.

CHRISTENSEN, L. R., JORGENSON, D. W., and LAU, L. J. (1973), 'Transcendental logarithmic production frontiers', *Rev. econ. Stat.*, vol. 55, pp. 28–45.

DIEWERT, W. E. (1971), 'An application of the Shephard duality theorem: a generalized Leontief production function', *J. pol. Econ.*, vol. 79, pp. 481–507.

DRIEHUIS, W. (1972), *Fluctuations and Growth in a Near Full Employment Economy*, Rotterdam University Press.

FELDSTEIN, M. S., and ROTHSCHILD, M. (1974), 'Towards an economic theory of replacement investment', *Econometrica*, vol. 42, forthcoming

Part One
Survey of Issues

The single paper in this part surveys the last decade's quantitative studies of aggregate investment. The survey concentrates on the main issues that must be faced in the specification and estimation of equations explaining fluctuations in aggregate investment. The issues are presented in roughly the same order in which they would present themselves to a research worker. The introduction is followed by a long section explaining the theory and data employed in the definition of the desired aggregate stock of capital. The subsequent sections deal with the process whereby *ex ante* capital shortages lead to capital expenditure, and with statistical issues involved in the estimation of investment equations.

1 J. F. Helliwell

Aggregate Investment Equations: A Survey of Issues

First published in this volume

I Introduction

The primary issue in applied econometrics involves decisions about what to assume and what to estimate. A notable feature of many recent econometric studies of investment behaviour is the extent to which explicit theory has been used to place constraints on the structure and functional form of the derived investment equations. A precise model of aggregate investment behaviour, in which output and relative prices play specific pre-ordained roles, requires a great number of simplifying assumptions. The more complete the set of prior assumptions, the less is left to be estimated from the data sample. In terms of the realism of the final equation, there may be either gains or losses from the use of additional prior assumptions. The gains may come because the assumptions reduce the number of parameters to be estimated. Since relevant aggregate data samples are inevitably few and small, any reduction in the number of coefficients to estimate increases the likely accuracy of estimation. In addition, the use of more *a priori* information also increases the precision of the estimation equation, as long as the prior information is correct. On the other hand, if the additional restrictions used are not correct, then the resulting equation may be less accurate in terms of either structure or prediction.

This survey of recent econometric studies of aggregate investment behaviour is intended to illustrate how the main problem noted above has been dealt with. Although all the bits of the investment process are intertwined, they will be dealt with serially to get some order into a jumble of description and commentary.

The survey is restricted to recent time-series studies of business fixed capital expenditures, either for total manufacturing or for all business investment. Some of the studies distinguish between non-residential construction (or structures) and machinery and equipment (producers' durables in US terminology), but most deal with the sum of the two. Studies prior to 1960 have been surveyed by Eisner and Strotz (1963). More recent studies at the industry and firm level have been surveyed by Jorgenson (1971). The primary object of the present effort is not to relate recent studies to one another, but to illustrate a number of important aspects of investment equations with references to recent aggregate empirical studies.

In keeping with its concern with research problems rather than with particular results, the survey will present the various issues roughly in the order they are faced by the research worker. Section II is concerned with the data and theoretical assumptions used to define a desired capital stock. Section III contains a discussion of the process by which investment expenditures are undertaken to move the actual level of the capital stock towards its desired level. Section IV contains a brief discussion of estimation problems, and there are concluding comments in Section V.

II Defining the desired capital stock
The framework for decisions

Goals of the investors. It is increasingly common in applied econometrics to explain aggregate expenditure series, whether for consumer services or business fixed investment, as being the result of purposive action. If there are enough common features in separate decisions to give some comparable content to the aggregate series, then there may be considerable scientific advance from evaluating the elements underlying decisions.

How important it may be to discover the motivation of decision-makers depends on how much scope they have for alternative actions. Economists often interpret a decision problem as the maximization of an objective function subject to constraints. The constraints may well be so specific as to allow little room for the investors' objectives to make much difference. For example, if the only available technology embodies a fixed capital/output ratio, and if output requirements are taken as given, then the required capital stock is the same whatever the private goals of the investor.

By the same token, if investors face a wide range of available technologies, and are able to determine the amount or price of output, then the size of the desired capital stock may depend more heavily on firms' objectives.

If there is a dominant feature of development of investment equations since 1960, it is the increasing use of more specific assumptions about objectives. Early quantitative studies of investment usually adduced profit maximization or cost minimization to support inclusion of the interest rate as a determinant of investment. In practice such studies were more heavily dependent on some variant of the acceleration principle, under which investment is proportional to the change in either current or expected future output. In these circumstances the exact form of the underlying objective function makes little difference, because most of the alternatives give the same predictions about the direction of the impact of, e.g. the cost of capital. The choice becomes more critical when the objective function is combined with specific assumptions about technology in deriving a precise definition of the desired capital stock.

The studies initiated by Jorgenson and several collaborators, e.g. Hall and Jorgenson (1971), Jorgenson (1963, 1965), Jorgenson and Stephenson (1967a, 1969), were among the first to derive desired capital/output ratios from specific assumptions about behaviour. These studies employ the general assumption that firms act so as to maximize the present value of net cash flow to the owners of the firm. However, dynamic considerations are short-circuited by the use of current prices and quantities alone. The Jorgenson studies make use of the partial conditions relating output prices and the cost of capital services. Some more recent studies have emphasized cost minimization to relate input prices to the relevant marginal physical products. As will be shown in Section II (pp. 29–33), these approaches normally give different results.

Although the maximization of net present value is the business goal typically assumed in normative studies of investment decisions, a number of other managerial utility functions have been alleged to be more descriptive of what firms actually do. The suggested goals have included sizes of sales or assets (Baumol, 1959), rate of growth (Marris, 1964), rate of profit, or some combination of factors entering a utility function (Williamson, 1963). These different maximands lead to different forms of investment behaviour. Alternatively, it has been suggested that firms attempt to attain minimum acceptable levels of performance, and do not attempt to maximize anything (Simon, 1962; Cyert and March, 1963). It is arguable that such satisficing behaviour is equivalent to optimization under restraint plus some lexico-graphical ordering in the choice of objective (Encarnación, 1964).

To date, aggregate investment studies that make direct use of an explicit objective function have assumed present-value maximization; typically only partial use has been made of the implied marginal conditions.

The time horizon. Aggregate investment studies have typically paid scant attention to the inter-temporal aspects of investment behaviour. The present-value technique is used to bring all future costs and revenues to the present but there is little said concerning the formation of expectations in this context. The mainly theoretical advances on the choice of an adjustment path are discussed in Section III (pp. 41–4). In general, quantitative studies have assumed stationary expectations, and thus have not considered how present and future actions interlock in the choice of an investment plan to satisfy an objective function.

The role of uncertainty. This important issue has also been dealt with principally by the handy assumption that the future will be like the present. In some cases, the future is represented by a weighted average of current and recent past values (Coen and Hickman, 1970). In no study is there any attempt to measure or consider the consequences of uncertainty about expectations. There is a certain amount of microeconomic work, chiefly theoretical, arguing that investments in real and financial assets ought to depend on more than just the mean values of the subjective probability distributions of future outcomes (Tobin, 1965; Arrow, 1964; Markowitz, 1959; Hirshleifer, 1965). Firms making capital expenditures are generally assumed, for a given expectation of return, to prefer an investment programme with lower variance in the subjective probability distributions of return. Firms are also supposed to prefer positive to negative skewness of the distribution (Hicks, 1967). These preferences are justified on two separate grounds. The primary justification is that purchasers of the bonds and shares have preferences which must be taken into account by those firms wishing to raise and invest financial capital efficiently (Helliwell, 1968, ch. 1). Second, there may be substantial personal incentives for managers to avoid bankruptcy, and therefore to keep the chance of excessive losses to a minimum (Roy, 1952). These hypotheses have not influenced the specification of aggregative time-series investment equations. It is difficult enough to define a reasonable process for single-valued expectations at the aggregate level. There is little or no evidence to support the estimation of higher moments of 'representative' probability distributions. Changes in risk assessments probably tend to coincide with changes in estimated mean values, so that the effects of the two could not be easily disentangled.

Aside from its influence on the incentive to invest, uncertainty about the product and technological mix of future output is likely to influence the present choice of technique. Special purpose machines that embody a particular technology can often produce at less cost than more flexible general-purpose equipment, but only as long as products and technology do not change. If uncertainty increases about the pace or direction of future innovations, there may be a premium placed on flexible capital and labour. To define the consequences of these for investment behaviour would require much more detailed specification of available techniques and expectations than is possible at the aggregate level.

Thus the influence of uncertainty is likely to remain far larger in the world of affairs than it is in the specification of aggregate investment equations.

Assumptions about technology

The assumed production function. The nature of the capital input to the productive process has not received much study in the investment literature. Georgescu-Roegen (1970) has recently emphasized the importance of distinguishing the effects of time and scale of activity when using both stock and flow magnitudes in a description of the productive process. The familiar simple production function relates to a per-period flow of output, Q, to a stock of capital, K, and a labour input L, which may be a stock or a flow:

$$Q = F(K, L). \qquad \qquad 1$$

To make the function invariant to the length of time period, it is necessary to specify K and L as per-period flows of services from capital and labour. The particular forms of this production function most often underlying investment equations are:

Cobb–Douglas,

$$Q = AK^a L^b; \qquad \qquad 2$$

Fixed proportion, or Leontief,

$$Q = \min(aK, bL); \qquad \qquad 3$$

Constant elasticity of substitution,

$$Q = \{aK^{(\sigma-1)/\sigma} + bL^{(\sigma-1)/\sigma}\}^{\sigma(\sigma-1)}, \qquad \qquad 4$$

where σ is the elasticity of substitution, $\sigma \neq 1$.

All three functions have a constant elasticity of substitution, but the range of possible values for σ is greater for the CES function (Arrow *et al.*, 1961; Brown and de Cani, 1963) in which it appears as a specific parameter. For the Cobb–Douglas function (Douglas, 1948) $\sigma = 1$, and for the Leontief (1951) function, $\sigma = 0$.

The first point to be made is that these simple two-factor production functions may omit too many important features. Among the omitted inputs are natural resources, inventories, financial working capital, and imports of intermediate products. No account is taken of waste and other non-saleable outputs. Capital is assumed to be a homogeneous mass in the simplest versions, although there have been attempts made to disaggregate by type (e.g. equipment and construction in Evans and Helliwell, 1969; Hall and Jorgenson, 1967, 1971; Helliwell and Glorieux, 1970; Helliwell *et al.*, 1969), and vintage (Bischoff, 1969, 1971; Helliwell *et al.*, 1971 and King, 1972), and to treat the stock of capital separately from its rate of utilization (Nadiri and Rosen, 1969). There have been parallel efforts, also bedevilled by measurement problems, to treat employment and average hours per employee as separate components of labour services (Feldstein, 1967; Nadiri and Rosen, 1969). Only rarely has the productive role of inventories and other working capital been even partly integrated with the demand for fixed assets (Schramm, 1970; Anderson, 1964).

It has already been noted that the capital services input is usually assumed, in most investment studies, to be proportional to a conventional measure of the capital stock. Aside from the well-known aggregation problems, the key difficulty with this approach arises from ignoring variations in the rate of utilization of capital. In a direct estimate of the production function, the procedure probably results in an overestimate of the marginal product of labour, or especially in the marginal product of average weekly hours if they are treated separately. If an assumed production function is used to derive a desired capital stock which is then used in an investment equation, failure to account for variations in the per-period flow of capital services per unit of the capital stock will lead to overstatement of the true investment lags, or an underestimation of the marginal capital/output ratio. Suppose, for simplicity, that a two-factor Cobb–Douglas production function applies to labour services $L = EH$, number employed (E) times average hours worked (H), and capital services KS, where K is the conventionally defined capital stock, S the per-period flow of services per unit of K, and KS the total per-period flow of capital services. Thus the production function is

$$Q = A(KS)^a L^b, \qquad\qquad 5$$

or in logs, and substituting the definition of L:

$$\log Q = \log A + a \log K + a \log S + b \log E + b \log H. \qquad 6$$

This can be solved for the required capital input:

$$\log K = 1/a \log Q - \log S - b/a \log E - b/a \log H - 1/a \log A. \qquad 7$$

If a first difference transformation of this relationship were estimated with S, E, and H omitted, it would resemble a crude accelerator model based on net investment. If S were positively correlated with Q, as it would normally be, especially in the short run, then such an equation could seriously overestimate the parameter a and hence underestimate the marginal capital/output ratio. Similar consequences follow from the omission of employment (E) and average hours (H) (or their prices), a matter which will be taken up in Section II (pp. 29–34). Here I am merely concerned to show that, even in the simplest investment model derived solely from the production function, the assumption of constant per-period services per unit of capital will bias parameter estimates if the assumption is false.

What are the facts of the matter likely to be? Most machines, factories and offices are normally used for less than three full shifts per day. When there is an increase in average weekly hours per employee, is it not likely that the average weekly hours of at least some items of capital equipment and buildings will increase in the same proportion? This is the extensive margin of capital utilization. There is also an intensive margin, presenting the possibility that under pressure of aggregate demand some machines are run at speeds greater than normal. These two ways of obtaining more services per time-period from a given capital stock must not be confused with the possibility that more output can be obtained from a given flow of capital services by combining it with a larger flow of labour services.

In investment equations derived from a combination of production function and price or cost conditions, the consequences of assuming capital services per unit per time period (S) to be constant may extend further. If S is really a variable, then the relevant price ratios will be misspecified if the rental price of capital goods (Section II, pp. 22–6 below) ignores any influence of S on the required amount of repair and replacement.

Factor substitution, ex ante *and* ex post. The three production functions considered above differ in the degree to which *ex ante* factor substitution is possible. As written, all three make no distinction between capital vintages, and hence assume that the amount of factor substitution is the same *ex ante* and *ex post*. If a Cobb–Douglas or CES function applies *ex ante* as well as *ex post*, the technology is known as 'putty-putty', implying that factories are designed so that factor proportions are as easily variable after construction as before. The Leontief technology is known as 'clay-clay' because there is no variability of factor proportions either before or after the capital is put in place.

A number of growth models and a few investment studies (Bischoff 1969, 1971; Helliwell *et al.*, 1971) have used the 'putty-clay' assumption that at the 'blueprint' stage the choice of factor proportions is unfettered, but becomes restricted once the chosen design has been implemented. In Bischoff's application, the *ex ante* production function is assumed to be CES, while the *ex post* function is Leontief. It has alternatively been suggested (Fuss, 1970) that some degree of substitution may be possible before and after investment, but that substitution is easier at the 'blueprint' stage.

As Bischoff (1969) points out, one major implication of differences between *ex ante* and *ex post* substitution possibilities is that a 'putty-putty' model involves a faster impact for relative prices than does a 'putty-clay' model. This is because factor proportions can be changed immediately (subject only to the usual investment lags) in response to price changes in a 'putty-putty' environment. Where there is no *ex post* substitution, the switch in factor proportions must await the appearance of gross investment

J. F. Helliwell 19

opportunities caused by growth in desired output or depreciation of the existing capital stock. (More on this in Section III, pp. 38–9.)

Assumptions about the degree of factor substitution are inevitably bound up with the role of relative prices in the investment decision. If output requirements are taken as given, as they are in almost all investment equations, then the required capital stock is defined directly from the production function conditions unless factor substitution is possible. Factor substitution provides scope for one ratio of relative prices, in a two-factor context, to influence the desired capital stock.

Technical change. Investment equations typically ignore technical change altogether, or deal with it in some way that is analytically convenient rather than empirically appropriate. There are good excuses at hand, for in the absence of reliable price series for used capital goods it is impossible to disentangle embodied and disembodied technical change and the rate of depreciation (Hall, 1968). The possible existence of technical changes embodied in new investment or newly trained labour has important implications for the theory of economic growth (e.g. Phelps, 1962) and raises difficulties for students of investment behaviour. It is difficult enough if each vintage of capital (the data problems in dealing with labour quality are even worse) has a preferred or required capital/labour ratio, but the complications are greater if a different value of some index of technical change must be associated with each block of investment. If the index itself were exogenous, complicated accounting could deal with the problem, but the index is likely to be endogenous and is unmeasured in any case.

In some studies the problems of disentangling the effects of technical change from those of relative prices have led to the definition of desired capital/output ratios on the basis of historical trends through points of equivalent capacity utilization. Most other studies have assumed technical change to be disembodied, and have not attributed it to either capital or labour. Sometimes information on income shares can be used as a guide in the attribution of disembodied technical progress. Researchers who worry about the right way of dealing with technical progress are likely to despair of finding any procedure that is appropriate at the aggregate level. The issue remains open, and solution probably awaits the appearance of better data on prices of used capital goods; even with such data the problems of heterogeneity and installation costs may prove insuperable. A number of the relevant issues have recently been surveyed by Nadiri (1970).

It should be noted that the type of technical progress assumed affects the appropriate definition of factor costs. For example, if Harrod-neutral (labour-augmenting) technical change is assumed, then the wage rate per man-hour of unchanged efficiency grows at a different rate than the wage per actual man-hour.

Defining the variables

Desired output. Desired output is that which determines current investment decisions. It ought to refer to a period far enough into the future that current investment decisions can lead to project completions just in time to provide the necessary output. Most investment studies do not use expectations processes with explicit horizons, so that this question is bypassed. The bulk of the existing studies use current demand or output (e.g. Jorgenson, 1963; Jorgenson and Stephenson, 1967), an average of current and lagged values (Coen and Hickman, 1970; Dhrymes, 1967), or an average with positive weights on several preceding periods (Eisner, 1967; Coen, 1968, 1971). Some studies use sales (Eisner, 1967) and others use output (Jorgenson, 1963) or new orders (Coen, 1968). If the investment demand equation is derived using a production function as a constraint, then output is obviously more appropriate. Yet some of the studies using production conditions also make use of conditions derived from a net revenue function involving sales (e.g. Jorgenson, 1963), and use a single variable as a proxy for both sales and output. This is another example of the general uncertainty about the appropriate way of handling inventory investment as part of the production process.

Whether sales or output is used as the 'demand' variable underlying the aggregate investment equation, the series in question is usually treated as exogenous to the investment process. There are three reasons for doubting this procedure. The first is the risk of simultaneous equations bias, caused by explaining investment by movements in an aggregate of which investment expenditure is a part. If current output does not appear in the equation, then this issue may be less important, depending on the existence of auto-correlated disturbances. If errors in the investment equation are auto-correlated, then even output in previous periods (which contain previous investment disturbances) will be correlated with the current disturbance in the investment equation. In any event, the problem can be met by use of appropriate simultaneous equation estimation techniques, as is common for investment equations imbedded in macroeconometric models.

The second reason (emphasized by Gould, 1969) is that if actual output is ever constrained by the availability of capital, then lagged responses in the investment process imply that actual output must at least occasionally differ from desired output. Thus the time series for actual output may not provide a suitable basis for expectations which determine desired future output. This issue arises only to the extent that output is ever limited by the existing capital stock. Such occasions are likely to be frequent if shifts in demand for output are not easily forecast and investment projects not efficiently carried out in a rush. Corrections, therefore, ought to be made to the actual output series to make it correspond more closely with demand and hence with desired output. In one model (Helliwell *et al.*, 1971), this has been done by subtracting a series for net unintended inventory changes.

The third reason for not treating output as exogenous is that if all marginal cost and profit conditions are taken into account by firms, the levels of output as well as inputs are thereby determined. If output and prices are taken as given the capital expenditure decision is overdetermined. The investment model can be made consistent only by suppressing the price of labour (as is done by Jorgenson, 1963; Bischoff, 1971), or the price of output (Coen, 1968; Coen and Hickman, 1970; Nadiri and Rosen, 1969; Helliwell *et al.*, 1971). The literature contains little in the way of justification for suppressing one of the marginal conditions rather than the other. One alternative procedure (see Section II, pp. 29–31) is to use all the marginal cost and revenue conditions taking prices as given, and thereby to exclude desired output entirely from the definition of the desired capital stock.

The cost of capital services. If this cost is measured, as it usually is, as a per-period proportion of the capital stock, it has two main components. One is the amount of physical capital 'used up' by use, deterioration, or obsolescence during the period. The other is the opportunity cost of the financial capital tied up in capital goods. Both components are multiplied by the investment goods price-deflator, because the capital stock is usually measured in constant prices.

The cost of capital services relevant to investment decisions is that applicable over the lifetime, somehow defined, of the related investment projects. If investment goods could be bought and sold, or rented, with no delays, transaction costs, or installation costs, then only the current cost of capital services would be relevant, and firms would simply rent or buy as much capital equipment and building space as seemed desirable at the current prices. But there are substantial delays and costs in establishing a plant, and the markets for second-hand establishments are imperfect enough to justify treating fixed-investment decisions as long-term commitments. However, the length of effective commitment is dictated as much by various cost and market considerations as it is by the physical lifetime of the investment goods, so there is no easy choice of a horizon over which to define the relevant cost of capital services. Some average values must be taken unless there is some way of defining and using separate expected values for the cost of capital services for each time period within the investment horizon.

In many recent investment studies, the cost of capital services has been based on a measure derived by Jorgenson (1965), Hall and Jorgenson (1971), Bischoff (1971) and others. It is sometimes referred to as the 'user cost of capital' and sometimes as the 'implicit rental price of capital services'. Ignoring for the time being any component based on expected capital gains, this measure is frequently defined as

$$c = \{q(r+\delta)(1-uz)/(1-u)\}, \qquad\qquad 8$$

where δ, the depreciation rate, and r, the cost of capital, correspond to the two above-mentioned components of the cost of capital services. As for the other variables, q is the price of capital goods, u the corporation tax rate, and z is the present value of depreciation allowances allowed for tax purposes. See Hall and Jorgenson (1971, pp. 14–22) and Bischoff (1971, pp. 65–6) for examples of the more complicated expressions required if there are investment tax credits or similar tax concessions.

As written above, the expression for c assumes that there are no tax reductions related to the cost of capital, r. If r is measured as the cost of capital with no tax allowances, then it should be multiplied by a factor $(1-uw)$ where w is the proportion of r that is deductible for corporation income tax purposes. Because of the problems of estimating what r would be in the absence of any tax deductions for interest payments, some researchers (Hall and Jorgenson, 1971; Bischoff, 1971) assume that measured r reflects the tax treatment at the corporate level, and ignore any possible consequences for r of changes in w or u. Further complications arise from differential personal tax treatment of interest, dividends, and retained earnings. See, for example, Feldstein and Flemming (1971) and King (1972).

The $(1-u)$ term in the denominator of the expression for c is not a direct part of the price of capital services, but a consequence of a wish to compare the product price p with the cost of capital services by means of a simple price ratio c/p. It is perhaps clearer to separate the taxability of sales revenues from the tax treatment of capital services by rewriting the price ratio as $c'/p(1-u)$, making c' the cost of capital services after corporation tax allowances and $p(1-u)$ the after-tax return from sales. With this revision, we have

$$c' = q(r+\delta)(1-uz). \qquad\qquad 9$$

On the assumption that capital goods involve no commitment, then all the components of c' take their current values. If we adopt the more plausible convention that capital goods are purchased in the likelihood that they will be kept and used under most circumstances by the purchasing firm, the time dimension becomes more tricky. The relevant price for capital goods is the expected price for future delivery. Although contracts may be made at the present time, the price is not likely to be the same as that applicable to investment goods presently being put in place, since their prices were presumably negotiated on prior dates.

If there are initial allowances, investment allowances, or variable rates of depreciation then only a present-value calculation can adequately encompass their net effects in a simple way. The discount rate used for calculating the present value of tax allowances for depreciation ought itself to be a variable, as ought the expected tax rates over the lifetime of the asset. Whether simplifying assumptions would give rise to important errors is a question that may have a different answer according to the details of each case.

One advantage of calculating separately the present value of tax allowances is that it permits the distinction between the depreciation rate assumed for tax purposes and the combined effects of wear-and-tear, obsolescence, and the passage of time, representing the actual consumption of capital goods. What rate ought to be used for the rate of capital consumption? Under the assumption of costless transactions in capital goods, δ should include al the deterioration and other costs associated with the current rate of use (Taubman and Wilkinson, 1970). If, on the other hand, the goods are bought to be kept and used until scrapping time, then δ ought to be some average rate of depreciation based on the expected average running speeds, and number of hours of use per week. If there are long-term trends in the rate of usage of capital goods, then they ought to be taken into account if their effect on depreciation can be established. Feldstein and Rothschild (1974) emphasize that the rate at which the productive capacity of the capital stock declines also depends on the rate of scrapping, which ought in turn to depend on a variety of cost factors.

The above discussion assumes that depreciation can be represented by some proportion δ of the replacement price q. This does not mean that flows of capital services need depend on some current or average value of δ. The actual flow of services from a particular investment good may (as suggested by Griliches, 1963) be more closely related to the number of machines in operation than to their exponentially depreciated capital value. (See pp. 27–9 below.)

There is an extensive literature about the appropriate value of r, the cost of capital, to use in public investment decisions (e.g. Feldstein, 1971) and in private investment decisions (Miller and Modigliani, 1966). In empirical work relating to business investment, the most frequent candidates are a long-term bond rate or some weighted average of an equity dividend/price ratio and a long-term bond rate. Is the current rate of interest for a serial obligation of the same maturity as the investment project, an appropriate measure of the cost of borrowing? If the bond and project maturities match, then an expectations theory of interest rates suggests that the current rate of interest is appropriate, because the long rate in question is supposed to be, apart from a liquidity premium, a weighted average of expected future short-term borrowing-rates. Individual borrowers may be able to do better by altering the term structures of their debts as interest rates change, but for the market as a whole this is not possible. When the cost of equity capital is taken into account, it is not possible to match maturities.

If debt and equity yields are allowed to influence r, how should they be combined? There are non-comparable features of the two yields. If some representative earnings/price ratio is used as a starting point, some account must be taken of the expected rate of growth of the earnings or dividend stream. The aggregate earnings stream will grow, in the absence of re-investment or new net investment, if there are corresponding increases in prices and costs, or changes in income distribution in favour of capital. These sources of growth do not apply to the yields from bonds or non-participating preferred shares, because interest payments, in the absence of escalator provisions, are fixed in nominal terms. If the stream of equity returns is assumed to have a perpetual growth rate, then the sum of the growth rate and a typical year's return (as a proportion of market value) defines a rate of return that may be compared to a nominal interest rate. This adjustment is made by Helliwell *et al.* (1971) and in the investment equations of the MPS model (Ando and Rasche, 1971) but not in other studies attempting to use interest rates as well as equity yields. At the margin, the costs of bonds and equities should be equal, when properly measured.

The comparability of debt and equity yields is further disturbed by provisions of corporation and personal income taxes. In most countries, interest payments are an expense allowable for corporation tax purposes; dividends, on the other hand, must be paid out of post-tax income. Retained earnings, however, are capitalized in share prices to the extent that they are expected to lead to increases in future earnings and dividends. The resulting capital gains may be treated, under the personal income tax, more favourably than dividends. This fact, along with transaction costs, is used to support models in which investment expenditure is largely determined by the flow of internally generated funds. Dividends may be treated more or less favourably than interest payments under the personal income tax. The shortage of data on the tax position of marginal shareholders has led researchers to mention some of these facts and then to continue using a bond rate of interest. Feldstein and Flemming (1971), in their study of UK investment, have taken some pains to specify the effects of taxation at the personal as well as the company level. When tax rates are brought into the definition of r, they should be expected rates, not necessarily those currently in force.

A final component of the cost of capital services is the expected after-tax rate of capital gain. If resale markets are good, then the rate of capital gain is an appropriate element to include, as it offsets any increase in the nominal cost of capital, r, as a consequence of an increase in the expected rate of inflation. If the firm is 'buying for keeps', then price expectations ought to influence the capital expenditure decision in some other way. Any positive influence of expected inflation on investment will operate either through a higher expected future output-price or wage rate, in either case relative to a current or delivery date price of capital goods. Alternatively, if current prices of inputs and output are being used for comparison, then the nominal cost of capital, r, should be reduced by the expected rate of inflation.

The price of output. This variable enters any investment model employing the marginal condition that capital should be added until its marginal revenue product equals its marginal cost. Once again, the question of horizon is important. If investment and employment decisions are easily reversible, then a near-term output price ought to be used. If transaction costs are high enough to commit firms for the expected lifetime of an investment project, then expected output prices over that horizon ought to be taken into account. To make models reasonably simple and operational, 'representative' values may be used for expected output price. If current output price is used to represent expected future output price (Jorgenson, 1963; Bischoff, 1971), the model will understate the incentive to invest if output prices are expected to rise over the lifetime of the investment project.

The costs of substitute factors. If aggregate capital and labour are assumed to be the only inputs to the production function, then labour is the only substitute factor whose price could enter the investment equation. If there is more than one kind of capital or labour, then several substitute factor prices may help to determine the desired amount of any type of capital. Other factor prices (as opposed to 'own price') influence investment in any model employing the marginal conditions that the ratio of marginal products of any two factors should equal the ratio of their marginal costs.

The appropriate horizon for expectations again depends on the degree of commitment implied by the investment decision, as well as the potential degree of *ex post* factor substitution. If investment goods can be sold easily, and if factor substitution is as easy *ex post* as it is *ex ante*, then it is appropriate to use the current wage rate as the price of a substitute factor. Low transaction costs for capital goods is not by itself enough, because capital goods with fixed factor proportions would still be subject to capital gains or losses, if factor prices changed after the project was finished.

If factor proportions are fixed at the time of investment decision, then the wage rates relevant for comparison with the cost of capital services are those over the entire lifetime of the capital goods. If the depreciation process operates so as to reduce the productive potential of the capital goods steadily over their lifetimes (and the required labour inputs, given our fixed proportions assumption) then the near-term wage rates should have extra weight. By contrast, if the capital goods are 'one-hoss shays' that perform as new until they collapse all at once, the wage-rate expectations should have corresponding weights.

Freedom to change factor proportions *ex post* reduces the importance to be attached to expected wage rates in the distant future. This is especially true if demand is expected to rise fast enough to absorb any excess plant capacity created by a decrease in the price of labour services relative to that of capital services. The rate of decline in the importance of far-future wage rates thus ought to depend on the expected growth of demand, the nature and rate of depreciation, and the relative ease of *ex ante* and *ex post* factor substitution. Because there is little *a priori* guidance about the parameters of the wage expectations process, the choice of a particular time horizon for wage expectations may become rather arbitrary. Almost any reasonable expectations process will make expected future wages different from current wages, especially where there are widespread expectations of a continued inflationary trend. When arbitrary choices must be made, some expected future wage rate is likely to be more appropriate than a current wage rate in models using the marginal factor substitution conditions for cost minimization.

The stock of capital. The problems involved in defining an aggregate stock of capital are formidable. The theoretical problems are most forcefully presented by Robinson (1965). The stringent conditions required for consistent capital aggregation are rigorously treated by Gorman (1968); while Fisher (1971) has used simulation experiments to show how difficult it is to distinguish 'good' aggregates from 'bad' ones. The student of investment behaviour cannot escape from these dilemmas except by assuming that the existing stock of capital is always fully employed. Without this convenient but often misleading simplification, it is necessary to somehow use data on past investment to derive some idea of the desired productive capacity of the existing capital stock.

Griliches has pointed out (1963) that the 'best' definition of the stock of capital may depend on the use to which the numbers are to be put. For inclusion in production relations, the stock ought to be defined in units which are homogeneous with respect to marginal productivity and the degree of possible factor substitution. If there is capital-embodied technical progress at some steady rate, this may require continual writing down of the value of earlier vintages to ensure comparability. (Unless the adjustment is made in the price index. See the next paragraph.) This adjustment may not serve to define a homogeneous capital stock, with respect to marginal productivity, even if embodied technical progress proceeds at a regular rate. If factor proportions are built into capital goods, even partially, then any possibility of changes in relative prices makes it necessary to keep the various vintages of capital goods separate.

The units of measurement of the capital stock are usually constant dollars, or some other currency unit at constant prices. This raises the question of how capital goods are priced in the national accounts. If machines are defined in terms of what they will do, then technical progress is defined as a reduction in the price of machines. Other measures of the 'size' of a capital good may not lead to price adjustments for increases in embodied efficiency. Thus the amount of capital services (in terms of productive power) from constant-price increments in the capital stock may or may not be an increasing function of the rate of capital-embodied technical progress, depending on the methods used to construct the price index. If the technical progress is matched by corresponding price reductions, then it would be double-counting to also write down the value of earlier vintages to account for the same changes.

To summarize, if embodied technical progress is identified with price reductions in capital goods, then the constant price measure of the capital stock is the right measure of productive potential, for any given rate of capital utilization. If the price index is otherwise defined, then comparability is obtained by writing down earlier vintages by the appropriate rate of obsolescence. In this case the 'efficiency units' of capital services will be in increasing proportion to the constant price measure of the capital stock, by an amount determined by the rate of obsolescence.

We now turn to consider deterioration through time and use. Assume no technical progress of any sort, so as to put aside the problems raised in the preceding paragraph. Most investment studies employ a measure of the net capital stock, either in a term defining a gap between desired and existing capacity, or as a base for assumed replacement investment, or both. Often, investment equations are estimated with the dependent variable being gross investment less some proportion of the net capital stock. The proportion is the rate of depreciation, assumed equal to the rate of replacement. This matter is discussed below in Section III, pp. 40–41. When defining the net capital stock for all these purposes, it is important to take account of the effect of use. The net capital stock is usually defined according to the expression

$$K_t = (1-\delta)K_{t-1} + I_t.$$

10

The depreciation rate used in the definition of the net capital stock is the actual current rate, while the δ used in the cost of capital services should be some expected average over the commitment horizon of the investment decision.

If the effects of use can be quantified, then the depreciation rate δ can be made a function of the appropriate utilization rates. If capital goods collapse like one-hoss shays rather than decaying like radioactive isotopes, the measurement of depreciation in proportionate terms is only an approximation. Jorgenson has argued (1965, p. 51) that if the aggregate capital stock contains goods with a reasonably wide distribution of average lives, the number of machines collapsing at any point in time approaches a proportion independent of cycles in investment expenditure. It is still possible, of course, to have this proportion depend on the intensity of use of the capital stock.

Combining the assumptions to determine a desired capital stock

Using prices of outputs and inputs. This type of model takes account of the production function and prices of output and inputs.

As emphasized throughout this section, the choice of a desired capital stock is an intertemporal allocation problem. The assumed goal of decision-makers is a present value of net revenues. To compress the time dimension is tricky but necessary if a reasonably simple investment model is to be derived. It can be done fairly well by using appropriate expectations horizons for each of the expected prices and costs, and then solving the model for the capital stock desired at the end of the construction period. We leave to Section III our discussion of the determination of the construction period or 'lead time'. Consider a simple net revenue function of the form

$$R = p(1-u)Q - (1-u)wL - c'K, \qquad \qquad 11$$

where R is net revenue after corporation tax, p the expected output price during the life of the investment (output assumed equal to sales), w the expected hourly wage rate over a similar horizon, c' the price of capital services expressed per unit of the capital stock, u the expected rate of corporation income tax, Q the quantity of output, L the labour input in man-hours, and K the net capital stock. The general production function is

$$Q = f(KS, L). \qquad \qquad 12$$

This simple version skirts some important issues in order to clarify the exposition. A single labour input L is used, thereby assuming that the productivity of a given number of man-hours is not affected by its split between number employed and average hours per employee. The capital services input to the production function is the product of the capital stock,

K, and S, the index of capital services per unit of the capital stock. There are two possible alternative justifications for making S equal to 1 in the following analysis. One is that S is not a long-term decision variable, because of either institutional rigidities or cost factors that make one average value preferred under all conditions. An alternative supposition is that c', the cost of capital services per unit of capital, has an elasticity of 1·0 with respect to changes in S. If this unlikely situation were true, and the other determinants of c' were exogenous, there would be no possible gain from altering the average value of S. To treat S explicitly would impose the complications of a third input factor, which is avoided at this stage. The first order condition for a maximum of R is that

$$dR = p(1-u)dQ - w(1-u)dL - c'dK = 0. \qquad\qquad 13$$

The corresponding total differential of the production function is

$$dQ = F_L dL + F_K dK, \qquad\qquad 14$$

where F_K and F_L are the partial derivatives of F with respect to K and L. The necessary pairwise conditions from the revenue function, with respect to the capital input are:

(holding L constant) $dK/dQ = p(1-u)/c'$,
(holding Q constant) $dK/dL = -w(1-u)/c'$.

The corresponding ratios derived from the production function are:

(holding L constant) $dK/dQ = 1/F_K$,
(holding Q constant) $dK/dL = -F_L/F_K$.

The two conditions obtained by holding L constant are those employed in the models used by Jorgenson and others, and are referred to by them as the profit-maximizing conditions. In our notation, they combine to give

$$F_K = c'/p(1-u). \qquad\qquad 15$$

The two conditions obtained by holding Q constant are those employed by Coen and Hickman (1970), Nadiri and Rosen (1969), and Helliwell *et al.* (1971), and are referred to as the cost minimization conditions. They combine to give

$$F_K/F_L = c'/w(1-u). \qquad\qquad 16$$

It is important to note that under stationary conditions of pure competition and constant returns to scale the cost minimization and profit-maximization models are formally identical. Under these conditions:

$$Q = (w/p)(L) + [c'/p(1-u)]K,$$

and $\quad Q = F_L L + F_K K,$

so that $\quad (F_L - w/p)L + [F_K - \{c'/p(1-u)\}]K = 0.$

If **15** holds, then the above expression implies $F_L = w/p$, which in conjunction with **15** gives **16**. In general, one has to choose between **15** and **16**, if output is treated as exogenous. Either **15** or **16** may be used, in conjunction with a production function and a desired output series, to derive a desired capital stock. These models are discussed below in Section II (pp. 32–3). If both **15** and **16** are imposed, then desired output must be made endogenous. If output is made endogenous, any twice-differentiable production function with diminishing marginal products and diminishing returns to scale can be used to solve for the desired capital stock. For example, from the Cobb–Douglas production function of equation **2** we have:

$$F_K = aQ/K; \; F_L = bQ/L. \tag{17}$$

When **17** is substituted in **16** and **15** and solved for L and Q in terms of K, we get

$$Q = Kc'/ap(1-u); \; L = Kbc'/aw(1-u). \tag{18}$$

The expressions **18** can then be solved for the desired levels of output and labour input. Substituting the expressions **18** into the production function **2**, and solving for K gives:

$$K = [\{Aap(1-u)/c'\}\{bc'/aw(1-u)\}^b]^{1/(1-a-b)}. \tag{19}$$

As noted above, and previously by Jorgenson (1967) and Coen (1969), the desired capital stock in this type of model is only defined for production functions with decreasing returns to scale. As constant returns are approached, $(a+b) \to 1$, the desired capital stock becomes infinitely large. The revenue function does not have a maximum in the case of increasing returns to scale, with fixed prices for inputs and output. Thus we see one of the possible problems in assuming full 'neoclassical' price-taking behaviour at the aggregate level: the perfectly price-elastic supplies of factors and demand for output require decreasing returns to production if an equilibrium is to be defined. In reality, of course, all prices and wages are endogenous to the markets for goods and services, so that upward-sloping supply curves for factors or downward-sloping demand curves for output could serve to define a neoclassical equilibrium even under increasing returns to scale. To apply an essentially microeconomic neoclassical theory of optimal capital accumulation at the aggregate level requires us either to suppress the endogenous price movements or to specify particular forms for the aggregate supplies of capital goods and labour, and the aggregate demand for output.

The only empirical applications of this type of model have been by Schramm (1970, 1972), although a similar qualitative model is considered in Jorgenson (1967). More common, and empirically successful, have been models suppressing either the output price or the wage rate, and then treating desired output as exogenous to the investment decision.

Using desired output, output price, and the cost of capital. This type of model employs the profit maximization conditions in equation 15 obtained by holding L constant. Using the Cobb–Douglas production function assumed by Jorgenson and others, 15 can be combined with the first expression in 17 to give the desired capital stocks as:

$$K = ap(1-u)Q/c'. \qquad\qquad 20$$

This model assumes that the partial elasticity of desired capital stock with respect to the price of capital services is equal to $-1\cdot0$. It has been criticized by Eisner and Nadiri (1968, 1970), Bischoff (1969), Coen (1969) and Rowley (1970), all of whom argue for a less restrictive form of production function. The use of a constant-returns Cobb–Douglas form has been defended by Jorgenson (1972), and Jorgenson and Stephenson (1969a) with reference to production function studies. The model has a positive unit elasticity of K with respect to Q. There is no direct effect of the wage rate on K, as w does not enter equation 20. In a macro context, changes in wage rates will lead directly or indirectly to changes in output prices, capital goods prices, interest rates, and so on, but these channels of influence cannot be traced without a complete macro model.

Using desired output, and prices of inputs. These models employ the cost minimization conditions 16 obtained by holding Q constant. If a Cobb–Douglas production function is assumed, the conditions 17 can be substituted in 16 and solved for L in terms of K:

$$L = \{c'b/aw(1-u)\}K. \qquad\qquad 21$$

This can be substituted into 2 so that desired K can be expressed in terms of expected Q and the cost and production parameters.

$$K = [(Q/A)\{aw(1-u)/c'b\}^b]1/(1-a-b). \qquad\qquad 22$$

There are several notable differences between this expression and equation 20. In 22, the elasticity of K with respect to Q is no longer 1 but $1/(a+b)$. These elasticities are the same only if the production function has constant returns to scale. The elasticity of K with respect to the price of capital services is not -1 but $-b/(a+b)$. These differences should be borne in mind when reading the exchanges between Jorgenson and Stephenson (1969a) on the one hand and Eisner and Nadiri (1968, 1970) on the other. Their discussion reveals that a CES production function with σ less than one is sufficient to make the partial elasticity of K less than one with respect to c', using either 15 or 16. Expressions 20 and 22 above show that such a conclusion is also consistent with a Cobb–Douglas production function, with or without constant returns to scale, if the cost minimization condition 16 is used.

As already shown, however, under constant returns to scale, perfect competition and stationary expectations, the wage rate and the price level are related so as to make equations 20 and 22 equivalent. The existence of such links between variables outside the investment sector should make one wary of any single-equation calculations of the partial elasticity of one endogenous variable with respect to another. In the world of fact, where firms face downward-sloping demand curves, the cost-minimizing framework of equation 22 seems more appropriate than equation 20 because only the former is consistent with both price-making and price-taking conditions in the markets for output.

Using desired output only. Prices and costs can be removed from the determination of K if the production function used does not permit any *ex ante* factor substitution. For example, if the production function is of the Leontief form, and there is no labour constraint operating, then $F_k = a$. Thus if the aggregate production function 3 is to hold, the following must be true:

$$K \geqslant Q \, 1/a. \qquad\qquad 23$$

If current output is used to represent desired output, if there are no lags in the adjustment process and if output is rising, inequality 23 reduces to a crude accelerator investment equation:

$$\Delta K = \Delta Q(1/a).$$

Within the framework of this section, the accelerator could be generalized by substituting expected output for current output. This is, of course, one way of bringing distributed lags into the investment process if expectations are based on several past values. Other extensions to the crude accelerator involve expenditure lags, partial adjustment models, and non-linearities allowing for excess capacity caused by gross investment being always non-negative. These matters are considered in Section III.

The accelerator model shown above was due to strict limits on the technological possibilities for factor substitution. Irrelevance of aggregate prices and costs could also be derived by assuming that measured profits and costs have no systematic effects on investment, or that the expected price variables, although theoretically important, have no systematic variance. A final rationale might be that at the aggregate level the impacts of a multitude of prices of goods and services, and rates of return, are so entangled with shifts in technology and output mix that one might as well represent the net effects of all the forces by trends based on historical experience of capital/output ratios. Such compromises may be practical and accurate in a fairly short-term forecasting context, but have obvious shortcomings for simulation studies concerned with the investment and output consequences of various public policies.

Other models. The general framework employed above takes for granted that measured prices and costs can provide a valid basis for expectations, which in turn can be used to help derive a desired capital stock based on particular revenue and production functions. A substantial and growing number of studies follow this procedure, the authors hoping that the resulting explicit structure is not thereby rendered seriously misleading. Many of the earlier studies attached more concern to the variety of observed behaviour, in terms of goals and expectations, and less value to having a final structure closely derived from underlying theory.

'Liquidity' theories of investment emphasize the lower monetary and psychological costs of internally generated funds; 'profits' theories use recent profits history as a proxy measure of the returns available from future investment. Grunfeld (1960) used the market value of the firm's securities to represent the discounted present value of future profits. This variable confounds supply and demand factors, for high expected profits (at the margin) increase the marginal revenue product of capital goods, while higher share prices (for a given expected profits stream) lower the price of capital services purchased by the firm.

A paper by Jorgenson and Siebert (1968) considers some of these factors as mutually-exclusive alternatives, while de Leeuw (1962) tests them jointly on the reasonable assumption that some combination of plausible influences is likely to explain more than any single factor.

III The adjustment process

In the previous sections it has been assumed that it takes time to translate a change in the desired capital stock into a change in the actual stock. This assumption is a necessary feature of investment theory. If finite changes in the desired capital stock could be translated with no lags into changes in the actual stock, the rate of investment would be unbounded. In this section, three aspects of the adjustment process are considered. First there is a discussion of the stages in the investment process with an eye to the amount and variability of calendar time required at each stage. There follows an assessment of how the size and nature of the existing stock of assets, work-in-progress, and plans for replacement serve to create, in conjunction with the desired stock, an *ex ante* capital stock 'gap' to be filled. Finally, on pages 41–4 there is a discussion of the various fixed and flexible lag distributions that have been used to represent empirically the adjustment of the capital stock to a new desired level.

Stages in the investment process

Decision. This is an amorphous stage in the process; it need not be important except to the extent that there are subsequent reductions in the efforts devoted to canvassing alternatives. For investment equations, the timing of this stage is relevant because it defines the data available as a basis for expectations about the relevant costs and revenues. Because of the detailed planning and information gathering often required, decisions may lag some time behind the perception of some need for the project in question.

Appropriation. This stage is important because it often provides the first quantitative evidence that decisions have been made. An appropriation approves an expenditure of funds on a particular project, and usually receives approval (if it is for a large amount) at the highest levels of management. Studies using distributed lags to link US appropriations data to actual investment outlays (Almon, 1965; Sachs and Hart, 1967) provide evidence of a fairly stable lag structure linking the two stages. The intermediate-stage information is useful in helping to separate expectations lags from expenditure lags. Sachs and Hart (1967) use appropriations in conjunction with other variables to explain actual expenditures. Their finding that other variables (cash flow and the change in share prices) add explanatory power to an initial equation based on appropriations alone suggests that firms have some scope to alter the timing of expenditures. The costs involved in altering the normal length of the construction period, or in cancelling appropriations, are apparently high enough to restrict the flexibility of response. In the study mentioned above, for example, the best investment equation based on appropriations and other variables has an explained variance only 3 per cent greater than an equation based solely on appropriations (Sachs and Hart, 1967, p. 509).

Contracts. The appropriations mentioned above are planning documents internal to the firm. The approval of an appropriation request usually provides authority (sometimes after the event) for contracts to be let for construction or delivery of building or equipment. Time series for contracts awarded, where they exist, are likely to refer to construction rather than machinery and equipment. In the case of construction there is more likely to be a single reported contract covering a fairly high proportion of the total expenditure on a project. If the reporting were good, contracts might explain expenditures better than do appropriations, since there are usually penalties levied for non-fulfilment.

J. F. Helliwell 35

Expenditure, anticipated and actual. Anticipated and actual expenditures have been described by Jorgenson (1965, p. 37) as separate stages in the investment process, but I prefer to regard them as estimates, made from different vantage points, of the same stage in the process. Investment anticipations and investment forecasts are synonymous expressions for the results of surveys asking firms and other investors what their capital outlays are likely to be in one or more future time periods.

Forecasts and actual expenditures refer to the total of expenditure in a certain time period, based on investment appropriations in that and several prior periods. The total of appropriations in one time period, by contrast, relates to expenditures spread out over a number of subsequent time periods.

As usually measured in national accounts, investment expenditure refers to work put in place, so that machinery being custom-built by the supplier would appear in the national accounts as inventory investment until the time of delivery and installation, when inventories would drop and fixed capital expenditure would rise. On-site work presumably is recorded as investment when it is taking place.

Completion. Although there are no aggregate time series for this stage of business fixed investment, the completion or 'going on stream' of a plant presumably marks the time when a cumulant of expenditure on a project ought to be considered a productive part of the capital stock. When one is calculating capital services available for production, the best capital stock to use would be the depreciated cumulant of projects completed; although for tax depreciation and obsolescence the cumulants of expenditure or starts may be more relevant. In the absence of completions data, net capital stocks will continue to be measured as the depreciated cumulant of investment outlays.

In none of the stages described above is any split made between projects intended for 'replacement' and those intended for 'expansion'. Only rarely can investment projects be usefully split into such categories, and even then the changes in technology and product mix since an original investment are likely to make its 'replacement' difficult to define. More on this in Section III (pp. 40–41).

Legacies from history

Backlog of uncompleted projects. The appropriate definition of this backlog depends on the definition used for the capital stock, and on the extent of freedom to alter projects once started. The usual definition employed by Jorgenson and others assumes no freedom to alter projects once started, and uses expenditures rather than completions to define increments to the capital stock. Thus the backlog comprises the total of expenditures yet to be made on projects started but not completed. If the capital stock were defined by completions rather than expenditure, then the backlog would comprise all expenditure relating to projects started but not completed, whether or not such expenditures had been made.

The backlog concept has been used (see de Leeuw, 1962) to develop a model of net investment via new appropriations for net investment. If desired capital stock, K^*, differs from the capital stock on hand at the beginning of the period by more than the backlog of investment approved but not put in place, then new appropriations for net investment (ANI_t) are made sufficient to fill the gap. If it takes j periods to complete investment projects the value of K^* should be that desired for period $t+j$ as seen at time t. This series is denoted by $K^*_{t+j,t}$ to show that expectations underlying the K^* series are formed at the time appropriations are made. Thus new appropriations for net investment are equal to the change, since last period, in the capital stock desired j periods ahead.

$$\text{ANI}_t = K^*_{t+j,t} - K^*_{t+j-1,t-1}. \qquad\qquad 24$$

If the lag distribution of actual net investment behind appropriations follows a fixed pattern of weights $W_0, W_1, \dots, W_{j-1}$ over j periods, then net investment NI in any period is

$$\text{NI}_t = \sum_{i=0}^{j-1} W_i(\text{ANI}_{t-i}). \qquad\qquad 25$$

Thus an equation for net investment can be defined in terms of changes in K^*.

$$\text{NI}_t = \sum_{i=0}^{j-1} W_i(K^*_{t+j-i,t-i} - K^*_{t+j-i-1,t-i-1}). \qquad\qquad 26$$

Note that this equation is based on the assumption that nothing can be done about changes in expectations that influence present or near-term future (i.e. closer than $t+j$) values of K^*. As shown in Helliwell and Glorieux (1970), the model must become far more complicated if it is possible to do something about the near-term shortages or excesses of capital stock. (See pp. 44, 306–29 below.)

The framework underlying equation **26** also assumes that K will not change unless there are changes in K^*, thus presupposing replacement investment equal to depreciation. The corresponding equation for gross investment can be written:

$$I_t = \sum_{i=0}^{j-1} W_i(K^*_{t+j-i,t-i} - K^*_{t+j-i-1,t-i-1}) + \delta K_{t-1}. \qquad\qquad 27$$

In applications of this model, $K_{t+j,t}^*$ is usually replaced by K_t^*, based on current Q, with or without some multiplicative impact from relative prices. The equation usually fitted is thus:

$$I_t = \sum_{i=0}^{j-1} W_i(K_{t-i}^* - K_{t-i-1}^*) + \delta K_{t-1}. \qquad 28$$

The substitution of K_t^* for $K_{t+j,t}^*$ is common, but it leaves us wondering whether the backlog has been properly accounted for after all. The same doubts carry over to the version in which K_{t-1} is used instead of K_{t-1}^*.

The implication of this model is that projects are always initiated to fill an *ex ante* gap, and that the lag distribution of resulting expenditures is fixed. In the case of net expansion, these assumptions may be reasonable, but if ever K^* decreases from one period to the next the model implies that the decrease is followed by the same fixed lag distribution, now comprising bits of net disinvestment. The conceptual foundations of the fixed lag distribution simply do not apply to decreases in K^*. The model equation 27 is sometimes defended on the grounds that aggregate net investment is seldom if ever negative. But the lag distribution assumptions are mistaken if ever K^* falls; and if capital stock cannot be shifted easily from one industry to another and/or K^* drops for any major industrial sector, the model is in danger. Evidence from equations fitted to successive samples of cross-section data (Meyer and Kuh, 1957; Meyer and Glauber, 1964) suggests that downward movements in K^* have been, at least in the United States, great enough to make the investment response asymmetric.

In the next paragraphs we shall consider the extent to which investment models explicitly including the lagged value of the capital stock can overcome the shortcomings of the symmetric models based entirely on changes in K^*.

Existing capital stock. The likelihood that the lags in the accumulation of capital stock are different in nature from those governing reductions in the stock has been recognized for many years. Indeed, a number of aggregate non-linear trade cycle models (Hicks, 1950; Goodwin, 1951) make important use of the resulting asymmetry.

If the capital stock cannot be reduced as fast as it can be increased, or if the rate of reduction depends on different factors from the rate of increase, then the actual capital stock will not be based simply on a weighted average of successive values of K^*. In these circumstances, the constraint which the existing capital stock imposes on the process of attaining K^* cannot be properly represented by the model of equation **28**. This explains why 'capacity' versions (Chenery, 1952), of the accelerator making use of the actual capital stock fit better than versions depending solely on expected changes in output. The version of the capital-stock adjustment model most closely corresponding to equation **28** is:

$$I_t = \sum_{i=0}^{j-1} W_i(K^*_{t-1} - K_{t-i-1}) + \delta K_{t-1} \qquad\qquad 29$$

in which actual K_{t-1} is used instead of K^*_{t-1} inside the distributed lag 'gap' variable. By including the lagged actual rather than the lagged desired capital stock as the 'starting point' from which adjustments are made, it partially removes the errors that arise if there are asymmetries in the accumulation process. However, although this equation may fit better than equation **28**, it will not simulate or forecast any more accurately, because both models involve the same symmetric response mechanism.

There is a big difference between equations **28** and **29** if a constant term or separate variables intended to alter the timing of investment outlays are included. The latter case is considered in Section III below (pp. 43–4). When an equation of the form of **28** has a positive constant term, then the actual capital stock would rise continually even if K^* were constant. This increase in the actual capital stock would in turn induce an increase in replacement investment. By contrast, a positive constant term in equation **29** would cause K, in equilibrium, to be above K^* by a constant amount. This is much preferable to the continual divergence of K from K^* implied by a linear constant term in equation **28**.

Another important difference between **28** and **29** arises if the estimated sum of the W_i lag weights differs from unity. If the sum of the weights is less than 1·0, then a change in K^* leads eventually to a corresponding change in K in **29** but not in **28**. Even in **29**, of course, the time pattern of the full adjustment will be more extended than the W_i distribution.

If a model were to be specified to take proper account of the constraint imposed by the actual capital stock, it would have to involve different lag distributions for increases than for decreases in K^*, and would have to permit replacement investment to drop in the presence of excess capacity. Some possibilities will be outlined in pages 40–44.

Existing employment, hours worked, and rates of production. The investment equations fitted by Jorgenson and others have taken no account of labour costs in the investment decision, on the assumption that the labour input can be instantaneously and costlessly adjusted to the level desired. Most employment equations, however, have shown substantial lags in the adjustment of actual to supposedly desired levels (Kuh, 1965). This result hints, reasonably enough, that there are costs involved in full short-term labour adjustment because of hiring costs, overtime premiums, specialized skills acquired in a job, notice payments, and so on. The fact that both labour and capital are relatively fixed factors has been used to argue that output cannot be exogenous (Gould, 1969), and that labour and capital demands are determined jointly rather than independently (Coen and Hickman, 1970; Helliwell *et al.*, 1971). The likelihood that the variability of adjustment speeds differs for capital, employment, and rates of utilization has been used to argue that the adjustment paths of all factors ought to be estimated interdependently (Nadiri and Rosen, 1969; Schramm 1970). These points are well taken, but the quantitative importance, for the investment equation, of interdependent adjustment paths has not been proven. For example, the Nadiri and Rosen equation for capital accumulation depends only weakly on output, and not significantly on the inputs of other factors.

Depreciation and replacement investment. As already explained, most investment equations are based on a theory of net investment, and are completed by the assumption that replacement investment regularly equals depreciation. If gross investment equations have been fitted, the lagged capital stock is included and a similarity between its coefficient and the assumed depreciation rate is used to support the theory of replacement investment. Occasionally, studies have chosen the depreciation rate so as to obtain convergence between it and the coefficient of replacement investment. The proportional model of replacement has been supported by Jorgenson (e.g. 1963, 1971a) on the grounds that the infinite series of replacement for any stock of assets with probabilistic lives approaches a constant proportion of that stock. There are several objections to this approach.

Helliwell and Glorieux (1970) doubt the existence of any meaningful distinction between expansion investment and replacement investment, and argue that a uniform model of gross investment ought to explain how the *ex ante* gap is filled between a desired capital stock and an expiring stock of existing capital. Faster depreciation forces a higher rate of gross investment to provide any particular series of desired capital stocks, but this does not rationalize a split between one type of investment done automatically and immediately and another done subject to lags. The first underlying behavioural assumption must be that equipment and building failures can be foreseen, and replacements planned to coincide. This requires a second assumption that demand will be high enough to justify at least that level of capital stock. All other increases in demand, by contrast, are unforeseen, so that perceived changes in output lead to a distributed lag of expansion investment. These assumptions are especially suspect when aggregate demand is dropping fast. Equations **27** and **28** would show a continuing level of replacement investment, offset by a distributed lag of net disinvestments in response to a drop in demand. A more plausible model would show no new projects started (assuming that expected demand dropped in all sectors), either for 'expansion' or 'replacement'. The capital stock would then drop at a rate determined by depreciation less the remaining expenditures on projects started but not completed. If there were some scope for cancellations, faster reductions would be possible in the capital stock.

Feldstein and Foot (1971) have argued along different lines. Making use of questionnaire data about the split of expenditure between 'expansion' on the one hand, and 'replacement and modernization' on the other, they have fitted equations for the latter category. They find systematic explanatory roles for economic variables and conclude that the proportional replacement assumption is mistaken. Similar results were subsequently obtained by Eisner (1972), and a broader range of tests is reported by Feldstein (1972). Advocates of equation **28** or **29** would presumably reply that the split between replacement and expansion is a convenience, justified or not by the success of the resulting explanation of gross investment. If Feldstein and Foot could use a questionnaire splitting of investment into two segments as a basis for a more accurate explanation of gross investment, then the proponents of equations **28** and **29** would have to reconsider. In any event, whether or not there is any useful distinction to be drawn between the 'replacement' and 'expansion' elements of gross investment, there is little reason to assume *a priori* that 'replacement' investment is equal to depreciation.

Feldstein and Rothschild (1974) have made a useful summary of the types of 'depreciation' to which capital goods are subject and present a variety of reasons why most types of depreciation ought to vary with price and cost conditions. They focus most of their attention on 'output decay', the rate of decline in the output of an ageing machine, with other inputs held constant. This type of depreciation, which is the one implicitly referred to by most investment studies, is associated by Feldstein and Rothschild with 'replacement investment' as a matter of definition. Whether this is the most useful way of defining replacement is questionable (see for example Nerlove, 1972, p. 224). In times of falling demand, there is every reason not to replace capacity lost through output decay.

The timing of outlays behind decisions

Fixed lag patterns. Most investment equations have supposed that outlays follow decisions according to a fixed pattern of non-negative weights. The recent literature, following Jorgenson (1966), has made use of a general operator notation to describe the alternative patterns of weights. LX is X_{t-1} and $W(L)$ is the general lag distribution of expenditures after the point of decision. Although the expectations schemes in most investment equations are not made explicit, I shall interpret the lag distributions employed as though they were lags of expenditures behind decisions or appropriations.

The geometrically declining weight pattern was one of the first employed in econometric studies, sometimes representing adaptive expectations (Cagan, 1956) and sometimes partial adjustment (Nerlove, 1958; de Leeuw, 1962). If both processes are assumed to operate simultaneously, then two lagged values of the dependent variable are required (Waud, 1968; Feige, 1967). Return to equation 28, and convert it to a net investment equation as follows:

$$NI_t = I_t - \delta K_{t-1} = W(L)(K_t^* - K_{t-1}^*). \tag{30}$$

Under the geometric lag, first used in an investment equation by Koyck (1954), $W(L) = (1-\lambda)(1+\lambda L+\lambda^2 L^2+...)$, $0 \leqslant \lambda < 1$, where the weights $W_i = (1-\lambda)\lambda^i$, and $\lambda W_i = W_{i-1}$. Following Jorgenson (1966) and Griliches (1967), this distribution can be written as a polynomial in the lag operator L for $W(L)X = (1-\lambda)(1+\lambda L+\lambda^2 L^2+...)X = \{(1-\lambda)/(1-\lambda L)\}X$. Hence

$$NI_t = \{(1-\lambda)/(1-\lambda L)\}(K_t^* - K_{t-1}^*). \tag{31}$$

One shortcoming with this distribution as written is that the weights $W_i = (1-\lambda)\lambda^i$ decline continually, and cannot represent a humped distribution, in which the weights first rise and then fall. Koyck (1954) applied the geometric lag in a slightly more flexible way by allowing the first weight to be unconstrained by estimating

$$NI_t = [\{W_0+(W_1-\lambda W_0)L\}/(1-\lambda L)](K_t^* - K_{t-1}^*). \tag{32}$$

This provides a simple example of a lag function which is a polynomial in the distributed lag operator. Its estimating form involves the current and one lagged value of the independent variable as well as one lagged value of the dependent variable. Ratios of higher-order polynomials have been used by Jorgenson and others in their investment equations. Higher-order polynomials involve further lagged values, and thereby allow more flexible lag shapes. An alternative two-parameter infinite lag distribution, the general Pascal distribution, has been suggested by Solow (1960) and applied recently to an investment equation by Feldstein and Flemming (1971). It takes the form

$$NI_t = \left\{ \frac{a(1-\lambda)^r}{(1-\lambda L)^r} \right\} (K_t^* - K_{t-1}^*). \tag{33}$$

In contrast to the infinite lag distributions mentioned above, the approximation procedure suggested by Almon (1965) permits the estimation of quite general polynomial distributions with pre-set starting and ending points. The Almon technique uses only linear combinations of various lagged values of the independent variables and has gained considerable favour for this reason. The possible problems arising from using lagged dependent variables in estimation will be mentioned in the next section.

Some of the other finite lag distributions used in investment equations have been the rectangular and inverted V (both by de Leeuw, 1962).

Flexible lag distributions. An early objection to fixed lag distributions was expressed by Eisner and Strotz (1963), who argued that the time it takes to adjust the capital stock to a new desired level is not fixed rigidly, any more than is the desired capital/output ratio. They argue that fixed lag distributions arise only as special cases contingent on specific forms of cost function relating to different adjustment speeds. It has since been shown that even their own results are special cases depending heavily on the convexity of the assumed cost function (Rothschild, 1971).

The theory underlying costs of adjustment is rather vague. We do know from the studies relating appropriations and expenditures that fairly stable outlay distributions do exist, but we do not have tractable and testable models of how the shapes of these distributions are determined. Reference is made to delivery lags, necessary sequences in the construction process, bottlenecks in the supplying industries, costs of overtime work, planning lags, and so on. But the range of potentially relevant factors is not easily represented by a simple function spelling out the costs of alternative adjustment speeds.

In part, the issue is bound up with the expectations process. If there is a least-cost time pattern of investment outlays for particular projects, then such projects ought to be started so many periods before they are needed. But if expectations are uncertain, and increasingly so as they go farther into the future, then there will be an incentive to defer commencements awaiting more accurate information about future demand, technology, and prices.

A number of theoretical papers (Gould, 1968; Treadway, 1969; Lucas, 1967, 1967a), have considered the influence of adjustment costs on adjustment speeds. Among the empirical studies, there have been several methods of allowing for variable adjustment paths. The factor demand models of Nadiri and Rosen (1969), Schramm (1970) and Brechling and Mortensen (1971) have relied on the assumption of differing adjustment costs for capital, labour, and utilization to justify making factor adjustment paths interdependent.

Alternatively, there have been models making the adjustment speed a function of supply constraints (Tinsley, 1967) or financial variables (Greenberg, 1964; Coen, 1971).

Finally, there are some capital stock adjustment models (e.g. Helliwell *et al.*, 1971) that vary the adjustment path by adding separate independent variables affecting the current flow of investment without influencing the desired stock. If such variables are being added to an equation, it makes a great deal of difference whether or not the lagged actual stock of capital is included. If a one-shot 'timing' variable is added to equation **28** it would alter permanently the net capital stock. If it were added to equation **29** in which the actual lagged stock of capital appears, it would alter the capital stock in the same way, in the first period. But then the higher value of the lagged capital stock would reduce subsequent net investment so that the final net capital stock would be unchanged, unless K^* itself were altered during the process. Nerlove (1972) surveys many of the procedures noted above, and presents some alternative ways of linking distributed lags more closely to the investment decision process.

The influence of changes in expectations. In the usual models making the capital stock gap a function of current values of output and prices, the lag distributions are either fixed or variable in one of the ways outlined above. But if the relevant time horizons are specified, and investment is planned now in order to fill an *ex ante* capital shortage, there arises the problem of how to deal with changes in expectations after projects are started but before they are completed. If expectations change about desired output, can the scale of the projects be partially or fully altered? If factor costs change, can the factor proportions be altered?

Some indirect evidence of these issues is provided by the various surveys of investment intentions. If actual expenditures differ from those forecast by the survey respondents, the differences ought to be explicable in terms of changes in expectations. The term 'realization function' has been used by Modigliani and Cohen (1961), and Eisner (1965), to describe equations explaining the processes linking anticipated and actual expenditures. To derive an explanation of the process in terms of explicit changes in expectations, as in Helliwell and Glorieux (1970) is rather complicated, but provides the best way of assessing the influence of changes in expectations occurring while the investment process is going on. Here, as elsewhere, there are too many alternative models to test with too little data.

IV Estimation problems
Stochastic assumptions

An assumed stochastic disturbance, hopefully with zero mean, constant variance, and zero covariance with all included variables, is a necessary feature of any equation to be estimated. Most investment models have been developed with little rationale given for the assumed stochastic properties of the estimating equations. This is slightly surprising, in view of the long history of attention to the corresponding features of production functions (e.g. Marschak and Andrews, 1944; Nerlove, 1965), and the rapidly growing body of econometric knowledge of the importance of stochastic specification in empirical work.

Why might the data generated by the economy fail to conform exactly to an aggregate investment equation? To merely ask this question is to lose confidence in any simple assumption about stochastic properties. There are aggregation errors involved in all the related prices and quantities; the assumed production function would be approximate for a single process, let alone for total production; the assumed expectations processes are prone to errors from aggregation, non-stationarity, and the influence of extraneous events; the lag distributions are approximations; and so on.

The simplest and most usual stochastic assumption is to add a random error term to the estimating equation for net or gross investment. If the errors are serially independent and uncorrelated with the independent variables, then equations like **28, 29** or **30** can be estimated by the ordinary least squares method if all the independent variables are exogenous, or by a simultaneous equations method if there is an important feedback from investment to the independent variables. These assumptions greatly simplify the estimation procedure, but they are highly restrictive and often unrealistic. Bischoff (1971), using an equation with the capital stock as the dependent variable, has generalized the stochastic assumption slightly, permitting the error term to follow a first-order autoregressive progress with a coefficient of autocorrelation $-1 \leqslant \rho \leqslant 1$, and estimating ρ and the behavioural parameters using a method suggested by Hildreth and Lu (1960). Bischoff's experiments indicated that values of between 0 and 1 were much more likely than either zero or one. Feldstein and Flemming (1971) introduce two assumed error terms, a multiplicative error term in the definition of the desired capital stock, and an additive error term in the definition of the actual capital stock as a distributed lag on past levels of the desired capital stock. The latter error term is equivalent to that in Bischoff's model when $\rho = 1$. The additional supposition by Feldstein and Flemming that the desired capital stock K^* is not an exact function of expected output and relative prices is very appropriate. However, if such an error term is due to approximations in aggregate expectations processes, shifts in the aggregate production mix, etc., then it cannot be accurately represented as a simple multiplicative term with constant mean and zero covariance with the other determinants of K^*. Even the simple version which they propose has to be assumed away in their actual estimation process, because any error term in the definition of K^* leads to autocorrelated disturbances in the investment equation. No simple transformations are adequate to account for this autocorrelation, for it is of first, second and all higher orders up to the number of time periods included in the lag distribution.

It is also a matter of convenience, in most cases, to assume an autoregressive error. For in most models involving lags, the logical error structure is a moving average process or perhaps a mixed process. Unfortunately, such processes are comparativly unfamiliar in econometrics and comparatively difficult to handle in estimation. Nevertheless, methods are available (see Trivedi, 1970) to handle these, and other problems. There is much scope for the development and application of estimation methods and equation specifications that employ more realistic stochastic assumptions than those used to date in investment equations.

Estimation of distributed lags

The preceding discussion suggests strongly that it is wise to avoid estimation methods whose results are biased if the error terms are subject to higher-order autocorrelation. When ordinary least squares are applied, it is well known that coefficients on lagged dependent variables are biased even in large samples if there is autocorrelation of the error term in the equation estimated (e.g. Griliches, 1961, 1967). It is feasible to apply the search technique suggested by Hildreth and Lu (1960) to account for first-order autocorrelation and technically possible to account for first-, second- and higher-order autocorrelation, but the scale of the necessary search procedure becomes excessive as the assumed autocorrelation process is made more general. Although it is possible to avoid using rational distributed lags or other methods requiring the use of a lagged dependent variable – the Almon technique providing the most flexible alternative currently available – it is less easy to avoid using the lagged capital stock. The lagged capital stock is used either in the definition of the capital stock 'gap' (as in equation 29), or as an assumed determinant of replacement investment, or both. The most straightforward way of dealing with this problem is to use instrumental variables (described in Sargan, 1958; and Griliches, 1967, pp. 41–2) to insulate the parameter estimates from the effects of autocorrelated errors transmitted by lagged values of investment or capital. However, such methods are not fully efficient and, more important, they do not permit proper estimation of standard errors without fully specifying and evaluating the covariance structure of errors. In other words, while instrumental variable estimators may be obtained which are unbiased in large samples, the problem of serial correlation is not fully and properly accounted for in the standard errors. Such methods therefore pave the way for incorrect inferences, even though large sample unbiasedness is achieved. There seems no escape from cumbersome search methods if serially correlated errors are obtained and we are to guard against making false inferences. Incidentally, while search methods are undoubtedly cumbersome, they do permit, in some cases, the identification of parameters that would otherwise be unidentifiable.

Whatever method of lag estimation is used, the results may not be decisively in favour of a particular lag shape (see Griliches and Wallace, 1965). There is no available experimental evidence to suggest which, if any, methods of estimating distributed lags are relatively precise.

V Concluding comments

At the beginning of this survey, the main problem in investment studies was alleged to be that of choosing what theory to impose *a priori* and what to leave to be determined by the data.

There is an evident trend, in the recent quantitative studies, to use more explicit assumptions about technology and behaviour. Perhaps the chief motivation for this trend has been a desire to measure the effects of government policies designed to influence investment expenditure. (See, for example, the papers and discussion in Fromm, 1971.) Such measurements are more confidently made using an explicit model in which policy variables enter the equation in a clearly defined manner consistent with the underlying theory. Estimation of the total effects of government policies influencing investment naturally requires that the investment equations be simulated in the context of a macro-model (as is done by Klein and Taubman, 1971) to allow appropriate accelerator and supply influences to come into play. As indicated by Harberger's comments in Fromm (1971), most existing macro-models depict accelerator influences more accurately than the relevant aggregate supply constraints, so that the impact of investment incentives on real output is likely to be overstated.

One of the consequences of using more explicit models is that the nature of their assumptions is made clear for all to see. Thus there is a second round of studies under way, which aim to test or to generalize the more restrictive or implausible of the assumptions employed in the earlier studies. There have already been attempts to increase the number of factors involved in the production function, to allow for differing degrees of factor substitution *ex ante* and *ex post*, to make expectations explicit and thereby to emphasize the forward-looking nature of investment behaviour, to make the adjustment process more flexible, and to make the stochastic assumptions more realistic. Further progress at the aggregate level is bedevilled by inadequate data samples and by aggregation problems. There are not enough observations to permit estimation of an aggregate model that generalizes several assumptions at once, and the available data are often not consistently defined. For example, it is usually difficult to obtain employment, investment, and output data that refer to the same time periods and establishments. Where these data are available, the associated prices are not, and there are enormous problems in measuring the various working capital and raw material inputs to the production process. Some of the problems are conceptual ones, while others exist mainly because the present national systems for collecting statistics were put in place before there were such obvious needs for consistency among the various series.

If good data can be developed at the industry level, it may be plausible to make progress there in the estimation of more realistic investment models. At the industry level it may be possible to use more *a priori* specification of the production process, and thereby to conserve data. If behaviour could be fairly accurately explained at the disaggregated level, then these results could be consistently combined to obtain more specific restrictions on the aggregate equations. Another way of conserving scarce data may be to use Bayesian estimation procedures to make use of prior information about the probability of various models and parameter values (e.g. Leamer, 1970; Zellner, 1971).

Useful empirical statements about a fast-changing economy will always require cunning use of the available information. In the field of investment behaviour, we can see some of the improvements in theory, data, and estimation techniques required for further progress. Even with these improvements, there will never be enough data to estimate appropriate models and to test them adequately against feasible alternatives. This makes the future course of research difficult either to predict or to prescribe. Ten years ago there was probably too little emphasis placed on the theoretical underpinnings of investment equations, while many of the more recent studies may well place too much faith in untested neoclassical assumptions. That we can never be entirely confident in such judgements is evidence in favour of another view (which I hold with more assurance) that there is and must be at least as much art as science in applied econometrics.

References

ALMON, S. (1965), 'The distributed lag between capital appropriations and expenditures', *Econometrica*, vol. 33, pp. 178–96.

ANDERSON, W. H. L. (1964), *Corporate Finance and Fixed Investment*, Harvard University Press.

ANDO, A., and RASCHE, R. (1971), *Equations in the MIT-Penn-SSRC Econometric Model of the United States*, Mimeo.

ARROW, K. J. (1964), 'The role of securities in the optimal allocation of risk-bearing', *Rev. econ. Stud.*, vol. 31, pp. 91–6.

ARROW, K. J., CHENERY, H. B., MINHAS, B. S., and SOLOW, R. M. (1961) 'Capital–labor substitution and ecomomic efficiency', *Rev. econ. Stat.*, vol. 43, pp. 225–50.

BAUMOL, W. J. (1959), *Business Behaviour, Value and Growth*, Macmillan.

BISCHOFF, C. W. (1969), 'Hypothesis testing and the demand for capital goods', *Rev. econ. Stat.*, vol. 51, pp. 354–68.

BISCHOFF, C. W., (1971), 'The effect of alternative lag distributions', in G. Fromm (ed.), *Tax Incentives and Capital Spending*, Brookings Institution, North-Holland.

BRECHLING, F. R., and MORTENSEN, D. T. (1971), 'Interrelated investment and employment decisions', Paper presented at the North American meetings of the Econometric Society, New Orleans.

BROWN, M., and DE CANI, J. S. (1963), 'Technical change and the distribution of income', *Inter. econ. Rev.*, vol. 4, pp. 289–309.

CAGAN, P. (1956), 'The monetary dynamics of hyperinflation', in M. Friedman (ed.), *Studies in the Quantity Theory of Money*, University of Chicago Press.

CHENERY, H. B. (1952), 'Overcapacity and the acceleration principle', *Econometrica*, vol. 20, pp. 1–28.

COEN, R. M. (1968), 'Effects of tax policy on investment in manufacturing' *Amer. econ. Rev.*, vol. 58, pp. 200–211.

COEN, R. M. (1969), 'Tax policy and investment behavior: comment', *Amer. econ. Rev.*, vol. 59, pp. 370–79.

COEN, R. M. (1971), 'The effect of cash flow on the speed of adjustments', in G. Fromm (ed.), *Tax Incentives and Capital Spending*, Brookings Institution, North-Holland.

COEN, R. M., and HICKMAN, B. G. (1970), 'Constrained joint estimation of factor demand and production functions', *Rev. econ. Stat.*, vol. 52, pp. 287–300.

CYERT, R. M., and MARCH, J. G. (1963), *A Behavioral Theory of the Firm*, Prentice-Hall.

DE LEEUW, F. (1962), 'The demand for capital goods by manufacturers: a study of quarterly time series', *Econometrica*, vol. 30, pp. 407–23.

DHRYMES, P. J. (1967), 'Adjustment dynamics and the estimation of the CES class of production functions', *Inter. econ. Rev.*, vol. 8, pp. 209–17.

DOUGLAS, P. H. (1948), 'Are there laws of production?', *Amer. econ. Rev.*, vol. 38, pp. 1–41.

EISNER, R. (1965), 'Realization of investment anticipations', in J. S. Duesenberry et al. (eds.), *The Brookings Quarterly Econometric Mode of the United States*, Rand NcNally, pp. 95–108.

EISNER, R. (1967), 'A permanent income theory for investment: some empirical explorations', *Amer. econ. Rev.*, vol. 57, pp. 363–90.

EISNER, R. (1969), 'Tax policy and investment behavior: comment', *Amer. econ. Rev.*, vol. 59, pp. 379–88.

EISNER, R. (1972), 'Components of capital expenditures: replacement and modernization versus expansion', *Rev. econ. Stat.*, vol. 54, pp. 297–305.

EISNER, R., and NADIRI, M. I. (1968), 'Investment behavior and neoclassical theory', *Rev. econ. Stat.*, vol. 50, pp. 369–82.

EISNER, R., and NADIRI, M. I. (1970), 'Neoclassical theory of investment behavior: comment', *Rev. econ. Stat.*, vol. 52, pp. 216–22.

EISNER, R., and STROTZ, R. H. (1963), 'Determinants of business investment', in Commission on Money and Credit, *Impacts of Monetary Policy*, Prentice-Hall, pp. 59–337.

ENCARNACIÓN, J. (1964), 'Constraint and the firm's utility function', *Rev. econ. Stud.*, vol. 31, pp. 113–20.

EVANS, R. G., and HELLIWELL, J. F. (1969), *Quarterly Business Capital Expenditures*, Bank of Canada Staff Research Studies, no. 1, Ottawa.

FEIGE, E. L. (1967), 'Expectations and adjustments in the monetary sector', *Amer. econ. Rev.*, vol. 57, pp. 462–73.

FELDSTEIN, M. S. (1967), 'Specification of the labour input in the aggregate production function', *Rev. econ. Stud.*, vol. 34, pp. 375–86.

FELDSTEIN, M. S. (1971), 'Financing in the evaluation of public expenditures', Harvard Institute of Economic Research, Discussion Paper no. 132.

FELDSTEIN, M. S. (1972), 'Tax incentives, stabilization policy and the proportional replacement hypothesis: some negative conclusions', Harvard Institute of Economic Research, Discussion Paper no. 256.

FELDSTEIN, M. S., and FLEMMING, J. S. (1971), 'Tax policy, corporate savings and investment behaviour in Britain', *Rev. econ. Stud.*, vol. 38, pp. 415–34.

FELDSTEIN, M. S., and FOOT, D. K. (1971), 'The other half of gross investment: replacement and modernization expenditures', *Rev. econ. Stat.*, vol. 53, pp. 49–58.

FELDSTEIN, M. S., and ROTHSCHILD, M. (1974), 'Towards an economic theory of replacement investment', *Econometrica*, vol. 42, forthcoming.

FISHER, F. M., (1971), 'Aggregate production functions and the explanation of wages: A simulation experiment', *Rev. econ. Stat.*, vol. 53, pp. 305–25.

FROMM, G. (ed.), (1971), *Tax Incentives and Capital Spending*, Brookings Institution, North-Holland.

FUSS, M. A. (1970), 'The structure of technology over time: a model for testing and the "putty clay" hypothesis', Harvard Institute of Economic Research, Discussion Paper no. 141.

GEORGESCU-ROEGEN, N. (1970), 'The economics of production', *Amer. econ. Rev.*, vol. 60, pp. 1–9.

GOODWIN, R. M. (1951), 'The nonlinear accelerator and the persistence of business cycles', *Econometrica*, vol. 19, pp. 1–17.

GORMAN, W. M. (1968), 'Measuring the quantities of fixed factors', in J. N. Wolfe (ed.), *Value, Capital, and Growth: Papers in honour of Sir John Hicks*, Aldine.

GOULD, J. P. (1968), 'Adjustment costs in the theory of investment of the firm', *Rev. econ. Stud.*, vol. 35, pp. 47–55.

GOULD, J. P. (1969), 'The use of endogenous variables in dynamic models of investment', *Q. J. Econ.*, vol. 83, pp. 580–99.

GREENBERG, E. (1964), 'A stock-adjustment investment model'. *Econometrica*, vol. 32, pp. 339–57.

GRILICHES, Z. (1961), 'A note on serial correlation bias in estimates of distributed lags', *Econometrica*, vol. 29, pp. 65–73.

GRILICHES, Z. (1963), 'Capital stock in investment functions: some problems of concept and measurement', in C. F. Christ *et al.* (eds.), *Measurement in Economics*, Stanford University Press.

GRILICHES, Z. (1967), 'Distributed lags: a survey', *Econometrica*, vol. 35, pp. 16–49.

GRILICHES, Z., and WALLACE, N. (1965), 'The determinants of investment revisited', *Inter. econ. Rev.*, vol. 6, pp. 311–29.

GRUNFELD, Y. (1960), 'The determinants of corporate investment', in A. C. Harberger (ed.), *The Demand for Durable Goods*, University of Chicago Press.

HALL, R. E. (1968), 'Technical change and capital from the point of view of the dual', *Rev. econ. Stud.*, vol. 35, pp. 35–46.

HALL, R. E., and JORGENSON, D. W. (1967), 'Tax policy and investment behavior', *Amer. econ. Rev.*, vol. 57, pp. 391–414.

HALL, R. E., and JORGENSON, D. W. (1969), 'Tax policy and investment behavior: reply and further results', *Amer. econ. Rev.*, vol. 59, pp. 388–401.

HALL, R. E., and JORGENSON, D. W. (1971), 'Application of the theory of optimal capital accumulation', in G. Fromm (ed.), *Tax Incentives and Capital Spending*, Brookings Institution, North-Holland.

HELLIWELL, J. F. (1968), *Public Policies and Private Investment*, Clarendon Press.

HELLIWELL, J. F., and GLORIEUX, G. (1970), 'Forward-looking investment behaviour', *Rev. econ. Stud.*, vol. 37, pp. 499–516.

HELLIWELL, J. F., OFFICER, L. H., SHAPIRO, H. T., and STEWART, I. A. (1969), *The Structure of RDX1*, Bank of Canada Staff Research Studies, no. 3, Ottawa.

HELLIWELL, J. F., SHAPIRO, H. T., SPARKS, G. R., STEWART, I. A., GORBET, F. W., and STEPHENSON, D. R. (1971) *The Structure of RDX2: Part 1 and Part 2*, Bank of Canada Staff Research Studies, no. 7, Ottawa.

HICKMAN, B. G. (1965), *Investment Demand and US* ed *Economic Growth*, Brookings Institution.

HICKS, J. R. (1950), *A Contribution to the Theory of the Trade Cycle*, Clarendon Press.

HICKS, J. R. (1967), 'The pure theory of portfolio selection', in J. R. Hicks, *Critical Essays in Monetary Theory*, Clarendon Press.

HILDRETH, C., and LU, J. Y. (1960), *Demand Relations with Autocorrelated Disturbances*, Michigan Agricultural Experiment Station Technical Bulletin 276 Michigan State University.

HIRSHLEIFER, J. (1965), 'Investment decision under uncertainty: choice theoretic approaches', *Q. J. Econ.*, vol. 79, pp. 509–36.

JORGENSON, D. W. (1963), 'Capital theory and investment behavior', *Amer. econ. Rev.*, vol. 53, pp. 247–59.

JORGENSON, D. W. (1965), 'Anticipations and investment behavior', in J. S. Duesenberry *et al.* (eds.), *The Brookings Quarterly Econometric Model of the United States*, Rand McNally, pp. 35–92.

JORGENSON, D. W. (1966), 'Rational distributed lag functions', *Econometrica*, vol. 34, pp. 135–49.

JORGENSON, D. W. (1967), 'The theory of investment behavior', in R. Ferber (ed.), *Determinants of Investment Behavior*, Columbia University Press.

JORGENSON, D. W. (1971), 'Econometric studies of investment behavior: a survey', *J. econ. Lit.*, vo.. 9, pp. 1111–47.

JORGENSON, D. W. (1971a), 'The economic theory of replacement and depreciation', Harvard Institute of Economic Research, Discussion Paper no. 203.

JORGENSON, D. W. (1972), 'Investment behavior and the production function', *Bell J. econ. man. Science*, vol. 3, 220–51.

JORGENSON, D. W., and SIEBERT, C. D. (1968), 'A comparison of alternative theories of corporate investment behavior', *Amer. econ. Rev.*, vol. 58, pp. 681–712.

JORGENSON, D. W., and STEPHENSON, J. A. (1967), 'The time structure of investment behavior in United States manufacturing, 1947–1960', *Rev. econ. Stat.* vol. 49, pp. 16–27.

JORGENSON, D. W., and STEPHENSON, J. A. (1967a), 'Investment behavior in US manufacturing, 1947–1960', *Econometrica*, vol. 35, pp. 169–220.

JORGENSON, D. W., and STEPHENSON, J. A. (1969), 'Anticipations and investment behavior in US manufacturing, 1947–1960', *J. Amer. stat. Assoc.*, vol. 64, pp. 67–89.

JORGENSON, D. W., and STEPHENSON, J. A. (1969a), 'Issues in the development of the neoclassical theory of investment behavior', *Rev. econ. Stat.*, vol. 51, pp. 346–53.

KING, M. A. (1972), 'Taxation and investment incentives in a vintage investment model', *J. pub. Econ.*, vol. 1, pp. 121–47.

KLEIN, L. R., and TAUBMAN, P. (1971), 'Estimating effects within a complete econometric model', in G. Fromm (ed.), *Tax Incentives and Capital Spending*, Brookings Institution, North-Holland.

KOYCK, L. M. (1954), *Distributed Lags and Investment Analysis*, North-Holland.

KUH, E. (1965), 'Income distribution and employment over the business cycle', in J. S. Duesenberry *et al.* (eds.), *The Brookings Quarterly Econometric Model of the United States*, Rand McNally.

LEAMER, E. E. (1970), 'Bayesian model selection with applications', Harvard Institution of Economic Research, Discussion Paper no. 151.

LEONTIEF, W. W. (1951), *The Structure of the American Economy, 1919–1939*, Oxford University Press.

LUCAS, R. E., JR (1967), 'Optimal investment policy and the flexible accelerator', *Inter. econ. Rev.*, vol. 8, pp. 78–85.

LUCAS, R. E., JR (1967a), 'Adjustment costs and the theory of supply', *J. pol. Econ.*, vol. 75, pp. 321–34.

MARKOWITZ, H. M. (1959), *Portfolio Selection: Efficient Diversification of Investments*, Wiley.

MARRIS, R. (1964), *The Economic Theory of 'Managerial' Capitalism*, Macmillan.

MARSCHAK, J., and ANDREWS, W. H. (1944), 'Random simultaneous equations and the theory of production', *Econometrica*, vol. 12, pp. 143–205.

MEYER, J. R., and GLAUBER, R. R. (1964), *Investment Decisions, Economic Forecasting, and Public Policy*, Harvard University Press.

MEYER, J. R., and KUH, E. (1957), *The Investment Decision: An Empirical Study*, Harvard University Press.

MILLER, M. H., and MODIGLIANI, F. (1966), 'Some estimates of the cost of capital to the electric utility industry, 1954–1957', *Amer. econ. Rev.*, vol. 56, pp. 333–91.

MODIGLIANI, F., and COHEN, K. J. (1961), *The Role of Anticipations and Plans in Economic Behavior and Their Use in Economic Analysis and Forecasting*, University of Illinois, Bureau of Economic and Business Research.

NADIRI, M. I. (1970), 'Some approaches to the theory and measurement of total factor productivity: a survey', *J. econ. Liter.*, vol. 8, pp. 1137–77.

NADIRI, M. I., and ROSEN, S. (1969), 'Interrelated factor demand functions', *Amer. econ. Rev.*, vol. 59, pp. 457–71.

NERLOVE, M. (1958), *Distributed Lags and Demand Analysis for Agricultural and Other Commodities*, US Government Printing Office, Washington. (Agricultural Handbook no. 141, Agricultural Marketing Service, United States Department of Agriculture.)

NERLOVE, M. (1965), *Estimation and Identification of Cobb–Douglas Production Functions*, North-Holland.

NERLOVE, M. (1972), 'Lags in economic behavior', *Econometrica*, vol. 40, pp. 221–51.

PHELPS, E. S. (1962), 'The new view of investment: a neoclassical analysis', *Q. J. Econ.*, vol. 76, pp. 548–67.

ROBINSON, J. (1965), *The Accumulation of Capital*, Macmillan.

ROTHSCHILD, M. (1971), 'On the cost of adjustment', *Q. J. Econ.*, vol. 75, pp. 605–22.

ROWLEY, J. C. R. (1970), 'Investment functions: which production function?', *Amer. econ. Rev.*, vol. 60, pp. 1008–12.

ROY, A. D. (1952), 'Safety first and the holding of assets', *Econometrica*, vol. 20, pp. 431–49.

SACHS, R., and HART, A. G. (1967), 'Anticipations and investment behavior: an econometric study of quarterly time series for large firms in durable goods manufacturing', in R. Ferber (ed.), *Determinants of Investment Behavior*, Columbia University Press.

SARGAN, J. D. (1958), 'The estimation of economic relationships using instrumental variables', *Econometrica*, vol. 26, pp. 393–415.

SCHRAMM, R. (1970), 'The influence of relative prices, production conditions and adjustment costs on investment behaviour', *Rev. econ. Stud.*, vol. 37, pp. 361–76.

SCHRAMM, R. (1972), 'Neoclassical investment models and French private manufacturing investment', *Amer. econ. Rev.*, vol. 62, pp. 553–63.

SIMON, H. A. (1962), 'New developments in the theory of the firm', *Amer. econ. Rev.*, vol. 52, pp. 1–15.

SOLOW, R. M. (1960), 'On a family of lag distributions', *Econometrica*, vol. 28, pp. 393–406.

TAUBMAN, P., and WILKINSON, M. (1970), 'User cost, capital utilization, and investment theory', *Inter. econ. Rev.*, vol. 11, pp. 209–15.

TINSLEY, P. A. (1967), 'An application of variable weight distributed lags', *J. Amer. stat. Assoc.*, vol. 62, pp. 1277–89.

TOBIN, J. E. (1965), 'The theory of portfolio selection', in F. Hahn and F. R. Brechling (eds.), *The Theory of Interest Rates*, Macmillan.

TREADWAY, A. B. (1969), 'On rational entrepreneurial behaviour and the demand for investment', *Rev. econ. Stud.*, vol. 36, pp. 227–39.

TRIVEDI, P. K. (1970), 'Inventory behaviour in UK manufacturing, 1956–67', *Rev. econ. Stud.*, vol. 37, pp. 517–36.

WAUD, R. N. (1968), 'Misspecification in the "partial adjustment" and "adaptive expectations" models', *Inter. econ. Rev.*, pp. 204–17.

WILLIAMSON, O. A. (1963), 'Managerial discretion and business behavior', *Amer. econ. Rev.*, vol. 53, pp. 1032–57.

ZELLNER, A. (1971), *Bayesian Inference in Econometrics*, Wiley.

Part Two
An Eclectic Approach

Prior to the 1960s, empirical studies of investment behaviour were limited, like all other applied econometric work, by data shortages, especially of quarterly data, and by slow and expensive computing facilities. De Leeuw's paper in this part, the earliest work reprinted in this volume, illustrates flexible and imaginative adaptation to these limitations. The paper is useful for present-day students for two reasons. First, it summarizes and synthesizes the alternative hypotheses that were prevalent at the time. Second, the 'investment backlog' concept used, and the flexible combination of prior information and experimental evidence in the choice of suitable lag structures jointly provide useful emphasis on the disequilibrium character of investment decisions.

2 F. de Leeuw

The Demand for Capital Goods by Manufacturers: A Study of Quarterly Time Series[1]

F. de Leeuw, 'The demand for capital goods by manufacturers: a study of quarterly time series', *Econometrica*, vol. 30, 1962, pp. 407–23.

I Introduction

Quarterly time series for all manufacturing are used in this study to test the relationship between plant and equipment expenditures and (a) output and capacity, (b) the flow of internal funds, and (c) the level of corporate bond yields. The study makes use of a newly derived capacity index for all manufacturing and experiments with a number of different lag distributions.

The purpose of this paper is a simple one: to confront some widely held hypotheses about the demand for capital goods with some widely used quarterly figures measuring business investment. The hypotheses relate to the influence on investment of output and capacity, of gross profits less dividends, and of rates of interest. The figures are the Commerce–SEC quarterly series on capital expenditures by manufacturers, and other manufacturing statistics. The figures and the hypotheses are so often used together in analyzing current business developments that it seems profitable to attempt to relate them systematically.[2] In doing so, furthermore, by-products of interest will be developed, namely, an index of manufacturing capacity and some experimentation with lag distributions.

Section II of the paper will present the hypothesis to be tested and reduce it to a form which relates to available quarterly time series. The

1. The views expressed in this paper are my own. I should like, however, to acknowledge the valuable suggestions of Bert Hickman, David Staiger, and William Waldorf.
2. Most recent studies of business investment have made use of other figures. For example, Eisner (1960) and Meyer and Kuh (1957) use annual cross-section data for individual firms; and Clark (1953), Chenery (1952), Hickman (1957), Koyck (1954), and Kisselgoff and Modigliani (1957) use annual physical output and capacity data for relatively homogeneous industries. Klein (1951) and Klein and Goldberger (1955) use annual expenditure data. Quarterly and semiannual investment spending figures have been used in recent studies by Gehrels and Wiggins (1957) and Hickman (1959), but with important differences in hypothesis and technique from the present paper.

third section will develop and modify the quarterly time series for manufacturing so that they relate as closely as possible to the final hypothesis of
Section II. The fourth section will present the results of testing the hypothesis. The principal substantive indication of the paper will be that under
certain assumption as to lags, a modified acceleration principle variable
('capital requirements'), the flow of internal funds, and the level of bond
yields all appear to be significantly related to capital spending.

II The hypothesis
The determinants of investment

A traditional hypothesis about the demand for new capital goods is that it
is a function of the rate of interest on long-term private borrowing, a function described by the schedule of the marginal efficiency of capital. In
recent decades, this hypothesis has found little acceptance, perhaps
fundamentally because of the apparent failure of low interest rates to
stimulate capital spending during the 1930s.[3]

One alternative hypothesis has emphasized shifts in the marginal
efficiency schedule, due to changes in output, in the degree of excess
capacity, and in the rate at which capital is wearing out. Under the names
of the modified acceleration principle, the capacity principle, or the capital
requirements theory, this approach has been widely investigated in recent
years.[4] Another approach has emphasized imperfections in the capital
market and risks associated with increasing the ratio of debt to earnings,
leading to a sharp distinction between internally and externally financed
investment. In line with this emphasis, a number of recent studies have
tested the relationship between internal funds and capital expenditures.[5]

The present study, drawing from all these various approaches, takes as
its basic hypothesis that investment demand is related to industrial bond
yields, to output and capacity (the term 'capital requirements' will be used
and explained below), and to the flow of internal funds. As a linear equation (passing over the difficulties of aggregating individual firms to the
level of all manufacturing), the hypothesis states that

$$D_{t+1} = a + b_c C_t + b_f F_t + b_r R_t + U_t \qquad\qquad 1$$

3. The renewed attention paid to interest rates in the last few years, however, has
found some reflection in investment studies. See, for example, Gehrels and Wiggins
(1957) and White (1956, 1958).
4. See Chenery (1952), Clark (1953), Eisner (1960), Hickman (1957, 1959), Kisselgoff
and Modigliani (1957), Koyck (1954), and Meyer and Kuh (1957).
5. See Eisner (1960), Klein (1951), Klein and Goldberger (1955), and Meyer and
Kuh (1957). There are other hypotheses also consistent with an association between
profits and investment. On all these relationships, see Duesenberry (1958, chapters
4 and 5).

in which C_t refers to capital requirements during period t, F_t to internal funds during t, and R_t to industrial bond yields during period t. U is a random disturbance, and a and the bs are parameters. The dependent variable, D_{t+1}, will be explained in the following section.

The dependent variable and the expenditure lag

D_{t+1}, investment demand, does not refer to investment expenditures in period $t+1$. Rather, it refers to the backlog of investment projects decided on, less the amount already spent on them, at the start of period $t+1$ (the end of period t). Between an initial decision to buy a capital good and the final expenditure, there lie many time-consuming steps. There are often detailed engineering plans to be drawn, bids to be taken, orders placed, financing arranged, and complex industrial structures or items of equipment to be produced. Because of this lag, it seems realistic to consider ' D ' in the basic equation as the total planned additions to the capital stock and to use the symbol ' I ' for actual investment spending.

Manufacturers are assumed to adjust this backlog, D, so that its total is in line with capital requirements, with the flow of internal funds, and with the yield on industrial bonds. If the backlog is already appropriate to current levels of capital requirements and other variables, no new capital projects are indicated. If the total is too small or too large, new projects or postponements and cancellations are indicated. Total planned additions, D, are subject to immediate control (except for a reduction sharper than any experienced in the post-war period), while current investment expenditures, I, often refer to a stage of commitment and completion too late to control closely, as evidenced by the frequent lag of capital spending behind general business conditions.

While the basic equation refers to the backlog of projects, the quarterly time series under investigation refers to actual expenditures on these projects. The problem raised by the expenditure lag for capital goods is therefore to transform equation 1 into terms involving expenditures, I, rather than projects, D. Since investment represents a translation into actual shipments of past additions to the backlog, the problem can be thought of as finding a set of coefficients representing the lag of expenditures behind additions to the backlog D.

Proceeding in this way, let the value of new projects added to the backlog D in period t be represented by N_t (defined net of cancellations and including revaluations). The value of subtractions from the backlog is, of course, actual investment during t, or I_t. Under these definitions, D_{t+1} is equal to D_t plus N_t minus I_t, or

$$N_t = D_{t+1} - D_t + I_t = \Delta D_{t+1} + I_t. \qquad 2$$

Now let I_t include some proportion, k_1, of projects added in the previous period, N_{t-1}; a proportion, k_2, of N_{t-2}; k_3 of N_{t-3}; and so forth back to period $t-n$, where n represents the number of periods over which new projects generate expenditures. Since N is defined net of cancellations, these proportions, k, must add up to one, and

$$I_t = \sum_{i=1}^{n} k_i N_{t-i}. \qquad\qquad 3$$

Combining **2** and **3**, we have

$$I_t = \sum_{i=1}^{n} k_i \Delta D_{t+1-i} + \sum_{i=1}^{n} k_i I_{t-i}. \qquad\qquad 4$$

Shifting the last term to the left side of **4** and substituting equation **1** for D gives the final equation:

$$I_t - \sum_{i=1}^{n} k_i I_{t-i} = \sum_{i=1}^{n} k_i (b_c \Delta C_{t-i} + b_t \Delta F_{t-i} + b_r \Delta R_{t-i} + \Delta U_{t-i}). \qquad\qquad 5$$

Current investment minus a weighted average of past investment, according to this equation, depends on weighted averages of past changes in capital requirements, in internal funds, in bond yields, and in random disturbances. The parameters to be estimated are the bs, which measure the influence of the independent variables, and the ks, which describe the lag structure.

III The data

The four variables of this study – investment spending, capital requirements, internal funds, and bond yields – are quarterly, seasonally adjusted, constant-dollar (except for bond yields) series for the period 1947 to 1959. Three of the variables are readily described. Capital spending, I, is the Commerce–SEC series generally used in current analysis, deflated by the implicit GNP deflator for producers' durable equipment and non-residential construction. The flow of internal funds, F, is defined as retained earnings (profits after taxes less dividends) plus depreciation allowances. Its dollar value is estimated from FTC–SEC quarterly reports for manufacturing firms, adjusted for changes in sample in 1951 and 1956, and deflated by the same GNP deflator as is used for capital spending. The adjustment for sample change was made on the assumption that the difference between new and old samples in overlapping quarters was a bias in old sample levels which had grown linearly since the sample initiation. The bond yield, R, is Moody's series for industrial bonds.

Manufacturing capacity

The remaining variable, capital requirements, depends in part on an index of manufacturing capacity to be used in conjunction with the Federal

Reserve Board index of manufacturing production. This capacity index will be described before taking up the complete capital requirements series.

Three sets of figures were used to estimate capacity. The first was the Commerce Department's estimates of manufacturers' fixed capital stock in 1954 dollars. The second was the McGraw-Hill index of manufacturing capacity, based on an annual mail survey including a question as to the percentage increase in the physical volume of capacity during the past year. Both these series were assumed to have a gradually shifting relationship to the desired capacity measure, on the grounds that many of their differences from the desired measures – differences in weighting, in treatment of capital retirements, in implied treatment of quality changes – would have effects which develop gradually over time. Both series showed a steady upward trend, with the McGraw-Hill series growing at about $2\frac{1}{2}$ per cent per year more than the Commerce series.

The third ingredient of the capacity measure was based on answers to another McGraw-Hill question: 'How much of your capacity were you operating at the end of 19—?' The Federal Reserve output index divided by the aggregate 'rate of operations' is a third capacity measure available beginning only with January, 1955. Since this measure is directly tied to the output index, its bias relative to the desired measure should not change greatly over time. However, it is probably subject to more short-term random influences than the other two series. The response rate is lower to this than to other McGraw-Hill questions, and the index varies significantly depending on whether 'end of year' is taken to refer to December, to the last week of December, to December–January, to a seasonally adjusted, or to an unadjusted output rate.

In view of these different sources of bias, the desired capacity measure was estimated by assuming that the ratio of the third measure above to each of the other two measures depended on time and a random disturbance. Specifically, the following two equations, converted to logarithms, were fitted to five observations starting with the beginning of 1955:

$$y_{3t} \div y_{1t} = a_1 b_1{}^t u_t,$$
$$\text{and} \quad y_{3t} \div y_{2t} = a_2 b_2{}^t v_t.$$

The Commerce series was y_1, the McGraw-Hill capacity index y_2, the indexes based on the McGraw-Hill rate-of-operations figures y_3, u and v were random disturbances, and the as and bs were regression coefficients. From estimates of the as and bs, two values of y_3 (one from each equation) were calculated for all years, and the average of these two was taken as the final capacity measure. The final measure grew at about $1\frac{1}{2}$ per cent per year less than the McGraw-Hill capacity index, and at about 1 per cent per year more than the Commerce stock series.

The output index divided by the final capacity series yields a 'rate of operations' which ranges from 74 per cent of capacity in the second quarter of 1958 to 96 per cent in the second quarter of 1953, with a 1947–59 average of 86 per cent. It should scarcely be necessary to add that these figures are much more of an approximation than most of the other figures in this study.

Capital requirements

'Capital requirements', a term taken from Clark's (1953) study of the telephone industry, is defined as the constant-dollar volume of projects which will bring capacity into an optimum relationship to output. Since capital projects decided on in quarter t are assumed not to be fully completed until quarter $t+n$, the definition is interpreted to refer to the volume of projects that will bring capacity into an optimum relation to expected output n quarters hence – the difference, in other words, between desired capital stock in period $t+n$ and actual capital stock currently. Capital requirements may be thought of as consisting of three components: (a) projects needed to bring capacity into optimum relation to present output; (b) projects needed to take account of expected changes in output; and (c) projects needed to offset the continual wearing-out of the present capital stock.

The 'optimum' output-capacity relationship referred to above is estimated from McGraw-Hill data collected in its 1957 survey of investment plans. In the aggregate, manufacturers responding to the survey were indicated to prefer a rate of operations of 90 per cent, or a capacity level equal to 111·1 per cent of output. This figure is many steps removed from actual average and marginal cost data; but it may be hoped that it is a pale reflection of the notion that some rates of operation are more efficient than others. A different figure would not greatly affect the regression coefficient for capital requirements.

Given this optimum relationship, the per cent change in capacity (it can be positive or negative) needed to bring capacity to its optimum relationship to present output is equal to the output index times 1·111 minus the capacity index, expressed as a per cent of present capacity. In the post-war period, according to the figures used in the present paper, this quantity has ranged from a plus 5 per cent to a minus 18 per cent.

The expected rate of increase in output has simply been taken as 4 per cent per year at all times. Four per cent per year represents the average rate of growth of total manufacturing output during the post-war period. In view of the mildness of cyclical fluctuations and the widespread confidence in the persistence of long-term growth during the period, this crude allowance for expected rises in output is probably an acceptable approximation. One of its consequences is that the *level* of capital requirements depends on the value of n. In a more refined, less aggregated study it might be possible to experiment with weighted averages of past growth rates as a separate independent variable.

The 4 per cent assumption yields a per cent figure which was added to the previously described per cent change needed to bring capacity to its optimum relation to present output. The total of these two per cent figures was then multiplied by the constant-dollar value of the capital stock for each quarter (Commerce estimates interpolated quarterly) to give the total projects required for net additions to the capital stock.

What is missing from this total is projects required to offset worn-out capital. Two assumptions about the rate of wearing-out seem plausible and have often been made: first, that it is proportional to the rate of output, and second, that it depends on the age of the items in the capital stock. A measure suitable for the first assumption is simply the Federal Reserve output index for manufacturing. A measure based on the age assumption (though purporting to reflect depreciation rather than the conceptually preferable retirement) has been calculated annually by the Commerce Department in building up its capital stock series. The two measures both have a 4 per cent per year upward trend since 1947, and for this study indexes of the two (with output seasonally adjusted and depreciation interpolated) were averaged for each quarter.

The resultant measure of capital wearing-out was converted to dollar figures by assuming that on the average (but not for each individual quarter) it was 2·357 times the level of capital requirements for net additions, described above. The figure of 2·357 refers to the average post-war level of depreciation relative to net additions in the Commerce constant-dollar series for changes in manufacturing capital. Since this ratio is based on actual rather than planned changes, no further adjustment for expected changes in capital wearing-out was required. The net additions component and the replacement component were simply added together into a capital requirements total.

This step-by-step explanation of the derivation of the capital requirements series has perhaps failed to give a feel for what actually accounts for its movements. Essentially, it is moved by (a) the sharply fluctuating estimates of output in relation to capacity, described in the previous section, and (b) various smoother series measuring level of output, of depreciation, and of the manufacturing capital stock, all of them growing at about 4 per cent per year. Its performance in the regressions below can be regarded, at a minimum, as a measure of the relationship of these aggregate figures to capital spending.

Whether the regressions below can be regarded as more than this minimum – specifically, as a crude test of an elaborated acceleration-principle theory of investment behavior – is more questionable. One important difficulty is that the assumed optimum relation of output to capacity (the estimate of which was shaky to begin with) may have changed during the post-war years in response to technological developments, shifts in the scale and composition of output, or other factors. All that can be offered in reply is that to the extent that such changes are gradual, the capital requirements series remains useful as a short-run approximation, though it loses validity over longer periods. Other criticism might relate to the weakness of the assumptions as to replacement needs and growth needs, the quality of the depreciation figures and the capital goods deflators used, and the usual aggregation difficulties.[6] In all, it would seem advisable to treat the empirical results below very cautiously with regard to any structural implications as to the determinants of investment.

IV The results

In introducing the results of applying the data described above to the basic hypothesis, it may be helpful to look at the actual behavior of the four variables under investigation. Three waves in the dependent variable, capital spending, appear in Figure 1. The first plotted quarters are near the crest of the early post-war wave; the capital spending line then proceeds through the Korean and post-Korean waves, and the observation period ends with the moderate upswing after the 1958 recession. The waves have been four to five years long. The quarters since 1959, not included in the original calculations, were used to test the regression estimates based on 1947–59 figures.

Capital requirements could also perhaps be interpreted as tracing out three waves, but fluctuations in requirements have been less smooth than the waves in capital spending. In 1951–3, an extra fluctuation in requirements, reflecting the 1951–2 weakness in many consumer goods markets and the subsequent 1952–3 strength, found no echo in the Commerce–SEC plant and equipment series. In no quarter have capital requirements had a negative value. The timing of capital requirements cycles has led that of actual spending, as would be expected from the lags which characterize capital goods planning and production.

The flow of internal funds has had about the same amplitude of swing as

6. A further difficulty might arise from an identification problem; namely, that levels of depreciation and of the capital stock (which enter into the capital requirements estimates) depend in part on past investment in addition to their hypothesized influence on the current investment backlog. However, past investment enters equation 5 above with a negative sign; and since capital requirements turns out to have a significant positive coefficient, this possible criticism is much reduced in force.

capital spending, but has been more choppy from quarter to quarter. The timing of internal funds has also been early, and its relatively depressed level for four years after the 1950 peak is quite different from the behavior of capital spending.

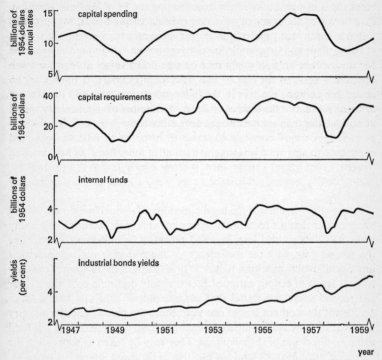

Figure 1 Quarterly, seasonally adjusted capital spending and related series

Industrial bond yields have gradually moved upwards since 1950, with some acceleration during 1956-9. Cyclical fluctuations were also intensified during the late 1950s. The simple relationship between yields and spending seems restricted to a bulge in yields toward the end of each wave of spending.

The lag structure

The final equation of Section II, it will be remembered, involved not only the *b*-coefficients attached to the three independent variables, but also a series of lag coefficients symbolized by *k*s. To estimate these lag coefficients, alternative simplifying assumptions were made about the shape of the lag distribution, and the coefficients of multiple correlation yielded by these assumptions were compared. After this step, the values of the b-coefficients were examined both for the 'best' lag distribution and for various other distributions.

Such independent evidence as exists relating to the shape of the investment lag is of only limited help in estimating the ks of the basic equation. In a survey of about seventy-five new manufacturing plants, Mayer (1960) found a 'mean lead time' of a little over seven quarters between the start of drawing plans and the completion of construction. This would suggest that for the average firm, ks might take on significant values at least for seven quarters – perhaps for one or two additional quarters, if there were an added lag between changes in the independent variables and the start of drawing plans. For the total of all firms, the number of significant ks would be still greater than for the average firm, since those firms with larger-than-average lags would continue to invest in response to past changes (and contribute to aggregate investment) even after other firms' ks had dropped to zero. From Mayer's study, then, it seems probable that k_1 to at least k_7, and probably several additional ks as well, should all be significantly positive.

Eisner (1960) estimated the lag distribution of annual investment behind annual sales changes for a cross-section of large manufacturing and utility firms. His data yielded long lags and generally declining coefficients after the second year, with the coefficients for the first year varying somewhat among different regressions. Koyck's (1954) study of the relation of capacity to past levels of output assumed geometrically declining coefficients after the second year, and found that current output generally had a lower coefficient than output lagged one year. Since the models and the industry coverage of these studies differed somewhat from the present one, it is hard to make direct use of their findings. They may be taken as supporting the inference from Mayer's study of positive ks for more than seven quarters. Perhaps Eisner's study may also be taken to imply declining values of k after some point – say after six or eight quarters – with various alternatives possible for earlier ks.

One lag distribution consistent with these findings is a Koyck (1954) distribution consisting of a geometrically declining series of coefficients. The ks, in this distribution, take on values of a, ra, r^2a, r^3a,..., r^na with r less than one. Since the sum of all the ks is equal to one, it can be shown that $a+r$ is also equal to one. The final equation from Section II (equation 5) becomes

$$I_t - a \sum_{i=1}^{n} r^{(i-1)} I_{t-i} = a \sum_{t=1}^{n} r^{(i-1)} (b_t \, \Delta C_{t-1} + b_t \, \Delta F_{t-1} + b_r \, \Delta R_{t-1}$$
$$+ \Delta U_{t-i}). \quad \textbf{6}$$

Multiplying each term in the equation for period $(t-1)$ by r and subtracting from **6** leads to

$$I_t-(a+r)I_{t-1} = a(b_c\,\Delta C_{t-1}+b_t\,\Delta F_{t-1}+b_r\,\Delta R_{t-1}+\Delta U_{t-1}),\qquad 7$$

assuming n is large enough so terms involving r^n can be ignored. Equation **7** can be rewritten as

$$\Delta I_t = ab_c\,\Delta C_{t-1}+ab_t\,\Delta F_{t-1}+ab_r\,\Delta R_{t-1}+\Delta U_{t-1}.\qquad 8$$

Thus, a Koyck distribution implies a simple relation between investment changes and changes in the independent variables lagged one period.

A second lag distribution which leads to a simple transformation of the basic data is a rectangular distribution in which $k_i = 1/n$ for $1 \leqslant i \leqslant n$ and zero otherwise. Applying this distribution to equation **5** gives

$$I_t-\frac{1}{n}\sum_{i=1}^{n} I_{t-i} = \frac{1}{n}\{b_c(C_{t-1}-C_{t-n-1})+b_f(F_{t-1}-F_{t-n-1})$$
$$+b_r(R_{t-1}-R_{r-n-1})+(U_{t-1}-U_{t-n-1})\}.\qquad 9$$

A third distribution consistent with the findings above and statistically manageable is an 'inverted V' distribution, in which the first half of the ks are proportional to the rising series $1, 2, 3,..., n/2$ (for even values of n) and the last half proportional to the declining series $n/2, n/2-1,..., 3, 2, 1$. This distribution implies that initially the investment effects of a change in the backlog are small, that they gradually (linearly) build up to a maximum, and then gradually decline to zero. It leads to an equation for even values of n of the form

$$I_t-r\sum_{j=t-(n/2)}\sum_{i=1}^{n/2} I_{j-i} = r\Bigg\{b_c\sum_{i=1}^{n/2}(C_{t-i}-C_{t-i-(n/2)-1})$$
$$+b_f\sum_{i=1}^{n/2}(F_{t-i}-F_{t-i-(n/2)-1})$$
$$+b_r\sum_{i=1}^{n/2}(R_{t-i}-R_{t-i-(n/2)-1})$$
$$+\sum_{i=1}^{n/2}(U_{t-i}-U_{t-i-(n/2)-1})\Bigg\}\qquad 10$$

in which r, the proportionality factor which makes the ks sum to one, is equal to $4\div(n^2+2n)$.

In all of these distributions, it should be noted, the presence of lags between the independent variables and investment justifies the use of single-equation regressions.

The results of fitting the three types of lag distribution represented by equations **8**, **9**, and **10** to the quarterly data for 1947 to 1959 favored the last of the alternatives, the 'inverted V' distribution. As Table 1 shows, this distribution gave the highest squared coefficient of multiple correlation, by a sizable margin. Equation **8**, based on a geometrically declining lag, gave a value of R^2 of only 0·332. If instead of using the first differences shown

Table 1 Squared coefficients of multiple correlation

Geometrically declining lag distribution	n	Rectangular lag distribution	Inverted V lag distribution
	6	0·588	0·629
(a) 0·332	8	0·751	0·726
(b) 0·572[a]	10	0·667	0·817
	12	0·458	0·872
	14	0·348	0·865

All coefficients are adjusted for the number of observations
[a] See text for explanation of the two values for R^2

in equation **8**, in which random influences might be of greater weight than in some of the other transformations, the levels of the four variables were used, the value of R^2 was raised to 0·572. Equation **9**, based on a rectangular distribution, reached a maximum R^2 of 0·751 for n equal to eight quarters. Equation **10**, based on an inverted V distribution, reached a still higher maximum, 0·872 ($R = 0·939$) for n equal to twelve quarters, with all b-coefficients of the expected sign. Odd values of n from seven to thirteen were tried for the inverted V distribution, and still left $n = 12$ as the maximum.

These three distributions cover a wide range of possible shapes for the manufacturing investment lag, and it appears likely that most plausible shapes could be approximated by one or another of the three. By combining the rectangular and inverted V equation, it would be possible to test for various degrees of dispersion around a central mean; and by combining these equations with the geometrically declining one, it would be possible to test for various degrees of skewness. In view of the many shortcomings of the basic data and hypothesis it would seem impossible to specify the correct lag distribution with great precision; for this reason, estimates based on combined equations were not attempted. The regressions which were tried, however, seem to suggest the conclusion that the inverted V distribution provides a better approximation to the manufacturing investment lag than either the geometrically declining or the rectangular distribution.

The regression coefficients

For the inverted V distribution with n equal to twelve quarters, all three of the independent variables – capital requirements, internal funds, and bond yields – had b-coefficients of expected signs and more than twice as large

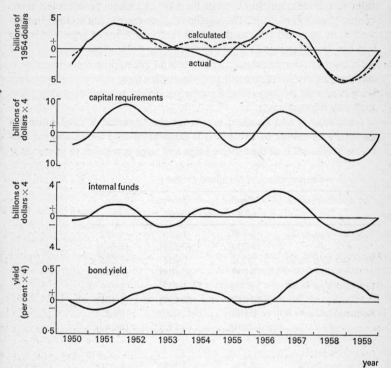

Figure 2 Quarterly, seasonally adjusted, capital spending and related series: 'inverted V' transformation, $n = 12$ quarters

as their standard errors. The transformed series underlying these coefficients are shown in Figure 2[7] along with the calculated values of investment based on the three other variables.

The coefficient of capital requirements was 0·347, implying that in any one quarter a rise of a billion dollars in capital requirements would increase the backlog of investment projects by $347 million. The fact that the

7. Based on data shown in Figure 1, transformed according to equation **10** for n equal to 12 ($r = 0·0238$). The independent variables have not been multiplied by their b-coefficients, but they have been multiplied by four to take account of the fact that capital spending is measured at annual rates.

coefficient is well below unity might be taken to suggest that current changes in the output–capacity ratio are in the first instance discounted rather heavily in planning for new investment. The coefficient of internal funds was 1·266, implying that the full effect (in fact, slightly more than the full effect, if the coefficient is taken literally) of a rise in profits is felt in the capital spending backlog. This coefficient, however, is not so high in relation to its standard error as the others. The coefficient of bond yields was −4·892, implying that a rise of one percentage point in the industrial bond yield has been associated with a decline of $4 892 million in the investment backlog. Intercorrelation coefficients among the three independent variables were moderate, with the largest coefficient, 0·544, relating capital requirements to internal funds.

b-coefficients and standard errors for the 'inverted V' and other lag distributions appear in Table 2. It is noteworthy that the capital requirements coefficient is of the expected sign and large in relation to its standard

Table 2 b-coefficients and standard errors

Lag distribution	Capital requirements	Internal funds	Bond yields
Inverted V, $n = 12$	0·347	1·266	−4·892
	(0·035)	(0·594)	(0·943)
Inverted V, $n = 10$	0·326	0·615	−3·065
	(0·038)	(0·605)	(0·944)
Inverted V, $n = 14$	0·329	1·627	−7·586
	(0·042)	(0·699)	(1·161)
Rectangular, $n = 8$	0·090	−0·055[a]	0·623[a]
	(0·010)	(0·145)	(0·240)
Geometrically declining (based on levels, letting $a = 0·25$)	0·824	−0·208[a]	0·051[a]
	(0·118)	(0·176)	(0·130)

[a]'Wrong' signs
Standard errors in parentheses

error for all of the distributions shown. The coefficient of internal funds is positive and more than twice its error for two of the five distributions, while bond yields have negative coefficients more than twice their standard error for three of the distributions.

Two other features of the regressions deserve mention. One is that constant terms were several times their standard errors in most of the regressions, although equations 8–10 do not imply significant constant terms. Constant terms could reflect biases in the levels or trends of the four basic series, or they might reflect incorrect specifications in the basic hypothesis or in the lag assumptions.

More serious is the presence of positive serial correlation in residuals based on all the regressions.[8] In the case of the inverted V distribution, equation 10 indicates that the moving average transformation of the error term, U, might introduce serial correlation even if there had not been any in the basic equation 5; however, this argument would not apply to the other distributions. Other causes of serial correlation – incorrect specification and systematic influences on investment not measured by the three independent variables – are certainly present to some extent in the regressions. The presence of serial correlation in a study of quarterly aggregate time-series, though disturbing, is hardly surprising. It may be some encouragement to note that if the quarterly residuals based on the inverted V distribution for n equal to twelve are combined into semi-annual residuals, the Durbin–Watson test is inconclusive. The serial correlation seems to be mainly a short-run matter.

Further results

The regressions above were all based on the four time series described in Section III. A large number of regressions were tried using other series – both other independent variables and other measures of manufacturing investment. The results will be summarized briefly.

Two other independent variables tested were the net liquidity of manufacturing corporations, defined as current assets, except for inventories, less current liabilities; and the ratio of capital goods prices to wage rates. The former was measured by FTC–SEC quarterly figures, seasonally adjusted and deflated; the latter by the ratio of the implicit GNP deflator for producers' durables and 'other' construction to a BLS-index of manufacturing wage rates, excluding the effects of overtime rates and inter-industry shifts. Both variables were tested for inverted V lag assumptions with various values of n; and in both cases the signs of the b-coefficients were opposite to expectation.

Two other investment series in addition to the basic Commerce–SEC series were also tested. One was based on data from the Census Bureau annual surveys of manufacturers, with a quarterly interpolation using the Commerce–SEC series. The other was based on the quarterly FTC–SEC financial surveys of manufacturing corporations, using depreciation plus the change in book value of net plant and equipment as an approximation to capital expenditures. The FTC–SEC spending series, like the internal funds series already described, was adjusted for sample changes in 1951 and

8. For the five distributions in Table 2, the Durbin–Watson ratios, in order, were 0·42, 0·43, 0·33, 0·49, and 0·26.

1956. Both these alternative series were lower in 1952–3 and higher in 1954 than the Commerce–SEC series, and both showed more growth than the Commerce–SEC series after 1955.

Both series were tested against the three basic independent variables using inverted V lag distributions of various lengths. Highest multiple correlations were found for a length of twelve quarters in both series, and all three independent variables again had the expected signs and were more than twice their standard errors. Both series showed a much higher coefficient for internal funds than the Commerce–SEC series, with other coefficients lower. In the case of the FTC–SEC series, this finding might be attributable to correlated errors of measurement, since the internal funds series and the FTC–SEC investment series had as their largest component the identical depreciation estimates. The Census investment series, however, was derived independently of the internal funds series.

A final test applied to the Commerce–SEC series was a comparison of actual and calculated values since 1959, the last year covered by the regres-

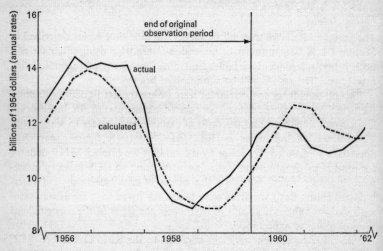

Figure 3 Quarterly, seasonally adjusted, actual and calculated investment

sions. The test was made using the inverted V distribution with n equal to twelve quarters. Data revisions affecting the capital requirements estimates were handled by linking a revised series to the old series in the fourth quarter of 1959. The actual and calculated series are plotted in Figure 3[9]

9. 'Actual' figures for the last two quarters shown are Commerce–SEC anticipations as of December, 1961, deflated by an extrapolated price index. 'Calculated' figures for these quarters are based partly on preliminary estimates.

in terms of levels of investment (that is, the moving-average investment term in equation **10** was shifted to the right side of the equation).

The results were generally favorable to the basic hypothesis. The residuals, on the average, were no larger after 1959 than during the regression period, and the calculated series indicated the two turning-points during 1960–61. However, the calculated series showed a distinct lag behind actual spending levels.

V Conclusions

The hypothesis developed in Section II of this paper was that the demand for capital by manufacturers depends on capital requirements, on the flow of internal funds, and on the industrial bond yield. The principal conclusion of this paper is that under certain assumptions as to lags, 1947–59 data for all manufacturing were consistent with the basic hypothesis. Capital requirements, internal funds, and bond yields were each found to be associated with capital spending. The association with capital requirements appeared under a variety of lag assumptions while association with internal funds and bond yields appeared only under the assumption of an 'inverted V' lag distribution. High serial correlation characterized all the regressions calculated.

The association of capital requirements or of internal funds with capital spending is a finding of many recent studies. In cross-section studies of manufacturing firms, Eisner (1960) has emphasized an explanation akin to the capital requirements one, while Meyer and Kuh (1957) have emphasized internal funds. In time-series studies Klein and Goldberger (1955) have emphasized profits, while in studies, using physical capacity figures, Chenery (1952), Clark (1953), Kisselgoff and Modigliani (1957), and Koyck (1954) have emphasized capital-requirements-type combinations of variables.

The association of interest rates (or of the credit situation they indicate) and capital spending by manufacturers is not so common a finding of recent studies, although Gehrels and Wiggins (1957), using time series similar to some of the ones in this study, do find a significant association. White (1958) has suggested that increasing exactness in planning investment programs in recent years may have increased the influence of interest rates. In the present study, the long lags play a major part in the finding as to the role of bond yields.

References

CHENERY, H. B. (1952), 'Overcapacity and the acceleration principle', *Econometrica*, vol. 20, pp. 1–28.

CLARK, P. G. (1953), 'The telephone industry: a study in private investment', in W. W. Leontief *et al.* (eds.), *Studies in the Structure of the American Economy*, Oxford University Press, pp. 243–94.

DUESENBERRY, J. S. (1958), *Business Cycles and Economic Growth*, McGraw-Hill.

EISNER, R. (1960), 'A distributed lag investment function', *Econometrica*, vol. 28, pp. 1–29.

GEHRELS, F., and WIGGINS, S. (1957), 'Interest rates and fixed investment', *Amer. econ. Rev.*, vol. 47, pp. 79–93.

HICKMAN, B. G. (1957), 'Capacity, capacity utilization and the acceleration principle', in Conference on Research in Income and Wealth, vol. 19, *Problems of Capital Formation*, Princeton University Press, pp. 419–49, and ensuing discussion.

HICKMAN, B. G. (1959), 'Diffusion, acceleration, and business cycles', *Amer. econ. Rev.*, vol. 49, pp. 535–65.

KISSELGOFF, A., and MODIGLIANI, F. (1957), 'Private investment in the electric power industry and the acceleration principle', *Rev. econ. Stat.*, vol. 39, pp. 363–79.

KLEIN, L. R. (1951), 'Studies in investment behavior', in Universities-National Bureau Committee for Economic Research, *Conference on Business Cycles*, pp. 233–303, and ensuing discussion.

KLEIN, L. R., and GOLDBERGER, A. S. (1955), *An Econometric Model of the United States, 1929–52*, North-Holland, pp. 10–13, 51, and 66–8.

KOYCK, L. M. (1954), *Distributed Lags and Investment Analysis*, North-Holland.

MAYER, T. (1960), 'Plant and equipment lead times', *Journal of Business of the University of Chicago*, vol. 33, pp. 127–32.

MEYER, J. R., and KUH, E. (1957), *The Investment Decision: An Empirical Study*, Harvard University Press.

WHITE, W. H. (1956), 'Interest elasticity of investment demand – the case from business attitude surveys re-examined', *Amer. econ. Rev.*, vol. 47, pp. 565–87.

WHITE, W. H. (1958), 'The rate of interest, the marginal efficiency of capital, and investment programming', *econ. J.*, vol. 68, pp. 51–9.

Part Three
Costs of Adjustment

The two papers in this part are the only ones that are purely
theoretical in nature. They are included so that the reader may be
exposed to the complexities involved if the lags between investment
decisions and expenditure are to be determined by economic variables.
In a fundamental sense, the lags in the investment process must be
related to the costs of building at different speeds, which in turn must
depend upon the amount of excess capacity in the industries producing
investment goods. Thus if the relevant costs of adjustment could be
measured, then supply conditions could be included more realistically in
the determination of aggregate investment.

We are at present a long way from such a goal. Even the theoretical
papers in this part are microeconomic in character, while many of the
important supply constraints are aggregate in nature.

Existing empirical work skirts this important problem. This may be
partly justified on the strength of several studies indicating rather stable
lag distributions between investment appropriations and expenditure,
(see Section III, p. 35 of Reading 1) suggesting that adjustment
speeds may not be greatly affected by normal variations in supply
conditions.

3 R. E. Lucas

Adjustment Costs and the Theory of Supply[1]

R. E. Lucas, 'Adjustment costs and the theory of supply', *Journal of Political Economy*, vol. 75, 1967, pp. 321–34.

I Introduction

This paper contains a re-examination from a dynamic point of view of some familiar problems in the theory of supply. In particular, it is concerned with the response of firms in a competitive industry to once-and-for-all shifts in the industry demand curve, to changes in the *rate of shift* in this demand curve, and to changes in the prices of factors of production. In most respects, our discussion of these issues will proceed along the lines of the traditional Marshall–Viner theory of supply. The novelty of our treatment will lie in its attempt to introduce the relative 'fixity' of capital explicitly into the formulation of the firm's maximum problem and to use this formulation to obtain a precise definition of the industry's 'short-run' and 'long-run' equilibrium positions and an analysis of the passage from one to the other.[2]

Aside from its theoretical interest, such a revision of the theory of a competitive industry appears to be necessitated by recent empirical work in industrial organization. Traditional supply theory affords a full explanation of firm and industry behavior only for the case in which each firm's long-run average cost curve is 'U-shaped'. In this case, the theory predicts that profit-maximizing behavior on the part of both existing and potential firms will lead firms to operate at the minimum point of this U-shaped

1. Some of the material in this paper is taken from the author's 'Constant Returns to Scale and Measurement of Technological Change', given at the March 1966 conference of the Inter-University Research Program on the Micro-Economics of Technological Change and Economic Growth. I would like to thank Sidney Winter for his helpful comments on the earlier paper.
2. The principal result concerning the relation of the long run to the short run is the famous 'envelope theorem' relating long- and short-run average cost curves, each of which is obtained from an appropriate cost minimization problem (see Samuelson, 1947, p. 34). Aside from the fact that this theorem sheds no light on the way in which fixed inputs become 'unfixed' through time, there is no reason to believe the equilibrium indicated by the solution to a 'long-run cost minimization problem' will coincide with the equilibrium which arises from a succession of 'short-run' decisions. This point has been well developed in a different context in Phelps (1961, pp. 638–43) and Pearce (1962, pp. 1088–97).

curve. This prediction is certainly at variance with the casual observation that in most industries the bulk of demand increases is met by existing firms rather than by new entrants. More systematic investigation is similarly unfavorable to the notion of an optimal firm size. The studies of Stigler, Simon and Bonini, Mansfield, and others,[3] while differing widely in conception and execution, all indicate that, with the exception of very small firms, the percentage rate of firm growth is roughly independent of its size. All of these authors have interpreted these findings as evidence in favor of constant returns to scale over a wide range of firm sizes.[4]

This evidence cannot be regarded as refuting traditional supply theory, since this theory nominally treats all conceivable sorts of average cost curves, but it must certainly call into question the empirical usefulness of this theory. With constant or increasing returns to scale, one can draw short- and long-run cost curves and discuss, in loose terms, long-run *tendencies* for the output of individual firms, but a unique long-run equilibrium cannot be exhibited on this diagram nor can it be obtained analytically by solving a 'long-run maximum problem'. Thus except for the case of 'U-shaped cost curves', the traditional theory yields no unambiguous testable implications. One may also 'reconcile' the industrial organizational evidence with U-shaped cost curves by supposing that these curves differ across firms in an industry and that they shift unpredictably over time, but such a reconciliation would only rob the hypothesis of whatever content it now has.

II Production possibilities with 'fixed' inputs

In order to develop a supply theory in which adjustments to demand shifts are staggered over time, it is first necessary to define the terms 'fixed' and 'variable' inputs and to determine the sorts of production possibilities or market opportunities under which a particular input will fall into one or the other of these two categories. In this section, after a discussion of notational matters, we shall examine a fairly recent view of the firm in which *all* inputs are variable and then discuss a modification of this theory which introduces 'fixity' of one of the inputs.

Consider a firm whose net receipts at time t are given by sales less labor costs less investment goods purchases, or:

$$R(t) = p(t)Q(t) - w(t)L(t) - v(t)I(t),$$

3. See Simon and Bonini (1958); Stigler (1958); Mansfield (1962). The cost curve evidence surveyed and augmented in Johnston (1960), while more difficult to interpret, also appears to support the constant-returns hypothesis for all but very small firms.
4. Hymer and Pashigian (1962) interpreted data similar to Mansfield's as evidence for *increasing* returns to scale. Their conclusion is disputed in Simon (1964).

where $Q(t), L(t), I(t)$ denote output, labor input, and gross investment; and $p(t)$, $w(t)$, and $v(t)$ are the respective prices of these goods. If the firm finances entirely by borrowing at a fixed rate r, its present value at time 0 is:

$$V(0) = \int_0^\infty e^{-rt} R(t) dt.$$

We shall assume that the firm selects $Q(t), L(t)$, and $I(t)$, for $t \geq 0$, so as to maximize $V(0)$ subject to a *production possibility constraint* relating these three flows, or time paths, and given suitable assumptions on *market opportunities* indicating how the three prices will vary over time. For the latter, it is assumed throughout this paper that in drawing up a plan at time 0, the firm regards these prices as beyond its control, and, further, it behaves as though the present price levels will be maintained forever.[5] It remains then only to characterize the firm's production possibilities.

The most familiar way to complete this model is to define the firm's capital stock by the declining balance formula:[6]

$$\frac{dK(t)}{dt} = I(t) - \delta K(t), \qquad\qquad 1$$

and an initial stock $K(0)$, and to assume that output is produced according to a production function:

$$Q(t) = F\{L(t), K(t)\}, \qquad\qquad 2$$

which relates output to current labor and capital inputs. Under these assumptions, it is known that if a rental price or user cost of capital is defined by $v(r+\delta)$, then present value is maximized by the policy which maximizes:

$$pF\{L(t), K(t)\} - wL(t) - v(r+\delta)K(t)$$

at each point in time, $t > 0$.[7] With constant prices, this rule determines an optimal stock K^* which will be held for all $t > 0$, and this stock will equal

5. An alternative to this assumption of 'static expectations' which is more attractive from some points of view is the hypothesis that firms' price expectations are rational, as defined by Muth (1961), or that future prices are correctly anticipated. I have developed some of the implications of this alternative hypothesis in 'Optimal Investment with Rational Expectations', unpublished Carnegie Tech research memorandum, 1966. If expectations are taken to be rational, however, one cannot in general obtain the supply and factor demand functions for the individual firms in an industry (although one *can* characterize the behavior of industry output and price through time) so that some of the parallels between traditional, static theory and the theory developed here cannot be exhibited.
6. If capital is regarded as an observable magnitude, equation 1 is an assumption rather than a definition.
7. This result is given in Haavelmo (1960).

the historically given $K(0)$ only by coincidence. If we define a variable input as one whose optimal level at $t > 0$ is independent of its level at $t = 0$, it is thus clear that capital and labor are, in this theory, both variable inputs, regardless of the institutional fact that one is owned by the firm and the other is hired. There is then *no* distinction between short- and long-run supply behavior: following a once-and-for-all change in prices, the firm proceeds *immediately* to its new long-run position.

If one wishes to build the 'fixity' of capital explicitly into the formulation, one must introduce costs per unit of gross investment which *rise* with the investment rate, either by postulating monopsonistic capital goods markets (letting v be a rising function of I) or by introducing internal costs of investment in the form of output foregone. In this paper, capital fixity will be treated as arising from such internal costs,[8] with the production function **2** replaced by:

$$Q(t) = F\{L(t), K(t), I(t)\}. \qquad \qquad 3$$

The investment rate is assumed to enter F with a negative and decreasing marginal productivity. For fixed $I(t)$, capital and labor have positive and diminishing marginal productivities.

The inclusion of the gross investment rate in the production function may be motivated by some examples. First, consider a firm composed of a production division and a planning division, each of which uses the same inputs, $L(t)$ and $K(t)$. The production division produces an output $Q(t)$ according to an ordinary production function, while the activity of the planning division is proportional to the firm's investment rate (that is, a unit of investment requires a fixed amount of planning). Suppose that both divisions operate under decreasing returns to scale. Then an increase in investment for *fixed* levels of L and K requires a withdrawal of labor and capital from the production division, reducing output $Q(t)$. Because of decreasing returns, additional increases in investment require successively

8. There are a number of alternative ways to introduce capital fixity into the firm's maximum problem, ranging from inequality constraints on the rate of investment to various types of 'smooth' adjustment cost hypotheses. The formulation used here is adopted from Eisner and Strotz (1963). One can also motivate the distinction between short- and long-run firm behavior by reference to more specific aspects of the production process, as Alchian (1959) does with his distinction between the rate of output (of a particular process within a firm) and the scheduled volume of output. The virtue of an approach such as Alchian's is that by being specific about the source of the short-run–long-run distinction one is able to get some 'feel' for the shapes of the functions involved. The difficulty with this approach, as opposed to the one used here, is that the resulting theory cannot be applied to data at the balance sheet and income statement aggregation level or at higher levels of aggregation.

larger output sacrifices. (If the firm 'hires' planning services from the outside, at rising unit costs, one would observe a similar effect.)

As a second example, suppose that the introduction of new capital goods introduces new production methods and that new capital becomes fully effective only after a learning period. In particular, suppose that current investment goods yield a fraction k, $0 < k < 1$, of the productive services they will ultimately provide. Then from 1, measured capital stock at time t is

$$K(t) = K(0)e^{-\delta t} + \int_0^t e^{-\delta(t-s)}I(s)ds,$$

while 'effective' capital is $K^e(t) = K(t) - (1-k)I(t)$. Inserting $K^e(t)$ in place of $K(t)$ in the static production function 2 yields a special instance of 3.

In either of these examples, one might argue that only *net* investment should enter into F, since replacement involves neither planning nor learning. This argument has some force if one thinks of replacement as typified, say, by changing a light bulb. It has less appeal if one thinks of replacing a computer with a newer model. In any case, the choice between gross and net investment is not crucial to any of the arguments which follow.

One could proceed immediately to obtain necessary conditions for the maximization of $V(0)$ under production possibilities given by 1 and 3, but without further restrictions on the production function F, it will be difficult to proceed beyond an empty statement of marginal equalities. In addition, the conditions so derived will not in general be consistent with the independence of firm growth and size. Accordingly, we shall add the assumption that $F(L, K, I)$ is *homogeneous of degree one* in its three arguments. It will be noted that this restriction differs from constant returns to scale in the usual sense, since a doubling of capital and labor *and* the investment rate will double output, but a doubling of capital and labor with a fixed investment rate will yield more than a doubled output.

III The present value-maximization problem for a single firm

In the preceding section, we defined production possibilities of a particular type (equations 1 and 3) and asserted that a single firm with these production possibilities, operating in competitive product and factor markets, would regard capital as a fixed input in the sense that its optimal capital stock for at least some positive t would depend on its initial stock $K(0)$. In this section, we shall work through in detail the present value-maximization problem for such a firm. In the course of this discussion, the assertion that capital is (partially) fixed under 1 and 3 will be proved, and the dependence of the firm's output supply, labor demand, and investment demand on prices, the interest rate, and the initial capital stock will be examined. In other words, we shall derive the short- and long-run supply and factor demand functions for the firm.

The maximum problem of the firm has been stated in piecemeal fashion in the preceding section. It will be helpful here to collect these assumptions. The firm's objective at time 0 is to choose continuous investment and labor force plans, $I(t)$ and $L(t)$, $t \geqslant 0$, so as to maximize:

$$V(0) = \int_0^\infty e^{-rt}[pF\{L(t), K(t), I(t)\} - wL(t) - vI(t)]dt,$$

where r, p, w, and v are current ($t = 0$) prices and where F is homogeneous of degree one with continuous first and second derivatives satisfying:

$$F_L > 0, F_K > 0, F_I < 0, F_{LL} < 0, F_{KK} < 0, F_{II} < 0. \qquad \textbf{4}$$

To simplify the analysis somewhat, it will be assumed that F can be written as a sum of an ordinary production function, with arguments L and K, and an internal 'adjustment cost function', with arguments I and K, or that:

$$F_{LI} = 0. \qquad \textbf{5}$$

Next, F is required to be concave in the following sense: let (L_0, K_0, I_0) and (L_1, K_1, I_1) be any two input combinations, let $L_\theta = \theta L_0 + (1-\theta)L_1$, and define K_θ and I_θ similarly. Assume that:

$$F(L_\theta, K_\theta, I_\theta) \geqslant \theta F(L_0, K_0, I_0) + (1-\theta)F(L_1, K_1, I_1), \qquad \textbf{6}$$

with equality if and only if (L_0, K_0, I_0) and (L_1, K_1, I_1) are proportional.

Finally, the derivatives of F are required to satisfy:

$$F_L(I, K) \to 0 \text{ as } L/K \to \infty;$$
$$F_L(L, K) \to \infty \text{ as } L/K \to 0; \qquad \textbf{7}$$
$$F_I(K, I) \to -\infty \text{ as } I/K \to r+\delta-a,$$

where a is some positive number.

Under these conditions, it is shown in the Appendix to this paper that a plan $\{L(t), I(t)\}$ with $L(t)$ and $I(t)$ strictly positive and $0 \leqslant I(t)/K(t) < r + \delta - a$, for all t, is optimal if and only if it satisfies:

$$pF_L(L, K) = w, \qquad \textbf{8}$$

$$pF_K(L, K, I) = \{v - pF_I(K, I)\}(r+\delta), \qquad \textbf{9}$$

in addition to the depreciation formula **1**.

Equation **8** is simply the usual marginal productivity condition for labor. The left side of **9** is the value of the marginal product of capital. The right side of **9** may be termed the 'marginal user cost' of capital and may be interpreted by analogy to the expression $v(r+\delta)$ for user cost to which pF_K is equated when capital is variable. In either case, the term $r+\delta$ converts a stock price to a flow price. The term $v-pF_I$ is the marginal cost of accumulating capital, with v measuring cash outlay per unit of investment goods, and $-pF_I$ measuring the value of output foregone with each unit of investment.

Next we derive from **1**, **8**, and **9** the firm's short-run labor demand function, its short-run supply function, its investment demand function, and its long-run growth plan. Since F is homogeneous of degree one, its first derivatives can be treated as functions of the ratios L/K and I/K. From **4** and **7**, **8** can be solved for a positive value of L/K for any price ratio w/p. The short-run demand curve for labor is then:

$$L(t) = K(t)D_1(w/p), \; D'_1(w/p) < 0. \tag{10}$$

A change in w/p thus induces an instantaneous movement of L along this curve; as capital is adjusted, this demand curve will shift proportionally.

To determine the investment demand function, rearrange **9**, apply Euler's Theorem to F, and use **10** to eliminate L/K to obtain:

$$p\left[F\left\{1, D_1\left(\frac{w}{p}\right), \frac{I}{K}\right\} - D_1\left(\frac{w}{p}\right)\frac{w}{p} + \left(r+\delta-\frac{I}{K}\right)F_I\left(\frac{I}{K}\right)\right] = v(r+\delta). \tag{11}$$

The left side of **11**, which we shall call $G(I/K, w, p)$ is drawn in Figure 1. The downward slope of G, as a function of I/K, follows from **4**. The fact

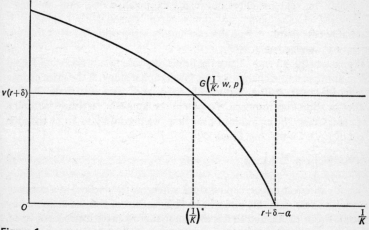

Figure 1

that G must cross the I/K axis to the left of the point $r+\delta-a$ follows from **7**. It may also be verified that $\partial G/\partial w < 0$ and $\partial G/\partial p > 0$. For any fixed w, there will be some critical price p_c (say) such that if $p > p_c$, **11** yields a positive solution for I/K. As indicated earlier, this analysis will consider *only* prices above this critical level. Then if $p > p_c$, **11** may be solved for the investment demand function:

$$I(t) = K(t)D_2\left(\frac{w}{p}, \frac{v}{p}, r, \delta\right),\qquad\qquad 12$$

where $\partial D_2/\partial(w/p) < 0$, $\partial D_2/\partial(v/p) < 0$, and $\partial D_2/\partial r = \partial D_2/\partial \delta < 0$.

Inserting these solutions for L/K and I/K into the production function gives the short-run supply function of the firm:

$$Q(t) = K(t)F\left\{1, D_1\left(\frac{w}{p}\right), D_2\left(\frac{w}{p}, \frac{v}{p}, r, \delta\right)\right\}.\qquad\qquad 13$$

Output will be a rising function of r, δ, and v/p, but the effect on $Q(t)$ of changes in w/p is indeterminate. This leads to the odd possibility that the slope of the short-run supply curve (the derivative of Q with respect to p) may have either sign. This result – which is of course at variance with the implication of conventional theory that the short-run supply curve must slope upward – arises from the presence of investment in the production function and from the role that price plays as a perfect indicator of future price. The initial effect of a price increase is to induce the firm to expand its labor force to meet current demand and *also* to increase the investment rate so as to be prepared to meet future demand. These two responses affect current output in opposite directions. While one might strain for examples in which the negative effect outweighs the positive one, thus making a downward sloping short-run supply curve 'reasonable', I think it is probably best simply to rule this case out by assumption. In what follows, then, it is assumed that $\partial Q/\partial p > 0$.

Equations **10**, **12** and **13** give the firm's response to any once-and-for-all price or interest rate change for any given capital stock. If the price change occurs at $t = 0$, $K(0)$ is historically fixed, and these equations give the initial or short-run response. To obtain the long-run response, assuming the new prices to be maintained over time, we need only to know the time path of $K(t)$. Combining **1** and **12**:

$$\frac{\dot{K}(t)}{K(t)} = D_2\left(r, \delta, \frac{w}{p}, \frac{v}{p}\right) - \delta.\qquad\qquad 14$$

Thus for constant prices, capital stock will grow (or decline) at a constant percentage rate, and this rate will be independent of size (as measured by assets). From **10**, **12**, and **13** it is evident that gross investment, labor force, and output will all grow at the rate $D_2 - \delta$ as well.

IV The organization of a competitive industry

In the last section, we determined the optimal growth plan for a single firm with a particular type of production possibilities. In this section, we examine an industry composed of a large number of such firms, each with identical production functions as given by **3** and each faced with the same set of prices p, w, v, and r, but with possibly different capital stocks.

Before deriving the supply curve of the industry, it is important to inquire whether the composition of the industry will remain the same in the face of shifting demand or, in particular, to raise the issues of merger and dissolution of firms and of entry and departure. A natural way to deal with both these questions is to examine the way in which present value under an optimal policy will vary with initial capital stock. Retaining the assumption of constant prices, **7** and **8** imply that the optimal ratios of labor to capital and gross investment to capital remain constant over time. Then if $R^*(t)$ and $K^*(t)$ denote receipts and capital stock at t under the optimal policy, the ratio R^*/K^* will remain constant, with both R^* and K^* expanding at the percentage rate $D_2-\delta$, as given in **14**. Then present value under the optimal policy is:

$$V^*\{K(0)\} = (r+\delta-D_2)^{-1}\frac{R^*(t)}{K^*(t)}K(0). \qquad \textbf{15}$$

Thus if each firm is selecting inputs optimally, the present value of *all* of the firms in the industry will be independent of how the industry's capital stock is distributed across firms.[9] There is, therefore, no incentive for firms to merge or dissolve, regardless of the initial asset distribution.

From **15** it is evident that the value of a firm with *no* capital is zero, so that mere membership in the industry has no value. From this, one is tempted to conclude that there will be no incentive for new firms to enter the industry and begin accumulating capital 'from scratch'. Unfortunately, the entry problem cannot be handled quite so neatly for reasons which will be clearer after industry growth in the absence of entry is discussed.

Assume an industry-wide demand function of the form:

$$Q(t)e^{-\lambda t} = z(t) = h\{p(t)\}, \qquad \textbf{16}$$

where h is required to satisfy:

$$h'(p) < 0, \quad h(0) = \infty, \quad \text{and} \quad h(\infty) = 0. \qquad \textbf{17}$$

If one thinks of GNP growth as the principal factor shifting the demand curve, the growth of demand λ can be thought of as the product of the

9. The proportionality of present value to initial capital stock as in **15** is not generally true with adjustment costs. In fact, with depreciation as assumed in **1**, it will hold if and only if the function F is homogeneous of degree one. This is shown in the paper cited in footnote 1.

growth rate of income times the income elasticity of demand for the industry's product.

The growth rate of output supplied is given by the right side of **14** in the previous section. For fixed levels of r, w, v, and δ, this rate may be written $D_2(r, w/p, v/p, \delta) = g(p)$, where $g'(p) > 0$ (see Figure 1). Then assuming the product market to be cleared at each point in time, the industry supply function is:

$$\frac{\dot{z}(t)}{z(t)} = g\{p(t)\} - \lambda. \qquad \textbf{18}$$

The initial value $z(0)$ is given by the intersection of the short-run supply function **13** and the demand curve **16**.[10]

The behavior of price and industry output over time can now be handled geometrically with a slightly modified supply-and-demand diagram (Figure 2).[11] The downward sloping curve in Figure 2 is obtained from **16**

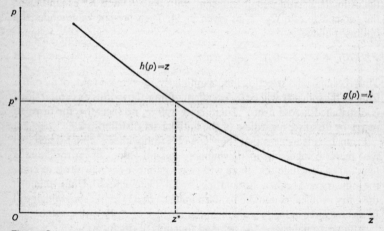

Figure 2

and **17**: it is the relative (to the 'size of the market') demand curve facing the industry, with price on the vertical axis and $z = Qe^{-\lambda t}$ on the horizontal axis. The horizontal line on Figure 2 gives that value of p which satisfies

10. Under the assumptions used here, there must be at least one such intersection, but the possibility of multiple short-run equilibria is not ruled out.
11. With rational rather than static expectations (see footnote 5), Figure 2 remains an accurate description of price–quantity movements in the industry. In general, the initial (short-run) response is different in the two cases, and the speed of adjustment along $z = h(p)$ will differ. In the context of this model, the equilibrium (p^*, z^*) is stable under either expectations hypothesis.

$g(p) = \lambda$, for fixed $\lambda \geqslant 0$. To draw this line above the z axis requires the assumption that a positive price is needed to induce firms to grow at a non-negative rate. Since $g'(p) > 0$, an increase in λ will shift this line upward. Under these assumptions, the curve $z = h(p)$ will intersect the line $g(p) = \lambda$ at exactly one value of z, say z^*. At this point, **18** implies $\dot{z} = 0$. For values of z to the left of z^*, product price (which is read off the relative demand curve) will exceed the price p^* which satisfies $g(p) = \lambda$, so that $g(p)$ will exceed λ. From **18** this implies that $\dot{z} > 0$. Similarly, if $z < z^*$, $\dot{z}$ will be negative. Thus z^* is a position of stable equilibrium for the industry, and the corresponding price p^* is the equilibrium price.

Using Figure 2, we can analyze the effects of either a shift in the relative demand curve or of a change in the demand growth rate λ. The first of these problems is depicted (for an upward demand shift) in Figure 3. Consider an industry initially in a long-run equilibrium position (such as z^* in Figure 2). Suppose that demand shifts as shown from $h_0(p)$ to $h_1(p)$, the rate λ remaining the same. The industry will *immediately* move to a

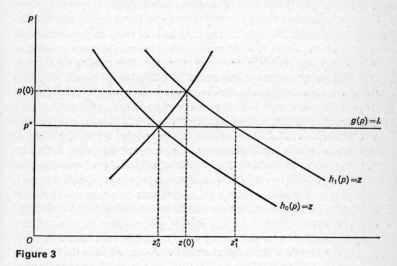

Figure 3

new short-run equilibrium position $z(0)$, $p(0)$ which, if the short-run supply curve is upward sloping, will be to the right of the former equilibrium z_0^*. The industry will then move to the right along $h_1(p)$ until it reaches the new equilibrium z_1^*, with the speed of approach governed by **18**. Thus the analysis of a once-and-for-all shift in relative demand proceeds exactly as in the traditional treatment of a constant cost industry.

The analysis of a change in the rate of demand growth, λ, is simpler, since in this case there is no short-run change in z or p. A rise in λ will raise the line $g(p) = \lambda$ but leave $h(p)$ unaffected. The industry will move left along the relative demand curve until the new equilibrium is reached, at a higher equilibrium price and lower z than before. This latter case helps to illustrate both the similarities and the differences between the line $g(p) = \lambda$ and the traditional flat supply curve of a constant-cost industry. For λ fixed at zero, the price p which satisfies $g(p) = 0$ is a supply price in the traditional sense: it is the price at which firms will be willing to supply an output to the market on a continuing basis, and as in the usual constant-cost case, this price is the same for all outputs. Unlike the usual constant-cost case, however, this supply price cannot be derived from a static, long-run cost minimization problem. In addition, if one considers positive values of λ, it is seen that supply price is a rising function of the growth rate of the industry. The height of the curve $g(p) = \lambda$, unlike the height of the usual average cost curve, depends on the rate of shift of demand as well as on cost considerations.

This concludes the analysis of the response of industry output to demand changes, under the assumption that these shifts do not induce new firms to enter the industry. We now turn to the effects of entry on the conclusions of this analysis. From **15** and from Figure 2, one sees that at a position of industry equilibrium in the *absence* of entry, the curve relating the value of each firm under optimal management $[V^*\{K(0)\}]$ to its assets, $K(0)$, is a straight line passing through the origin whose slope is higher, the higher is the rate of demand shift λ. Thus the value of a unit of capital in an industry will depend upon how fast demand is growing in that industry *and* upon the ease with which this demand growth can be satisfied by existing firms. If capital goods were freely transferable, at constant unit cost, across industries (that is, if capital were a variable input) and if entry were free, the ratio $V^*\{K(0)\}/K(0)$ would be equated across industries. If capital is *not* a variable input, then one must treat each means of accumulating capital differently, so that internal investment by an established firm is associated with one set of adjustment costs, merger with another set of costs, and entry of new firms with still a third set of costs. We have treated formally only the first mode of capital accumulation. As remarked at the beginning of this section, firms will have no incentive, on our model, to merge even in the absence of costs associated with mergers, so that the introduction of such costs would imply that firms will *never* merge. To deal with entry, some additional theory is needed.

We shall not attempt to develop a theory of entry from notions of the 'optimal behavior of potential firms', but the outlines of what a reasonable entry hypothesis should look like are easily sketched. First, while one cannot assert that $V^*\{K(0)\}/K(0)$ should equalize across industries, the birth rate of firms should certainly be a rising function of this ratio. For fixed factor prices, this ratio in turn is a rising function of output price. Then if $b(p), b'(p) > 0$ is the increment to output from new firms relative to current industry output, equation **18** is replaced by:

$$\frac{\dot{z}(t)}{z(t)} = g\{p(t)\}+b\{p(t)\}-\lambda. \qquad \qquad \textbf{19}$$

The construction of Figure 2 and the subsequent analysis then proceeds as before. The effect of replacing **18** with **19** is to make the equilibrium product price less sensitive to changes in the growth rate λ. If, as one might expect, $b(p)$ becomes infinitely elastic at some price p_0 (whose value would of course depend on prices in other industries), then under **14** the horizontal line in Figure 1 would have to lie under the line $p = p_0$, regardless of the size of λ. In the limit, as costs of shifting capital between industries go to zero, the height of the horizontal line in Figure 1 would be fixed exactly by prices and costs in other industries, and changes in λ would affect *only* the entry rate.

V Investment demand in a competitive industry

Once the behavior of industry output over time is determined, it is not difficult to obtain the industry factor demand functions. In view of the recent interest in the theoretical foundations of econometric investment functions, most of which have been estimated from industry or even sectoral time series, it may be worthwhile to examine the implications for investment demand of the analysis of the preceding two sections. In so doing, we neglect the effects of entry of new firms.

From equation **12**, which is readily aggregated over all firms, we have the gross investment function for the industry as a function of output price and other variables:

$$\frac{I(t)}{K(t)} = D_2\left(r, \frac{w}{p}, \frac{v}{p}\right). \qquad \qquad \textbf{20}$$

From **16** and **18**, $p(t)$ is obtained as a function of $p(t)$ and λ. For econometric purposes, then, **20** and this first-order equation in $p(t)$ would be approximated by convenient linear or log-linear forms, and $p(t)$ eliminated between the two equations. The industry investment demand function so obtained will be a first-order differential (or difference) equation in $I(t)/K(t)$ with the levels and rates of changes of the factor prices w, v, and r as 'forcing variables' and with the rate of demand shift, λ, as an additional variable. The properties of this investment function are easily developed from the preceding analysis and need not be discussed here.

Two important differences between the industry demand function for capital goods and the demand function for a single firm may be noted. First, the firm's demand function, equation **20**, regarded as a differential equation in capital stock, is a first-order equation as is the familiar flexible accelerator. When one looks at adjustment from an industry-wide viewpoint, regarding product price as an 'endogenous' variable, the order of the differential (or difference) equation in capital stock goes up by one. Second, when one aggregates from the firm to the industry, the rate of shift in the industry's demand curve, λ, becomes an argument in the investment function. The presence of λ in this function was, of course, a feature of the early formulations of the accelerator hypothesis.[12]

VI Conclusion

This paper has been an attempt to clarify some familiar notions of the theory of supply, in particular the concepts of short- and long-run adjustments to demand shifts, through the assumption of production possibilities which induce present value-maximizing firms to 'stagger' their responses to price changes. Insofar as the effort has been successful, it seems to me to have relevance for empirical study of industrial organization and of the demand for investment goods.

First, the present value-maximization problem of the firm as we have formulated it yields an optimal investment plan characterized by the independence of firm size and the percentage growth rate of the firm. Such a model, if made stochastic in an appropriate way, has the empirical advantages of the 'Gibrat's Law' theories of firm growth as well as the other well-known virtues of a hypothesis based on the assumption of maximizing behavior. In addition, it has been found that if firm growth is independent of size, the ratio of a firm's market value to the replacement value of its assets is also independent of size.

From the point of view of empirical investment studies, the approach taken here has two advantages over an approach based on the theory of a single firm's behavior. First, the industrial organizational evidence is highly relevant to any investment theory (indeed, Gibrat's Law *is* an investment theory), and restricting oneself to investment hypotheses which are consistent with this evidence provides a useful discipline in theoretical work. Second, in view of the aggregate nature of the time series used in most empirical investment studies, there are obvious advantages to developing an investment demand for an industry rather than for a single firm.

Finally, we have shown that in the presence of costs of adjustment the long-run supply price for a competitive industry cannot be interpreted as an average cost curve derived from a 'long-run cost minimization problem'.

12. See, for example, Clark (1917) and Samuelson (1939).

If the industry's long-run equilibrium position is not attained immediately, then the nature of this equilibrium depends on the costs of approaching and maintaining it.

Appendix

Derivation of equations 8 and 9

It will be convenient to approach the maximum problem stated in Section III of the text in two steps: first, at each point in time, choose $L(t)$ so as to maximize $R(t)$ for arbitrary $K(t)$ and $I(t)$; second, use the solution to the first problem to eliminate $L(t)$ from the problem, and choose a path $I(t)$, $t \geq 0$, so as to maximize $V(0)$.

The first of these problems is:

$$\max_{L(t)} [pF\{L(t), K(t), I(t)\} - wL(t)].$$

Clearly, **8** is a necessary condition for this problem. From **4** and **7**, **8** has exactly one solution $L_0\{K(t), w/p\}$, as given in **10**, and this solution yields a maximum to receipts for given $K(t), I(t)$.

Let

$$G\{K(t), I(t)\} = pF\left[L_0\left\{K(t), \frac{w}{p}\right\}, K(t), I(t)\right] - wL_0\left\{K(t), \frac{w}{p}\right\} - vI(t).$$

Then using **10**, it is easily verified that G is homogeneous of degree one, that:

$$G_K > 0, \ G_I < 0, \ G_{KK} < 0, \ G_{II} < 0,$$

and $\quad G_I\left(\dfrac{I}{K}\right) \to -\infty \quad$ as $\quad \dfrac{I}{K} \to r + \delta - a.$ **A1**

Further, if $0 < \theta < 1$, $I_\theta = \theta I_0 + (1-\theta)I_1$, and $K_\theta = \theta K_0 + (1-\theta)K_1$,

$$G(K_\theta, I_\theta) \geq \theta G(K_0, I_0) + (1-\theta)G(K_1, I_1),$$ **A2**

with equality if and only if (K_0, I_0) and (K_1, I_1) are proportional.

The problem is now reduced to that of selecting a continuous investment plan $I(t)$, $t \geq 0$, satisfying $0 \leq I(t)/K(t) < r + \delta - a$, so as to maximize:

$$W = \int_0^\infty e^{-rt} G\{K(t), I(t)\} dt,$$

subject to **1** and given $K(0)$. For any admissible plan $I(t)$, present value may be regarded as a functional $W\{I(t)\}$ of $I(t)$. In view of the bounds on $I(t)/K(t)$, $W(I)$ will have a finite value for all admissible plans. Let $I^*(t)$ be the solution to **11**, satisfying $I^*(t) > 0$ for all t. (Recall that the existence of such a solution rests on an additional assumption that p is above some critical value p_c.) Let $I_1(t)$ be any admissible plan. Then if θ is sufficiently small, $I_\theta(t) = (1-\theta)I^*(t)+\theta I_1(t)$ is also admissible, and $f(\theta) = W\{I_\theta(t)\}$ is well defined. We then show that $f'(0) = 0$ (that is, that $I^*(t)$ satisfies the Euler necessary condition and the transversality condition) and, further, that $W\{I^*(t)\} > W\{I(t)\}$ for *all* admissible $I(t)$ with $I(t) \neq I^*(t)$ for some t.

Form the Lagrangian expression:

$$\mathscr{L}(K, I, \lambda, t) = e^{-rt}\{G(K, I)+\lambda(\dot{K}-I+\delta K)\}.$$

Then if a continuous plan $I(t)$, $I(t) > 0$ for all t, maximizes $W(I)$, there must exist a multiplier function $\lambda(t)$ such that the following conditions are met:

$$0 = \frac{\partial \mathscr{L}}{\partial I} = e^{-rt}\{G_I(K, I)-\lambda\}, \tag{A3}$$

$$0 = \frac{\partial \mathscr{L}}{\partial K}-\frac{d}{dt}(\partial \mathscr{L}/\partial \dot{K})$$

$$= e^{-rt}\{G_K(K, I)+\lambda\delta\}-\frac{d}{dt}e^{-rt}\lambda, \tag{A4}$$

$$0 = \frac{\partial \mathscr{L}}{\partial \lambda} = e^{-rt}(\dot{K}-I+\delta K), \tag{A5}$$

$$0 = \lim_{t\to\infty} (\partial \mathscr{L}/\partial \dot{K}) = \lim_{t\to\infty} e^{-rt}\lambda(t). \tag{A6}$$

Since G is homogeneous of degree one, the derivatives G_I and G_K are functions of I/K, and **A3** and **A4** involve only the variables I/K and λ. Setting $\dot{\lambda} = 0$ and eliminating λ between these two equations gives an equation in I/K. Using the definition of G in terms of F, this equation is found to be equivalent to **11**. Hence if **11** has a solution $I^*(t)$, this solution also satisfies **A3** and **A4**. Then the associated capital plan satisfies **A5**, and since $I^*(t)$ is constant, **A6** is satisfied. This proves that $f'(0) = 0$, where $f(\theta) = W\{I_\theta(t)\}$.

We next show that $W(I)$ is a *strictly* concave functional of $I(t)$. Let I_0 and I_1 be distinct (for some interval of time) admissible plans, and let $I_\theta = \theta I_0+(1-\theta)I_1$, where $0 < \theta < 1$. Let K_t be the capital plan implied by **1** and I_t ($i = 0, 1, \theta$). Since **1** is linear, $K_\theta = \theta K_0+(1-\theta)K_1$. Then:

$$W(I_\theta)-\theta W(I_0)-(1-\theta)W(I_1)$$

$$= \int_0^\infty e^{-rt}\{G(K_\theta, I_\theta)-\theta G(K_0, I_0)-(1-\theta)G(K_1, I_1)\}dt \tag{A7}$$

By **A2**, the right side of **A7** is non-negative and is strictly positive unless (K_0, I_0) and (K_1, I_1) are proportional. Let t_0 be the lower end point of the first interval on which $I_0 \neq I_1$, and let t_1 be the right end point of this interval. Suppose that $I_0(t) = a(t)I_1(t)$, $a(t) \neq 1$, on (t_0, t_1). Then if (K_0, I_0) and (K_1, I_1) are proportional, we must have $K_0(t) = a(t)K_1(t)$ or:

$$e^{-\delta(t-t_0)}K(t_0) + \int_{t_0}^{t} e^{-\delta(t-s)}a(s)I_1(s)ds$$

$$= a(t)\{e^{-\delta(t-t_0)}K(t_0) + \int_{t_0}^{t} e^{-\delta(t-s)}I_1(s)ds\},$$

for all $t_0 < t < t_1$, where $K(t_0)$ is the common value of K_0 and K_1 at t_0. But this equality implies $a(t) \equiv 1$ on (t_0, t_1). Hence (K_0, I_0) and (K_1, I_1) cannot be proportional for all t, which proves that the right side of **A7** is strictly positive, or that $W(I)$ is strictly concave.

Next, let $I^*(t)$ be the solution to **11** as before, and suppose that $I_1(t)$, with $I_1(t) \neq I^*(t)$ for some t, is another admissible plan with $W\{I_1(t)\} > W\{I^*(t)\}$. Let $I_\theta(t) = (1-\theta)I^*(t) + \theta I_1(t)$, for $0 < \theta < 1$. Then:

$$\frac{f(\theta) - f(0)}{\theta} = \theta^{-1}[W\{I_\theta(t)\} - W\{I^*(t)\}]$$

$$> \theta^{-1}[(1-\theta)W\{I^*(t)\} + \theta W\{I_1(t)\} - W\{I^*(t)\}]$$

$$= W\{I_1(t)\} - W\{I^*(t)\}$$

$$> 0.$$

But since $f'(0) = 0$, this is a contradiction.

Alternatively, if $W\{I_1(t)\} = W\{I^*(t)\}$ one can (by the strict concavity of W) construct a plan $I_\theta(t) = \theta I^*(t) + (1-\theta)I_1(t)$ such that $W\{I_\theta(t)\} > W\{I^*(t)\}$. Hence this case is also ruled out by the argument above.

This proves that the solution found in Section III gives the unique optimal policy.

References

ALCHIAN, A. A. (p. 277) (1959), 'Costs and outputs', in M. Abramovitz (ed.), *The Allocation of Economic Resources: Essays in Honor of B. F. Haley*, Stanford University Press.

CLARK, J. M. (1917), 'Business acceleration and the law of demand: a technical factor in economic cycles', *J. pol. Econ.*, vol. 25, pp. 217–35.

EISNER, R., and STROTZ, R. H. (1963), 'Determinants of business investment', in Commission on Money and Credit, *Impacts of Monetary Policy*, Prentice-Hall.

HAAVELMO, T. (1960), *A Study in the Theory of Investment*, University of Chicago Press.

HYMER, S., and PASHIGIAN, P. (1962), 'Firm size and the rate of growth', *J. pol. Econ.*, vol. 70, pp. 556–69.

JOHNSTON, J. (1960), *Statistical Cost Analysis*, McGraw-Hill.

MANSFIELD, E. (1962), 'Entry Gibrat's law, innovation and the growth of firms', *Amer. econ. Rev.*, vol. 52, pp. 1023–51.

MUTH, J. F. (1961), 'Rational expectations and the theory of price movements', *Econometrica*, vol. 29, pp. 315–35.

PEARCE, I. F. (1962), 'The end of the golden age in Solovia: a further fable for growthmen hoping to be "One Up" on Oiko', *Amer. econ. Rev.*, vol. 52. pp. 1088–99.

PHELPS, E. S. (1961), 'The golden rule of accumulation: a fable for growthmen', *Amer. econ. Rev.* vol. 51, pp. 638–43.

SAMUELSON, P. A. (1939), 'Interactions between the multiplier analysis and the principle of acceleration', *Rev. econ. Stat.*, vol. 21, pp. 75–8.

SAMUELSON, P. A. (1947), *Foundations of Economic Analysis*, Harvard University Press.

SIMON, H. A. (1964), 'Comment: firm size and the rate of growth', *J. pol. Econ.*, vol. 72, pp. 81–2.

SIMON, H. A., and BONINI, C. P. (1958), 'The size distribution of business firms', *Amer. econ. Rev.*, vol. 47, pp. 607–17.

STIGLER, G. J. (1958), 'Economies of scale', *J. Law and Econ.*, vol. 1, pp. 54–71.

4 J. P. Gould

Adjustment Costs in the Theory of Investment of the Firm[1]

J. P. Gould, 'Adjustment costs in the theory of investment of the firm',
Review of Economic Studies, vol. 35, 1968, pp. 47–55.

Introduction

Consider a rationally managed firm in a competitive industry, acting to maximize the present value of all future net cash flows, this present value being given by the functional

$$V = \int_0^\infty e^{-R(t)}\{P(t)Q - w(t)L(t) - C(I)\}dt. \qquad \mathbf{1}$$

In **1**, $R(t) = \int_0^t r(\xi)d\xi$ is the discount factor at time zero for cash flows to be

received at t where $r(\xi)$ is the instantaneous interest rate prevailing at time ξ.[2] $P(t)$ is the price of output as a function of time, Q is output, $w(t)$ is the wage rate, $L(t)$ is labour input, and $C(I)$ represents the costs associated with investing in capital stock at the gross investment rate I. Output is related to the labour and capital inputs by the production function $Q = F(K, L)$ and $I = \dot{K} + D(K)$ where $D(K)$ is the level of replacement investment needed to maintain a capital stock K.[3] In a certainty world, the firm chooses the functions $K(t)$ and $L(t)$ to maximize **1**.

There are a number of economic implications associated with **1** that are worthy of comment. The underlying motivation for this kind of model is the desire to reduce, if not eliminate, some of the difficulties associated with the *ad hoc* dynamic theory frequently used in studies of investment

1. I am indebted to M. Miller, Z. Griliches, P. Pashigian, Arnold Zellner, and especially to the participants in the Symposium on the Theory of Optimum Economic Growth for their comments, suggestions, and criticism. All errors are my responsibility.
2. For a discussion of this method of discounting cash flows when the interest rate is assumed to vary over time see Massé (1962, pp. 16–17).
3. A dot over a variable indicates its time derivative.
4. The bibliography of such studies is too vast to give here. The interested reader should examine the very thorough review of this body of literature by Eisner and Strotz (1963).

behaviour.[4] The standard approach in these studies has been to derive desired capital stock, K^*, from comparative static profit maximization considerations and then to use this K^* as the 'long-run' desired capital stock in some auxiliary adjustment mechanism to determine the firm's investment path. An example of such an auxiliary adjustment mechanism is the geometrically declining distribution lag which may be stated in continuous form by

$$\dot{K} = \gamma(K^* - K). \qquad\qquad 2$$

The shortcomings of this approach stem largely from the fact that K^* is determined without regard to the auxiliary adjustment mechanism which will, however, constrain the rate of capital accumulation or disposal. One resulting difficulty is that many of the variables used to define K^* such as sales or profits are in fact affected by 2 and hence do not reflect the 'true' desired capital stock at any point on the investment path before full equilibrium has been achieved. Stated another way, the actual investment path is in itself a decision which will affect profits and therefore should be either in the criterion function or recognized as a constraint on the maximization of this function.

One way to deal with this problem is to hypothesize that the average economic price of capital goods increases as the rate of investment increases. Eisner and Strotz (1963) and Lucas (1967) have examined models of this kind and have found, interestingly enough, that in a number of cases the investment path has the functional form of equation 2. The theoretical insight provided by these articles represents an important contribution to the literature on investment behaviour and indicates that the use of adjustment costs in the criterion functional is worthy of additional consideration.

The cost of adjustment

In both the Strotz–Eisner and Lucas papers, the cost of adjustment is assumed to be a function of *net* investment. The correctness of this specification depends on which factors are assumed to make greater rates of investment more expensive. Lucas suggests that this cost behaviour can be thought of as a sum of purchase costs (with either perfect or imperfect factor markets) and installation costs which are internal to the firm. From the purchase cost viewpoint it makes no difference if the capital is acquired for purposes of expansion or replacement – a given rate of investment will cost the same amount in either case. This is less obviously true with regard to internal costs, since it is possible that once a firm adjusts to a given level of capital its average replacement cost will be independent of the level of replacement. However, since the total cost of adjustment contains both external and internal costs, this total cost will be treated as a function of gross investment as indicated by **1**. This assumption has some distinct advantages.[5] First, since replacement investment is included in gross investment the firm will have some positive costs even if it is not expanding its capital stock. If the cost of adjustment function is such that average costs are greater for higher level of I this will introduce diseconomies of scale thereby giving the firm a determinate size even if the production function is homogeneous of degree one. In addition to putting a bound on the size of the firm it will be seen shortly that this assumption permits us to avoid nonlinearities in the Euler differential equations and hence explicit rather than approximate growth paths can be derived.

The most important question remains to be answered, namely, what is the correct mathematical specification of the adjustment cost function? The choice of this function for econometric work clearly depends on empirical considerations and, like the demand function, will no doubt vary over industries. For the present purpose of theoretical analysis this cost function should be general enough to approximate the actual function in a fairly wide range of empirical situations and yet be specific enough to derive some behavioural implications from the mathematical analysis. For obvious reasons the cost function $C(I)$ should be such that for $I > 0$,

$$C(I) > 0, \; C'(I) > 0, \quad \text{and} \quad C(0) = 0.$$

In addition it seems reasonable to require, as do the above authors, that

$$C''(I) > 0$$

reflecting the assumption that cost of adjustment will be greater on the average the greater the rate of (dis)investment. This is equivalent to the assumption that there are diseconomies of scale associated with more rapid

5. It also has distinct disadvantages. For example, the implication that the *average* cost of replacement investment increases with the size of the capital stock may be precisely the opposite of what happens in many industries. It is quite reasonable to believe that a large firm can replace worn-out capital at the same price per unit as a small firm and it may very well be able to perform this function at a lower average cost than the small firm. Moreover, adjustment costs might be associated with the proportional rate of change in capital stock, not the absolute rate of change: The acquisition of a milling machine may be a much easier task for a firm already owning 999 of them than for a firm that doesn't own any.

It should be mentioned that while there are these interesting economic reasons for considering other cost of adjustment functions such as $C(I/K)$ (i.e. the cost depends on the relative rate of expansion, not the absolute rate of expansion) such specifications usually lead to non-linear differential equations and the attendant difficulties of establishing existence and uniqueness of optimal growth paths. In order to keep the mathematical exposition as simple as possible we do not consider such models in the present paper.

changes in capital stock. The simplest function with these characteristics is the quadratic

$$C(I) = q_0 I + q_1 I^2. \qquad 3$$

One feature of this specification is worth commenting on in the case of the individual firm where net disinvestment is possible (i.e. I may be negative). In this case it may be that for low rates of net disinvestment $-C(I)$ may be positive. This reflects the revenue that may be obtained as capital is sold off. It is possible, however, that all changes in capital stock are costly, in which case $q_0 = 0$.[6]

While there is no reason to expect that a quadratic cost function will be correct in all circumstances, Holt, Modigliani, Muth, and Simon found it to be a good approximation to a wide range of similar costs such as hiring and layoff costs, overtime costs, inventory costs, and machine setup costs. These authors state:

Since the optimality of the decision rules depends on the accuracy with which the mathematical cost function approximates the true structure of costs, we would like to know how close the approximation really needs to be. It turns out that fairly large errors in estimating the cost relations and in approximating them with quadratic functions lead to relatively small differences in the decisions (Holt *et al.*, 1960, p. 43).

Furthermore, as will be seen in the following analysis, the gains in mathematical tractability from using the quadratic cost function offer substantial compensation for the error that may be introduced by their use.[7]

Determining the proper specification of the depreciation rate is not a trivial matter from an economic point of view, as Griliches (1963) has cogently argued. Nonetheless, a thorough examination of this problem would take us too far afield and so the following analysis is based on the usual assumption that depreciation is a constant percentage of capital stock, i.e. $D(K) = \delta K$. The production function is taken to be homogeneous of degree one.[8]

6. If $q_0 = 0$ then, for all $I \neq 0$, $C(I) > 0$ and $C''(I) > 0$. Also, $C'(I) \gtrless 0$ accordingly as $I \lessgtr 0$.
7. Whether this compensation is enough to outweigh the approximation error is, as mentioned above, an empirical question that should be faced whenever the model is used in econometric work.
8. It should be emphasized that an important advantage of using a quadratic cost function and a linear homogeneous production function is that under these assumptions an exact solution to the Euler equations can be found. This means that the model yields qualitative economic implications for both the short-run and the long-run in contrast to, say, Lucas' version where it is necessary to resort to a long-run approximation by linearizing the system around its long-run stationarity in order to say very much about the qualitative aspects of the model.

The optimum capital accumulation path

The criterion functional **1** may be written

$$V = \int\limits_{0}^{\infty} H(K, L, \dot{K}, t)dt.$$

The Euler differential equations that must be satisfied by the functions which maximize this integral are

$$\frac{\partial H}{\partial L} = e^{-R(t)}\left[P\frac{\partial F}{\partial L} - w\right] = 0 \qquad\qquad\qquad\quad \textbf{4}$$

and $\quad \dfrac{\partial H}{\partial K} - \dfrac{d}{dt}\dfrac{\partial H}{\partial \dot{K}} = e^{-R(t)}\left[P\dfrac{\partial F}{\partial K} - (r+\delta)C' + (\dot{K}+\delta\dot{K})C''\right] = 0. \qquad \textbf{5}$

From equation **4** it follows that the value of the marginal product of labour should equal the wage rate everywhere on the optimum path.[9] Since $F(K, L)$ is homogeneous of degree one, its first partial derivatives are functions which are homogeneous of degree zero so that

$$\frac{\partial F}{\partial L} = F_L(K, L) = F_L\left(\frac{K}{L}\right).$$

Thus equation **4** determines the capital–labour ratio at every point in time;

$$\frac{K}{L} = F_L^{-1}\left(\frac{w}{P}\right). \qquad\qquad\qquad\qquad\qquad\qquad \textbf{6}$$

The partial derivative F_K is also homogeneous of degree zero and hence may similarly be treated as a function of the capital–labour ratio. Thus, substituting from **6** we obtain

$$PF_K(K, L) = PF_K\left(\frac{K}{L}\right) = PF_K\left[F_L^{-1}\left(\frac{w}{P}\right)\right]. \qquad\qquad \textbf{7}$$

Using this result and the quadratic cost of adjustment function, equation **5** becomes the second-order linear differential equation,

$$\ddot{K} - r\dot{K} - (r+\delta)\delta K + \frac{PG\left(\dfrac{w}{P}\right) - q_0(r+\delta)}{2q_1} = 0, \qquad\qquad \textbf{8}$$

9. It is assumed that labour can be adjusted freely and instantaneously so the initial labour force is not a boundary condition for the problem.

where $G\left(\dfrac{w}{P}\right) = F_K\left[F_L^{-1}\left(\dfrac{w}{P}\right)\right]$. Introducing the identity $\dot{I}(t) = \ddot{K} + \delta\dot{K}$,

7 is equivalent to the first-order differential equation

$$\dot{I} = [r(t) + \delta]I - f(t) \qquad\qquad \textbf{9}$$

where $\quad f(t) = \dfrac{P(t)G\left(\dfrac{w}{P}\right) - q_0[r(t)+\delta]}{2q_1}.$ [10]

Assuming that the time paths of the economic variables appearing in $f(t)$ are such that this function is continuous, positive, and bounded, the general solution to **9** is

$$I(t) = I_0 \exp -\left\{\int\limits_t^{t_0} (r(\xi)+\delta)d\xi\right\} + \int\limits_t^{t_0} f(s)\exp\left\{\int\limits_s^t (r(\xi)+\delta)d\xi\right\}ds$$

where the solution passes through (t_0, I_0). Since we assume an infinite horizon, the specific solution which maximizes **1** is

$$I(t) = \int\limits_t^{\infty} f(s)\exp\left\{-\int\limits_t^s (r(\xi)+\delta)d\xi\right\}ds. \qquad\qquad \textbf{10}$$

As a check we can ask if this solution satisfies the transversality condition. The transversality condition is that

$$\lim_{t\to\infty}\begin{bmatrix} H_{\dot{K}} \\ H_{\dot{L}} \end{bmatrix} = \mathbf{0}.$$

From **1** $\quad H_{\dot{L}} = 0$

$$H_{\dot{K}} = e^{-R(t)}[-q_0 - 2q_1(\dot{K}+\delta K)]$$
$$= e^{-R(t)}[-q_0 - 2q_1 I]. \qquad\qquad \textbf{11}$$

Hence the transversality requires that

$$\lim_{t\to\infty} e^{-R(t)}[-q_0 - 2q_1 I] = 0. \qquad\qquad \textbf{12}$$

10. I am indebted to a referee for suggesting this transformation which not only allows generalization of the model but also simplifies the task of analysing its economic implications.

Assuming that the interest rate is always positive we immediately get $\lim_{t \to \infty} e^{-R(t)} q_0 = 0$. It is easy to see that the second term in **12** also goes to zero; since $f(s) < M$ for all s,

$$0 \leqslant I \leqslant M \int_t^{\infty} e^{[R(t) - R(s)] + \delta(t - s)} ds = \frac{M}{r(t) + \delta},$$

and $\lim_{t \to \infty} e^{-R(t)} \dfrac{M}{r(t) + \delta} = 0.$

Thus, the solution **10** satisfies the transversality condition.

Constant prices

One of the most interesting things about **10** is that it clearly indicates the dependence of current investment on the *entire* future paths of price, wages, and interest rates. Before considering the effects on investment of changes in these paths in the general case it is interesting to examine the frequently assumed special case of constant values over time for these quantities. In this case

$$I(t) = \frac{\left[PG\left(\frac{w}{P}\right) - q_0(r + \delta) \right]}{2q_1} \int_t^{\infty} e^{(r + \delta)(t - s)} ds$$

or $\quad I^* = \dfrac{PG\left(\dfrac{w}{P}\right) - q_0(r + \delta)}{2q_1(r + \delta)}$ **13**

which is a constant. From **8** it follows that when all net investment is completed (so that $\dot{K}$ and $\ddot{K}$ are zero) the long-run desired capital stock is given by the right side of **13** divided by δ. Thus in the case of constant prices over time

$$I^* = \delta K^* \qquad\qquad\qquad \textbf{14}$$

which says simply that the optimum rate of investment will be the amount needed to just maintain the long-run capital stock indefinitely. This does not mean that capital stock is held constant over time, however. Using the identity $I = \dot{K} + \delta K$ we see that **14** implies the path

$$\dot{K} = \delta(K^* - K) \qquad\qquad \textbf{15}$$

for capital stock.

As could be anticipated from the Strotz–Eisner and Lucas findings, **15** has the form of a distributed lag with declining weights. The above analysis indicates that this is a rather special case, however, which depends critically on the highly unrealistic assumption that output prices, wages, and interest rates remain unchanged over time. Nonetheless, it is interesting to investigate the comparative dynamics of this particular version of the model by considering the effect on investment of changes in the economic parameters.

The results of this analysis must be interpreted with caution. Consider, for example, the effect of an increase in the wage rate w. The wage rate affects K^* only through its impact on $G\left(\dfrac{w}{P}\right)$ and

$$\frac{\partial G}{\partial w} = F_{KK} \times F_{LK}^{-1} \times \frac{\partial\left(\dfrac{w}{P}\right)}{\partial w} < 0.^{11} \tag{16}$$

Thus, we have from **13** and **16** that an increase in wages will *decrease* the rate of investment. To see why this decrease occurs it is useful to consider the effect of the wage increase in two parts – a substitution effect and a scale effect. If output remained constant, there would be no scale effect and the convexity of the production function isoquants would induce a profit-maximizing firm to increase capital and decrease labour following a wage increase. However, given constant returns to scale, this wage increase also increases marginal costs, thereby inducing the firm to reduce output. Since output price remains constant, the scale effect swamps the substitution effect and the firm decreases both capital and labour inputs. However, if the firm being considered is a typical one in its industry and if the wage increase is industry-wide, then it would seem more reasonable, economically speaking, to recognize that the increase in wages will increase costs for every firm. In most cases this will cause an industry-wide reduction in output and consequently an increase in output price. Since $\partial K^*/\partial P > 0$, this price increase will increase K^* for each firm and may lessen the scale effect to the extent that at the new equilibrium the typical firm uses more capital relative to labour than it did before w increased.[12] We now can examine the effect of various parameter changes keeping in mind that the fixed price assumption limits somewhat the inferential value of the results.

11. This results from (a) $F_{KK} < 0$ (by assumption of diminishing marginal returns), (b) $F_{LK}F_{LK}^{-1} = 1$ (unique inverse of F_{LK}), and (c) $F_{LK} = -(K/L)F_{KK} > 0$ (since F is homogeneous of degree one).
12. In one comparative-static version of this model it can be shown that this 'industry effect' will result in a substitution of capital for labour after w increases if the price elasticity of demand is less than -1. It is interesting to observe that there has been a strong *a priori* assumption in the empirical literature to the effect that an increase in wages must always lead to an increase in the amount of capital employed.

Since $\partial K^*/\partial q_0 < 0$ and $\partial K^*/\partial q_1 < 0$, it follows that increasing the costs of adjusting capital stock reduces the rate of investment. An increase in r will have a similar effect while increases in P increase I. The derivative

$$\frac{\partial I^*}{\partial \delta} = \frac{-PG\left(\dfrac{w}{P}\right)}{2q_1(r+\delta)^2}$$

is negative, indicating that an increase in the depreciation rate decreases gross investment.[13] These findings are gratifying since they show, at least for the case of constant prices, that the recognition of adjustment costs in the criterion function leads to a well-defined investment function for the firm which displays the commonly assumed kinds of responsiveness to changes in economic variables such as the interest rate. We now consider how these results extend to the more general case of time dependent prices.

Time dependent prices

In the more realistic case where prices, wages, and interest rates are allowed to vary over time, **10** will not lead, in general, to any simple adjustment scheme such as **15**. Indeed, the rate of investment will depend on the entire path of prices so that even in the case where, say, two alternative time-paths of prices ultimately lead to the same long-run level of capital stock the firm's adjustment to that long-run level will be affected by differences which may occur at any point along the price paths. Thus, in contrast to Arrow's results in which the firm is myopic when determining investment, the introduction of adjustment costs forces the firm to consider profit potentials over its entire horizon (thus requiring both myopia and hyperopia) when making current investment decisions.[14] The reason for this is that, so long as there is nothing such as an adjustment cost which links current and future profits, the firm can blithely ignore the future and chose the strategy which maximizes its current profit since when the environment changes it can adjust instantaneously and costlessly to the new profit-maximizing position. An interesting implication of this distinction is that if adjustment is costless and instantaneous it does not pay the firm to forecast. Viewed another way, the amount of time and effort expended in increasing the accuracy of economic forecasts in an uncertain world will be a function of the costs of adjustment and the degree of variation expected in the values of relevant economic variables.

13. It can also be shown than an increase in the depreciation rate will *increase* the short-run net investment rate and decrease the long-run net investment rate.
14. Arrow (1964) defines cash flow at time t as $P[K(t), t] - I(t)$ where $P[K(t), t]$ represents profits as a function of capital stock and time. The myopic decision rule arises because profits are not a function of $\dot{K}$.

In order to determine the effect on investment of variations in the time-dependent price paths consider two alternative paths for $P(t)$, say $P_1(t)$ and $P_2(t)$, where

$$P_1(t) \begin{cases} = P_2(t) & t \leqslant t_1 \\ \leqslant P_2(t) & t_1 \leqslant t \leqslant t_2. \\ = P_2(t) & t_2 \leqslant t \end{cases}$$

The difference in the corresponding investment paths, $I_1(t)$ and $I_2(t)$, is then given by

$$I_2(t) - I_1(t) = \begin{cases} \displaystyle\int_t^{t_2} \frac{P_2 G\left(\dfrac{w}{P_2}\right) - P_1 G\left(\dfrac{w}{P_1}\right)}{2q_1} \exp\{-[R(s) - R(t) + \delta(s-t)]\}ds & \\ & t \leqslant t_2 \quad \textbf{17} \\ 0 & t_2 \leqslant t. \end{cases}$$

Since the kernel of the integral in **17** is somewhere positive and nowhere negative we see that $I_2 > I_1$ everywhere before t_2 and $I_2 = I_1$ everywhere after t_2. This result is depicted in Figures 1 and 2 where it can be seen that the greater price along path two from t_1 to t_2 induces the firm to increase investment *everywhere* before t_2.

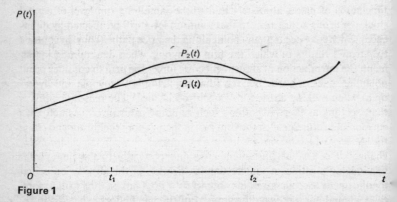

Figure 1

Similar analysis shows that if the path of interest rates or wages were increased over some time interval investment would be reduced everywhere before that interval.[15] Thus, the results of the constant-price case extend in a natural way to time-dependent prices.

15. As in the case of constant prices these results must be interpreted with some caution. If wages did increase over some interval, presumably all firms would reduce output thus resulting in an increase in the price of output which would have an offsetting effect on investment.

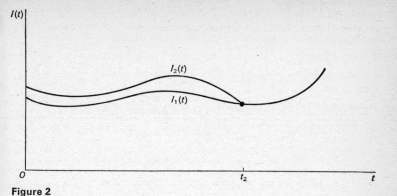

Figure 2

Summary

It appears from these results that the justification provided by the Strotz–Eisner and Lucas papers for the geometrically declining distributed lag form of the investment function depends critically on the assumption of fixed prices. In a dynamic world, however, it seems more realistic to assume time dependence in economic variables. When time-dependent prices are introduced, the investment path is no longer a geometrically declining distributed lag and there is little evidence to indicate that an auxiliary adjustment mechanism of any fixed form will work for all firms and at all times. Of course, it is possible to introduce a changing K^* into a distributed lag investment mechanism which is *defined* so as to make the resulting path optimal. However, it would be surprising to find that past or present levels of sales, profits, market value, or any of the other variables frequently used as estimators of desired capital in econometric work would work very well in this regard. The determination of the seriousness and extent of such misspecification falls in the realm of empirical rather than theoretical analysis, however. It is entirely possible that auxiliary adjustment mechanisms, while possibly embodying the above sources of error, give a sufficiently good approximation to such a broad range of underlying cost of adjustment situations that their use is justified on the principle of Occam's Razor.

Although no simple, unique form of the investment path can be derived from the model discussed in this paper, it is possible to establish some qualitative relationships between investment and other economic variables which are useful in theoretical work. Among the most important of these relationships is the finding that investment will be increased if the path of output prices is anywhere increased and decreased if the path of interest rates is anywhere increased.

References

ARROW, K. J. (1964), 'Optimal capital policy, the cost of capital, and myopic decision rules', *Annals of the Institute of Statistical Mathematics*, vol. 16, nos. 1–2, Tokyo.

EISNER, R. and STROTZ, R. H. (1963), 'Determinants of business investment', in Commission on Money and Credit, *Impacts of Monetary Policy*, Prentice-Hall, pp. 59–337.

GRILICHES, Z. (1963), 'Capital stock in investment functions: some problems of concept and measurement', in C. F. Christ *et al.* (eds.), *Measurement in Economics*, Stanford University Press.

HOLT, C., *et al.* (1960), *Planning Production, Inventories, and Work Force*, Prentice-Hall.

LUCAS, R. E. (1967), 'Optimal investment policy and the flexible accelerator', *Inter. econ. Rev.*, vol. 8, pp. 78–85.

MASSÉ, P. (1962), *Optimal Investment Decisions*, Prentice-Hall.

Part Four
Testing Neoclassical Assumptions

One of the key features of applied econometrics during the 1960s was
the increasing use of explicit theory to derive equations for estimation.
Investment studies have been prominent in this regard; the largest group
of examples being the studies by Jorgenson and several collaborators
(see the references section of Reading 1) based on profit-maximizing
behaviour, a Cobb–Douglas production function, and a variety of other
assumptions in the neoclassical spirit. In most of these studies, the large
number of specific assumptions are tested as a group. Other researchers
have questioned one or more aspects of the particular neoclassical
model used, and have sought to test them separately. The two papers in
this part are concerned chiefly with just one aspect – whether it is more
appropriate to assume a Cobb–Douglas production function rather than
one with a lower elasticity of substitution between capital and labour.
This is probably not the most important issue at stake, but the papers,
especially that by Bischoff, do help to show the difficulties, as well as the
desirability, of testing separately the more crucial features of a theory.

5 R. Eisner and M. I. Nadiri

Investment Behaviour and Neoclassical Theory

R. Eisner and M. I. Nadiri,[1] 'Investment behavior and neo-classical theory'
Review of Economics and Statistics, vol. 50, 1968, pp. 369–82.

Introduction

The role of relative prices as a determinant of factor demand has received wide attention in recent work. Major contributions have been made by Jorgenson who, either alone (1963, 1965, 1966, 1967) or with associates (Jorgenson and Stephenson, 1967, 1967a; Hall and Jorgenson, 1967), has presented, along with various empirical results and certain policy conclusions, what is called 'a theory of investment behavior based on the neoclassical theory of optimal accumulation of capital' (Jorgenson, 1963, p. 248.)

We shall endeavor in this paper to direct a number of tests to critical points of departure in the Jorgenson model. This task has been greatly facilitated by Jorgenson, who has made available to us his own basic quarterly data for total United States manufacturing, thus permitting our re-examination to go forward without confusing the analysis with questions of data comparability.[2]

The essential burden of Jorgenson's argument is that substitution parameters have been improperly neglected or ignored in most work on the investment function. He accepts the widely held view of the demand for capital stock as a function of the output produced but argues that it is also a function of the relative price of output and capital. Investment itself then consists of the replacement of depreciating capital stock and a distributed lag adjustment of capital to its (usually changing) equilibrium value.

1. The authors have benefited particularly from research grants of the National Science Foundation and the Ford Foundation (Eisner) and the Graduate School of Northwestern University and the National Bureau of Economic Research (Nadiri), computational assistance of Betty Benson and Jon Rasmussen, and comments by Otto Eckstein, Robert Gregory, T. N. Srinivasan and Robert H. Strotz.
2. While satisfying ourselves that the additional observations made no important difference we have, however, used all of the data through 1962, which Jorgenson gave us, rather than observations extending only to 1960, on which the papers by Jorgenson, and Jorgenson and Stephenson were generally based. We describe the data briefly in our Appendix. Most of them are explained in more detail in the 'Statistical Appendix' to Jorgenson and Stephenson (1967a).

Jorgenson also argues that, in quarterly data at least , a particular generalization of the techniques by Chenery and Koyck for estimating distributed lag relations is essential.

Jorgenson seeks to capture the price or substitution effect in investment with various measures of, or proxies for, the 'implicit rental or "shadow price" of a unit of capital services' (Jorgenson, 1965, p. 58). In his original formulation (Jorgenson, 1963, p. 249) this depends upon the price of capital goods, q, the rate of depreciation, δ, the rate of interest, r, the relative rate of change of capital goods prices, $\dot{q}/q$ (capital gains), the rate of direct business taxation, u, and the proportions, v, w, and x, of depreciation, cost of capital, and capital losses (gains) chargeable against taxable income; his rental price for capital services is

$$c = q\left\{\left(\frac{1-uv}{1-u}\right)\delta + \left(\frac{1-uw}{1-u}\right)r - \left(\frac{1-ux}{1-u}\right)\frac{\dot{q}}{q}\right\}.\qquad 1$$

The capital gains term, however, is generally ignored in the empirica analysis.

Assuming that the production function is Cobb–Douglas, Jorgenson writes the desired amount of capital stock as

$$K^* = a\frac{pQ}{c},\qquad 2$$

'where the *parameter a* is the elasticity of output with respect to capital' (Jorgenson and Stephenson, 1967, p. 17, italics added). Then, embodying a distributed lag response of actual net investment to changes in the desired stock of capital, the investment function becomes

$$\omega(S)(I_t - \delta K_t) = \gamma(S)(K_t^* - K_{t-1}^*),\qquad 3$$

where S is a lag operator, I_t are gross capital expenditures of the period (quarter) t, δ is a constant proportionate rate of capital stock decay or depreciation, and K_t is the capital stock at the beginning of period t. Hence $I_t - \delta K_t = K_{t+1} - K_t$, the actual net change in capital stock over the period t. We may thus write

$$\begin{aligned} I_t - \delta K_t &= K_{t+1} - K_t \\ &= \mu(S)(K_t^* - K_{t-1}^*)\qquad 4 \end{aligned}$$

where[3]

$$\mu(S) = \frac{\gamma(S)}{\omega(S)}.\qquad 4.2$$

3. Essentially these symbols are to be found in Jorgenson and Stephenson (1967, pp. 17–18).

The pattern of responses of gross investment is found by adding to the net investment the assumed depreciation on new additions to capital stock. Equations 3 and 4 conform to what Jorgenson calls a 'general Pascal distributed lag function', which includes as special cases both the Koyck geometric lag function and the finite distributed lag function employed on a number of occasions by one of the current authors.

In connection with application of this model to United States data, Jorgenson and associates have indicated the following.

1 '. . . A theory of investment behavior based on the neoclassical theory of optimal accumulation of capital provides a highly satisfactory explanation of actual investment expenditures for our sample period' (Jorgenson and Stephenson, 1967a, p. 216). This is presumably to be understood in the context of Jorgenson's statement, 'The central feature of a neoclassical theory is the response of the demand for capital to changes in relative factor prices or the ratio of factor prices to the price of output' (Jorgenson, 1963, p. 247).

2 There are substantial short-run responses and elasticities of investment with respect to the price of output, the price of capital goods, the rate of interest, the income tax rate, and various tax incentives, particularly the investment tax credit and the rate of tax depreciation (Jorgenson, 1963, pp. 258–9; 1965, pp. 86–9; Hall and Jorgenson, 1967). Jorgenson and Stephenson conclude, 'Our results suggest that policy instruments that play a role in the determination of investment expenditures include the tax structure and instruments that affect the cost of capital' (Jorgenson and Stephenson, 1967a, p. 217).

3 'Our results show that approximately three quarters elapse between the change in desired capital and the first actual investment expenditures' (Jorgenson and Stephenson, 1967, p. 21).

The analysis which follows seeks to demonstrate that these conclusions are not sustained by Jorgenson's data. Rather, it appears, they follow from crucial, *a priori* constraints put upon parameters. Indeed, in most critical instances, it will be found that empirical tests contradict Jorgenson's assumptions and with them the deductively derived conclusions.

The neoclassical model and the role of relative prices

A first critical test of Jorgenson's formulation must relate to the elasticity of capital stock with respect to both output and relative prices. Jorgenson, it may be noted in equation 2, has *assumed* that the elasticity of desired capital stock with respect to both output and relative prices is unity. This may be written simply as

$$E_q = \frac{\partial \ln K^*}{\partial \ln Q} = 1 \qquad\qquad 5$$

and

$$E_p = \frac{\partial \ln K^*}{\partial \ln (p/c)} = 1. \qquad\qquad 6$$

All of Jorgenson's empirical 'findings' with respect to the roles of relative prices and output depend upon these assumptions. The unitary elasticity with respect to output would follow from any homogeneous production function of the first degree. But the unitary elasticity with respect to relative prices would contradict the growing if still uncertain evidence from estimates of constant-elasticity-of-substitution (CES) production functions that the elasticity of substitution is less than unity.[4] For a direct test of Jorgenson's essential assumptions and constraints, we substitute equation 2 into equation 4 and, shifting to logarithmic relations,[5] obtain:

$$\Delta \ln K_t = \sum_{i=m}^{n} \gamma_i \, \Delta \ln \left(\frac{pQ}{c}\right)_{t-i} + \sum_{j=1} \omega_j \, \Delta \ln K_{t-j} + u \qquad\qquad 7$$

and

$$\Delta \ln K_t = \sum_{i=m}^{n} \left\{ \gamma_{pi} \, \Delta \ln \left(\frac{p}{c}\right)_{t-i} + \gamma_{qi} \, \Delta \ln Q_{t-i} \right\}$$

$$+ \sum_{j=1}^{s} \omega_j \, \Delta \ln K_{t-j} + v. \qquad\qquad 8$$

It will be noted that both of these equations employ the general Pascal lag estimator, with the question of which coefficients are to be constrained to zero for the moment left open. Confirmation of Jorgenson's assumptions would then be found in equation 7 if the estimated long-run elasticity of demand for capital stock with respect to pQ/c approximated unity, that is,

$$\hat{E}_{\frac{pQ}{c}} = \frac{\sum_{i=m}^{n} \hat{\gamma}_i}{1 - \sum_{j=1}^{s} \hat{\omega}_j} \cong 1, \qquad\qquad 9$$

or that there are no statistical grounds for rejecting the hypothesis that $1 - \Sigma(\gamma_i + \omega_j) = 0$. More discriminating and perhaps more powerful tests of the separate roles of relative prices and of output may be found in the

4. For a CES function with constant returns to scale, $K^* = \beta(p/c)^\sigma Q$, where σ is the elasticity of substitution, as noted by Dhrymes (1967, p. 215). As will be seen below, our results are reasonably consistent with this formulation.
5. See footnote 8.

estimates of elasticity with respect to relative prices and output derived from equation **8**, as written in **10** and **11**,

$$\hat{E}_p = \frac{\sum_{i=m}^{n} \hat{\gamma}_{pi}}{1 - \sum_{j=1}^{s} \hat{\omega}_j} \overset{?}{\cong} 1 \qquad\qquad 10$$

$$\hat{E}_q = \frac{\sum_{i=m}^{n} \hat{\gamma}_{qi}}{1 - \sum_{j=1}^{s} \hat{\omega}_j} \overset{?}{\cong} 1. \qquad\qquad 11$$

Estimated elasticities may, of course, prove less than unity because of errors in the variables, which might bias downward estimates of the γ_i, or misspecification of the lag structure which would prevent capture of the full long-run effect on capital stock. As for the first possibility, Jorgenson and Stephenson recognize it in their own low implicit estimates of the elasticity of output with respect to capital.[6]

In Table 1 we present a number of estimates of the elasticity of capital stock with respect to pQ/c_1, for the quarterly data of total manufacturing used by Jorgenson and Stephenson.[7] It is to be noted that for an analog of the lag structure for which estimates were presented by Jorgenson and Stephenson, specified by the assumptions that $m = 4$, $n = 7$ and $s = 2$, the estimated elasticity is only 0·088. A precise estimate of the standard error of this estimated elasticity has not been calculated but, on the assumption of zero covariance between $\Sigma\gamma_i$ and $\Sigma\omega_j$, we may note that adding two

6. In Jorgenson's formulation, since $K^* = a\,pQ/c$, with a a parameter, the elasticity of capital with respect to desired capital, which must be unity, must also equal the elasticity with respect to pQ/c. Hence,

$$\sum_{i=0}^{\infty} \mu_i' = \frac{\sum_{i=m}^{n} (\gamma_i' a)^*/a}{1 - \sum_{j=1}^{s} \hat{\omega}_j'} = E_K^* = E_{pQ/c} = 1. \qquad\qquad 12$$

The $\hat{\omega}_j'$ and the $(\gamma_i' a)^*$ come from the regressions. No separate estimates of γ_i' and a are given. The imposition of the constraint that $\sum_{i=0}^{\infty} \mu_i' = 1$ permits estimates of a, but the resulting figures are generally far lower than those usually associated with the constant elasticity of output to capital input of the Cobb–Douglas production function; for total manufacturing, for example, Jorgenson and Stephenson (1967a, p. 215) report $\hat{a} = 0·05813$.

7. Where the cost of capital entering into the rental price, c_1, is r_1, 'the ratio of corporate profits after taxes and net monetary interest to the value of all outstanding securities' (Jorgenson and Stephenson, 1967, p. 17, footnote 7).

Table 1 Estimates of elasticity $(\hat{E})$ of capital stock (K) with respect to product of relative prices and output (pQ/c_1)

(1) m	(2) s	(3) $\sum \hat{\gamma}_i$	(4) $\sum \hat{\omega}_j$	(5) SEE	(6) $\hat{E}$	(7) $1 - \sum(\hat{\gamma}+\hat{\omega})$
0	3	0·0265 (0·0099)	0·8804 (0·0428)	0·0012545	0·221 [0·211]	0·0931 (0·0431)
0	2	0·0279 (0·0097)	0·8862 (0·0418)	0·0012475	0·245 [0·233]	0·0859 (0·0416)
1	2	0·0241 (0·0092)	0·8801 (0·0417)	0·0012546	0·201 [0·188]	0·0958 (0·0410)
0[a]	3	0·0297 (0·0094)	0·9121 (0·0275)	0·0012535	0·338 [0·360]	0·0582 (0·0236)
0	1	0·0478 (0·0107)	0·8972 (0·0509)	0·0015214	0·464 [0·435]	0·0551 (0·0501)
2	2	0·0232 (0·0086)	0·8784 (0·0408)	0·0012422	0·191 [0·161]	0·0985 (0·0395)
3	2	0·0175 (0·0085)	0·8624 (0·0417)	0·0012907	0·127 [0·122]	0·1201 (0·0397)
4	2	0·0132 (0·0081)	0·8498 (0·0414)	0·0013072	0·088 [0·098]	0·1370 (0·0386)
4	1	0·0338 (0·0092)	0·8444 (0·0525)	0·0016589	0·217 [0·212]	0·1218 (0·0489)
4[a]	2	0·0127 (0·0085)	0·9254 (0·0297)	0·0013740	0·170 [0·181]	0·0619 (0·0257)

$$\hat{E} = \sum_{i=m}^{7} \hat{\gamma}_i \Big/ \left(1 - \sum_{j=1}^{s} \hat{\omega}_j\right),$$

$$\Delta \ln K_t = \sum_{i=m}^{7} \hat{\gamma}_i \, \Delta \ln \left(\frac{pQ}{c_1}\right)_{t-i} + \sum_{j=1}^{s} \hat{\omega}_j \, \Delta \ln K_{t-j} + u$$

[a] Constant term constrained to zero

c_1 involves interest and earnings as in Jorgenson and Stephenson (1967, 1967a). Standard errors of $\sum \hat{\gamma}_i$ and $\sum \hat{\omega}_j$ in parentheses. SEE = unbiased standard error of estimate of regression. Estimates in all tables are based on fifty-six quarterly observations from the first quarter in 1949 to the last in 1962. Tables have also been prepared from regressions of observations through 1960 only, as in Jorgenson and Stephenson (1967, 1967a), and show essentially the same results as tables presented in this paper. Estimated elasticities based on the fewer observations are given here in brackets in column 6; the reader may see readily that the additional observations were not critical.

standard errors to the estimated values of $\sum \gamma_i$ and $\sum \omega_j$ would still yield an estimated elasticity well under 0·5. The column 7 value of 0·1370 for $1 - \sum(\hat{\gamma}+\hat{\omega})$, more than three times its standard error of 0·0386, in any event argues strongly for rejection of the hypothesis of unitary elasticity.

Jorgenson and Stephenson point out that the general Pascal lag estimator permits approximation of any arbitrary lag distribution to any desired degree of accuracy. To minimize suspicion that the low estimated elasticity is due to misspecification of the lag structure, we therefore also present in Table 1 estimates of the elasticity for nine other lag distributions in this general class with which we experimented. In all cases, it can be seen quickly, the estimated elasticities are well below unity, and perusal of column 7 makes clear that the departures from unity are usually of substantial statistical significance. Indeed, the highest estimate, 0·464, is found in the Koyck estimator (where $m = 0$ and $s = 1$), which had been dismissed by Jorgenson and Stephenson as not 'satisfactory' for these data (Jorgenson and Stephenson, 1967, p. 23). Using their criterion for specification of the lag structure – minimization of the estimated standard error of the regression, attributed by them to Theil (1961; cited in Jorgenson and Stephenson, 1967a, p. 181–2) – we may note that the preferred specifications would be $m = 0$, $n = 7$ and $s = 2$, or $m = 2$, $n = 7$ and $s = 2$; the estimated elasticities [8] for these two equations are respectively 0·245 and 0·191.

8. Elasticities are more directly and efficiently estimated from the equations, linear in the logarithms, which we have used. The reader may be assured, however, that the arithmetic relation, in precisely the form set forth by Jorgenson, yields similar estimates. The estimate of elasticity calculated at the means of capital stock and pQ/c may then be written as

$$\hat{E} = \left(\frac{dK}{d(pQ/c)}\right)^*_{LR} \times \frac{\text{Mean } pQ/c}{\text{Mean } K}, \qquad 13$$

where $\left(\dfrac{dK}{d(pQ/c)}\right)^*_{LR} = \dfrac{\sum\limits_i (a\hat{\gamma}_i')^*}{1 - \sum\limits_j \hat{\omega}_j'}$ 14

s the estimated long-run derivative of capital stock with respect to pQ/c and $(a\hat{\gamma}_i')^*$ and $\hat{\omega}_j'$ are coefficients in Jorgenson's arithmetic relation, e.g. (26) in Jorgenson and Stephenson (1967), corresponding to our logarithmic equation 7. For the 1949 to 1960 observations used in Jorgenson and Stephenson (1967) we find:

$$\sum_{i=0}^{7} (a\hat{\gamma}_i')^* = 0·0133, \quad \sum_{j=1}^{2} \hat{\omega}_j' = 0·7688,$$

$$\left(\frac{dK}{d(pQ/c_1)}\right)^*_{LR} = 0·0575,$$

Mean $K = 82·609$

and, for observations from 1947 through 1960 in order to give due weight to lagged values, Mean $pQ/c_1 = 354·847$. Hence, $\hat{E}$, the estimate of elasticity, is 0·247. This is very close to the corresponding estimate of 0·233 from our logarithmic equation.

In general, Jorgenson's arithmetic formulation is

$$\Delta K_t = a \sum_{i=0}^{\infty} \mu_i' \Delta \left(\frac{pQ}{c}\right)_{t-i} \qquad 15$$

Continued overleaf

Something is clearly wrong. According to Jorgenson's model, we should get an elasticity of one with respect to pQ/c and, by his assumption of a Cobb–Douglas production function on which his substantive conclusions rest, the elasticities of capital stock should be unity with respect to *both* p/c and Q. Let us therefore proceed to estimates of equation 8, which will offer empirical findings bearing directly on the critical elasticities which Jorgenson and his associates have assumed.

Estimates of the elasticity of capital stock with respect to p/c and Q, $\hat{E}_p$ and $\hat{E}_q$, are presented in Table 2. The elasticities with respect to output are generally considerably higher than those with respect to relative prices – in a number of instances in at least a broadly defined neighborhood of unity – while elasticities with respect to relative prices (p/c) are low.[9]

---

which, on the assumption that the variance of the ratio of pQ/c to its mean value is relatively small, may be written approximately as

$$\frac{K_t}{K_{t-1}} = 1 + \sum_{i=0}^{\infty} \mu_i' \left(\frac{\Delta(pQ/c)_{t-i}}{(pQ/c)_{t-i-1}} \right). \qquad 16$$

Our own logarithmic relation may be written in corresponding form as

$$\frac{K_t}{K_{t-1}} = \prod_{i=0}^{\infty} \left\{ (pQ/c)_{t-i}/(pQ/c)_{t-i-1} \right\}^{\mu_i}. \qquad 17$$

Jorgenson's equation relating the adjustment of capital stock to a weighted arithmetic mean of arithmetic changes in pQ/c is thus essentially the same as ours, involving a weighted geometric mean of relative changes (or ratios) of pQ/c. One might argue that our equation is somewhat more plausible, as desired capital stock relates essentially to projections of the future which would seem more likely to be perceived in percentage or proportional terms (thus offering the usually convenient first degree homogeneity properties eliminating scale effects).

It would appear that over the range of data with which we are concerned, the two formulations should yield approximately the same results. (If they did not, because of small sample oddities involving some extremely large arithmetic but smaller relative variations in pQ/c, stemming from possibly sharp changes in c, our logarithmetic formulation would again appear superior.) When it comes to the separate or partial elasticities of capital stock with respect to the relative price and output components, p/c and Q, with which this paper is primarily concerned, the logarithmic formulation has the distinct further advantage of avoiding ambiguous cross product terms, and is generally easier to handle and interpret. Nevertheless, we have completed a series of re-estimates of all of our equations using arithmetic variables in the form $\Delta x/x$, with results similar to those presented in this paper.
9. As suggested above (footnote 4), our results are roughly consistent with the implications of a first degree CES production function, where

$$K^* = \beta \left(\frac{p}{c} \right)^{E_p} Q, \qquad 18$$

but not with its special case, the Cobb–Douglas function, since $E_p = \sigma$ is clearly less than unity. It is perhaps interesting to note that if one could argue that, with non-constant returns, the marginal productivity of capital must equal the rental

We may note further in Table 2 that the criterion of minimization of the standard error of estimate leads us to reject the usual Jorgenson–Stephenson constraint which causes the first several lag coefficients to be zero. Best fits are obtained by allowing the γ_i to run from 1 to 7. The best fit, without elimination of the constant term, is then obtained when ω_j for $j > 1$ is constrained at zero. With this Koyck lag the elasticity of capital stock with respect to output is estimated at 0·8158, while that with respect to relative prices is 0·1576. When two lagged values of the dependent variable are utilized ($\omega_j = 0$ only for $j > 2$), the estimated elasticity of capital stock with respect to output is 0·6889 while the estimated elasticity with respect

---

price or user cost of capital, whatever the fate of the marginal condition for labor (or other factors), our results are all the more consistent with a CES function of degree greater than unity. From the general CES, two-factor function,

$$Q = \gamma\{\delta K^{-\rho}+(1-\delta)L^{-\rho}\}^{-v/\rho}, \tag{19}$$

where v = the degree of the function and $\rho = \dfrac{1}{\sigma}-1$, we have

$$\frac{\partial Q}{\partial K} = \delta v\gamma^{(1-\rho/v)}Q^{(1+\rho/v)}K^{-(1+\rho)}. \tag{20}$$

Then, setting

$$\frac{\partial Q}{\delta K} = \frac{c}{p} \tag{21}$$

and writing $\delta v\gamma^{(1-\rho/v)}$ as $\beta^{1+\rho}$, we find that desired capital is

$$K^* = \beta\left(\frac{p}{c}\right)^{\sigma}Q^{\{\sigma+(1-\sigma)/v\}}. \tag{22}$$

For Jorgenson's special Cobb–Douglas case, where $\sigma = 1$, this reduces to

$$K^* = a\frac{pQ}{c}.$$

If $v = 1$, we of course have the constant returns case already noted. For $E_p = \sigma < 1$, and $v > 1$, however, we note that

$$E_q = \sigma+\frac{1-\sigma}{v} = 1 +\frac{(1-v)(1-\sigma)}{v} < 1, \tag{23}$$

and we have precisely the empirical results which we observe. Indeed if one could really accept the marginal condition $\partial Q/\partial K = c/p$, one could use this investment function to estimate the degree as well as the elasticity of substitution of the CES production function. For then,

$$v = (1-E_p)/(E_q-E_p). \tag{24}$$

Using the 'best-fitting' estimates, $\hat{E}_p = 0·1306$ and $\hat{E}_q = 0·5873$ shown in Table 2, where $m = 1$, $s = 2$ and the constant term is constrained to zero, we thus have $v = 1·84$. Taking the best-fitting estimates when the constant term is not deleted, $\hat{E}_p = 0·1576$, $\hat{E}_q = 0·8158$ and $v = 1·28$.

Table 2 Estimates of elasticities of capital stock with respect to relative price ($\hat{E}_p$) and output ($\hat{E}_q$), c_1 based on r_1, involving interest and earnings

(1) m	(2) s	(3) $\Sigma \hat{\gamma}_{pi}$	(4) $\Sigma \hat{\gamma}_{qi}$	(5) $\Sigma \hat{\omega}_j$	(6) SEE	(7) $\hat{E}_p$	(8) $\hat{E}_q$	(9) $1 - \Sigma(\hat{\gamma}_p + \hat{\omega})$	(10) $1 - \Sigma(\hat{\gamma}_q + \hat{\omega})$
1	2	0·0192 (0·0093)	0·0902 (0·0252)	0·8691 (0·0441)	0·0012191	0·1470	0·6889	0·1117 (0·0436)	0·0407 (0·0446)
1	1	0·0211 (0·0090)	0·1092 (0·0155)	0·8661 (0·0439)	0·0012162	0·1576	0·8158	0·1128 (0·0434)	0·0247 (0·0408)
1[a]	2	0·0187 (0·0091)	0·0840 (0·0226)	0·8570 (0·0359)	0·0012073	0·1306	0·5873	0·1243 (0·0348)	0·0590 (0·0235)
2	2	0·0200 (0·0091)	0·0440 (0·0193)	0·8722 (0·0459)	0·0012791	0·1562	0·3444	0·1078 (0·0447)	0·0838 (0·0424)
3	2	0·0157 (0·0092)	0·0205 (0·0147)	0·8668 (0·0474)	0·0013415	0·1176	0·1539	0·1175 (0·0457)	0·1127 (0·0427)
4	1	0·0280 (0·0099)	0·0391 (0·0137)	0·8392 (0·0582)	0·0016711	0·1739	0·2433	0·1328 (0·0553)	0·1217 (0·0513)
4[a]	2	0·0112 (0·0089)	0·0084 (0·0128)	0·9346 (0·0340)	0·0014048	0·1714	0·1286	0·0542 (0·0309)	0·0570 (0·0271)
4	2	0·0119 (0·0086)	0·0117 (0·0123)	0·8585 (0·0471)	0·0013471	0·0844	0·0825	0·1296 (0·0446)	0·1298 (0·0414)
1	3	0·0195 (0·0097)	0·0914 (0·0296)	0·8695 (0·0448)	0·0012348	0·1492	0·7006	0·1111 (0·0446)	0·0391 (0·0483)
4	3	0·0102 (0·0090)	0·0084 (0·0134)	0·8545 (0·0477)	0·0013556	0·0701	0·0574	0·1353 (0·0457)	0·1372 (0·0431)

$$\Delta \ln K_t = \sum_{i=m}^{7} \{\gamma_{pi} \Delta \ln (p/c_1)_{t-i} + \gamma_{qi} \Delta \ln Q_{t-i}\} + \sum_{j=1}^{s} \omega_j \Delta \ln K_{t-j} + v$$

$$\hat{E}_p = \frac{\sum_{i=m}^{7} \hat{\gamma}_{pi}}{1 - \sum_{j=1}^{s} \hat{\omega}_j} \qquad \hat{E}_q = \frac{\sum_{i=m}^{7} \hat{\gamma}_{qi}}{1 - \sum_{j=1}^{s} \hat{\omega}_j}$$

[a] Constant term constrained to zero.
SEE is unbiased standard of estimate of regression. Standard errors of indicated sums of coefficients in brackets.

to relative prices is only 0·1470. Estimates of these elasticities are respectively 0·5873 and 0·1306 in the corresponding (and best-fitting) regression with the constant term constrained to be zero. Ratios of $1-\Sigma(\hat{\gamma}_p+\hat{\omega})$ to their standard errors are such as to indicate rejection at 0·01 probability levels, and better, of the hypothesis of unitary elasticity with respect to relative prices. Further, on the assumption that $\Sigma\,\hat{\gamma}_{pt}$ is independent of $\Sigma\,\hat{\gamma}_{qi}$, the differences in the estimated elasticities are clearly significant. For the top line in Table 2, for example, where $s = 2$, the critical difference in the $\Sigma\,\hat{\gamma}$ is 0·0710 and the standard error of that difference on the indicated assumption would be only 0·0278. It is clear that the estimated elasticity of capital stock with respect to output permits the operation of a potent flexible accelerator, to be examined further in connection with estimates of the lag structure. The low estimates of the elasticity of capital stock with respect to relative prices indicated in Table 2 offer only slight confirmation of a significant role for relative prices, and a small role at that.

Even this small role for relative prices is called into some question by further reflection upon the nature of the cost of capital, r_1, which enters into this particular measure of Jorgenson's rental price of capital, c_1, and by findings based on a different measure. We have so far been using the Jorgenson definition of cost of capital 'as the ratio of corporate profits after taxes and net monetary interest to the value of all outstanding securities . . .' (Jorgenson and Stephenson, 1967, p. 17, footnote 7). As has been pointed out elsewhere (Eisner, 1967, pp. 378–9), this measure of 'cost of capital' is also an implicit measure of expected future profits. For the higher that earnings are expected to be in the future the higher will be the value of equity and hence the lower will be this 'cost of capital'. Yet the true cost of capital to a firm must include the share of the future earnings to which it expects to entitle holders of equity. Hence high future earnings as mirrored in value of equity do not imply a low cost of capital. They may, however, be associated with high expected profits on investment or a high marginal efficiency of investment; indeed, the market may well tend to rate highly the stock of companies with sufficient confidence in their own prospects of earnings to engage in large capital expenditure programs.

In some of his papers (e.g. 1963, 1965) Jorgenson uses as his measure of the cost of capital the United States Government long-term bond rate.[10] Since he has also made this measure available to us, we have been able to use it in an alternate set of estimates of elasticities of capital stock with respect to relative prices and output. While, of course, the cost of capital to business is more than the United States Government long-term bond rate, it may well be some more or less constant proportion of that interest rate, with the factor of proportionality more than one. For one may generally

10. Which we shall designate r_2.

Table 3 Estimates of elasticity of capital stock with respect to relative prices ($\hat{E}_p$) and output ($\hat{E}_q$), c_2 involving interest rate only

(1) m	(2) s	(3) $\Sigma \hat{\gamma}_{pi}$	(4) $\Sigma \hat{\gamma}_{qi}$	(5) $\Sigma \hat{\omega}_j$	(6) SEE	(7) $\hat{E}_p$	(8) $\hat{E}_q$	(9) $1 - \Sigma(\hat{\gamma}_p + \hat{\omega})$	(10) $1 - \Sigma(\hat{\gamma}_q + \hat{\omega})$
1	2	0·0066 (0·0121)	0·0751 (0·0276)	0·8742 (0·0439)	0·0012791	0·0525	0·5974	0·1192 (0·0472)	0·0506 (0·0432)
1	1	0·0058 (0·0122)	0·1040 (0·0159)	0·8665 (0·0438)	0·0012891	0·0432	0·7786	0·1278 (0·0471)	0·0296 (0·0403)
1[a]	2	0·0066 (0·0119)	0·0770 (0·0240)	0·8773 (0·0373)	0·0012633	0·0535	0·6273	0·1161 (0·0418)	0·0457 (0·0246)
2	2	0·0070 (0·0124)	0·0134 (0·0205)	0·8796 (0·0476)	0·0013922	0·0577	0·1117	0·1135 (0·0508)	0·1070 (0·0427)
3	2	0·0071 (0·0113)	−0·0026 (0·0131)	0·8894 (0·0462)	0·0013777	0·0645	−0·0231	0·1035 (0·0491)	0·1131 (0·0417)
4	1	0·0152 (0·0140)	0·0128 (0·0135)	0·9096 (0·0610)	0·0018578	0·1679	0·1415	0·0753 (0·0639)	0·0777 (0·0554)
4[a]	2	0·0102 (0·0108)	−0·0058 (0·0105)	0·9691 (0·0305)	0·0014171	0·3288	−0·1870	0·0208 (0·0344)	0·0367 (0·0267)
4	2	0·0105 (0·0103)	−0·0018 (0·0101)	0·8925 (0·0446)	0·0013573	0·0981	0·0171	0·0970 (0·0468)	0·1094 (0·0390)
1	3	0·0079 (0·0122)	0·0651 (0·0303)	0·8708 (0·0443)	0·0012846	0·0612	0·5043	0·1213 (0·0475)	0·0640 (0·0464)
4	3	0·0103 (0·0103)	−0·0042 (0·0107)	0·8843 (0·0461)	0·0013638	0·0887	−0·0361	0·1054 (0·0483)	0·1199 (0·0433)

$$\Delta \ln K_t = \sum_{i=m}^{7} \left\{ \gamma_{pi} \Delta \ln \left(\frac{p}{c_2}\right)_{t-i} + \gamma_{qi} \Delta \ln Q_{t-i} \right\} + \sum_{j=1}^{s} \omega_j \Delta \ln K_{t-j} + v$$

$$\hat{E}_p = \frac{\sum_{i=m}^{7} \hat{\gamma}_{pi}}{1 - \sum_{j=1}^{s} \hat{\omega}_j} \qquad \hat{E}_q = \frac{\sum_{i=m}^{7} \hat{\gamma}_{qi}}{1 - \sum_{j=1}^{s} \hat{\omega}_j}$$

[a] Constant term constrained to zero

expect market arbitrage to preserve a fairly constant ratio between the interest rate and the ratio of *expected* earnings to the price of equity. Measures of the elasticity of capital stock with respect to the interest rate might hence be expected to be identical to those measured with respect to the ratio of *expected* earnings to the value of equity but would lack the bias introduced by the ratio of *actual* earnings plus interest involved in the Jorgenson–Stephenson measure.[11] Table 3 presents a set of estimates involving a relation identical to that in Table 2 except for the use of the United States Government long-term bond rate, r_2, in calculation of a rental price of capital, c_2. It is then found that in no case does the estimated elasticity of capital stock with respect to relative prices differ significantly from zero and in the best fitting equations, corresponding to those considered in Table 2, the estimated elasticities of capital stock with respect to relative prices are in the order of 0·05. The estimated elasticities of capital stock with respect to output, however, are again relatively high. All in all, there appears to be scant *empirical* support for the usefulness of 'the neoclassical model of capital accumulation'.[12]

11. The effect on $\hat{E}_p$ of using r_2 instead of r_1 will also depend on its mean value since, as seen in equation **1**, c is not proportional to r.

12. Jorgenson and Stephenson (1967a, p. 215) suggested 'errors of measurement in the observed values of changes in desired capital' as an explanation of their low estimates of the elasticity of output with respect to capital input. A corresponding explanation may now be offered for the relatively low estimates of the elasticity of capital stock with respect to the product of relative prices and output noted in Table 1. This explanation, however, runs in terms of misspecification of the role of relative prices in the investment function. If desired capital stock is not a first degree, homogeneous function of relative prices and output, but rather is of the form $K^* = \beta(p/c)^{\gamma_p} Q^{\gamma_q}$, with γ_p markedly less than γ_q (and perhaps differing little from zero), then the substantial variance in p/c over time introduces a substantial error in Jorgenson's measure of desired capital. This causes a major downward bias in his unconstrained estimates of the elasticity of actual capital stock with respect to desired capital.

As Martin Feldstein has reminded us, the errors in variables will not *generally* contribute to a downward bias in the estimates of elasticity. In this case, if the regression of $\Delta \ln p/c$ on $\Delta \ln Q$ were negative, and sufficiently so to outweigh high ratios of the variance of $\Delta \ln p/c$ to $\Delta \ln Q$, the bias could be upward. In fact, however, while $\Delta \ln p/c$ is apparently negatively related to $\Delta \ln Q$, the ratio of the variance of $\Delta \ln p/c$ to that of $\Delta \ln Q$ is relatively high. A very rough suggestion of the nature of the bias, ignoring all lagged variables other than $\Delta\ln (p/c)_{t-1}$ and $\Delta \ln Q_{t-1}$, may be found by noting that if we consider the true relation to be

$$\Delta \ln K_t = \eta \, \Delta \ln Q_{t-1} + e$$

but use $\{\Delta \ln Q_{t-1} + \Delta \ln (p/c)_{t-1}\}$ as our independent variable, we have the simple errors-in-variable system:

$$y = \eta z + e; \quad z = x + u; \quad u = hx + v.$$

Continued overleaf

Lag distributions, the putty-clay hypothesis, and replacement

Jorgenson and Stephenson state, 'Our results show that approximately three quarters elapse between the change in desired capital and the first actual investment expenditures' (Jorgenson and Stephenson, 1967, p. 21). However, they have constrained their estimators so that no investment expenditures could be shown for the first several quarters – not until the fourth quarter for total manufacturing. According to their criterion of minimum standard errors of estimate this constraint is not justified. With the original arithmetic formulation by Jorgenson and Stephenson, the standard error of estimate, when γ_i is constrained to be zero for $i < 4$ and $i > 7$, is 0.09146 (rounded to 0.0915, as reported in Jorgenson and Stephenson, 1967, Table 3), while the standard errors of estimate when the first non-zero y_i is allowed to be y_1, y_2, or y_3 are 0.09127, 0.09085, and 0.09087, respectively. Our estimates of the Jorgenson–Stephenson equations (3 and 4, above) indicate that the ratio, to total net investment, of the sum of net investment induced up to the fourth quarter following a stimulus to

---

Least squares estimation of $y = \eta' z + e'$ will then, if plim $\Sigma xe =$ plim $\Sigma ue = 0$, yield estimates of η' such that

$$\text{plim } \hat{\eta} = \eta \left\{ \frac{\text{plim } (1+h)}{1+2 \text{ plim } h + \text{plim } (\Sigma u^2/\Sigma x^2)} \right\}.$$

Taking the variance and covariance statistics involving $\Delta \ln Q_{t-1}$ and $\Delta \ln (p/c)_{t-1}$ associated with Table 2 as if they were probability limits, we have

$$\text{Est. plim } \hat{\eta} = \eta \left\{ \frac{1+(-0.840723)}{1+2(-0.840723)+(0.00447348/0.00172129)} \right\}$$
$$= 0.08306 \, \eta.$$

We may then offer the further rough calculation that estimates of E in the relation

$$K^* = \beta \left(\frac{pQ}{c} \right)^E$$

(where Jorgenson, as noted, takes $E = 1$), will yield, if the true relation is $K^* = \beta (p/c)^{\gamma_p} Q^{\gamma_q}$,

$$\hat{E} = \gamma_p + 0.08306 \, (\gamma_q - \gamma_p).$$

Substituting our estimates of γ_p and γ_q from line 1 of Table 2, we have

$$\hat{E} = 0.1470 + 0.08306 \, (0.6889 - 0.1470) = 0.192,$$

which does indeed come close to the corresponding $\hat{E}$ of 0.201 to be found in line 3 of Table 1.

Our results with Jorgenson's quarterly data for manufacturing have been interestingly foreshadowed in Hickman's (1965) careful development and analysis of post-war annual data of all industries. He found elasticities of capital stock with respect to output sufficiently close to unity to warrant constraining them at that value, while '. . . in most sectors the price variables were of the wrong sign, were statistically insignificant, or both' (p. 53).

demand for capital is 0·120, 0·097, or 0·057, depending whether the *assumptions* permit investment to begin to take place during the quarter of the stimulus, the first following quarter, or the second following quarter.

These differences in estimates of the lag structure become sharper when we turn to the logarithmic form of the equation we have estimated in **8**. Here we find, for example, that for $m = 0$, $n = 7$, and $s = 3$, which in estimating freely the largest number of γs and ωs offers a relative minimum of constraints to our estimator, with the end of the third quarter following a stimulus the ratio of the sum of net investment to the total eventually achieved has reached 0·267. (See Table 4.) By the end of the fifth quarter, that ratio is 0·600, compared to a ratio of only 0·203 with the Jorgenson–Stephenson constraints of $m = 4$, $n = 7$ and $s = 2$. Net investment indeed reaches its peak in the fourth quarter following a stimulus. The estimated median lag of net investment, it may be noted, is 4·40 quarters as against 6·89; the estimated mean lag is 4·49 quarters versus 6·78. We should not want the reader to attach great confidence to these specific results. We report them merely to demonstrate that a sound *empirical* basis has not been furnished for the conclusion offered by Jorgenson and Stephenson that appropriate policy 'changes result in a relatively short sharp boom in investment beginning approximately a year after the policy measures are put into effect and building up to a peak approximately two years after the policy measures are undertaken'. [13]

The problem of estimation of the lag structure, however, becomes intertwined with the matter of basic model specification. For along with 'the neo-classical model' involving relative prices, it may be appropriate to utilize a 'putty-clay' hypothesis which would distinguish between the responses of investment to changes in relative prices and the responses to changes in output. If new capital can be molded into any shape (putty) but once installed is not malleable (clay), then changes in relative prices leading to changes in the equilibrium stock of capital (a movement from wood buildings to longer-lasting brick buildings as a result, perhaps, of a fall in the cost of capital) would be effected to a large extent only as the older capital (wooden buildings) wore out. In the case of increases in output, however, additional capital would be desired at once. A change in relative

13. Jorgenson and Stephenson (1967, p. 26). Curiously, conflicting results, consistent with ours but not with Jorgenson and Stephenson's, are drawn by Hall and Jorgenson (1967, p. 40) from annual data; they report, 'A substantial part of the investment takes place during the year in which the change in desired capital occurs'. Hall and Jorgenson preface this statement with the claim that 'The general shape of the distributed lag functions coincides with previous results based on quarterly data', despite the report by Jorgenson and Stephenson (1967, p. 21), 'Our results show that approximately three quarters elapse between the change in desired capital and the first actual investment expenditures'.

Table 4 Distributed lag coefficient: effect of removing zero constraints on initial coefficients and ω_3

(1)	(2)	(3)	(4)	(5)	(6)	(7)
	$\hat{\mu}_i$		$\sum_{k=0}^{i} \hat{\mu}_k$		$\sum^{i} \hat{\mu}_k / \sum^{\infty} \hat{\mu}_k$	
	$m = 4$	$m = 0$	$m = 4$	$m = 0$	$m = 4$	$m = 0$
i	$s = 2$	$s = 3$	$s = 2$	$s = 3$	$s = 2$	$s = 3$
0	0·0000	0·0048	0·0000	0·0048	0·0000	0·0216
1	0·0000	0·0089	0·0000	0·0137	0·0000	0·0619
2	0·0000	0·0184	0·0000	0·0320	0·0000	0·1447
3	0·0000	0·0270	0·0000	0·0591	0·0000	0·2669
4	0·0077	0·0370	0·0077	0·0961	0·0878	0·4341
5	0·0102	0·0368	0·0179	0·1329	0·2033	0·6001
6	0·0118	0·0299	0·0297	0·1628	0·3370	0·7352
7	0·0162	0·0261	0·0459	0·1889	0·5209	0·8531
8	0·0166	0·0203	0·0624	0·2092	0·7088	0·9450
9	0·0143	0·0146	0·0767	0·2238	0·8710	1·0107
10	0·0107	0·0093	0·0874	0·2331	0·9927	1·0526
11	0·0069	0·0048	0·0943	0·2379	1·0705	1·0744
12	0·0034	0·0015	0·0977	0·2394	1·1090	1·0810
13	0·0007	−0·0009	0·0984	0·2385	1·1168	1·0769
14	−0·0011	−0·0024	0·0973	0·2361	1·1043	1·0663
15	−0·0021	−0·0031	0·0952	0·2330	1·0807	1·0525
16 to ∞	−0·0071	−0·0116	−0·0071 [a]	−0·0116 [a]	−0·0807 [b]	−0·0525 [b]

modal lag	8	4	
second modal lag	27 [c]	25 [d]	
median lag	6·8866	4·3971	
mean lag	6·7787	4·4866	

$$\Delta \ln K_t = \sum_{i=m}^{7} \gamma_i \, \Delta \ln \left(\frac{pQ}{c_1}\right)_{t-i} + \sum_{j=1}^{s} \omega_j \, \Delta \ln K_{t-j} + w$$

$$= \sum_{i=m}^{\infty} \mu_i \, \Delta \ln \left(\frac{pQ}{c_1}\right)_{t-i} + w'$$

[a] Summed from $k = 16$. [b] Numerator summed from $k = 16$. [c] $\hat{\mu}_{27} = 0·00031$.
[d] $\hat{\mu}_{25} = 0·00033$

prices would, of course, alter the equilibrium response of capital to a change in output, but this would be a relatively second-order effect.

In the context of the current work, the putty-clay hypothesis suggests that the short-run responses of investment to changes in output would be more rapid than those to changes in relative prices. In particular, an estimator which constrained investment to be zero in the first several quarters following a stimulus to the demand for capital would then bias particularly estimates of both the short-run and total response of investment to changes in output. The latter bias is indeed apparent in Table 2, where estimates of the elasticity of capital with respect to output are reduced sharply, from 0·6889 to 0·3444 to 0·1539 to 0·1286, as investment is constrained to be zero in all quarters following a stimulus up to the second, third, and fourth, respectively. Further, if variations in relative prices do not influence investment in the first several quarters, they constitute errors in the independent variables of equation 8 which may be expected to bias toward zero our estimates of γ_i for low values of i in equation 7. This might explain the low estimates of elasticities with respect to pQ/c, presented in Table 1, in those regressions where prompt investment response is not precluded. Such downward bias in estimates of elasticity, stemming from misspecification of initial lagged variables, may be viewed as a particular case of the bias if relative prices enter generally as an error in the lagged variables specified as affecting the demand for capital.

It is in fact the general bias which seems to dominate, and evidence of a particular role for relative prices in the putty-clay hypothesis is hard to come by. Table 5 compares the estimated responses of net investment to changes in relative price and output where the cost of capital is measured as the ratio of interest and earnings to the market value of securities. The total response to output changes, as noted earlier, is much greater than that with respect to changes in relative prices. The proportion of response occurring in the first quarter following a stimulus is indeed slightly greater in the case of output than relative prices: 0·0278 compared to 0·0225. Thereafter, however, the reaction to price changes, though in total less, is more rapid. This can be noted most directly by comparing columns 8 and 9; after four quarters, some 36 per cent of the response of investment to relative price changes has occurred while only 25 per cent of the total response to a change in output is achieved. It may also be noted that the modal, median, and mean lags of investment with respect to relative price changes are in all cases about one quarter less than that with respect to output changes.

Our earlier concern that the measure of cost of capital underlying Table 5 (and the Jorgenson–Stephenson papers) rather reflects market expectations would suggest that it is this anticipatory factor that reduces the relative lag of our 'relative price' variable. We therefore offer a similar comparison of responses to relative prices and output in Table 6, where relative price is derived from a cost of capital defined as the long-term US Government bond rate. Here the picture is indeed somewhat different. The response of net investment to changes in relative prices is markedly slower, and less rapid than the response to changes in output. The results, however, are far from clear. The total response of net investment to a change in relative

Table 5 Distributed lag coefficients: responses of investment to relative price and output changes compared, cost of capital involving interest and earnings

(1)	(2)	(3)	(4)	(5)	(6)	(7)	(8)	(9)	(10)
i	γ_{pt}	γ_{qt}	β_{pt}	β_{qt}	$\sum\limits_{k=1}^{i}\beta_{pk}$	$\sum\limits_{k=1}^{i}\beta_{qk}$	$\dfrac{\sum\limits_{1}^{i}\beta_{pk}}{\sum\limits_{1}^{\infty}\beta_{pk}}$	$\dfrac{\sum\limits_{1}^{i}\beta_{qk}}{\sum\limits_{1}^{\infty}\beta_{qk}}$	$\dfrac{\sum\limits_{1}^{i}\beta_{pk}}{\sum\limits_{1}^{i}\beta_{qk}}$ $\{(6) \div (7)\}$
1	0·0033	0·0192	0·0033	0·0192	0·0033	0·0192	0·0225	0·0278	0·1727
2	0·0090	0·0191	0·0124	0·0388	0·0157	0·0579	0·1067	0·0841	0·2709
3	0·0038	0·0151	0·0160	0·0518	0·0317	0·1098	0·2154	0·1593	0·2886
4	0·0066	0·0149	0·0210	0·0620	0·0527	0·1718	0·3583	0·2493	0·3067
5	−0·0039	0·0081	0·0152	0·0636	0·0678	0·2353	0·4614	0·3416	0·2883
6	−0·0034	−0·0036	0·0088	0·0591	0·0767	0·2944	0·5214	0·4274	0·2604
7	0·0039	0·0103	0·0106	0·0609	0·0873	0·3553	0·5934	0·5158	0·2456
8	—	—	0·0095	0·0532	0·0967	0·4085	0·6580	0·5930	0·2368
9	—	—	0·0081	0·0450	0·1048	0·4536	0·7128	0·6584	0·2311
10	—	—	0·0068	0·0379	0·1116	0·4915	0·7590	0·7134	0·2271
11	—	—	0·0057	0·0318	0·1173	0·5232	0·7978	0·7595	0·2242
12	—	—	0·0048	0·0267	0·1221	0·5499	0·8304	0·7982	0·2220
13	—	—	0·0040	0·0224	0·1261	0·5723	0·8577	0·8307	0·2204
14	—	—	0·0034	0·0188	0·1295	0·5911	0·8806	0·8580	0·2191
15	—	—	0·0028	0·0158	0·1323	0·6068	0·8998	0·8808	0·2180
16 to ∞	0·0	0·0	0·0147	0·0821	0·0147 [a]	0·0821 [a]	0·1002 [b]	0·1192 [b]	0·1795 [a]
Sum	0·0192 (0·0093)	0·0902 (0·0262)	0·1470	0·6889	0·1470	0·6889	1·0000	1·0000	0·2134

	(2)	(3)
modal lag	4	5
median lag	5·6436	6·8213
mean lag	7·8468	8·7234

$$\Delta \ln K_t = \sum_{i=1}^{7}\{\gamma_{pi}\,\Delta\ln(p/c_1)_{t-i} + \gamma_{qi}\,\Delta\ln Q_{t-i}\} + \sum_{j=1}^{2}\omega_j\,\Delta\ln K_{t-} + v$$

$$= \sum_{i=1}^{8}\{\mu_{pi}\,\Delta\ln(p/c_1)_{t-i} + \mu_{qi}\,\Delta\ln Q_{t-i}\} + v'$$

[a] Summed from k = 16. [b] Numerator summed from k = 16.

prices so measured is very small and not statistically significantly different from zero, as noted above. There is an abortive rapid response of investment to relative prices in the first two quarters, but this response is not statistically significant and is followed quickly by negative investment (also not statistically significant) which largely cancels the initial surge.

One would have to conclude again, from these estimates of the lag distributions, that the response of investment to changes in relative prices is small, and if one recognizes the possible role of market expectations in the Jorgenson–Stephenson measure of cost of capital, it is not confirmed at all. But then, correspondingly, one would find in the lag distributions estimated from these post-war quarterly data no evidence which would support the role of relative prices suggested by the putty-clay hypothesis.[14]

Turning to replacement investment, one may also question the Jorgenson–Stephenson conclusion that '. . . replacement is proportional to capital stock' (Jorgenson and Stephenson, 1967a, p. 211). The hypothesis is set forth first as '. . . a fundamental result of renewal theory' (Jorgenson, 1963, p. 251); it is later argued that 'if replacement is not proportional to capital stock, there is no reason for capital stock to appear in the [gross investment] regression with a non-zero coefficient' (Jorgenson, 1965, p. 75). The confirmation of proportional replacement is then based on empirical evidence of significantly positive regression values of δ, the coefficient of capital stock.

But the expected value of δ would be positive if there were any kind of positive relation between gross capital expenditures and capital stock, however far from a proportionate one. Proper tests of proportionality would entail a search for nonlinearities, which could hardly be ruled out *a priori* unless the regression fit were perfect.

The accuracy of the proportionality hypothesis comes into question initially when one distinguishes between the asymptotic property of a random process and the relatively short-run consequences of cyclical fluctuations in investment. If the probability of exhaustion of capital stock is very small in the early period of its life one should hardly expect replacement requirements to continue at a constant ratio of capital stock after a burst of investment which substantially alters the age distribution. Depreciation should approximate a constant proportion of some long-run or 'permanent' value for capital stock; it will be a smaller porportion of a temporarily younger capital stock resulting from higher than usual net

14. This may be contrasted with the conclusions offered by Bischoff (1966). In commenting on that paper one of the authors (Eisner) argued that Bischoff obtained his results in support of the putty-clay role of relative prices from the particular constraints introduced into the Almon lag estimator. Our results here with essentially similar data would appear to confirm that comment.

Table 6 Distributed lag coefficients: responses of investment to relative price and output changes compared, cost of capital involving interest rate only

(1) i	(2) γ_{pt}	(3) γ_{qt}	(4) μ_{pt}	(5) μ_{qt}	(6) $\sum_{k=1}^{i}\mu_{pk}$	(7) $\sum_{k=1}^{i}\mu_{qk}$	(8) $\dfrac{\sum^{i}\mu_{pk}}{\sum^{\infty}\mu_{px}}$	(9) $\dfrac{\sum^{i}\mu_{qt}}{\sum^{\infty}\mu_{qk}}$	(10) $\dfrac{\sum^{i}\mu_{pk}}{\{(6)\div(7)\}}$
1	0·0055	0·0215	0·0055	0·0215	0·0055	0·0215	0·1039	0·0360	0·2537
2	0·0027	0·0143	0·0087	0·0381	0·0141	0·0596	0·2693	0·0997	0·2372
3	−0·0080	−0·0093	−0·0003	0·0465	0·0145	0·1060	0·2757	0·1775	0·1364
4	−0·0013	−0·0054	−0·0003	0·0479	0·0142	0·1539	0·2699	0·2577	0·0920
5	−0·0072	−0·0084	−0·0076	0·0506	0·0066	0·2045	0·1253	0·3424	0·0321
6	−0·0029	−0·0086	−0·0054	0·0534	0·0011	0·2580	0·0215	0·4318	0·0044
7	0·0095	0·0077	0·0052	0·0550	0·0063	0·3130	0·1207	0·5239	0·0202
8	—	—	0·0070	0·0485	0·0133	0·3614	0·2541	0·6050	0·0369
9	—	—	0·0065	0·0409	0·0199	0·4023	0·3787	0·6734	0·0494
10	—	—	0·0056	0·0340	0·0255	0·4363	0·4856	0·7302	0·0584
11	—	—	0·0047	0·0281	0·0302	0·4644	0·5749	0·7773	0·0649
12	—	—	0·0039	0·0232	0·0340	0·4876	0·6490	0·8161	0·0698
13	—	—	0·0032	0·0192	0·0373	0·5067	0·7102	0·8482	0·0735
14	—	—	0·0027	0·0158	0·0399	0·5226	0·7608	0·8747	0·0764
15	—	—	0·0022	0·0131	0·0421	0·5356	0·8025	0·8966	0·0786
16 to ∞	0·0	0·0	0·0104	0·0618	0·0104 [a]	0·0618 [b]	0·1975 [b]	0·1034 [b]	0·1676 [a]
Sum	0·0066 (0·0121)	0·0751 (0·0276)	0·0525	0·5974	0·0525	0·5974	1·0000	1·0000	0·0879

	(4)	(5)
modal lag	2·8	7
median lag	10·1616	6·7408
mean lag	11·1320	8·3990

$$\Delta \ln K_t = \sum_{i=1}^{7} \{\gamma_{pt}\,\Delta\ln(p/c_2)_{t-i} + \gamma_{qt}\,\Delta\ln Q_{t-i}\} + \sum_{j=1}^{2} \omega_j\,\Delta\ln K_{t-j} + v$$

$$= \sum_{i=1}^{8} \{\mu_{pt}\,\Delta\ln(p/c_2)_{t-j} + \mu_{qt}\,\Delta\ln Q_{t-i}\} + v'$$

[a] Summed from $k = 16$. [b] Numerator summed from $k = 16$

investment and will be a higher proportion of a temporarily older capital stock resulting from less than normal net investment. The actual observed capital stock will then tend to include an error in the true variable, 'permanent' capital, a constant proportion of which would be replaced.

Our own further analysis of the data confirms the Jorgenson–Stephenson findings that the estimated or fitted value of depreciation is significantly less than the value of 0·0273 which they calculated by application of the perpetual inventory method to beginning and end points for capital stock. The errors-in-variable hypothesis argument we are advancing here against proportional replacement would also explain these downwardly biased estimates of the depreciation coefficient.

It is further claimed that the conclusion in favor of proportional replacement 'confirms the evidence against the so-called "echo effect"'' (Jorgenson, 1965, p. 75; see also Jorgenson and Stephenson, 1967a, p. 212), by which successive cyclic waves of investment would follow an initial stimulus. Failure to demonstrate proportional replacement would then correspondingly leave denial of the echo effect unconfirmed. Some positive suggestions of echo effects may in fact be noted when we abandon certain constraints on the lag estimator (particularly the Jorgenson–Stephenson requirement that $\omega_2 \geqslant -\frac{{\omega_1}^2}{4}$), which prevent the estimates of μ_i, the lag coefficients, from ever turning negative. Unconstrained estimates of the lag distribution for total manufacturing, which we present in Table 4, offer modest evidence of cyclical responses, which might conceivably reflect echo effects, but this evidence, it must be admitted, is very slight.

Summary and conclusion

We have utilized data furnished by Jorgenson to test the relevance of the assumptions and the accuracy of the conclusions of his 'neoclassical' theory of investment. Our results indicate:

1 The role of relative prices, the critical element of the neoclassical approach, is not confirmed. The elasticity of capital stock with respect to the ratios of the wholesale price index to Jorgenson's measures of the rental price of capital is far below the value of unity which he has *assumed* in his papers. For one of the measures used by Jorgenson, it does not differ significantly from zero.

2 Unconstrained estimates of the long-run elasticity of capital stock with respect to the product of relative prices and output, which are also far less than unity, suggest errors in Jorgenson's desired capital stock variables introduced by misspecification of the role of relative prices.

3 The elasticity of capital stock with respect to output is reasonably high, in a number of instances approaching unity. This is consistent with flexible accelerator models.

4 Results contradict Jorgenson's assumption of a Cobb–Douglas production function but are generally consistent with the implications of CES production functions with elasticities of substitution nearer zero than unity and, possibly, increasing returns to scale.

5 Conclusions by Jorgenson and Stephenson suggesting a delay of up to a year before the response of investment to changes in its determinants are found to follow from the constraints which they impose upon the lag distribution, and are contradicted by relatively free estimates from the data.

6 The role of relative prices suggested by the 'putty-clay hypothesis' is not confirmed by estimates utilizing the general Pascal lag distribution.

7 The hypothesis of proportional replacement of capital, along with rejection of 'echo effects', are left open to doubt.

Our results, it should be noted finally, call into question a number of conclusions by Jorgenson, himself and with Stephenson or Hall, regarding the implications of various fiscal and monetary policies for investment.[15] One may hope that further research will shed additional light on these matters as well as some of the basic questions regarding lag structure and the nature and role of substitution parameters in investment behavior.[16]

Appendix

The following quarterly data, generally from the first quarter of 1947 to the fourth quarter of 1962, were obtained from Jorgenson:

1 Gross investment from the OBE–SEC Quarterly Investment Surveys (reported in the *Survey of Current Business*), price deflated by a weighted average (q) of deflators for producers' durables and non-farm, non-residential construction from the United States National Product accounts.

15. The specific relevance of this to such issues as accelerated depreciation and the investment tax credit is considered by Eisner (1969).
16. Issues later raised by Bischoff (1969, reprinted as Reading 6 in this volume) have subsequently been discussed by Eisner and Nadiri (1970). They report on modification of the Jorgenson stochastic specification used in their original work and employment of a maximum likelihood estimator allowing for autoregressive disturbances as suggested by Bischoff. The new regressions with the Jorgenson data confirm fully the findings reprinted here, with little difference in estimated parameters. (Editor's note: This footnote was added by Eisner and Nadiri in 1974. See also the survey papers by Jorgenson and Klein listed among the suggestions for further reading.)

2 Capital stock net of depreciation at the beginning of 1948 and 1960 from the OBE Capital Goods Study (Jaszi *et al.* in *Survey of Current Business*, November 1962) with intervening quarterly values along with the rate of depreciation, δ, calculated from the recursive relation,

$$K_{t+1} = I_t + (1-\delta)K_t.$$

3 Gross value added – pQ – the sum of corporate and noncorporate profits before taxes, depreciation, net monetary interest, and total compensation of employees. These data for total manufacturing were allocated among quarters in proportion to the corresponding series in the FTC–SEC *Quarterly Financial Reports*.

4 A first measure of the rental price or user cost of capital, c_1, based on r_1, defined as (corporate profits after taxes plus net monetary interest)/the value of all outstanding securities. The value of equity was estimated as the ratio of corporate profits after taxes to the earnings–price ratio for manufacturing corporations reported by Standard and Poor's. The value of debt was estimated as the ratio of net monetary interest to the bond yield for manufacturing corporations.

5 A second measure of the rental price or user cost of capital, c_2, based on r_2, the United States Government Long-Term Bond Rate as reported in the *Survey of Current Business*.

All of these data are reported to be seasonally adjusted and flow variables are measured at quarterly rates. All price indexes take the value of unity in 1954.

The only additional variable introduced by Eisner and Nadiri is the wholesale price index, also given the value of unity in 1954. This index was considered to be p, and output of each quarter, Q_t, was then calculated by dividing the Jorgenson figure, $p_t Q_t$, by our p_t. Our measure of relative prices was p/c.

Fuller accounts of Jorgenson's data are to be found in various of the references cited but particularly in the 'Statistical Appendix' of Jorgenson and Stephenson (1967a, pp. 217–18).

References

BISCHOFF, C. W. (1966), 'Elasticities of substitution, capital malleability, and distributed lag investment functions', presented to the San Francisco Meetings of the Econometric Society.

BISCHOFF, C. W. (1969), 'Hypothesis testing and the demand for capital goods', *Rev. econ. Stat.*, vol. 51, pp. 354–68.

DHRYMES, P. J. (1967), 'Adjustment dynamics and the estimation of the CES class of production functions', *Inter. econ. Rev.*, vol. 8, pp. 209–17.

EISNER, R. (1967), 'A permanent income theory for investment: some empirical explorations', *Amer. econ. Rev.*, vol. 57, pp. 363–90.

EISNER, R. (1969), 'Tax policy and investment behavior: comment', *Amer. econ. Rev.*, vol. 59, pp. 379–88.

EISNER, R., and NAPIVI, M. I. (1970), 'Neoclassical theory of investment behaviour: comment', *Rev. econ. Stat.*, vol. 52 pp. 216–22.

HALL, R. E., NADIRI and JORGENSON, D. W. (1967), 'Tax policy and investmen behavior', *Amer. econ. Rev.*, vol. 57, pp. 391–414.

HICKMAN, B. G. (1965), *Investment Demand and US Economic Growth*, Brookings Institution.

JORGENSON, D. W. (1963), 'Capital theory and investment behavior', *Amer. econ. Rev.*, vol. 53, pp. 247–59.

JORGENSON, D. W. (1965), 'Anticipations and investment behavior', in James S. Duesenberry *et al.* (eds.), *The Brookings Quarterly Econometric Model of the United States*, Rand McNally, pp. 35–94.

JORGENSON, D. W. (1966), 'Rational distributed lag functions', *Econometrica*, vol. 34, pp. 135–49.

JORGENSON, D. W. (1967), 'The theory of investment behavior', in Robert Ferber (ed.), *Determinants of Investment Behavior*, Columbia University Press.

JORGENSON, D. W., and STEPHENSON, J. A. (1967), 'The time structure of investment behavior in United States manufacturing, 1947–1960', *Rev. econ. Stat.*, vol. 49, pp. 16–27.

JORGENSON, D. W., and STEPHENSON, J. A. (1967a), 'Investment behavior in US manufacturing, 1947–1960', *Econometrica*, vol. 35, pp. 169–220.

THEIL, H. (1961), *Economic Forecasts and Policy*, North-Holland.

6 C. W. Bischoff

Hypothesis Testing and the Demand for Capital Goods[1]

C. W. Bischoff, 'Hypothesis testing and the demand for capital goods', *Review of Economics and Statistics*, vol. 51, 1969, pp. 354–68.

I Introduction and summary

One of the basic facts of life confronting econometric researchers is that in order to test any hypothesis it is necessary to assume the validity of other assumptions which cannot be tested. An important part of the art of practical econometrics is knowing how much to include in the *maintained hypothesis*; if too much is assumed there may be little or nothing left to test while if too little is assumed it may be impossible to reach any conclusions, or else the analysis may become hopelessly complex.

In a recent article[2] Eisner and Nadiri have examined critically one of the essential maintained hypotheses used by Jorgenson, Stephenson, Hall, and Siebert in a substantial body of empirical research on the demand for capital goods.[3] This assumption maintains that the *long-run* partial elasticity of the flow of capital services, the stock of capital, the flow of gross investment demand, or the flow of net investment, with respect to the price of output (p) divided by the price of capital services (c) should be unity. By respecifying Jorgenson's model in a logarithmic form, Eisner and Nadiri have produced tests of the hypothesis that the long-run price elasticity of demand for capital stock is unity. Not only do they find that the estimated elasticity with respect to (p/c) is significantly less than one, but all of their preferred point estimates of this parameter are less than 0·16 and in some cases do not differ significantly from zero. The first of the seven conclusions

1. Support for this research was provided under contract DACA31–67–C–0141, US Army Corps of Engineers, for the Office of Emergency Planning, and by the National Science Foundation and Ford Foundation through grants to the Cowles Foundation for Research in Economics. I am very grateful to Professors R. Eisner, R. J. Gordon, D. Grether, D. Jorgenson, F. Modigliani, and M. Nerlove and to the members of the Workshop in Econometrics and Mathematical Economics of the University of Chicago, for criticisms of earlier versions of this paper, and to Petter Frenger for extremely helpful research assistance.
2. Eisner and Nadiri (1968), reprinted as Reading 5. These criticisms have been amplified in Eisner (1969, 1969a).
3. This body of research includes Hall and Jorgenson (1967, 1971), Jorgenson (1963, 1965), Jorgenson and Siebert (1968, 1968a), Jorgenson and Stephenson (1967, 1967a).

summarized by Eisner and Nadiri is that 'the role of relative prices, the critical element of the neoclassical approach, is not confirmed'.[4]

In principle, the Eisner–Nadiri goal of relaxing and testing crucial maintained hypotheses is a laudable one. Their conclusions, if they can be sustained, have far-reaching implications. If their estimated elasticities are correct, then fiscal and monetary policy-makers have little, if any, *direct* influence on investment expenditures. A cautious approach to the importance of the Eisner–Nadiri conclusions would seem justified, however, in view of the fact that others have also undertaken the task of critically examining the maintained hypotheses in the Jorgenson model. While none of the other critics of Jorgenson has defended the precise manner in which he has specified his model, without exception the results have been favorable to the essence of the 'neoclassical approach' to investment functions – the assumption that relative prices do matter.[5]

The next section of this paper is essentially an exercise in detective work aimed at finding out why Eisner and Nadiri obtained results contrary to the body of other research. The analytical method used is to carry the goal of Eisner and Nadiri – relaxing and testing maintained hypothesis – one step further. The maintained hypothesis I relax and test involves the assumption of serially independent errors.[6] In a sense, the exercise succeeds only partially; some of the empirical results are even more peculiar than those reported by Eisner and Nadiri.

In the context of a maintained hypothesis about the errors which is only slightly more general than the one used by either Eisner and Nadiri or Jorgenson and Stephenson, but otherwise using the Eisner–Nadiri model, the empirical results are somewhat startling. The summary of conclusions drawn by Eisner and Nadiri includes seven separate paragraphs. For one or two similar sets of data, *four* of these conclusions simply no longer follow, if the more general stochastic specification is applied.[7] For the second set of data, at least two of the conclusions are reversed. Unfortunately, however, the noise level for the data and model analysed becomes so high that the

4. Eisner and Nadiri (1968, p. 380).
5. See Bischoff (1971), Coen (1968, 1971), Evans (1968). Some of this evidence is discussed briefly in section III below. The evidence on demand for factors other than capital, and on direct estimation of CES production functions, is also relevant, at least indirectly. See Jorgenson and Stephenson (1969) for discussion of this evidence.
6. As I note below, the stochastic assumption I make – that the errors are a first order autoregressive process – is only one step more general than that used by Eisner and Nadiri. I do not wish to imply that this stochastic assumption is anything more than a minimal improvement; the only reasons for not using other types of assumption was my desire to minimize computational problems.
7. See below, section II, for a precise statement of the conclusions which are called into question.

final conclusion of the second section must be completely agnostic with respect to what *really* influences the demand for capital.

In an attempt to draw conclusions less ambiguous than those derived from the data Eisner and Nadiri have analysed, I have applied the same model to a different set of data in the third section. For reasons which may have to do with the construction or quality of the time series, the sample period, or both, the noise level is much lower when the model is applied to the economy-wide demand for equipment for the period 1949–66. Both output and relative prices appear to have statistically significant effects on equipment demand and the point estimates of parameters are almost precisely what one would expect if the data had been generated by a model including a Cobb–Douglas production function with constant returns to scale.

None of this, of course, should be interpreted as positive support for the policy conclusions emphasized by Jorgenson and Stephenson (1967, p. 26) on the basis of the lag patterns reported in their first article. What is being defended is the 'neoclassical approach' to the study of investment behaviour.

II A re-examination of the Eisner–Nadiri conclusions about the demand for capital in manufacturing

The model of the demand for capital goods which Eisner and Nadiri employ involves the assumption that, in the long run, capital stock, K, will be related to output, Q, the price of output, p, and the rental price of capital services, c, according to

$$K = A(p/c)^{E_p}Q^{E_q}, \qquad\qquad 1$$

where A is a constant and E_p and E_q are the elasticities of capital stock with respect to the price ratio p/c and output, respectively.

If firms are constrained by a CES production function, and if the flow of capital services is proportional to the stock of capital, then E_p may be interpreted as an estimate of the elasticity of substitution, σ, and $E_q = \sigma + (1-\sigma)/v$, where v is the degree of homogeneity of the function. Because Jorgenson develops his model from an assumption that the production function is Cobb–Douglas, both E_p and E_q in his model are specified to be equal to 1, and this holds regardless of whether or not the production function is homogeneous of degree one.

In the short run, it is not assumed that a relationship such as 1 will always hold; instead a distributed lag relationship is postulated by Eisner and Nadiri in which

$$\Delta \ln K_t = \sum_{i=m}^{\infty} \{\mu_{pi} \Delta \ln (p/c)_{t-i} + \mu_{qi} \Delta \ln Q_{t-i}\}, \qquad\qquad 2$$

where K_t represents capital stock at the end of period t,

$$\sum_{i=m}^{\infty} \mu_{pi} = E_p,$$

and $$\sum_{i=m}^{\infty} \mu_{qi} = E_q.$$

Equation 2 also should include some sort of disturbance term. Note that after taking logarithms, all of the variables have been first-differenced, so that the variable on the left-hand side is the natural logarithm of one plus the ratio of net investment in period t to capital stock at the end of period $t-1$.

As it stands, equation 2 is too general to permit parameter estimation; it has an infinite number of parameters. Following Jorgenson, Eisner and Nadiri assume the μ_{pi} and μ_{qi} weights may be approximated by a general rational lag distribution.[8] The equation which emerges is one of two which they employ for their empirical tests, but the other equation is a special case of this one:[9]

$$\Delta \ln K_t = \sum_{i=m}^{n} \{\gamma_{pi} \Delta \ln (p/c)_{t-i} + \gamma_{qi} \Delta \ln Q_{t-i}\} + \sum_{j=1}^{s} \omega_j \Delta \ln K_{t-j} + u_t. \quad 3$$

The lag parameters μ_{pi} and μ_{qi} in 2, as well as the elasticities E_p and E_q, may be derived on the basis of estimates of the parameters γ_{pi}, γ_{qi}, and ω_j.

Eisner and Nadiri estimate the parameters of 3 by ordinary least squares. There is no discussion of assumptions about the distribution of the disturbance term u. However, as is well known, ordinary least squares estimates of equations with lagged endogenous variables on the right-hand side will not even be consistent unless the errors are serially independent.[10] It should be noted that in this equation, in addition to the lagged values of $\Delta \ln K$, the lagged values of $\Delta \ln (p/c)$ and $\Delta \ln Q$ must also be considered as endogenous variables in the system of equations of which 3 is a part.

In this context, then, the assumption of independent disturbances is a crucial one if meaningful results are to be obtained. Ideally, in order to justify application of standard test statistics, one would hope that the disturbance vector would have a multivariate normal distribution, with all disturbances having mean zero and the same variance, and each disturbance being independent of all the others. Implicitly, these properties have

8. See Jorgenson (1966) for a discussion of properties and estimation techniques for lag distributions of this class.
9. My equation 3 corresponds to equation 8 in Eisner and Nadiri (1968). The other specification used by Eisner and Nadiri is given in their equation 7.
10. See, for example, Griliches (1961).

no doubt been assumed. In doing this, Eisner and Nadiri are following standard procedure; in the published research on distributed lag investment functions with lagged dependent variables on the right-hand side, only Koyck (1954) has given explicit consideration to the possibility of nonindependent disturbances.[11]

It is not difficult, of course, to develop a rationale for the assumption that the disturbances in equation 3 should be independent. One might hypothesize, for example, that the rate of investment (relative to capital stock) is partially adjusted each quarter from the rate which prevailed in the previous quarter towards the rate of net investment necessary to match increments in p/c and Q. The errors in such an adjustment process might well be thought to be independent from quarter to quarter. At the same time, an equally convincing (or unconvincing) rationale could be developed for the assumption that the disturbances w in

$$\ln K_t = a + \sum_{i=m}^{n} \{\gamma_{pi} \ln (p/c)_{t-i} + \gamma_{qi} \ln Q_{t-i}\} + \sum_{j=1}^{s} \omega_j \ln K_{t-j} + w_t, \qquad 4$$

should be serially independent. This equation is identical to 3 except for the fact that the first-differencing operation has not been performed. Equation 4 may be interpreted as a capital stock demand equation, or a 'capital stock adjustment' model.

Unfortunately, it is not possible for both 3 and 4 to have independent errors, at least for the same values of the indices m, n, and s. For given values of these indices

$$u_t = w_t - w_{t-1}. \qquad 5$$

If the disturbances w are independent, then the disturbances u will be a moving average of independent errors, leading to biased and inconsistent parameter estimates. On the other hand, if the disturbances u are independent and of constant variance, then the disturbances w will be generated by an unstable autoregressive process, and will be very badly autocorrelated.

In general, ordinary least squares parameter estimation will be inappropriate for *at least one* of the two specifications 3 or 4. It is quite possible that neither will have independent errors.

Since each specification is theoretically plausible, the choice between them must be made on empirical grounds. Fortunately, it is easy to formulate a general model which includes both 3 and 4 as special cases. Using this slightly more general model provides an appropriate test to discriminate between 3 and 4 and perhaps to reject them both.

11. Hall and Jorgenson (1967), Klein and Taubman (1971) and Evans (1968) have estimated investment functions assuming autoregressive errors.

The model is a standard one. If the disturbance w is defined by the equation

$$w_t = \rho w_{t-1} + \varepsilon_t \qquad\qquad 6$$

in which $|\rho| \leqslant 1$ and ε is normally and independently distributed with mean zero and variance σ^2, ordinary least squares estimation of the parameters of **3** will be optimal only if $\rho = 1$; ordinary least squares estimates using **4** will be optimal only if $\rho = 0$.

Hildreth and Lu (1960) have shown that in an equation of the form

$$y_t = X_t \beta + w_t, \qquad\qquad 7$$

where X represents a vector of independent variables and w has the distribution indicated above, then maximum likelihood estimates of ρ and the coefficient vector β, conditional on a fixed value of w_1, may be obtained by minimizing $e'e$, the sum of squared residuals in

$$y_t - \hat{\rho} y_{t-1} = (X_t - \hat{\rho} X_{t-1})\hat{\beta} + e_t.\text{[12]} \qquad\qquad 8$$

Minimizing the sum of squared residuals in such an equation is a nonlinear problem, and solution of it by standard nonlinear estimation techniques involves the risk that there may be more than one local minimum of the function. This difficulty may be circumvented by simply specifying a number of trial values of ρ in the admissible range $-1 \leqslant \rho \leqslant 1$, and transforming each of the variables as in equation **8**. This method will provide at least approximate maximum likelihood estimates, and the approximation may be improved by successive searches with smaller and smaller increments in ρ.

The precise specification of the equation whose parameters I estimate is completed by rewriting equation **4** in the form of equation **8**, and choosing values of m, n, and s, the parameters which relate to the degree of the numerator and denominator polynomials in the rational lag distribution. I have chosen $m = 1$, $n = 8$, $s = 2$. Except for the stochastic specification (and the consequent estimation of ρ) the equation differs from the one on which Eisner and Nadiri base most of their conclusions only in being a bit

12. See Hildreth and Lu (1960). Although they do not discuss the case in which lagged dependent variables appear on the right-hand side, it is trivial to show that in this case as well the procedure leads to maximum likelihood estimates. Hildreth (1966) has investigated the asymptotic distribution of the estimators in the case in which all the right-hand variables are known; for this case the asymptotic covariance matrix is the same as that of the best linear unbiased estimates for a model with known ρ. With lagged dependent variables the asymptotic covariance matrix of the estimators has not, to my knowledge, been investigated, although some research has been done on the properties of maximum likelihood estimates for models similar except in the way the first disturbance is treated.

more general; I use eight lagged values of p/c and Q, instead of seven. The equation is thus

$$\ln K_t - \rho \ln K_{t-1} = a(1-\rho) + \sum_{i=1}^{8} [\gamma_{pi}\{\ln (p/c)_{t-i} - \rho \ln (p/c)_{t-i-1}\}$$

$$+ \gamma_{qi}\{\ln Q_{t-i} - \rho \ln Q_{t-i-1}\}]$$

$$+ \sum_{j=1}^{2} \omega_j\{\ln K_{t-i} - \rho \ln K_{t-i-1}\} + \varepsilon_t.$$

9

As noted above, with $\rho = 1$, 9 corresponds to 3; with $\rho = 0$, 9 corresponds to 4.

The sample includes quarterly data from the second quarter of 1949 to the end of 1962. The dependent variable, $\ln K_t$, is the natural logarithm of a constant dollar measure (in 1954 dollars) of the net stock of manufacturing capital at the end of period t, calculated by Jorgenson. The output measure Q_t is derived by using the wholesale price index to deflate gross value added by manufacturing firms, also calculated by Jorgenson. The price index p_t is the wholesale price index, rebased to $1954 = 100$ by Eisner and Nadiri. Two different measures of the rental price of capital services are used: c_1, in which the discount rate for investment decisions is defined as corporate profits plus net monetary interest divided by the value of outstanding securities, and c_2, in which the yield on long-term government bonds is used to approximate this discount rate.[13] These data, with the exception of the wholesale price index, not required for their model, had been used by Jorgenson and Stephenson, although only c_1 was used as a measure of the price of capital services.[14]

I have estimated the autoregressive parameter, ρ, using a grid of twenty-one trial values, spaced at intervals of length 0·1 in the domain $-1 \leqslant \rho \leqslant 1$. The results for a selection of trial values, including those closest to the maximum of the likelihood function, are given in Table 1. For the data set using c_1, the first set of trial values showed two local maxima of the likelihood function, at $\rho = 0.9$ and at $\rho = 0.2$. The maximum at $\rho = 0.2$ appeared to be the better one, but to verify this the intervals $0.8 \leqslant \rho \leqslant 1.0$ and $0.1 \leqslant \rho \leqslant 0.3$ were explored using grids with intervals of length 0·01. This second stage established that the global maximum, to the nearest 0·01, was at 0·20, while the maximum at 0·92 was an inferior one.

13. The sources of the data are described in the appendix to Eisner and Nadiri (1968).
14. See Jorgenson and Siebert (1968a), Jorgenson and Stephenson (1967). In Jorgenson (1963, 1965), however, c_2 is used.

Only a cursory glance at Table 1 is required to see that some of the point estimates look very peculiar. The data set using c_1 provides the best explanation of the dependent variable, by a margin of about 10 per cent in terms of the sum of squared residuals. The point estimates of the parameters,

Table 1 Maximum likelihood estimation of autoregressive parameter, Jorgenson–Stephenson data, demand equation for manufacturing structures and equipment[a]

ρ	$\Sigma\, e^2$	$\hat{E}_p$	$\hat{E}_q$
Data set using c_1 as price of capital services			
$1 \cdot 0$[b]	$0 \cdot 5684 \times 10^{-4}$	$0 \cdot 125$	$0 \cdot 686$
$0 \cdot 3$	$0 \cdot 5060$		
$0 \cdot 2$	$0 \cdot 5043$	$0 \cdot 358$	$0 \cdot 028$
$0 \cdot 1$	$0 \cdot 5067$		
$0 \cdot 0$	$0 \cdot 5139$	$0 \cdot 629$	$-0 \cdot 434$
Data set using c_2 as price of capital services			
$1 \cdot 0$[b]	$0 \cdot 6049 \times 10^{-4}$	$0 \cdot 037$	$0 \cdot 604$
$0 \cdot 6$	$0 \cdot 5526$		
$0 \cdot 5$	$0 \cdot 5513$	$0 \cdot 072$	$0 \cdot 739$
$0 \cdot 4$	$0 \cdot 5519$		
$0 \cdot 0$	$0 \cdot 5805$	$0 \cdot 117$	$0 \cdot 773$

[a] The specification used is given in equation 9. The sample period includes the fifty-five quarters from the second quarter in 1949 to the last in 1962
[b] Constant was not suppressed. Within the context of equation 9 the only possible interpretation of the constant when $p = 1$ is that a time trend has been added. The constant is completely insignificant, but results with the constant included are used to preserve comparability with the Eisner–Nadiri results

however, appear quite nonsensical. The maximum likelihood estimate of E_q, $0 \cdot 028$, if correct would indicate that in the long run the level of capital stock is virtually independent of output. Using the underlying marginal productivity condition and solving back for the implied parameters of the supposed underlying CES production function, the implication is that the elasticity of substitution is $0 \cdot 358$ and that the function is homogenous of degree $-1 \cdot 95$. This is *not* a sensible production function!

Before jumping to any conclusions on the basis of the point estimates, the question of sampling variability must be considered. The burden of the next few paragraphs is that neither of the nonsensical point estimates $E_q = 0.028$ and $E_p = 0.358$ is, using conventional significance levels, significantly different from unity; if one started with the Cobb–Douglas model as a null hypothesis it could not be rejected. Before establishing this, a brief excursion is required into the realm of hypothesis testing and confidence interval derivation for nonlinear models.

First, consider the question of statistical inference about the autoregressive parameter ρ. In the context of the error specification adopted, estimates conditional on values of ρ very close to 1 (and also between -0.2 and -1.0) may be rejected because they result in significant increases in the sum of squared residuals.

An exact test of the null hypothesis that ρ takes a particular value is not possible without knowledge of the exact distribution of the likelihood ratio between the value of the likelihood function under the null hypothesis and the maximum value of the function under the alternative hypothesis that $-1 \leqslant \rho \leqslant 1$. Asymptotically, if the null hypothesis is true the statistic

$$-2(L_0 - L_1),$$

where L_0 is the log of the likelihood function under the null hypothesis and L_1 is the log of the likelihood function using the maximum likelihood estimate of ρ, will have a χ^2 distribution with 1 degree of freedom. For finite samples this test is not exact, and it may be very badly biased. An alternative approach is suggested by Beale (1960), based on the fact that for linear models the exact test involving the likelihood ratio uses the F distribution. Following Beale's suggestions, it appears that for this particular model his recommended procedure for small sample asymptotic tests involves using exactly the same F ratio which would be appropriate if the model were completely linear.[15]

Proceeding, then, as if the model were linear, for the first data set the hypothesis $\rho = 1$ may be rejected at the 0.05 significance level; the test statistic F is 4.45, or slightly larger than 4.12, the critical value of $F(1, 35)$. An approximate 95 per cent confidence interval for ρ would include $0.97 \geqslant \rho \geqslant -0.2$, for this data set. For the data set using c_2 a similar confidence interval would include $1.0 \geqslant \rho \geqslant -0.2$.

Thus, my conclusion is that a wide range of values for ρ are consistent with the data, although the 'level' specifications give somewhat better explanations of the data than do the 'first-difference' specifications. The evidence, especially for the second data set, would not be strong enough to reject *either* the hypothesis $\rho = 1$, or the hypothesis $\rho = 0$, if there was any good reason for giving either one the strong presumption that is usually

15. A fuller discussion of why this is the case is contained in a more extensive multilithed version of this article, available from the author.

accorded a null hypothesis. My point, however, is that no such reason exists, except for computational convenience. If the true value of ρ is somewhere between 0 and 1, then the errors entering the level specification will be autoregressive and the errors entering the first difference specification will be a mixed autoregressive moving average process. In neither case will ordinary least squares be optimal for providing point estimates of parameters or providing the raw material for hypothesis testing. Instead, it seems desirable to me to proceed only on the maintained hypothesis that the errors are a first-order autoregressive process. Nevertheless, if only in order to be able to compare my results to those of Eisner and Nadiri, I will also test various models within the contexts of two other maintained hypotheses: (1) $\rho = 1$, and (2) $\rho = 0$.

Proceeding conditionally on each of these three stochastic specifications there are a number of interesting hypotheses about the other parameters which may be tested. The hypotheses which Eisner and Nadiri attempt to test formally are:

(a) $E_p = 1$ (by seeing whether $1 - \Sigma (\hat{\gamma}_p + \hat{\omega})$ differs significantly from 1);

(b) $E_q = 1$ (by seeing whether $1 - \Sigma (\hat{\gamma}_q + \hat{\omega})$ differs significantly from 1);

(c) $E_p = E_q = 1$, conditional on the hypothesis that $\gamma_{pi} = \gamma_{qi}$, for all i (by seeing whether $1 - \Sigma (\hat{\gamma} + \hat{\omega})$ is significantly different from 1 in regressions where all of the γ_{pi} are constrained to be equal to the γ_{qi}).

The test statistics which Eisner and Nadiri use are all t statistics which are appropriate for testing a single linear restriction on the coefficients. All the above hypotheses, and a number of others which require *more* than one linear restriction, may be tested using statistics which will have F distributions in the event the hypothesis is true.

For the purpose of testing a wide range of hypotheses which various investigators, including Eisner or Jorgenson, might want to put forth as null hypotheses, I have computed sums of squared residuals for twelve alternative models in addition to the basic one specified in equation 9 above. Several of the models are special cases of other ones, and any particular investigator probably would not want to use more than one of them as a null hypothesis.[16]

16. To conserve space, only eight of the alternative models are discussed in this paper, and only three of them are considered in this section. Readers interested in the other models are referred to the more extensive version of the paper which may be obtained from the author.

Eisner and Nadiri, who are worried about (a) the possibility that relative prices may have no effect; (b) the possibility that even if there is an effect, it may only be on the timing of investment expenditures;[17] or (c) the possibility that the underlying function is CES with constant returns to scale but $\sigma < 1$, would presumably wish to use either (a) model 3, in which no relative price terms appear, or (b) model 5, in which $E_p = 0$, or model 11 in which $E_p = 0$ and $E_q = 1$, or (c) model 8 in which $E_q = 1$ and E_p is not restricted.

None of the models corresponds exactly to the Jorgenson–Stephenson model, since their specification is linear in the variables rather than linear in the logarithms of the variables. However, model 10, in which $E_p = E_q = 1$ and the lag distribution for the relative price terms is the same as the lag distribution for output, comes closest to being the embodiment of all of their maintained hypotheses. Model 9, with $E_p = E_q = 1$, includes the Cobb–Douglas part of their hypothesis but relaxes the assumption of identical lag distributions. Model 4 maintains the assumption of identical lag distributions, but relaxes the assumption that the elasticity of K with respect to pQ/c is unity. Model 6 has $E_p = 1$ with E_q unrestricted; the interpretation of this model is unclear for if E_p is 1 the underlying model implies that E_q should also be 1.

Only models 1, 6, 8, and 9 are applied to the data for manufacturing capital stock. Because the results are so inconclusive, extensive exploration of all the other models does not seem justified with these data. In Section III the other models are applied to a set of data which permits sharper discrimination between them.

Applying these models to the question of statistical inference about the elasticities E_p and E_q, Table 2 gives information about: (a) whether or not a one-dimensional 95 per cent confidence interval about the maximum likelihood estimate of E_p would include the point $E_p = 1$; (b) whether or not a one-dimensional confidence interval drawn about the maximum likelihood estimate of E_q would include the point $E_q = 1$; and (c) whether or not a two-dimensional confidence interval would include the point $E_p = 1$, $E_q = 1$. Because the Cobb–Douglas specification fixes both elasticities, I feel that (c) is the most meaningful question to ask with respect to Jorgenson's maintained hypothesis. This question was never examined by Eisner and Nadiri, but examination of part 1 of Table 2 indicates that if it had been asked the answer would have been no, within the context of their maintained hypothesis about the errors. Thus, a researcher who only

17. The notion that relative prices may affect capital stock in the short run but not in the long run, was formally developed by Eisner and Strotz (1963). The theoretical model is one in which the speed of adjustment of actual to 'desired' capital stock is a function of the interest rate.

examined the first differenced data would feel quite secure in concluding, as they did, that 'the role of relative prices is not confirmed', 'the elasticity of capital stock with respect to output is reasonably high . . .', and 'results contradict Jorgenson's assumption of a Cobb–Douglas production function . . .' Eisner and Nadiri (1968, pp. 380–81).[18]

By way of contrast, a researcher examining only the regressions using levels of all the variables (see part 2 of Table 2) would conclude, for the first

Table 2 Test statistics for alternative models of demand for manufacturing capital, given alternative maintained hypothesis about stochastic specification[a]

Model number	$\Sigma e^2 \times 10^4$	F statistic for H_0: model i; H_1: model 1	Critical value of F (0·05 level)	Result of test
(1) Maintaining the hypothesis $\rho = 1$				
1 (no restrictions)	0·56848			
6 ($E_p = 1$)	0·66353	6·02	4·11[c]	reject model 6
8 ($E_q = 1$)	0·58386	0·97	4·11[c]	do not reject
9 ($E_p = E_q = 1$)	0·69203	3·87	3·26[d]	reject model 9
(2) Maintaining the hypothesis $\rho = 0$				
1 (no restrictions)	0·51389			
6 ($E_p = 1$)	0·51447	0·04	4·11[c]	do not reject
8 ($E_q = 1$)	0·57286	4·13	4·11[c]	reject model 8
9 ($E_p = E_q = ·1$)	0·58162	2·37	3·26[d]	do not reject
(3) Maintaining the hypothesis that errors are a first order autoregressive process				
1 (no restrictions)	0·50426 ($\hat{\rho} = 0·2$)			
6 ($E_p = 1$)	0·50822 ($\hat{\rho} = 0·3$)	0·27	4·12[b e]	do not reject
8 ($E_q = 1$)	0·56220 ($\hat{\rho} = 0·2$)	4·02	4·12[b e]	do not reject
9 ($E_p = E_q = 1$)	0·56416 ($\hat{\rho} = 0·3$)	2·08	3·27[b f]	do not reject

[a] Data set using c_1 as price of capital services
[b] Significance level is only approximate for this test
[c] $F(1, 36)$. [d] $F(2, 36)$. [e] $F(1, 35)$. [f] $F(2, 35)$

set of data, that the estimated elasticity of capital stock with respect to relative prices was substantial (0·629), apparently confirming their role in the investment process. Furthermore, this point estimate is not even close to

18. Table 2 covers only the data set using c_1, but the same conclusion holds for the other data set. The test statistic for model 9 is 4·05, which exceeds the critical value of $F(2, 36)$ at the 0·05 level. Model 6 is also rejected, but model 8 is not.

being significantly different from one. Finally, he would be able to conclude that the Cobb–Douglas assumption was not contradicted, for the test statistic for model 9 is well below the critical level for rejection of the hypothesis at conventional levels. Of course, the point estimate of output elasticity (-0.434) might cause some concern; it is even more nonsensical than the maximum likelihood estimate. Certainly one might suspect something peculiar about the model or the data. On the other hand, one could blame the sample, in view of the large confidence intervals.[19] In this situation, not much empirical discrimination about the long-run elasticities is possible.

Using the second set of data, the point estimate of E_q is much more respectable (0.773), but although the point estimate of E_p is much smaller (0.117) the rest of the story would be the same; the confidence region for the long-run elasticities is very large. In particular, with either $\rho = 0$ or the first-order autoregressive assumption, model 9 is not rejected.[20]

Again, my point is that neither of these procedures is defensible. In order to avoid mistaken conclusions a stochastic specification *at least* as general as the autoregressive one used here would seem to be the minimum required. Ideally, one should specify a variety of behavioral models for generating the underlying lag distributions, and test a variety of stochastic specifications which make sense in view of the range of plausible hypotheses.[21] It is well known that partial adjustment or cost of adjustment distributed lag models suggest much different stochastic specifications than do expectational or 'permanent something' models. In addition distributed lag models for investment demand could arise simply because a single decision (a capital budget made up once a year; an order to begin construction leading to expenditures spread over several quarters) affects the dependent variable in several periods. This third type of distributed lag provides a third type of plausible stochastic specification, and perhaps the most difficult type to deal with because the errors would seem to be inherently a moving average process of perhaps the fourth order.

With due recognition, then, for the fact that the assumption of errors generated by a first-order autoregressive process may still be too special for use as a maintained hypothesis in this case, the results summarized in part 3 of Table 2 indicate that the conclusion a researcher would have drawn by

19. Although the results are not shown in Table 2, model 13, in which both elasticities are zero, is not rejected either. If one started out believing in such a model, analysis of these data would not contradict that belief.
20. With $\rho = 0$, the test statistic is 1.45, much less than 3.26, the critical value of $F(2, 36)$ at the 0.05 level. With the assumption of autoregressive errors, the test statistic for model 9 is 2.15.
21. Zellner and Geisel (1970) have recently provided a very interesting example of this sort of exploration using consumption functions.

focusing on the special case $\rho = 0$ are essentially the same as those which emerge from the more general specification. The conclusion – that in conventional statistical terms these data are not inconsistent with the assumption of a Cobb–Douglas production function – is diametrically opposed to the one which seems to be correct if only the special case $\rho = 1$ is considered.

All of this, of course, is at best backhanded support for the maintained hypothesis of a Cobb–Douglas production function employed in the Jorgenson model. Large confidence intervals or not, the point estimates of elasticities are nothing to write home about. The explanation may involve peculiarities of the sample period, or it may involve measurement errors in the data, but it cannot be said that the results reported in this section provide evidence for the model, or for the role of relative prices in investment demand.[22] All that I have attempted to do here is refute the statement that they provide convincing evidence against this model or this role.

To make clear exactly what this re-examination of the work of Eisner and Nadiri *does* show, it is useful to quote from several of their conclusions, and contrast them to what I have found. Eisner and Nadiri (1968, pp. 380–81) summarize their conclusions in seven paragraphs. Four of these conclusions are at issue. They state:

1 The role of relative prices ... is not confirmed. The elasticity of capital stock with respect to the ratios of the wholesale price index to Jorgenson's measures of the rental price of capital is far below the value of unity which he has *assumed* in his papers. ...

My finding is that, for one of the two sets of data, this is incorrect if $\rho \neq 1$. Using c_1 as the cost of capital, if $\rho = 0$, E_p is estimated to be equal to 0·629. The hypothesis $\rho = 0$ cannot be rejected, while the hypothesis $\rho = 1$ can. The maximum likelihood estimate of E_p, 0·358, *is* far below unity, but not significantly so.

Eisner and Nadiri conclude:

3 The elasticity of capital stock with respect to output is reasonably high, in a number of instances approaching unity. This is consistent with flexible accelerator models.

Using the first-order autoregressive specification, with c_1 as the cost of capital, E_q is estimated to be 0·028, far below unity. No model I know of would predict this.

22. Without fiddling with either the specification or the sample period, model 3, the model in which *no* relative price terms *at all* appear, cannot be rejected at any significance level smaller than 0·25. If, however, the number of values of (p/c) is reduced to four, or if the sample is reduced to exclude the period before the Treasury–Federal Reserve accord, the hypothesis of no relative price effects may be rejected at the 0·05 level.

With regard to the specific issue of hypothesis testing, the Eisner–Nadiri conclusion is:

4 Results contradict Jorgenson's assumption of a Cobb–Douglas production function. . . .

The basis for this conclusion is the fact that model 9 can be rejected given the stochastic specification $\rho = 1$. With an improved stochastic specification, the results do not contradict the Cobb–Douglas assumption using *either* measure of the cost of capital.

Finally, Eisner and Nadiri attempt to cast doubt on a particular hypothesis about the lag distributions for the p/c and Q terms, which I have advanced elsewhere (Bischoff, 1971). This hypothesis is dubbed the 'putty-clay hypothesis'. If it can be validated, the hypothesis would provide a serious criticism of some of the policy conclusions Jorgenson and others have drawn from their studies. It has not yet been fully tested, but the essential prediction is that relative prices should affect investment expenditures in a much different way, and with a generally much longer lag than output. The idea behind this hypothesis is that factor proportions are not variable after fixed capital has been put into place.[23]

On the basis of lag distributions reported in their tables 5 and 6, Eisner and Nadiri (1968, pp. 378–9) concluded:

6 The role of relative prices suggested by the 'putty-clay hypothesis' is not confirmed by estimates using the general Pascal lag distribution.

Again to conserve space, I am not including tables to conform to the ones Eisner and Nadiri included; one such table is included in the next section. Such tables, however, have been constructed, using the maximum likelihood estimates of the parameters of model 9, for both sets of Jorgenson's data. They conform almost exactly to the qualitative predictions on the 'putty-clay model' – the adjustment to changes in relative price is more gradual than the adjustment to changes in output.

Eisner and Nadiri have started toward the very laudable goal of testing Jorgenson's maintained hypothesis, and also peripherally, to explore the 'putty-clay hypothesis'. Their attempt has floundered because of an inadequate maintained hypothesis of their own about the errors entering their equation. If they had started with the hypothesis $\rho = 0$, or with the first-order autoregressive hypothesis, it seems doubtful that their paper ever would have been written.

23. See Bischoff (1971, pp. 4–24) for an extensive discussion developing the basis for expecting such a pattern of lagged effects.

III Application of the Eisner–Nadiri model to the demand for equipment

With respect to the value of the 'neoclassical approach', the results of Section II are inconclusive. The case for or against the Jorgenson model must rest on other evidence, including the predictive power to the model, with as many built-in assumptions as desired, relative to the predictive power of other models. The case for relative price effects – the effects of capital goods prices, wages, output prices, the cost of capital to firms, depreciation rules, profits tax rates, tax credits, etc. – must rest on other evidence than analysis of the single aggregate time series which Eisner and Nadiri re-examined and which I have re-re-examined. Other studies have been made, as mentioned above. These studies are not inconsistent with the view that the price elasticity of capital demand might be unity, although several of them suggest values slightly below unity.[24]

In a study of equipment demand for the period 1951/3–1965/4, I assumed a CES production function with constant returns to scale, and obtained an estimate of 1·002 for E_p (Bischoff, 1971, p. 66). I also concluded that the lag distributions conformed to the qualitative suggestions of the putty-clay hypothesis. Eisner has argued that this conclusion about the lag distributions is a statistical artifact, produced by 'the particular constraints introduced into the Almon lag estimator' (Eisner and Nadiri, 1968, p. 379).

Because the issues raised by Eisner and Nadiri are much broader than the narrow question of whether or not various maintained hypotheses of Jorgenson are correct, and because additional data may help to clarify what implications, if any, their model has for the question of the actual role of relative prices in the investment function, I have used data derived from my earlier study to estimate an economy-wide equipment demand function in the form of equation 9 above.

The data to be analysed in this section are as follows. The dependent variable, $\ln K_t$, is the natural logarithm of a constant dollar measure of the

24. The recent work of Evans (1968) covering quarterly time series for thirteen two-digit industries and the manufacturing aggregate, for the period 1952/1–1967/4, includes a term reflecting the inverse of p/c. The point estimate of elasticity of equilibrium capital stock with respect to p/c appears to be in the range between 0·5 and 0·8 (the model Evans uses is not a constant elasticity model, and the elasticity varies over the sample period). In Coen (1968, 1971), two models (for aggregate manufacturing, 1950/1–1966/3) are presented. The relative price term is the average *wage* divided by c. For Coen's preferred (and best-fitting) model the elasticity (measured at the point of means of all variables) of equilibrium capital with respect to (wage/c) is only 0·29. In his less-preferred model, which corresponds most closely to the Jorgenson model, this elasticity is 0·58. In comparing these elasticities to those for terms involving p/c, it should be noted that in a Cobb–Douglas model the expected elasticity of K with respect to w/c would be only $1/(1+a/\beta)$ where a and β are the elasticities of output with respect to capital and labor, respectively.

net stock of producers' durable equipment for the private sector of the United States economy. The output measure, Q_t, is constant dollar gross product of the business sector. The relative price term, $(p/c)_t$, includes several coefficients estimated in my previous study (including a trend term which is somewhat difficult to interpret, but which is relatively unimportant). The variable labelled p/c in this section is defined as:

$$(p/c)_t = e^{0.00178t}(p'_t/c'_t), \qquad\qquad 10$$

where p'_t is the implicit price deflator for business gross product and c'_t is the rental price of capital services, defined according to

$$c'_t = \frac{q_t(r_t + \delta)(1 - k_t - u_t z_t)}{1 - u_t}. \qquad\qquad 11$$

In 11, q_t is the implicit price deflator for producers' durable equipment, r_t is an approximation to the cost of capital of firms, based on the industrial bond yield and the dividend–price ratio,[25] δ is the rate of decline of the value of services provided by a unit of equipment, k_t is the effective tax credit against equipment purchases, u_t is the general rate of income taxation for corporations, and z_t is the present value per dollar of new equipment of the income tax deduction which can be taken for depreciation over the lifetime of the equipment.

As before, trial values of ρ spaced at intervals of length $0\cdot1$ in the domain $-1 \leqslant \rho \leqslant 1$ are used. The results are presented in Table 3. By fitting a quadratic to the three smallest values of $e'e$, it can be estimated that $e'e$ reaches a minimum at about $\rho = -0\cdot068$, and that the minimum of $e'e$ is about $0\cdot9956 \times 10^{-4}$.

As Table 3 shows, estimates of the price elasticity are extremely sensitive to the value of ρ. For values of ρ close to 1, the estimated price elasticity is very low. In the context of the error specification adopted, however, estimates conditional on large values of ρ may be rejected because they result in significant increases in the sum of squared residuals. The hypothesis $\rho = 1$ may be rejected at the $0\cdot001$ significance level. Using the regression with the constant suppressed, the test statistic for the hypothesis $\rho = 1$ is $19\cdot0$, much greater than the critical value of $F(2, 51)$ for the $0\cdot001$ significance level ($8\cdot0$). An asymptotic 95 per cent confidence interval for ρ would extend from about $+0\cdot35$ to about $-0\cdot42$.

Since estimating ρ in every case is a very time consuming process, and

25. The form of this approximation is $r_t = (c_0 + c_1 R_t + c_2 S_t + c_3 t)(1 - c_4 u_t)$, where R_t is the bond yield and S_t is the dividend–price ratio. In Bischoff (1971), the coefficients c_0, c_1, and c_2 were estimated by nonlinear methods, c_3 was set equal to zero, and c_4 was specified on the basis of casual empirical arguments. In this study all of these coefficients are taken as *a proiri* information.

since the estimate seems to be not at all significantly different from zero, all further results are based on the assumption that $\rho = 0$, and that the 'level' form of the equation is the most appropriate one. This is not the best statistical procedure, for I am shifting the hypothesis $\rho = 0$ into the main-

Table 3 Estimation of autoregressive parameter, demand equation for equipment, total private economy[a]

ρ	Σe^2	$\hat{E}_p$	$\hat{E}_q$
$1 \cdot 0$[b]	$1 \cdot 7384 \times 10^{-4}$	$0 \cdot 1356$	$1 \cdot 0434$
$1 \cdot 0$[c]	$1 \cdot 7251$	$0 \cdot 1139$	$0 \cdot 8945$
$0 \cdot 0$	$1 \cdot 0002$	$1 \cdot 0125$	$1 \cdot 0277$
$-0 \cdot 1$	$0 \cdot 9984$	$1 \cdot 0199$	$1 \cdot 0294$
$-0 \cdot 2$	$1 \cdot 0067$	$1 \cdot 0203$	$1 \cdot 0320$

[a] The specification used is given in equation 9. The sample period extends from the second quarter of 1949 to the fourth quarter of 1966
[b] Constant was suppressed
[c] Constant was not suppressed

tained hypothesis, and I have argued above that this is not legitimate. The results indicate, however, that all of the models rejected here would almost certainly still be rejected under the more general hypothesis; in view of the large saving on computation, I feel that this procedure may be defensible.

Proceeding conditionally on the stochastic specification $\rho = 0$, I have estimated the parameters of all of the alternative models mentioned above. Table 4 lists the sums of squared residuals derived by fitting the various restricted models to quarterly data on the stock of equipment, for the sample period 1949–66.[26] Estimates of E_p and E_q are also included; [a] indicates that the value represents an assumption built into the model in question. Every one of the alternative models is a special case of model 1. Thus, each of the restricted models may be used as a null hypothesis, with the alternative hypothesis being model 1. Values of the F statistic for each of these comparisons are given in column 5; critical values for rejecting the null hypothesis at the 0·05 significance level are given in column 6.

Adding the first quarter of 1949 to the sample results in a somewhat

26. Similar tests were carried out for sample periods encompassing 1949–62 and 1951/2–66. In both cases, all of the alternative models except models 6, 8, and 9 could be rejected. This is exactly the same result as is indicated in Table 4. Point estimates of elasticities derived from the shorter sample periods are $E_p = 0·6961$, $E_q = 1·0016$ for the 1949–62 sample and $E_p = 1·2202$, $E_q = 1·0153$ for the 1951/2–66 sample. None of these estimated elasticities differed significantly from 1.

lower estimate of E_p (0·8276 compared to 1·0002) and a slightly higher estimate of E_q (1·0339 compared to 1·0125), but these estimated elasticities are not in any case significantly different from one (the test statistics are far below the rejection level for models 6, 8, and 9). All of the other alternative models may be rejected at the 0·01 significance level. The conclusion is that this body of data may well be consistent with a variety of hypotheses about E_p (it seems likely that hypothesized values of E_p at least over the range from 0·5 to 1·2 could not be rejected), but it is not consistent with $E_p = 0$. Furthermore, the hypothesis of no relative price effects in the short or long runs (model 3) is rejected, although the test statistic shown in Table 4

Table 4 Test and elasticities for alternative models of demand for equipment[a]

Model number	$\Sigma e^2 \times 10^4$	$\hat{E}_p$	$\hat{E}_q$	F statistic for H_0: model j H_1: model 1	Critical value of F (0·05 level)	Result of test
1	1·0657	0·828	1·034	—	—	—
3	1·9400	0·0[b]	1·106	5·44	2·12[c]	reject model 3
4	2·4034	1·071	1·071	8·32	2·12[c]	reject model 4
5	1·6068	0·0[b]	1·099	26·91	4·02[d]	reject model 5
6	1·0680	1·0[b]	1·026	0·114	4·02[d]	do not reject model 6
8	1·0780	1·199	1·0[b]	0·609	4·02[d]	do not reject model 8
9	1·0825	1·0[b]	1·0[b]	0·419	3·17[e]	do not reject model 9
10	2·4592	1·0[b]	1·0[b]	7·70	2·06[f]	reject model 10
11	1·8250	0·0[b]	1·0[b]	18·88	3·17[e]	reject model 11

[a] The maintained hypothesis for all of these models includes $\rho = 0$. The sample extends from 1949/1 through 1966/4
[b] Indicates parameter value is assumed as part of model j
[c] $F(8,53)$.   [d] $F(1,53)$.   [e] $F(2,53)$.   [f] $F(9,53)$

should be adjusted in some way to allow for preprocessing of the data; as mentioned above, the relative price term p/c is not really known *a priori* but includes four coefficients estimated in a closely related regression (for the time period from the third quarter of 1951 to the fourth in 1965). Making a crude allowance for this, the hypotheses of no relative price effects is still decisively rejected.[27]

The portion of the Jorgenson–Stephenson hypothesis which is rejected is the hypothesis of identical lag distributions. Model 10 may be rejected in favor of model 1. If, instead, model 9 is used as the alternative hypothesis, model 10 is rejected in favor of model 9, a Cobb–Douglas model with separate lags for output and relative prices. The F statistic for this last comparison is 9·99, substantially exceeding $F_{.01}$ (7, 55) = 2·98. The difference between the two lag distributions may be examined in Table 5, which displays the distributions derived from model 1 in a format comparable to tables 5 and 6 of the Eisner–Nadiri article.[28] The qualitative features of the distributions are in accord with the suggestion of the 'putty-clay' hypothesis – that the relative price effect on investment should be more gradual than the effect of output. Eisner's suggestion, that in earlier work I obtained this result on the basis of constraints built into the distributed lag estimation technique I used, is incorrect, for the result shows up in the present estimation when a general rational distributed lag specification is substituted for the modified Almon distributed lag specification used earlier.

The results of analysing these data are extremely favorable to the role of relative prices in the investment function. The point estimates of elasticities conform almost exactly to the predictions of the Cobb–Douglas model. The noise level in the data is much lower than the noise level in the Jorgenson–Stephenson data. I can only speculate about why this should be the case. One possibility is that there may be significant differences between models which cover all fixed capital and models, like this one, which include only equipment. The measure of output may be better (deflating gross value added by the wholesale price index does not seem to me the best method to get at real output). The measure of rental price of capital incorporates improved specifications of the way taxes enter into the model, developed independently by Hall and Jorgenson (1967, 1971) and Coen (1968, 1971). Finally, the longer sample period, extending through 1966, includes a

27. The four coefficients in question are the time trend and the three coefficients which feed into the definition of r_t. If I had re-estimated them for each model, the results could only have been to make *all* models *except* model 3 fit better. This suggests that in comparing model 1 and model 3, an asymptotic test which would, if anything, be biased in favor of model 3, would be to proceed as if all of the nonlinear coefficients had been re-estimated in this study. The F ratio for the comparison would then be $(0·8743/12)/(1·0657/49) = 3·35$, which still exceeds the critical value of $F(12, 49)$ at the 0·01 significance level (2·57).

28. The lag distributions for model 9 are very similar. These lag patterns are not directly comparable to the lag distributions shown in tables 10 and 11 and figure 6 of Bischoff (1971), for those distributions show the time shape of the impact on *gross investment* whereas the current distributions involve the impact on net capital stock.

(1)	(2)	(3)	(4)	(5)	(6)	(7)	(8)	(9)	(10)
i	$\hat{\gamma}_{pi}$	$\hat{\gamma}_{qi}$	$\hat{\mu}_{pi}$	$\hat{\mu}_{qi}$	$\sum_{k=1}^{i}\hat{\mu}_{-pk}$	$\sum_{k=1}^{i}\hat{\mu}_{pk}$	$\dfrac{\sum_{8}\hat{\mu}_{pk}}{\sum\hat{\mu}_{pi}}$	$\dfrac{\sum_{8}\hat{\mu}_{qi}}{\sum\hat{\mu}_{qk}}$	Column 6 ÷ Column 7
1	0·0000	0·0785	0·0000	0·0785	0·0000	0·0785	0·0000	0·0759	0·0005
2	−0·0024	−0·0019	−0·0024	0·0975	−0·0024	0·1760	−0·0028	0·1702	−0·0013
3	−0·0134	−0·0194	−0·0165	0·0798	−0·0188	0·2558	−0·0228	0·2474	−0·0736
4	0·0214	−0·0217	0·0013	0·0492	−0·0176	0·3050	−0·0212	0·2950	−0·0576
5	0·0123	0·0067	0·0190	0·0442	0·0014	0·3491	0·0017	0·3377	0·0041
6	0·0163	0·0285	0·0400	0·0692	0·0414	0·4183	0·0501	0·4046	0·0990
7	−0·0130	−0·0208	0·0318	0·0531	0·0732	0·4715	0·0885	0·4560	0·1553
8	0·0147	−0·0049	0·0426	0·0409	0·1158	0·5124	0·1399	0·4956	0·2260
9			0·0441	0·0353	0·1599	0·5477	0·1932	0·5298	0·2920
10			0·0427	0·0321	0·2026	0·5798	0·2448	0·5608	0·3494
11			0·0404	0·0297	0·2420	0·6094	0·2935	0·5895	0·3986
12			0·0379	0·0276	0·2808	0·6371	0·3393	0·6162	0·4408
13			0·0355	0·0258	0·3163	0·6628	0·3822	0·6411	0·4772
14			0·0332	0·0241	0·3495	0·6369	0·4223	0·6644	0·5088
15			0·0311	0·0225	0·3306	0·7095	0·4598	0·6862	0·5364
16			0·0290	0·0211	0·4096	0·7305	0·4949	0·7066	0·5607
17 to ∞	0·0000	0·0000	0·4180	0·3033	0·4180[a]	0·3033[a]	0·5051[b]	0·2934[b]	1·3781
Sum	0·0359	0·0448	0·8276	1·0339	0·8276	1·0339	1·0000	1·0000	0·8005
Primary modal lag			9	2					
Secondary modal lag			6	6					
Median lag			16·21	8·13					
Mean lag			17·84	11·79					

$$\ln K_t = a_0 + \sum_{i=1}^{8}\{\gamma_{pi}\ln(p/c)_{t-i} + \gamma_{pi}\ln Q_{t-i}\} + \sum_{j=1}^{2}\omega_j \ln K_{t-j} + \omega_t.$$

$$= a_0' + \sum_{i=1}^{\infty}\{\mu_{qi}\ln(p/c)_{t-i} + \mu_{qi}\ln Q_{t-i}\} + \omega_t'$$

[a] Summed from $k = 17$

[b] Numerator summed from $k = 17$

$\hat{\omega}_1 = 1·2677 . \hat{\omega}^2 = -0·3111$

$\bar{R}^2 = 1·0000 . \text{SEE} = 0·001418$

D.W. = 2·2093

period in which major tax experiments substantially increased the variation in the p/c measure. For all of these reasons, the elasticities derived from these data are likely to be more reliable than those reported in Section II, but further research is needed to pin down the influence of the various factors.

My conclusions, from the analysis in this section, may be summarized as follows:

1 The stochastic specification is again crucial to the conclusions, but the specification which leads to a first-difference transformation of all variables is decisively rejected.

2 Point estimates of long-run elasticities of the stock of equipment with respect to either relative prices or output are very close to unity.

3 The hypothesis that either or both of these elasticities is zero may be rejected.

4 The hypothesis of no relative price effects may be rejected.

5 The lagged effect of relative prices on the stock of equipment operates more slowly than the lagged effect of changes in output, and the hypothesis that both act with the same lag distribution may be rejected.

IV Concluding remarks

The implications of this paper go far beyond the question of the validity of the Jorgenson model, narrowly defined.[29] The more basic questions involve whether or not relative prices play a role in factor demand, and how the dynamic mechanism works. There are also questions of how empirical research in this area ought to be carried out, and I have tried to illustrate some of the possible pitfalls of aggregative time series analyses of the type pursued by some researchers.

Two trite lessons are illustrated by the results. The first is the simple point, emphasized by Griliches (1967) in his survey article on distributed lags, that when using distributed lags, even more than in other time-series work, the stochastic assumptions are crucial. The second point is a homely note of caution. As we all know but perhaps too often forget, all statements about confidence intervals are only as good as the underlying assumptions – correctness of the functional form, no errors-in-variables, normality, independence and the rest. Statements about accepting and rejecting hypotheses may be useful ways to communicate, in a somewhat conventional way, certain information about the results of a regression analysis. We must not forget, however, the necessary pound of salt.

29. See Jorgenson and Stephenson (1969) for discussion of some of the questions relating specifically to this model.

References

BEALE, E. M. L. (1960), 'Confidence regions in non-linear estimation'
J. roy. stat. Soc., vol. 22, pp. 41–76. (Series B.)

BISCHOFF, C. W. (1971), 'The effect of alternative lag distributions', in
G. Fromm (ed.), *Tax Incentives and Capital Spending*, Brookings Institution,
North-Holland.

COEN, R. M. (1968), 'Effects of tax policy on investment in manufacturing',
Amer. econ. Rev., vol. 58, pp. 200–211.

COEN, R. M. (1971), 'The effect of cash flow on the speed of adjustment', in
G. Fromm (ed.), *Tax Incentives and Capital Spending*, Brookings Institution,
North-Holland.

EISNER, R. (1969), 'Investment and the frustrations of econometricians',
Amer. econ. Rev., vol. 59, pp. 50–64.

EISNER, R. (1969a), 'Tax policy and investment behavior: comment',
Amer. econ. Rev., vol. 59, pp. 379–88.

EISNER, R., and NADIRI, M. I. (1968), 'Investment behavior and
neo-classical theory', *Rev. econ. Stat.*, vol. 50, pp. 369–82.

EISNER, R., and STROTZ, R. H. (1963), 'Determinants of business investment',
in Commission on Money and Credit, *Impacts of Monetary Policy*,
Prentice-Hall, pp. 59–337.

EVANS, M. K. (1968), 'A further study of industry investment functions',
Department of Economics, University of Pennsylvania, Discussion Paper no. 93.

GRILICHES, Z. (1961), 'A note on serial correlation bias in estimates of
distributed lags', *Econometrica*, vol. 29, pp. 65–73.

GRILICHES, Z. (1967), 'Distributed lags: a survey', *Econometrica*, vol. 35,
pp. 16–49.

HALL, R. E., and JORGENSON, D. W. (1967), 'Tax policy and investment
behavior', *Amer. econ. Rev.*, vol. 57, pp. 391–414.

HALL, R. E., and JORGENSON, D. W. (1971), 'The quantitative impact of tax
policy on investment expenditures', in G. Fromm (ed.), *Tax Incentives and
Capital Spending*, Brookings Institution, North-Holland.

HILDRETH, C. (1966), 'Asymptotic distribution of maximum likelihood estimators
in linear models with autoregressive disturbances', RAND Corporation
Memorandum R M–5059–P R, Santa Monica, California.

HILDRETH, C. and LU, J. Y. (1960), *Demand Relations with Autocorrelated
Disturbances*, Michigan Agricultural Experiment Station Technical Bulletin 276,
Michigan State University.

JORGENSON, D. W. (1963), 'Capital theory and investment behavior',
Amer. econ. Rev., vol. 53, pp. 247–59.

JORGENSON, D. W. (1965), 'Anticipations and investment behavior', in
J. S. Duesenberry *et al.* (eds.), *The Brookings Quarterly Econometric Model
of the United States*, Rand McNally, pp. 35–94.

JORGENSON, D. W. (1966), 'Rational distributed lag functions', *Econometrica*,
vol. 34, pp. 135–49.

JORGENSON, D. W., and SIEBERT, C. D. (1968), 'A comparison of alternative
theories of corporate investment behavior', *Amer. econ. Rev.*, vol. 58, pp. 681–712.

JORGENSON, D. W., and SIEBERT, C. D. (1968a), 'Optimal capital accumulation
and corporate investment behavior', *J. pol. Econ.*, vol. 76, pp. 1123–51.

JORGENSON, D. W., and STEPHENSON, J. A. (1967), 'The time structure of
investment behavior in United States manufacturing, 1947–1960',
Rev. econ. Stat., vol. 49, pp. 16–27.

JORGENSON, D. W., and STEPHENSON, J. A. (1967a), 'Investment behavior in US manufacturing, 1947–1960', *Econometrica*, vol. 35, pp. 169–220.

JORGENSON, D. W., and STEPHENSON, J. A. (1969), 'Issues in the development of the neoclassical theory of investment behavior', *Rev. econ. Stat.*, vol. 51, pp. 346–53.

KLEIN, L. R., and TAUBMAN, P. (1971), 'Impact of accelerated depreciation and investment tax credit on investment and general economic activity', in G. Fromm (ed.), *Tax Incentives and Capital Spending*, Brookings Institution, North-Holland.

KOYCK, L. M. (1954), *Distributed Lags and Investment Analysis*, North-Holland.

ZELLNER, A., and GEISEL, M. S. (1970), 'Analysis of distributed lag models with applications to consumption function estimation', *Econometrica*, vol. 38, pp. 865–88.

Part Five
Effects of Tax Policy

One of the advantages of the increasing use of explicit investment
theory has been the greater usefulness of investment equations in
assessing the effects of tax policies designed to influence investment.
Theories are especially useful if they provide appropriate roles for cost
of capital and cash flow variables, as these are the most direct routes for
tax policies to influence investment. Each of the four Readings in this
part provides some contribution to theoretical development as well as to
empirical assessment of the effects of tax policy. The first two papers, by
Coen and Bischoff, deal with the effects of US investment tax credits.
The volume from which the Bischoff paper is reprinted also contains a
number of other important papers on the same topic. Readings 9 and 10
are concerned with the effects of UK tax policy, especially the changes
in the relative rates of taxation on distributed and undistributed
corporation income.

7 C. W. Bischoff

The Effect of Alternative Lag Distributions

Excerpts from C. W. Bischoff, 'The effect of alternative lag distributions', in
G. Fromm (ed.), *Tax Incentives and Capital Spending*, Brookings Institution,
North-Holland, 1971.

Fiscal and monetary policymakers share the desire to influence the flow of
business fixed investment. Their overall purposes may be for the short run
(for example, to counteract a business cycle) or the long run (to affect the
rate of growth of potential output). In the first case, it is desirable to apply
a policy tool with prompt, highly concentrated impact, for the cyclical
situation may have drastically changed by the time a policy with a long lag
takes hold. In the second, it is desirable to affect the flow of investment
more gradually, or else the policy itself may create short-run instability.
In either case, as Griliches and Wallace (1965, p. 328) have emphasized,
'whether or not a particular stabilization or growth policy will actually
do more harm than good depends crucially on the form of the lag
function'.

Through tax changes in 1954, 1962, and 1964, the federal government
has sought to encourage investment spending, presumably with long-run
goals in mind. On the other hand, monetary changes since the Treasury-
Federal Reserve accord in 1951 have presumably aimed at prompt and
reversible influence. Without doubt, the 1966 and 1967 offsetting changes
in the tax treatment of investment were explicitly designed to have short-
run effects on investment.

This Reading seeks to evaluate the direct effects of fiscal and monetary
instruments, as well as other determinants, on expenditures for producers'
durable equipment, the largest component of business fixed investment.[1]
In particular, it is concerned not only with *how much* a particular policy
affects investment, but also *when* the effect occurs. Jorgenson, in a series of
papers with several colleagues, has drawn the striking conclusion that 'any
measures which result in a once-over change in demand for capital will
result in a relatively short and sharp boom in investment demand followed

---

1. By the direct effect of a change in a policy parameter, I mean its effect with all
other determinants of investment unchanged. A tax credit stimulates investment
indirectly through feedbacks on the other determinants of investment, but the
magnitude of these feedbacks can be discussed only in the context of a complete
model.

by a lengthy period of steadily worsening stagnation induced by a decline in total investment expenditures relative to their peak levels.[2] This conclusion, if correct, has important policy implications. However, a controversial feature of the model from which it is derived is the assumption that all of the determinants of investment act with the same distributed lag. I have attempted to relax this restrictive assumption.

The model discussed in this reading is heavily influenced by Jorgenson's neoclassical investment model, in the extended version developed by Hall and Jorgenson to study the effects of tax policy on investment. All fiscal and monetary parameters in their model affect investment by means of changes in the imputed rent on the services of capital goods. By assumption, in their model the elasticity of investment demand with respect to this rent is unity, and thus the elasticity of investment demand with respect to each of the determinants of the rent is an assumed, rather than estimated, value. In removing this second restrictive assumption, I provide estimates of the direct effects of various policy changes that are less dependent on the particular way the model is put together.

The next section sets forth a rationale for the estimation of separate lag distributions for different determinants of investment. The rationale is stated in terms of a neoclassical model in which factor proportions are variable only up to the point when new machines are installed.[3] With the addition of assumptions about how machines wear out and how expectations about future prices are formed, this model implies that the short-run elasticity of investment demand with respect to changes in the rent will never exceed the long-run elasticity. This rationale, while plausible, is not, however, the only way in which a divergence in lag distributions could be justified.

The model is used to explain quarterly data for aggregate expenditures on producers' durable equipment. The long-run price elasticity of demand for equipment is estimated to be very close to unity, with the short-run elasticity considerably smaller. At the same time, the short-run elasticity of equipment demand with respect to output substantially exceeds the long-run elasticity. Tax parameters, the interest rate, and the yield on equities all appear to be important determinants of the level of expenditures, although the quantitative impact of the investment tax credit, adopted in 1962, appears to be greater than that of any of the other policy measures studied.

2. Jorgenson (1965). See also Jorgenson (1963), Jorgenson and Stephenson (1967, 1967a), and Hall and Jorgenson (1967, 1971).
3. For theoretical developments of this model, mostly in the context of long-run growth, see Johansen (1959), Solow (1962), Massell (1962), Phelps (1963), Kemp and Thanh (1966).

Specification of a distributed lag model

To provide policy makers with knowledge about the speed with which their actions can affect investment, it is necessary to estimate the parameters of a model of investment demand in which explicit attention is given to monetary and fiscal parameters. This section discusses the specification of such a model, in which a number of terms, reflecting relative prices, capital costs, and the effects of taxes, are combined into a single expression for the imputed rent on a piece of equipment. In the long run, it is assumed that the demand for equipment is a log-linear function of this rent, which is identified with the price of the services provided by a unit of equipment. In addition, the demand for equipment is assumed to be proportional to the sum of (a) desired changes in capacity and (b) replacement of capacity.

A crucial feature of this model is the assumption that changes in the determinants of the rent may affect investment expenditures with a lag distribution different from that which exists for changes in the determinants of desired capacity. Given the current state of knowledge about possibilities in the real world for changes in factor proportions, it cannot be assumed *a priori* that all of the determinants of investment affect expenditures with the same time pattern.

The stylized world on which the model of investment behavior is based is one in which a firm, at time t, must make investment decisions η periods ahead. Any equipment that is ordered in period t is delivered in period $t + \eta$ and can be put immediately into production. From the vantage point of period t, the firm knows that even if it orders no new equipment in period $t + \eta$ it will have a certain amount of equipment on hand. This equipment includes the machinery available in period t, plus the equipment previously ordered that will be delivered between t and $t + \eta$, less the equipment that will be retired during this same period. The factor proportions on all of this equipment are assumed to be fixed, although in general they will differ from machine to machine. Each machine, if operated for a period by the appropriate amounts of the cooperating factors, can produce a certain amount of output,[4] which is defined as the capacity of the machine.[5] The aggregate capacity of all the machines that will be in existence at the beginning of period $t + \eta$, with no new investment, is Q_{K0}.

With the assumption that the firm's objective in fixing factor proportions is the minimization of cost, it must decide (a) how much new capacity to order for delivery η periods later, and (b) what blueprint should be used to

4. For the present it is assumed there is only a single homogeneous output.
5. In fact, unless fixed capital is used on a twenty-four-hour basis, there is still no unique measure of capacity. It does not seem unreasonable, however, to assume that institutional patterns set a 'normal' degree of utilization that can be altered only by incurring higher costs.

specify the factor proportions on the new capacity. I assume that the two decisions are separable, and, given the amount of new capacity to be ordered, consider first the question of the blueprint.

Choice of factor proportions

In a situation in which relative prices will change over the lifetime of the capacity, it will be impossible, in general, to choose proportions that use the optimal amount of all factors at all times. In order to simplify the problem of choice, it is assumed that starting from an initial rent $c(0)$ earned by a new machine, the flow of rent is expected to decline exponentially, so that $c(t) = c(0)e^{-\delta t}$. This decline may result from physical deterioration of the capacity so that the flow of output it can produce becomes less over time, from rises in the wages or rents on nonfixed factors, from changes in the price of the output produced, or from other causes. This assumption is a very crude approximation, and may compromise the results.[6] If it is granted, however, the present value of the stream of rents earned (after deduction of income-taxes) by a unit of new capacity over its lifetime may be written (ignoring subscripts)

$$\int\limits_{0}^{\infty} e^{-rt}(1-u)c(0)e^{-\delta t}dt + kq + q(1-k')u \int\limits_{0}^{T} e^{-rs}D(s)ds, \qquad \textbf{1}$$

in which

$q =$ the price of the ith capital good (when new);

$k =$ the rate of tax credit on investment in the ith good;

$k' =$ the rate of tax credit that must be deducted from the depreciation base;

$r =$ the appropriate discount rate (including adjustment for risk);

$u =$ the rate of direct taxation of business income;

$T =$ the lifetime of the ith good prescribed for tax purposes;

$D(s) =$ the proportion of the depreciation base for an asset of age s that may be deducted from taxable income;

$\delta =$ the exponential rate of decline in the value of services provided by a unit of the ith good.

The first term in **1** is the discounted stream of quasi-rents, after deduction of direct taxes. The second term allows for tax credits of a certain proportion of the cost of the machine. The third term is the discounted value of

6. This assumption, in particular, implies that the quasi-rent will approach zero only asymptotically. However, if the reason for the expected decline in quasi-rent is, for example, an expected rise in all wages at a constant rate $\dot{w}$, then $c(t) = c(0)(1 - w_0 e^{\dot{w}t})$ (where w_0 is the initial wage share), and this function declines at an increasing rate and reaches zero in finite time.

the stream of taxes saved as a result of a deduction of depreciation expenses from taxable income.

If this present value is equated to q, the price of a new machine, it is possible to solve for $c(0)^*$, the quasi-rent that must be earned by a new machine to justify its purchase. If z denotes $\int_0^T e^{-rs} D(s) ds$, the present value of the depreciation deduction, the equality is

$$q(1-k-uz+uzk') = \int_0^\infty e^{-(\delta+r)t} c(0)^*(1-u) dt; \qquad\qquad 2$$

integrating the right-hand side leads to[7]

$$c(0)^* = \frac{q(r+\delta)(1-k-uz+uzk')}{1-u}. \qquad\qquad 3$$

The blueprints tell how much of the malleable output must be molded into each of the models of machinery that are available. In order to proceed further, it is assumed that at any particular point of time, the available blueprints correspond to a neoclassical production function of the special constant elasticity of substitution (CES) class[8] (in the first degree homogeneous version as originally developed by Arrow et al., 1961). With m factors, this function, with suitable normalization,[9] may be written

$$Q = \left\{ \sum_{i=1}^m a_i X_i^{(\sigma-1)/\sigma} \right\}^{\sigma/(\sigma-1)}, \qquad\qquad 4$$

in which Q = output in physical terms, X_i = the input of the ith factor,[10] σ = the elasticity of substitution, a_i = the distribution parameter for the ith factor (as noted below, these parameters may change over time).

7. This derivation closely follows that of Hall and Jorgenson (1967), and the formula arrived at differs from theirs only because I have distinguished between k and k'.
8. This m-factor constant-elasticity-of-substitution function, though itself a special case, is still relatively general compared with the two most popular alternatives, the Cobb-Douglas and Leontief production functions, both of which are a special cases of the class of CES functions.
9. As originally written by Arrow et al. (1961), the right-hand side was multiplied by a scaling (or so-called efficiency) parameter v, with the sum of the as set equal (normalized) to unity. With no loss of generality, the efficiency parameter may be set equal to unity. If the alternative normalization is adopted, the sum of all the distribution parameters (the as) is then equal to $v^{(\sigma-1)/\sigma}$.
10. This input may be thought of as a flow of services per unit of time, or, without loss of generality, as a stock of fixed factor that provides a flow of services proportional to the stock, with the proportionality factor normalized to unity by appropriate choice of units. Changes in units will, of course, change the distribution parameter for the factor in question, but as long as σ does not change over time, this will not cause any difficulty. The input of the factor 'machinery' in what follows is the number of units of the homogeneous output that are frozen into the machine of the particular blueprint chosen.

Suppose, for the moment, that no factor price is expected to vary over the lifetime of the capacity to be installed. In this case, the assumed decline in rent could come about if, for example, a certain portion of the capacity disappeared each period, thus reducing both the output and the costs by exactly the same proportion. For this special case, a single set of factor proportions will minimize costs at all times. Given knowledge of prices for a unit of the services of each of the factors (c_i, $i = 1,...m$), conditions for cost minimization subject to the production constraint **4** may be derived by forming the Lagrangian expression

$$COST = \sum_{i=1}^{m} c_i X_i + \Lambda \left\{ Q - \left(\sum_{i=1}^{m} a_i X_i^{(\sigma-1)/\sigma} \right)^{\sigma/(\sigma-1)} \right\},$$ **5**

and, as necessary conditions, setting the m first derivatives with respect to the X_i equal to zero. This leads to the equations

$$c_i - \Lambda a_i (Q/X_i)^{1/\sigma} = 0, \qquad i = 1,...m.$$ **6**

From **6** it would be possible to derive $m-1$ equations expressing the cost-minimizing ratios of each of the other $m-1$ factors to X_1 (numbering the factors so that equipment, the factor being studied, is the first);

$$X_i/X_1 = a_i^\sigma c_1^\sigma / a_1^\sigma c_i^\sigma, \qquad i = 2,...m.$$ **7**

Substituting these ratios into the production function leads to the expression

$$X_1/Q = \left\{ a_1 + \sum_{i=2}^{m} \frac{a_i^\sigma c_1^{\sigma-1}}{a_1^{\sigma-1} c_i^{\sigma-1}} \right\}^{\sigma/(\sigma-1)}$$ **8**

for the amount of the first factor to be embodied in (or needed to cooperate with) each unit of new capacity.

Not only is **8** very awkward, especially if the number of factors is greater than two, but also it is necessary to make assumptions about the time paths of each of the a_i in order to use it to derive the demand for a factor. Unless it is assumed that each of the distribution parameters is constant over time, or that each changes according to some exponential time pattern, **8** leads to hopeless difficulties. In addition, the choice of units in which to measure each of the other factors presents problems. In computing a wage rate, for example, should labor be measured in man-hours, or man-hours adjusted for education, or some other unit? Although it will certainly prove necessary to make arbitrary assumptions about smoothness with regard to technical changes in the distribution parameter for equipment, it seems desirable to make as few as possible.

Fortunately, the number of such assumptions can be decreased by using the economic interpretation of the Lagrangian multiplier Λ, and adding one plausible behavioral assumption. Note first that Λ represents the minimum average total cost of output produced with the newest technology. If the firm is investing in new equipment, this average cost must represent its marginal cost as well.[11] The interpretation of Λ as a minimum average cost may be verified by rewriting equation 6 in the form

$$c_i = \Lambda a_i \, X_i^{-(1/\sigma)} \left\{ \sum_{i=1}^{m} a_i X_i^{(\sigma-1)/\sigma} \right\}^{1/(\sigma-1)}, \qquad i = 1,\dots m, \qquad 9$$

multiplying both sides of each equation by X_i, and summing all m equations, to get

$$\sum_{i=1}^{m} c_i \, X_i = \Lambda \left\{ \sum_{i=1}^{m} a_i \, X_i^{(\sigma-1)/\sigma} \right\} \left\{ \sum_{i=1}^{m} a_i \, X_i^{(\sigma-1)/\sigma} \right\}^{1/(\sigma-1)}$$

$$= \Lambda \left\{ \sum_{i=1}^{m} a_i \, X_i^{(\sigma-1)/\sigma} \right\}^{\sigma/(\sigma-1)}$$

$$= \Lambda Q. \qquad 10$$

Thus $\quad \Lambda = \dfrac{\displaystyle\sum_{i=1}^{m} c_i \, X_i}{Q}, \qquad\qquad 11$

the average cost with the latest technology, assuming that static cost-minimizing factor proportions are used.

With the addition of the behavioral assumption that price p is set as a constant markup factor M on marginal or minimum average cost, so that

$$p = M\Lambda, \quad M \geqslant 1, \qquad\qquad 12$$

it is possible to use observed output price as a proxy for minimum average cost. If 12 is substituted into 6, only this one equation is required to write the demand for the first factor per unit of new capacity as a function of its rental, its distribution parameter, the price of output, and M. Thus

$$X_1/Q = [a_1 \, p/c_1 \, M]^\sigma. \qquad\qquad 13$$

The derivation of 13 has proceeded under the assumption of a static world, with no changes in prices or technology. In a time-series analysis, it

11. When the firm is investing in new machinery, the average *variable* costs on the oldest machinery in use cannot exceed the appropriate calculated average *total* cost using new machinery. The trick lies in calculating average total cost, which must include allowance for expected decreases in value of new machinery, without knowledge about expectations of future prices. The simplified rules of thumb I have assumed make the calculation easy, but they may not be at all appropriate.

C. W. Bischoff 165

is unrealistic to assume that the underlying production function will not change over time. As long as technical change is factor-augmenting only with respect to factors other than machinery, the marginal product of machinery will not, however, be changed.

Factor augmentation, in the sense used here, may be defined as follows. A change in one of the distribution parameters a_i cannot be distinguished from a change in the units in which the factor X_i is measured. Thus the production function 4, governing additions to capacity at time t, may be written with unchanged distribution parameters, but with scale factors that multiply the quantities of each factor when these quantities are measured in time-invariant units. These scale factors are functions of time, and thus the production function may be written

a_1 ?

$$Q_t = \left\{ a_i\{h_{1t} X_{1t}\}^{(\sigma-1)/\sigma} + \sum_{i=2}^{m} a_i\{h_{lt} X_{it}\}^{(\sigma-1)/\sigma} \right\}^{\sigma/(\sigma-1)}, \qquad 4.1$$

where the first factor is equipment. In 4.1 technical change that increases h_{it} is factor-augmenting with respect to the ith factor; a single unit of that factor goes further. Each of the derivatives of 4.1 with respect to any factor involves only the scaling of that particular factor, so that

$$\partial Q_t / \partial X_{1t} = a_1 h_{1t}(Q_t / h_{1t} X_{1t})^{1/\sigma}. \qquad 14$$

For equipment, therefore, a change in h_{it} ($i = 2, m$) is Harrod-neutral.[12]

If, however, there is a change in h_{1t} (including a Hicks-neutral technical change, in which all the h_{it} rise by the same proportion), the marginal product of a unit of equipment will change over time.[13] Without loss of generality, all equipment-augmenting technical progress may be treated as embodied in new equipment, for Hall has shown that 'given rates of embodied and disembodied technical change and a given deterioration function cannot be distinguished from a lower rate of embodied technical change, a higher rate of disembodied change, and a higher rate of deterioration' (Hall, 1968, p. 38). This means that the rate of disembodied equipment-augmenting change can be arbitrarily normalized to zero; ways to make old equipment more productive will simply show up as slower deterioration of the capacity embodied in that equipment.

12. Technical change is said to be Harrod-neutral if, at a constant rate of interest, technical change leaves the capital-output ratio unchanged. This condition will be satisfied if the marginal product of capital, as a function of the capital-output ratio, is unaffected by the technical change.
13. Technical change is said to be Hicks-neutral if, for a given set of factor proportions, the technical change does not affect the ratio of the marginal products of any pair of factors. Since the marginal product of the jth factor includes h_{it} raised to the power $(\sigma-1)/\sigma$, equal proportional changes in h_{it} and h_{lt} will not affect the ratio of the marginal product of the ith factor to the marginal product of the jth factor.

As soon as the possibility of technical change is admitted, the assumption that relative prices and factor costs do not change becomes untenable. In addition, if the model is to be applied empirically, there must be some recognition that prices are, in fact, constantly changing. If the production function and the costs of time t were to persist forever, the factor proportions that would minimize costs would be

$$X_{1t}/Q_t = (1/h_{1t})(h_{1t} \, a_1 \, p_t/c_{1t} \, M)^\sigma = V_t, \qquad\qquad \textbf{13.1}$$

but these will generally be the wrong proportions in a world of changing prices.

For purposes of estimation, it is assumed that entrepreneurs choose their factor proportions by a simple suboptimal rule of thumb. This rule involves factor proportions V_t^* which are calculated as a distributed lag function of past values of V, the *static* optimum amount of equipment per unit of capacity defined in output terms. Thus,

$$V_t^* = \sum_{k=0}^{\infty} \chi_k \, V_{t-k}. \qquad\qquad \textbf{15}$$

There is no particular reason why the weights χ should add up to one.

This rule is undoubtedly a vast oversimplification. It would be desirable to consider explicitly the ways in which expectations about interest rates, equipment prices, and prices of other factors are formed, and the choice of optimum proportions in the face of such expectations. However, such an explicit model would require many more specific assumptions than I have been willing to make.

Gross additions to capacity

The decision as to how much capacity to order at time t for delivery η periods later depends on how much is needed for replacement, and how much is desired for net additions. Replacement temporarily aside, desired net additions to capacity should equal the difference between the capacity the firm desired to have, and placed orders to achieve, in period $t+\eta-1$ and the capacity desired in period $t+\eta$. Desired capacity Q_K^* is assumed to be a roughly constant [14] multiple ($\zeta^* \geqslant 1$) of output planned for period $t+\eta$, $Q_{t+\eta}^*$, that is,

$$Q_{K_t+\eta}^* = \zeta^* Q_{t+\eta}^*. \qquad\qquad \textbf{16}$$

14. With fixed proportions prevailing *ex post*, there will be an optimal degree of excess capacity which depends on the certainty with which demand expectations are held, the costs, due to lost sales or overtime work, of not having enough capacity, and the cost of holding excess capacity. Thus, in general the desired capacity-output ratio ζ will be a function of relative prices, among other things, but for simplicity I assume it is approximately constant. For approaches to the problem of the optimal degree of excess capacity for relatively special cases, see Manne (1961) and Smith (1967).

Furthermore, Q^* may, it is assumed, be approximated by a function of past outputs

$$Q^*_{t+\eta} = \sum_{i=0}^{\infty} \xi_i\, Q_{t-i}.\qquad\qquad 17$$

Then net additions to desired capacity are

$$Q^*_{K_t+\eta} - Q^*_{K_t+\eta-1} = \zeta^* \left\{ \sum_{i=0}^{\infty} \xi_i(Q_{t-i} - Q_{t-i-1}) \right\}.\qquad 18$$

For different firms, and for different types of equipment within a firm, the lead time η will vary. Therefore, in deriving an aggregate model, it is desirable to specify that actual net additions to capacity are a distributed lag function of past desired net additions, with the weights adding up to one and with each particular weight ψ_j indicating the proportion of the capacity ordered in period t that is installed in period $t+j$. In other words, ψ_j represents the proportion of the equipment aggregate for which the waiting period η is equal to j. Thus an aggregate equation for actual net additions to capacity would be

$$Q_{K_t} - Q_{K_t-1} = \zeta^* \left\{ \sum_{j=0}^{\infty} \sum_{i=0}^{\infty} \psi_j \xi_i(Q_{t-i-j} - Q_{t-i-j-1}) \right\}.\qquad 19$$

This equation can be written in general form as

$$Q_{K_t} - Q_{K_t-1} = \zeta^* \left\{ \sum_{k=0}^{\infty} \varphi_k(Q_{t-k} - Q_{t-k-1}) \right\}.$$

The above equation, however, is nothing but a first-order difference equation with a very simple solution,

$$Q_{K_t} = \zeta^* \sum_{k=0}^{\infty} \varphi_k\, Q_{t-k} + Constant,\qquad\qquad 20$$

where the constant is arbitrary and must be zero if actual capacity is to equal desired capacity in a steady state.

If net additions to capacity actually follow such a pattern (either without error, or with very small, serially independent errors), current capacity can be adequately approximated as a function of past output levels. This approximation is not likely to be very good in the case of an individual firm or industry, or even in the aggregate in the face of a substantial downswing, for the lag between desired and actual net decreases in capacity cannot be expected to resemble the lag for net increases.[15] Nevertheless, in the absence of any direct measures of capacity or capacity utilization for the economy as a whole, an approximation of this sort is perhaps the best available measure.

The conceptual stock of capacity specified in equation 20 is the analogue in this model to the stock of capital that ordinarily appears in investment functions. The crucial difference is that in this model the amount of investment necessary to replace a unit of capacity that wears out or becomes obsolete will depend on recent relative prices rather than on the amount of investment that originally took place.

As to replacement demand, by far the simplest assumption is that the flow of services from a unit of capacity declines exponentially from the time the capacity is installed. Under static conditions, such a pattern would imply exponential decline in the prices of used machinery. Since existing evidence suggests that exponential decline may be an adequate approximation to the true pattern,[16] this assumption can be rationalized, and leads to the conclusion that the proportion of existing capacity to be replaced in a given time period may be adequately approximated by a constant (δ).[17] Then gross additions to capacity, or gross investment in capacity units I_{QK}, may be written as

$$I_{QK_t} = \zeta^* \sum_{k=0}^{\infty} \varphi_k(Q_{t-k}-Q_{t-k-1})+\delta\zeta^* \sum_{k=0}^{\infty} \varphi_k Q_{t-k-1}, \qquad 21$$

using 20 to express the net stock of capacity at the end of period $t-1$ (the beginning of period t).

Equipment expenditures

To derive an investment function, gross additions to capacity must be scaled by a factor that represents the incremental ratio of equipment to

15. This is the well-known problem of asymmetry in the operation of the acceleration principle. Aggregation, of course, does not solve the problem, except to the extent that some firms can sell their excess capacity to others. Nevertheless, the declines in aggregate net new orders for machinery in the post-Korean period, even in the worst recessions, have been moderate enough to encourage the feeling that the bias from this source will not be serious.

16. See, for example, Terborgh (1954), Griliches (1963), and Chow (1957).

17. A simplification of this sort may not be tenable, however, in a model with *ex post* fixed proportions, to the extent that rising variable costs eliminate the quasi-rents on old equipment even before it is physically worn out. In such circumstances, the proportion of capacity retired in any given period would be a function of relative prices, among other things. On the other hand, if there is some possibility of choosing the durability of machinery, and more durable machines cost more, one would expect that market forces would lead to the manufacture of capital goods in which the physical life is normally *less* than the economic life.

capacity considered optimal at the time the plans are made final. The rule of thumb for choosing this marginal ratio is given in **15**. As given in **15**, V_i^* must be multiplied by net additions to desired capacity in period $t+\eta$, as given by **17**, and also by the amount of replacement to take place in period t/η, which will be $\delta\zeta^*$ times the output planned for $t+\eta$. Thus, desired gross additions to capacity I_{QK}^* are given by

$$I_{QKt+\eta}^* = \zeta^* \sum_{i=0}^{\infty} \xi_i(Q_{t-i}-Q_{t-i-1})+\delta\zeta^* \sum_{i=0}^{\infty} \xi_i Q_{t-i-1} \qquad \textbf{22}$$

$$= \zeta^* \sum_{i=0}^{\infty} \xi_i\{Q_{t-i}-(1-\delta)Q_{t-i-1}\},$$

and planned expenditure $I_{t+\eta}^*$ is

$$I_{t+\eta}^* = \zeta^* \sum_{k=0}^{\infty} \chi_k V_{t-k} \sum_{i=0}^{\infty} \xi_i\{Q_{t-i}-(1-\delta)Q_{t-i-1}\}. \qquad \textbf{23}$$

If a lag is introduced between plans and expenditures, as before, *aggregate* equipment expenditures in period t are expressed in terms of past output levels and relative price ratios as

$$I_t = \zeta^* \sum_{j=0}^{\infty} \sum_{k=0}^{\infty} \sum_{i=0}^{\infty} \psi_j \chi_k \xi_i V_{t-k-j}\{Q_{t-i-j}-(1-\delta)Q_{t-i-j-1}\}. \qquad \textbf{24}$$

This expression may be thought of as a special case of the general form

$$I_t = \zeta^* \sum_{j=0}^{\infty} \sum_{i=0}^{\infty} \beta_{ij} V_{t-i} Q_{t-j}. \qquad \textbf{25}$$

The relationship between the coefficients β_{ij} in equation **25** and the coefficients of the equation that immediately precedes it is as follows:

$$\beta_{ij} = \sum_{k=0}^{\min[i,j]} \psi_k \chi_{i-k}\{\xi_{j-k}-(1-\delta)\xi_{j-k-1}\}. \qquad \textbf{26}$$

Equation **25** involves a large – indeed, in principle, infinite – matrix of coefficients β_{ij} of relative price and output terms. Unrestricted estimation of the matrix, however, is neither possible nor desirable.

The common-sense interpretation of **25** is that equipment spending is a complex weighted sum of the effects of lagged relative prices and output levels, interacting multiplicatively. But if quarterly changes in V and Q are small relative to their levels, **25** is approximately proportional to

$$I_t \approx \zeta^* \sum_{i=0}^{n} \lambda_i V_{t-i} \tilde{Q}_t+\xi^* \sum_{j=0}^{n} \mu_j Q_{t-j} \tilde{V}_t, \qquad \textbf{27}$$

in which $\tilde{Q}_t$ and $\tilde{V}_t$ are approximations to the levels of Q and V over the period $t-n, t$. On this interpretation

$$\lambda_i \approx \sum_j \beta_{ij} = \sum_{k=0}^{i} \delta \psi_k \chi_{i-k} \qquad \qquad 28$$

and $\quad \mu_j \approx \sum_i \beta_{ij} = \sum_{k=0}^{j} \psi_k \{\xi_{j-k} - (1-\delta)\xi_{j-k-1}\}; \qquad 29$

that is, the λs represent row sums of the β_{ij} coefficient matrix and the μs represent column sums. Since all of the ψs and χs are assumed positive, the λs should all be positive.[18] With respect to the μs, only the first nonzero μ_j weight can be specified *a priori* to be positive; nevertheless it seems likely that the first few μ_j would be positive, while the weights applied to more distant output effects would be negative. In other words, both recent and distant relative prices are expected to enter the equation with the same sign, but recent output levels are expected to have a positive effect on investment while past levels should have a negative effect. This simply reflects the familiar acceleration principle; for a given level of current output a higher level of past output means a smaller output rise and hence less investment. The distinction between the expected pattern of λs and the μs arises because without *ex post* substitution, investment reacts not to a change in relative prices but only to the level of the ratio.[19] In this model there is no acceleration effect with respect to relative prices.

Using **26**, Table 1 sets out a numerical example of what the full coefficient matrix β would be, with δ arbitrarily set at 0·10, and given the arbitrarily chosen sets of weights[20]

$$[\xi_0 \ \xi_1 \ \xi_2] = [0·5 \ 0·4 \ 0·15],$$
$$[\chi_0 \ \chi_1 \ \chi_2 \ \chi_3] = [0·4 \ 0·3 \ 0·2 \ 0·1],$$
$$[\psi_0 \ \psi_1 \ \psi_2] = [0·25 \ 0·5 \ 0·25]. \qquad 30$$

18. This statement requires amplification. The χ weights, which partly represent expectations about future relative prices, might conceivably contain negative terms. The assumption that they should all be positive implies that V_t^* is a positively weighted sum of past values of V_t, which may not be true.

19. To the extent that more capacity is replaced when V is rising, because old capacity (put in place when V was low) becomes uneconomical, I might react to changes in V even when *ex post* substitution does not exist. As noted earlier, the assumption of exponential retirement patterns excludes this possibility, but the assumption may not be valid.

20. These weights imply (a) that output planned at $t+\eta$ is one-half of output at t, plus 40 per cent of output at $t-1$, plus 15 per cent of output at $t-2$; (b) that $V_t^* = 0·4V_t + 0·3V_{t-1} + 0·2V_{t-2} + 0·1V_{t-3}$; and (c) that 25 per cent of orders placed in period t are filled in that period, 50 per cent in period $t+1$, and 25 per cent in period $t+2$.

In the example, the row sums are all positive, while the column sums are first positive and then negative. The same pattern is evident in each row across; the coefficients are first positive and then negative.

Table 1 Example of beta matrix with *ex post* fixed proportions

Number of periods factor proportions are lagged	Number of periods output is lagged						Total[a]
	0	1	2	3	4	5	λ_j
0	0·050	−0·005	−0·021	−0·014	0·000	0·000	0·010
1	0·038	0·096	−0·026	−0·052	−0·027	0·000	0·029
2	0·025	0·072	0·032	−0·043	−0·041	−0·014	0·032
3	0·012	0·049	0·027	−0·028	−0·029	−0·010	0·021
4	0·000	0·025	0·022	−0·013	−0·017	−0·007	0·010
5	0·000	0·000	0·012	−0·001	−0·006	−0·003	0·003
Total μ_i[a]	0·125	0·237	0·048	−0·151	−0·120	−0·034	0·105

Source: Equation **26**

[a] Details may not add to totals due to rounding

The standard neoclassical model

The functional forms **25** and **27** are particularly appropriate for testing the hypothesis that a more general functional form is needed than is provided by the standard neoclassical model, because the standard model can also be fitted into these forms. I identify the 'standard' model with the path-breaking work of Jorgenson, mentioned in the introduction to this study;[21] the most important particular in which it differs from the model I have specified is that in it factor proportions are assumed to be freely variable at all times. In this case, **13.1** would give the appropriate conditional operating rule for the cost-minimizing ratio of capital stock to output.[22]

Jorgenson recognizes, however, that there exists a lag – or series of lags – between the making of plans and the delivery of equipment. In the most rigid form of this model, plans are made without regard to this lag; one interpretation of this assumption would be that expectations are static,[23] that is,

$$Q_{t+n} = Q_t \qquad \qquad \mathbf{31}$$

21. See footnote 2, p. 160.
22. I am also assuming that the standard model includes enough assumptions to assure the existence of an aggregate capital stock. See Fisher (1965). The operating rule does not, however, specify how the optimum output is chosen.
23. Nothing would be changed if expectations embodied some sort of constant trend so that, for example, expected output Q^* was a constant multiple of current output. The constant trend factor could not, in the estimation, be untangled from the other coefficients.

and $V_t^* = V_t.$ **32**

A desired stock of equipment K^* is computed as

$$K_t^* = V_t^* Q_{t+\eta} = V_t Q_t. \qquad \textbf{33}$$

If equipment is ordered to cover any change in desired capital stock, and a proportion ψ_j of the aggregate total of equipment ordered in period t is delivered in period $t+j$, then

$$K_t - K_{t-1} = \sum_{j=0}^{\infty} \psi_j (V_{t-j} Q_{t-j} - V_{t-j-1} Q_{t-j-1}) \qquad \textbf{34}$$

and

$$K_t = \sum_{j=0}^{\infty} \psi_j V_{t-j} Q_{t-j}, \qquad \textbf{34.1}$$

where K_t is the aggregate stock at the end of period t.

Then, since **34** provides an expression for net investment in period t, and replacement in that same period will be δK_{t-1} if exponential retirement is assumed, this means

$$I_t = \sum_{j=0}^{\infty} \psi_j (V_{t-j} Q_{t-j} - V_{t-j-1} Q_{t-j-1}) + \delta K_{t-1}. \qquad \textbf{35}$$

If **35** is substituted for K_{t-1}, then

$$I_t = \sum_{j=0}^{\infty} \psi_j (V_{t-j} Q_{t-j} - V_{t-j-1} Q_{t-j-1}) + \delta \sum_{j=0}^{\infty} \psi_j V_{t-j-1} Q_{t-j-1}$$

$$= \sum_{j=0}^{\infty} \psi_j (V_{t-j} Q_{t-j} - [1-\delta] V_{t-j-1} Q_{t-j-1}). \qquad \textbf{36}$$

This corresponds to **25** with the matrix β simply

$$\begin{bmatrix} \psi_0 & 0 & 0 & \cdot & \cdot & \cdot \\ 0 & \psi_1 - (1-\delta)\psi_0 & 0 & & & \\ 0 & 0 & \psi_2 - (1-\delta)\psi_1 & & \cdot & \\ \cdot & & & & & \\ \cdot & & & \cdot & & \\ \cdot & & & & & \cdot \end{bmatrix}.$$

The row and column sums are obviously identical. The expected sign pattern of the weights on the main diagonal would be $\beta_{11} > 0$, $\beta_{22} > 0$ depending on whether or not $\psi_1 > (1-\delta)\psi_0$. All the weights could be positive if $\psi_{i+1} \geqslant (1-\delta)\psi_i$ for all i. But this would appear unlikely, for this restriction implies that the mean lag between orders and deliveries of equipment would have to be at least $1/\delta$ periods (that is, six to twelve years for plausible values of δ).

The lag pattern derived above depends not only on *ex post* variability of factor proportions but also on the existence of static expectations. There is no reason why the two assumptions should be connected, and relaxing the assumption of static expectations leads to a very different lag pattern. If, for example, price and output expectations are generated by processes of the form

$$Q_{t+\eta} = \sum_{i=0}^{\infty} \xi_i Q_{t-i}, \qquad\qquad 37$$

and

$$V_{t+\eta}^* = \sum_{k=0}^{\infty} \chi_k V_{t-k}, \qquad\qquad 38$$

then an argument precisely analogous to the one just given leads to the expression

$$I_t = \sum_{j=0}^{\infty} \sum_{k=0}^{\infty} \sum_{i=0}^{\infty} \psi_j \chi_k \xi_i [V_{t-k-j} Q_{t-i-j} - (1-\delta)V_{t-k-j-i} Q_{t-i-j-1}]. \qquad 39$$

If equation 39 is also considered a special case of

$$I_t = \sum_{j=0}^{\infty} \sum_{i=0}^{\infty} \beta_{ij} V_{t-i} Q_{t-j}, \qquad\qquad 39.1$$

the correspondence between the coefficients β_{ij} and the coefficients of 39 is

$$\beta_{ij} = \sum_{k=0}^{\min[i,j]} \psi_k [\chi_{i-k} \xi_{j-k} - (1-\delta)\chi_{i-k-1} \xi_{j-k-1}]. \qquad\qquad 40$$

In this case the row and column sums of the β matrix will not be identical unless the coefficients χ_k are identical with the coefficients ξ_i. A condition that is sufficient, though not necessary, to guarantee that all the row sums in the β matrix corresponding to 39 will be positive is that $\chi_{i+1} \geqslant (1-\delta)\chi_i$ for all i.

Table 2 gives a numerical example of a β matrix derived from equation 40 using the same sets of ψ, χ, and ξ weights that were used in deriving Table 1. In this example, both the row sums and the column sums are first positive and then negative, which would be the normal case.

To summarize, I have shown that in the most extreme form of the standard model (with the implicit assumption of static expectations) the jth row sum of the coefficient matrix of equation 25 would be identical to the jth column sum. In the less restrictive case in which expectations about both V and Q are formed as weighted averages of past observations on V and Q, with all the weights having positive signs, the presumption is that both the row sums and the column sums would be positive at first and then negative. This contrasts to the hypothesized sign pattern of row sums derived from a theoretical model in which *ex post* substitution is not possible. In that case, all the row sums would be positive.[24]

Table 2 Example of beta matrix for standard neoclassical model with nonstatic expectations

Number of periods factor proportions are lagged	Number of periods output is lagged						Total[a] λ_J
	0	1	2	3	4	5	
0	0·050	0·040	0·015	0·000	0·000	0·000	0·105
1	0·038	0·085	0·055	0·016	0·000	0·000	0·194
2	0·025	0·061	0·000	−0·020	−0·012	0·000	0·055
3	0·012	0·038	−0·004	−0·061	−0·045	−0·014	−0·074
4	0·000	0·014	−0·009	−0·045	−0·033	−0·010	−0·083
5	0·000	0·000	−0·010	−0·030	−0·021	−0·007	−0·068
6	0·000	0·000	0·000	−0·011	−0·009	−0·003	−0·024
Total[a] m_t	0·125	0·237	0·048	−0·151	−0·120	−0·034	0·105

Source: Equation **40**
[a]Details may not add to totals due to rounding

As noted in the introduction, policy makers should be concerned with whether a measure that affects the implicit rent on equipment sets off a short-lived investment boom. Thus, for the purposes of short-run policy, the most important thing is to be able to estimate the parameters of **25** or **27**, and to derive a qualitative (and quantitative) description of the λ weights. It would also, however, be desirable to be able to interpret the estimates and to draw conclusions about the sort of capital-theoretic model that generated the data. I have noted that an unambiguous interpretation will not generally be possible. All that can be said is that, if all the λ weights turn out to have the same sign, if only a few of them are negative, or if they differ very significantly from the distribution of the μ weights, then these results are not inconsistent with a model in which *ex post* substitution is not possible. In addition, this pattern would seem improbable in a model in which factor proportions could be easily altered even after fixed equipment was in place.

24. This is true, at least given the assumptions that V_t^* is a positively weighted average of past values of V, and that the amount of capacity desired is not a function of V.

Estimation of the parameters of the model
Restrictions on lag distributions

At the close of the first section, it was argued that the interesting parameters in equation **39.1** are the row and column sums of the β matrix – the λ and μ weights. One feasible method of approximation involves estimating two coefficients out of each row and column of the coefficient matrix β to act as proxies for all the rest of the coefficients in the row or column. Experimentation with various patterns reveals that the results are insensitive to the choice of coefficients to be estimated, as long as at least two coefficients in each row are estimated.[25] The practice of estimating two diagonal sets of coefficients $\beta_{i,i}$ and $\beta_{i,i-1}$ for $i = 2,\dots,n$ has been adopted for all regressions that are reported here. The maximum lag n has been chosen equal to 12, implying that the estimated value of equipment spending is based on values of V' and Q for the preceding three years.[26] Since $\mu_j = \beta_{jj} + \beta_{j+1,j}$ and $\lambda_k = \beta_{kk} + \beta_{k,k-1}$, the coefficients to be estimated determine μ_j for $j = 1, 12$, and λ_k for $k = 2, 12$.[27] Thus, the equation to be estimated, referred to as the expenditures equation, is

$$I_t = \sum_{i=2}^{12} \beta_{i,i-1} \, V'_{t-i} \, Q_{t-i+1} + \sum_{i=2}^{12} \beta_{i,i} \, V'_{t-i} \, Q_{t-i} + \varepsilon_t, \qquad \textbf{41}$$

in which I_t is expenditure for producers' durable equipment and Q_t is business gross product, both variables measured seasonally adjusted at annual rates, in billions of 1958 US dollars. ε_t is an independently distributed random error. V'_t is proportional to the equilibrium ratio of equipment to out-

25. Estimating more than two coefficients in each row and column produced negligible improvements in the unadjusted coefficient of determination and reduced the adjusted coefficient of determination in all cases in which it was tried.
26. In the theoretical development, all lag weights were specified to extend over the infinite past. For the purpose of estimation, an infinite lag specification could have been adopted. In this case, finite lags are more convenient, especially because there are several different lag distributions to be estimated. *A priori*, it is at least as plausible to assume that the effects of a change in a particular variable will become negligible after a finite period as it is to assume that the effects will continue forever. In addition, even though only a finite number of lagged values of Q enter equation **41**, it is shown in the section beginning on p. 185 that this does not generally imply that the *complete* adjustment of capacity to a change in output takes place within a finite period (see Table 7).
27. This estimation procedure requires the first row sum λ_1 to be zero. Alternative regressions in which this requirement was removed produced no evidence that λ_1, the row sum representing the effects of V' lagged only one quarter, was significantly different from zero. The regressions reported below show estimated values of λ_2 as well which are essentially zero; no significant effects of variations in relative prices are found until the third quarter after the change.

put, given the prices and technology of period t, and is obtained from equation 13·1 by assuming a_1 and M to be constants independent of time, giving

$$V'_t = h^{\sigma-1}_{1t} \, p^{\sigma}_t \, c^{-\sigma}_{1t}, \qquad\qquad 42$$

in which h_{1t} is a technical change parameter assumed to follow a smooth trend, p_t is the implicit deflator for business gross product, σ is the price elasticity of the demand for equipment, and c_{1t} is the imputed rent per unit of new equipment, as defined by equation 3. The unusual feature of the present application of equation 3 lies in the cost of capital r_t, defined as

$$r_t = (r_0 + r_1 R_t + r_2 S_t + r_3 T_t)(1 - r_4 u_t), \qquad\qquad 43$$

in which R_t is the industrial bond yield, S_t the dividend-price ratio, T_t a time trend equal to zero in mid-1958, u_t the rate of corporation income tax, and r_0, r_1, r_2, r_3, and r_4 are coefficients to be estimated. (Further explanation may be found on pp. 81–8 of the original paper.)

Multicollinearity would not permit the estimation of all twenty-two of the $\beta_{i,i-1}$ and $\beta_{i,i}$ coefficients in equation 41, and to overcome this difficulty, I have used the technique developed by Almon (1965). The $\beta_{i,i-1}$ coefficients are constrained to be values of a third-degree polynomial in i, with the additional constraint that the value of the polynomial for $i = 13$ should be zero. This last constraint has the effect of forcing the $\beta_{i,i-1}$ coefficients to approach zero as the index approaches 13. In mathematical form the constraints applied amount to

$$\beta_{i,i-1} = A_3(i^3 - 2197) + A_2(i^2 - 169) + A_1(i - 13) \text{ for } 2 \leqslant i \leqslant 13.$$

A similar constraint has been applied to the estimated $\beta_{i,i}$ coefficients:

$$\beta_{i,i} = B_3(i^3 - 2197) + B_2(i^2 - 169) + B_1(i - 13) \text{ for } 2 \leqslant i \leqslant 13.$$

With the insertion of these constraints into 41 all but six of the linear coefficients may be eliminated. The coefficients A_1, A_2, A_3, and B_1, B_2, B_3 could be estimated, or, as I have done, the constraints could be applied by making use of Lagrangian interpolation weights.[28] The six coefficients actually estimated, A'_1, A'_2, A'_3, and B'_1, B'_2, B'_3, are linear functions of, respectively, A_1, A_2, A_3, and B_1, B_2, B_3.

Preliminary exploration of the parameter space

Even with these simplifications, estimation of the parameters of 41 presents a complicated nonlinear problem. The variable V' is a nonlinear function

28. For a more extensive discussion of the use of these weights, see Almon (1965). Except for rounding error in computation, the alternative methods for eliminating all but six coefficients will produce identical results.

of σ, δ, r_0, r_1, r_2, r_3, r_4, and h'. If it is assumed that the error term ε in equation **41** is normally distributed with zero mean, constant variance, no serial correlation, and independent of all the right-hand variables, then maximum likelihood estimates of the parameters of **41** may be obtained by minimizing the sum of squared residuals with respect to all eight non-linear parameters and the six linear A' and B' parameters. The next section describes the simultaneous non-linear estimation of all these parameters (with the exception of r_3, r_4, and δ).

Nonlinear estimates of the model

An iterative technique has been used to obtain estimates of the parameters of the nonlinear version of the expenditures equation that maximize the likelihood function, at least locally. Because there may be several maxima, and because the iterative technique used cannot guarantee a global maximum, the process has been started from a number of initial sets of estimates, including all of the sets of parameters used in the preliminary trials. All have led to the same local maximum.

The technique used is called the 'maximum neighborhood' method by its originator, Marquardt (1963). It combines the favorable features of two better-known techniques for solving nonlinear equations, Gauss's method and the method of steepest ascent. Gauss's method involves linearization of the model by expanding it in a Taylor series about the initial guesses of the parameters (and truncating after the first order terms). The normal equations for the linearized model can be solved, and they provide a new set of parameter estimates which usually give a larger value for the likelihood function when they are inserted into the original model. The method can break down, however, if the linear approximation is not sufficiently good in the neighborhood of the 'corrected' parameter estimates: the new estimates may actually give a smaller value of the likelihood function.[29]

With the method of steepest ascent, however, it is always possible to improve the parameter estimates in such a way as to increase the likelihood function (except at a local maximum or a saddle point). The difficulty is that convergence may be extremely slow. Marquardt's method 'in effect performs an optimum interpolation between the Taylor series method and the gradient method, the interpolation being based upon the maximum neighborhood in which the truncated Taylor series gives an adequate representation of the nonlinear model' (Marquardt, 1963, p. 431).[30]

Convergence to a local maximum has been considered complete only

29. In this case, Hartley (1961) recommends correcting the parameter estimates by only a fraction of the vector of corrections provided by the linearized model.
30. The program I used embodies the Marquardt algorithm and is a slight revision of I B M Share Program No. S D A-3094-01.

when every one of the corrections estimated from the linearized model has passed the test

$$\frac{|b_i^{q+} - b_i^q|}{0.001 + |b_i^q|} < 0.00005,$$

where

b_i^q = the value of the ith parameter on the qth iteration

b_i^{q+} = the corrected value of the parameter.

Depending on the initial guesses, convergence for the model has involved as few as three iterations or as many as sixty.

Parameter constraints and estimates

In practice, it appears that convergence cannot be achieved if both the coefficient of the rate of technical change h' and the coefficient on the time trend in the discount rate equation r_3 are allowed to vary. Since both represent trend terms, the linearized model is too nearly singular to get meaningful results. Thus r_3 has been arbitrarily set at zero. Similarly, it has seemed necessary arbitrarily to normalize either the depreciation rate δ, the coefficient on the industrial bond yield r_1, or the coefficient on the dividend-price ratio r_2, and to estimate in effect, only the ratios r_1/δ, r_2/δ, and r_1/r_2. The parameter δ has therefore been set at 0.16 in all cases (some rough tests indicate that the results are not at all sensitive to the absolute value of δ, within the range 0.10–0.20). No attempt has been made to estimate the coefficient of the tax rate r_4 in the discount rate equation, which plays a very small role in the model in any case. Instead, this parameter has been set at 0.2 on the basis of rather casual examination of movements in debt-equity ratios at market value and book value.

Nonlinear solution of the model thus has involved obtaining least squares estimates of the parameters r_0, r_1, r_2, σ, and h', and of the A' and B' parameters. Asymptotic standard errors have been computed, but they are in fact only the standard errors of the parameter estimates as computed from the linearized model. The Taylor series model can be written

$$\hat{I} = f(Q, V'; \hat{\beta}) + \partial(\hat{\beta} - \beta), \qquad\qquad 44$$

in which $f(Q, V'; \hat{\beta})$ is the $m_2 \times 1$ vector of predicted values of I as a nonlinear function of the matrix of right-hand variables Q, V', and the $m_3 \times 1$ vector of final parameter estimates $\hat{\beta}$; $(\beta - \hat{\beta})$ is an $m_3 \times 1$ vector; and ∂ is the $m_2 \times m_3$ matrix of partial derivatives of the estimated values of I with respect to each of the parameters, evaluated at $\hat{\beta}$, that is,

$$\partial_{ij} = \frac{\partial f_i}{\partial \beta_j}\bigg|_{\hat{\beta}}. \qquad\qquad 45$$

In this case,

$$\frac{\sum\limits_{t=1}^{m}(I_t - \hat{I}_t)^2}{m_2 - m_3}(\partial'\partial)^{-1}$$

is the asymptotic variance-covariance matrix of the parameter estimates from which the asymptotic standard errors have been derived.

The fruits of the nonlinear estimation are given in (a) Table 3, which presents the estimated parameters and various summary statistics; (b) Table 4, which shows the estimated long-run elasticities of equipment

Table 3 Nonlinear estimates of parameters, asymptotic standard errors, and summary statistics for expenditures equation

Parameters and summary statistics	Value	Asymptotic standard error
Parameters		
r_0	−0·008	(0·002)
r_1 (bond yield)	0·535	(0·096)
r_2 (stock yield)	0·098	(0·028)
σ	1·022	(0·069)
h'	0·00182	(0·00030)
A'_1	0·0254	(0·0053)
A'_2	0·0184	(0·0032)
A'_3	0·0069	(0·0022)
B'_1	−0·0263	(0·0061)
B'_2	−0·0161	(0·0030)
B'_3	−0·0058	(0·0020)

Summary statistics	
coefficient of multiple determination[a]	0·98954
adjusted standard error of estimate[b]	$0·597 \times 10^9$
coefficient of variation[c]	2·00%
Durbin–Watson statistic	1·95
sum of squared residuals	$16·37 \times 10^{18}$
mean of dependent variable	$29·89 \times 10^9$
number of observations	57

Source: Expenditures equation **41**
[a] Unadjusted
[b] Square root of sum of squared residuals divided by number of observations minus 11
[c] Adjusted standard error of estimate divided by mean of dependent variable

Table 4 Estimates of long-run elasticities of equipment expenditures for selected determinants, at selected price levels, 1953–65

Determinant	1953/1 prices	1958/1 prices	1963/1 prices	1965/4 prices
output[a]	1·00	1·00	1·00	1·00
price of output	1·02	1·02	1·02	1·02
price of equipment	−1·02	−1·02	−1·02	−1·02
bond yield	−0·20	−0·21	−0·22	−0·23
dividend-price ratio	−0·07	−0·05	−0·04	−0·02
corporate tax rate	−0·20	−0·18	−0·17	−0·06
proportion of depreciation by accelerated methods	—	0·02	0·02	0·02
service lifetime for tax purposes	−0·10	−0·09	−0·09	−0·09
rate of tax credit	—	—	0·05	0·10
time[b]	0·01	0·01	0·01	0·01

Source: Data are derived from nonlinear parameter estimates for expenditures equation **41**

[a] By assumption

[b] Since the origin of the variable time is completely arbitrary, these elasticities have been calculated as $(\partial l/\partial t) \times (1/l)$ instead of $(\partial l/\partial t) \times (t/l)$. For the purposes of these calculations, time is measured in years, although for the other calculations it is measured in quarters

spending with respect to all of the important variables and policy parameters in the model; and (c) Figure 1, in which the fitted and actual values and the residuals are plotted.

Capital cost. The estimated values of both r_1 and r_2 are large compared with their asymptotic standard errors, but this is misleading, for these coefficients were quite unstable when small changes were made in the model or sample. The estimate of r_0 is negative, and the predicted result seems unreasonably low. But examination of the underlying model indicates that, of the two places in which the discount rate enters, its absolute level matters only when it is used to discount depreciation patterns in computing the present value of the depreciation deduction. In this role, a low discount rate may act primarily as an *ad hoc* adjustment to weaken the influence of changes in depreciation rules as a determinant of investment.[31] Thus, it decreases the elasticity of investment demand with respect to, for example, a change in guideline lives.

Technical change. The estimated trend term h' is positive, and indicates that with all other variables held constant, the ratio of equipment spending

31. At a discount rate of zero, all depreciation patterns have the same present value.

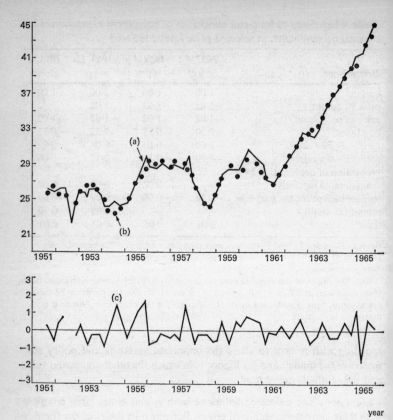

Figure 1 Equipment expenditures, third quarter 1951 through fourth quarter 1965, (a) actual, and (b) predicted, using expenditure equation. (c) Residuals (actual less predicted)

to output is estimated to rise at a rate of about 0·73 per cent per year. Although h' was included in the equation to allow for technical change, it would not be proper to interpret this parameter as a reliable measure of the degree to which technical change is capital-augmenting or capital-using.

Instead, the estimate of h' seems to reflect primarily an offset to trends in other variables. For example, the higher the estimate of r_1, the greater the weight given to the bond yield, which has a very definite uptrend, in the determination of the discount rate. Other things equal, then, the rent will become higher over time and the equilibrium equipment-output ratio lower. But if this ratio is not to fall over time (and Figure 2 indicates that it was about as high in 1965 as it was in 1948) then the estimate of h' must be higher, other things being equal, whenever r_1 is higher. If a high estimate of r_1 results from a high cyclical partial correlation between investment orders and the bond yield, the equilibrium effects are offset by an algebraically larger estimate of h'.

The relationship of all this to technical change seems rather remote. Despite the fact that it cannot be interpreted, it still seems useful to allow for a trend in order to minimize the danger of accepting one of the other variables as significant when it is really acting as a proxy for the trend.

Price elasticity. The estimated price elasticity is close to 1, and also close to the preliminary estimates. The estimated effect of the tax credit is relatively large; with repeal of the Long amendment, the elasticities in Table 4 indicate that repeal of the investment tax credit would lead eventually to a permanent reduction of about 10 per cent in equipment spending. Accelerated depreciation is estimated to have an effect that, while substantial, is considerably smaller than that of the tax credit. The impact of variations in guideline lives within the range that has been contemplated is also relatively small.

The very large change over time in the elasticity with respect to the corporate tax rate requires some comment. This elasticity is proportional to the derivative of the rent with respect to u. From 3, the expression for the rent, the relevant derivative is

$$\frac{q(r+\delta)(1-k-z+zk')}{(1-u)^2}.$$

Thus the elasticity is proportional to $1-k-z+zk'$, and when z, the present value of the depreciation deduction, is close to 1, the elasticity is quite sensitive to the value of k, the rate of tax credit. For a piece of equipment on which the whole credit of 7 per cent can be claimed, if z is greater than 0·93 and with k' equal to zero after repeal of the Long amendment, an increase in the tax rate should increase investment, for the discounted depreciation deductions exceed the cost of the machine (net of credit), and the higher the investment, the greater the savings on the excess deductions.

Relative factor proportions and lag distributions

The time path of V', which summarizes all of the relative price and trend effects, is plotted in Figure 2. Apart from the general downtrend of V' through most of the period, attributable to rising equipment prices (relative to the rest of output) and to rising interest rates, there are three major movements in the series, all primarily the results of changes in tax laws. In 1954–5, the adoption of accelerated depreciation provided a significant additional investment incentive. In the last half of 1962, adoption of the tax credit, along with liberalization of depreciation guidelines, provided another significant offset to rising costs; the repeal of the Long amendment in 1964, restoring the tax credit to the depreciation base, added to the value of this incentive. Finally, temporary repeal of the tax credit in late 1966 created a situation in which the indicated equilibrium ratio of equipment per unit of capacity was only slightly above its low levels of the late fifties and early sixties (with the improvement due to the relative stability of equipment prices since 1958).

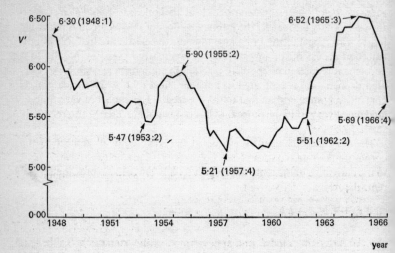

Figure 2 Time series of conglomerate relative prices V' as estimated from expenditure equation, 1948–66

Figure 2 is of particular interest in light of Hickman's (1965) conclusion, based on investment functions fitted for the period 1949–60, that the capital–output ratio in the United States was declining. If true, this proposition might mean that private investment demand would be insufficient to sustain full employment. Figure 2 indicates that the marginal capital–output ratio might well have declined during the period studied by Hickman, although not necessarily for technological reasons. But it also indicates that at least the desired ratio of equipment to output has been substantially affected by government policy since that time. Hickman did not allow for this effect (which was less important for his sample period), but it has played a significant part in the revival of investment demand since 1963.

Lag distributions. Table 5 gives estimates of the lag parameters derived from the nonlinear estimates of the $\beta_{i,t-1}$ and $\beta_{i,t}$ parameters. As suggested

Table 5 Lag distributions obtained from nonlinear estimation of expenditures equation

Period i	Coefficients of $V'_{t-i}Q_{t-i+1}$ $\hat{\beta}_{i,i-1}$	Coefficients of $V'_{t-i}Q_{t-1}$ $\hat{\beta}_{i,i}$	Column sums of β matrix $\hat{\mu}_i$	Row sums of β matrix $\hat{\lambda}_j$
0	—	—		
1	—	—	0·0254	—
2	0·0254	−0·0263	−0·0019	−0·0009
3	0·0245	−0·0238	−0·0011	0·0007
4	0·0227	−0·0210	−0·0007	0·0017
5	0·0203	−0·0181	−0·0007	0·0022
6	0·0174	−0·0151	−0·0009	0·0023
7	0·0143	−0·0121	−0·0011	0·0021
8	0·0110	−0·0093	−0·0014	0·0017
9	0·0079	−0·0067	−0·0016	0·0012
10	0·0050	−0·0043	−0·0017	0·0007
11	0·0026	−0·0024	−0·0015	0·0003
12	0·0009	−0·0009	−0·0009	0·0000
Total[a]	0·1520	−0·1400	0·0120	0·0120

Source: Data are derived from nonlinear parameter estimates for expenditures equation **41**
[a] Details may not add to totals due to rounding
$\Sigma\Sigma\,\hat{\beta}_{ij} = \Sigma\,\hat{\beta}_{i,i-1} + \Sigma\,\hat{\beta}_{i,i} = \Sigma\,\hat{\mu}_j = \Sigma_i\hat{\lambda} = 0.01197$

by the putty-clay model, and as illustrated in the example in Table 1, all of the row sums are either positive or insignificantly different from zero (the asymptotic standard error for the one row sum that is negative is 0·0012). Only the first column sum is positive while all the othes are negative. One might have expected the first two or three column sums to be positive, but the result may be occasioned by the particular approximating technique that was used.

Impact of changes in output and factor proportions

The sum of all the coefficients shows that a rise in output of $1 billion (1958 value) will eventually increase the flow of expenditures for producers' durable equipment by V' times $11·97 million, or, at the level of V' in the fourth quarter of 1965 (6·494), by roughly $78 million.[32] Due to the accelerator

32. If the depreciation rate δ is 0·16, this would correspond to an equipment-output ratio of about 0·49; if δ is 0·10, the ratio would be 0·78. The Commerce Department data on net stocks of equipment in 1966 (in 1958 dollars, with straight-line depreciation) show $221 billion, compared with private business product of $579 billion in that year, a ratio of 0·38.

effect, this response will be exceeded as capacity is initially adjusted upward, and only after three years will the response die down to the steady-state effect, which is replacement on the equipment needed to produce $1 billion of output. Table 6 gives the increments in spending for producers'

Table 6 Effects of sustained rise in output and changes in relative prices on equipment expenditures during next twelve quarters (percentage of steady-state response)

Quarter after change	Effect of change in physical output[a]	Effect of change in relative prices[b]
0	—	—
1	212	—
2	197	−5
3	188	2
4	182	17
5	176	35
6	169	53
7	159	70
8	148	83
9	134	92
10	120	98
11	108	100
12	100	100

Source: Simulation of equation 41, using the nonlinear parameter estimates shown in Tables 4 and 5
[a] Assuming no change in static optimum equipment per unit of capacity
[b] Assuming constant 4 per cent growth in physical output

durable equipment that would stem from a sustained rise in output, as percentages of the steady-state increment.

The most disturbing lag coefficient is the relatively large response of investment in the first quarter following a change in output. Some investment functions have specified *a priori* that no stimulus lagged less than two quarters can have *any* effect, in view of the supposed accuracy of investment anticipations. But Eisner and Evans and Green have found that unexpected rises in sales, or simply changes in sales occurring *after* anticipations have been reported, can enhance explanations based on anticipations alone

(Eisner, 1965; Evans and Green, 1966, pp. 104–16).[33] In principle, changes in output might well be reflected very rapidly in changes in orders (especially cancellations) and at least some of these orders could be promptly translated into expenditures. Although the elasticity of I_t with respect to Q_{t-1} seems too large to be reconciled with Eisner's estimates of the elasticity of I_t with respect to sales in period $t-1$, the constraint of this lag coefficient to zero, which is the principal feasible alternative, does not seem theoretically justifiable. In fact, even the requirement that changes in output cannot affect investment in the same quarter is hard to defend; this specification was adopted largely to minimize statistical problems resulting from simultaneous determination.

The distinction between output and sales should not, however, be overlooked. It is possible that changes in output (which, unlike sales, are under the control of the producer) are in fact correctly anticipated, and that their high correlation with nearly simultaneous investment is a result of this correct anticipation. Viewed in a slightly different way, changes in output may result from some external cause (say, changes in orders) which stimulates investment demand as well. If this is the case, orders themselves should be studied (though this can be done only on an industry level), but as a first approximation the linkage from aggregate demand (via orders) to output and then to investment may not be seriously misspecified if the intermediate orders stage is suppressed.

A less optimistic interpretation would point out that if serial correlation is present, lagging the endogenous output variable will not remove problems brought about by failure to consider all of the simultaneous equations in the underlying economic system. The presence of serial correlation in the empirical results must still be suspected because the Durbin–Watson test is not designed for use in equations that contain lagged endogenous variables. The difficulties may be compounded by the fact that the lagged output variable includes the dependent variable, equipment spending, as one of its components. Although estimation of a more complete system is not feasible in this study, a cautious interpretation of the lag distributions is certainly advisable.

Given relative prices, it is possible to compute the equilibrium increment to an imaginary net stock of equipment that will be brought about by a sustained unit change in output.[34] The lag weights, when combined with an

33. Eisner's conclusions were tempered by the relatively unsuccessful results of tests based on extrapolation beyond the sample period. But extrapolations with the functions estimated by Evans and Green generally produced better predictions than the anticipations did.
34. If both relative prices and technical change are held constant, it is possible to speak of a stock of equipment, since all machines are of the same model.

a priori value of the depreciation rate, can be used to derive an expression for the proportion of the adjustment from one equilibrium stock to another that will be completed within *n* quarters after the change in output. For the estimated weights, the results, as a function of the assumed δ, are shown in Table 7. For reasonable values of δ, in the range from 0·08 to 0·16, the

Table 7 Proportion of adjustment of stock of equipment to change in physical output completed after selected number of quarters, by selected depreciation rates (percentage of adjustment)

Number of quarters	Depreciation rate				
	0·04	0·08	0·12	0·16	0·20
4	8	15	22	29	36
8	13	25	36	46	55
12	17	32	45	56	66
16	20	37	51	63	72
20	23	42	57	68	77
40	37	61	76	86	92

Source: Expenditures equation **41**

adjustment seems relatively slow; only 42 per cent to 68 per cent of the adjustment takes place within the first five years, and it is more than ten years before the adjustment even approaches 90 per cent completion. Long lags in capital-stock adjustment models, of course, are nothing new, but it is these long lags that have led to criticism of many of the simpler versions of such models.

The speed of response of equipment spending to a change in V' varies with the rate of growth in output; the faster output grows, the faster substitution will take place. With investment running at a level of around $50 billion and with a 4 per cent growth in real output, a 1 per cent change in the interest rate (from the fourth quarter 1965 level of 4·72 per cent) would eventually change the flow of spending for producers' durable equipment by about 5 per cent (or $2·5 billion), but a year after the interest rate change, less than 20 per cent of the eventual effect would have been felt. If the change were then reversed, the effects of the original change would continue to build up and it would be more than a year after an equal deviation of interest rates in the opposite direction (from the normal level) before spending on equipment would return to the level that would have obtained had no changes taken place.[35] Table 8 gives the time pattern of effects for the sequence of interest rate changes assumed in this particular case; similar patterns can be computed from Table 6 for any desired sequence of changes.

Table 8 Effect on equipment spending of a change in relative prices followed after one year by a change in the opposite direction of twice the magnitude of the original change (percentage of steady-state effect of the original change)

Quarters after first change	Change in equipment spending[a]
1	—
2	−5
3	2
4	17
5	35
6	63
7	66
8	49
9	22
10	−8

Source: Based on Table 6
[a] Assuming a constant 4 per cent growth in output

Figure 3 compares the estimated short- and long-run responses of equipment spending to changes in V' and Q, based on the nonlinear estimates, to some previous estimates of lags in the investment process. The results are not comparable, especially inasmuch as the Jorgenson (1963) and Griliches

35. This research contributes to a larger project on monetary policy, the FRB–MIT quarterly economic model described in more detail in de Leeuw and Gramlich (1968), and in Rasche and Shapiro (1968). I have also, consequently, been concerned with the possibility that the effects of rationing, or availability of credit, might lead to more rapid monetary influences on investment. A variety of variables which have been suggested as likely to reflect such effects have been experimentally introduced into the model with very short lags, but none has come close to making a significant contribution to the explanation.

C. W. Bischoff 189

and Wallace (1965) models included structures as well as equipment.[36] The most recent estimates by Hall and Jorgenson, based on yearly data for equipment spending, conform only relatively well to my estimates of the lag for changes in output. But they exclude any possibility of interest rate effects; only changes in tax policy and the relative price of new equipment

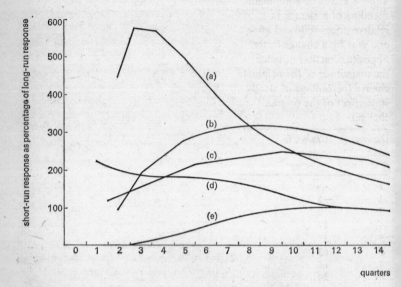

Figure 3 Selected lag distributions for capital expenditures. (a) Jorgenson's original model, manufacturing, all investment, quarterly, 1948–60. (b) Griliches and Wallace model, manufacturing, all investment, quarterly, 1948–62. (c) Hall and Jorgenson model, manufacturing, equipment only, yearly data. (d) Lags for changes in Q from equation **41**. (e) Lags for changes in V' from equation **41**

influence V' in their model. Their results are not inconsistent with the view that the relatively larger and more frequent fluctuations in output exerted a dominant influence in the estimation of the lag pattern. Granting this possibility, because no separate lag pattern was allowed for tax changes it would seem dangerous to base policy conclusions on the apparently large and rapid effects of tax policy found in their study.

36. In view, however, of the small proportion of construction in the total investment of manufacturers, the short-run response of construction to relative price changes would have to exceed the long-run response by a factor of ten or more to produce lag patterns for *total* investment like those implicit in the models cited. This seems unlikely.

Conclusions

The principal conclusions drawn from the empirical work presented in this study may be summarized as follows:

The value and efficacy of the neoclassical approach – the inclusion of relative prices in the investment function – are substantially confirmed. Relative prices appear to have a statistically significant effect on equipment expenditures. At least one tax measure, the investment tax credit, is independently shown to have a substantial effect on equipment expenditures.

The general neoclassical model provides an explanation of aggregate equipment expenditures superior to that given by either of the two most popular alternatives – the standard neoclassical model and the flexible accelerator model. As suggested by the putty-clay hypothesis, relative prices (including tax credits, interest rates, depreciation rules, and so forth) apparently affect equipment spending with a much longer lag than do changes in output.

The long-run elasticity of equipment spending with respect to the rental price of equipment services is estimated to be very close to unity, but this elasticity cannot be estimated with any great precision.

The investment tax credit adopted in 1962 has probably directly stimulated more investment spending than the policy has cost the government in taxes.

Variations in measures of the cost of capital seem to have the negative partial effect on equipment spending suggested by standard theory, but stable estimates of the effects of these variables have not been obtained.

The marginal ratio of equipment spending to output is apparently sensitive to direct fiscal and monetary policy measures, and there is no evidence pointing to a secular decline in this ratio. Attempts to manipulate this ratio for short-run purposes may, however, prove difficult to implement, due to lags in the response to the policy measures.

References

ALMON, S. (1965), 'The distributed lag between capital appropriations and expenditures', *Econometrica*, vol. 33, pp. 178–96.

ARROW, K. J., CHENERY, H. B., MINHAS, B. S., and SOLOW, R. M. (1961), 'Capital–labor substitution and economic efficiency', *Rev. econ. Stat.*, vol. 43. pp. 225–50.

CHOW, G. C. (1957), *Demand for Automobiles in the United States: A Study in Consumer Durables*, North-Holland.

DE LEEUW, F., and GRAMLICH, E. (1968), 'The federal reserve – MIT econometric model', *Federal Reserve Bulletin*, vol. 54, pp. 11–40.

EISNER, R. (1965), 'Realization of investment anticipations', in J. S. Duesenberry *et al.* (eds.), *The Brookings Quarterly Econometric Model of the United States*, Rand McNally, pp. 95–108.

EVANS, M. K., and GREEN, E. W. (1966), 'The relative efficacy of investment anticipations', *J. Amer. stat. Association*, vol. 61, pp. 104–16.

FISHER, F. M. (1965), 'Embodied technical change and the existence of an aggregate capital stock', *Rev. econ. Stud.*, vol. 32, pp. 263–88.

GRILICHES, Z. (1963), 'Capital stock in investment functions: some problems of concept and measurement', in C. F. Christ *et al.*, (eds.) *Measurement in Economics*, Stanford University Press, pp. 121–3.

GRILICHES, Z., and WALLACE,, N. (1965), 'The determinants of investment revisited', *Inter. econ. Rev.*, vol. 6, pp. 321–8.

HALL, R. E. (1968), 'Technical change and capital from the point of view of the dual', *Rev. econ. Stud.*, vol. 35, p. 38.

HALL, R. E., and JORGENSON, D. W. (1967), 'Tax policy and investment behavior', *Amer. econ. Rev.*, vol. 57, pp. 391–414.

HALL, R. E., and JORGENSON, D. W. (1971), 'Application of the theory of optimum capital accumulation', in G. Fromm (ed.), *Tax Incentives and Capital Spending*, Brookings Institution, North-Holland.

HARTLEY, H. O. (1961), 'The modified Gauss–Newton method for the fitting of nonlinear regression functions by least squares', *Technometrics*, vol. 3, pp. 269–80.

HICKMAN, B. G. (1965), *Investment Demand and US Economic Growth*, Brookings Institution.

JOHANSEN, L. (1959), 'Substitution versus fixed production coefficients in the theory of economic growth: a synthesis', *Econometrica*, vol. 27, pp. 157–76.

JORGENSON, D. W. (1963), 'Capital theory and investment behavior', *Amer. econ. Rev.*, vol. 53, pp. 247–59.

JORGENSON, D. W. (1965), 'Anticipations and investment behavior', in J. S. Duesenberry *et al.* (eds.), *The Brookings Quarterly Econometric Model of the United States*, Rand McNally, pp. 85–6.

JORGENSON, D. W. and STEPHENSON, J. A. (1967), 'The time structure of investment behavior in United States manufacturing, 1947–1960', *Rev. econ. Stat.*, vol. 49, pp. 16–27.

JORGENSON, D. W., and STEPHENSON, J. A. (1967a), 'Investment behavior in US manufacturing, 1947–1960', *Econometrica*, vol. 35, pp. 169–220.

KEMP, M. C., and THANH, P. C. (1966), 'On a class of growth models', *Econometrica*, vol. 34, pp. 257–82.

MANNE, A. S. (1961), 'Capacity expansion and probabilistic growth', *Econometrica*, vol. 29, pp. 632–49.

MARQUARDT, D. W. (1963), 'An algorithm for least-squares estimation of nonlinear parameters', *J. Soc. indust. appl. Math.*, vol. 2, pp. 431–41.

MASSELL, B. F. (1962), 'Investment, innovation and growth', *Econometrica*, vol. 30, pp. 239–52.

PHELPS, E. S. (1963), 'Substitution, fixed proportions, growth and distribution', *Inter. econ. Rev.*, vol. 4, pp. 265–88.

RASCHE, R. H., and SHAPIRO, H. T. (1968), 'The FRB–MIT econometric model: its special features', *Amer. econ. Rev.*, vol. 58, pp. 123–49.

SMITH, K. R. (1967), 'The determinants of excess capacity', paper presented to the North American Regional Conference of the Econometric Society, Washington.

SOLOW, R. M. (1962), 'Substitution and fixed proportions in the theory of capital', *Rev. econ. Stud.*, vol. 29, pp. 207–18.

TERBORGH, G. (1954), *Realistic Depreciation Policy*, Machinery and Allied Products Institute, chapters 4 and 5.

8 R. M. Coen

Effects of Tax Policy on Investment in Manufacturing[1]

R. M. Coen, 'Effects of tax policy on investment in manufacturing',
American Economic Review, vol. 58, 1968, pp. 200–211.

Tax incentives for investment have been in vogue in the United States since 1954 when firms were granted the opportunity to accelerate depreciation for tax purposes through use of the declining balance and sum-of-years-digits depreciation methods. More recently, firms have benefited from the 7 per cent investment tax credit (3 per cent for utilities) incorporated in the Revenue Act of 1962, the reductions in equipment lives for tax purposes permitted under the Treasury Department's Revenue Procedure 62-21 (released in July, 1962), and the tax rate reductions provided by the Revenue Act of 1964. The purposes of this study are (a) to determine the magnitude of the tax savings that manufacturing firms have enjoyed as a result of these policies, and (b) to determine the impact of tax incentives on plant and equipment expenditures in manufacturing.

Tax incentives are thought to stimulate capital expenditures in two ways. First, by reducing the amount of taxes that must be paid on income from assets, or by changing the timing of the tax payments in favor of the future, tax incentives increase the after-tax rate of return on capital. Second, by reducing tax liabilities, tax incentives increase a firm's cash flow (after-tax profits plus depreciation charges for tax purposes), which is one measure of internal funds available for investment and is thought by some to be an important determinant of investment expenditures. The rate-of-return effect is captured here in a 'user cost of capital' variable, i.e. an implicit rental price of capital, which enters the investment function as a determinant of the demand for capital. The internal-funds effect is captured by the inclusion of cash flow in the investment function as a determinant of the

1. This paper is a summary of an up-dated version of my doctoral dissertation, 'Tax policy and investment in manufacturing, 1954–66', presented at Northwestern University and published in 1971 by the Brookings Institution in a conference volume on tax policy and investment. I am indebted to Kenyon E. Poole and Robert H. Strotz for their helpful criticisms and suggestions, and I especially want to thank the director of my research, Robert Eisner, whose inspiration and guidance have been invaluable. Part of this work was done while I was a Research Fellow at the Brookings Institution, and I am very grateful to Brookings and to the Johnson Foundation for this support.

speed at which firms eliminate any gap between their desired and actual stocks of capital.[2] This seems to be the appropriate way of entering cash flow in the investment relation, since short-term financial considerations should primarily affect the timing of expenditures, not the desired stock of capital.

I Tax incentives and cash flow

Cash flow during period t can be written as

$$F_t = (1-u_t)(R_t-D_t)+D_t+C_t, \qquad 1$$

where u is the tax rate on business income, R is gross business income (gross of depreciation, but net of all other deductions), D is depreciation charges for tax purposes, and C is the amount of the investment credit. Suppose that if tax policy changes had not occurred relative to some selected base period, the tax rate faced by firms would have been u^*, their depreciation charges for tax purposes would have been D^*, and they would not have been permitted an investment credit. Thus, in the absence of the policy changes, cash flow would have been

$$F_t^* = (1-u_t^*)(R_t-D_t)+D_t^*, \qquad 2$$

and tax savings resulting from the policy changes are

$$F_t-F_t^* = \overbrace{(u_t^*-u_t)(R_t-D_t^*)}^{\substack{\text{savings due to tax} \\ \text{rate change only}}}+\overbrace{u_t^*(D_t-D_t^*)}^{\substack{\text{savings due to} \\ \text{accelerated de-} \\ \text{preciation only}}}-\overbrace{(u_t^*-u_i)(D_t-D_t^*)}^{\text{interaction term}}+\overbrace{C_t}^{\substack{\text{savings due} \\ \text{to tax credit}}}. \quad 3$$

Estimates of $F-F^*$ and its components for corporate manufacturing are presented in Table 1. As an approximation, the interaction between tax rate changes and depreciation accounting changes is distributed in proportion to the separate effects. The tax structure selected as the base is that prevailing at the end of 1953. The major computational task underlying these figures is estimation of the series D^*. This series was obtained by applying a straight-line depreciation formula to gross investment expenditures in manufacturing, assuming a useful life for tax purposes of twenty-five years for acquisitions through 1945 and eighteen years for post-war acquisitions. These tax lives were suggested by studies of corporate income

2. Pioneering studies of capital stock adjustment models in which economic variables influence the adjustment speed are those of Greenberg (1964) and Hochman (1966). A theoretical rationale for such models has been developed by Eisner and Strotz (1963).

and balance-sheet data carried out by Huntley (1961) and Hickman (1965), and they were found to work reasonably well in the sense that the series obtained approximated actual depreciation charges in the earlier post-war years quite closely, as it should.

Table 1 Tax savings resulting from tax incentives – all corporate manufacturing, 1954–66 (millions of dollars)

Year	Tax Savings				Equivalent rate reduction			
	Accelerated depreciation	Tax credit	Tax cut	Total	Accelerated depreciation	Tax credit	Tax cut	Total
1954	559			559	0·028			0·028
1955	816			816	0·029			0·029
1956	797			797	0·030			0·030
1957	711			781	0·031			0·031
1958	699			699	0·035			0·035
1959	592			592	0·022			0·022
1960	462			462	0·020			0·020
1961	382			382	0·017			0·017
1962	927	421		1348	0·035	0·014		0·049
1963	840	573		1413	0·029	0·018		0·047
1964	933	680	648	2261	0·028	0·021	0·020	0·069
1965	1155	819	1540	3514	0·029	0·021	0·039	0·089
1966[a]	977	731	1271	2979	0·030	0·022	0·039	0·091

[a] First three quarters only

Tax savings resulting from the 1954 acceleration of depreciation peaked in 1955 at $816 million, then tapered off to $382 million in 1961.[3] The new depreciation guidelines gave depreciation charges another shot in the arm and, with aid from the tax credit, boosted tax savings in 1962 to $1348 million. The tax cuts of 1964 and 1965 made for continued growth in tax savings – to a level of $3514 million in 1965. Perhaps more interesting and more meaningful than the absolute savings are the 'equivalent rate reductions' shown in Table 1. These figures indicate the reduction in the tax rate on corporate income that would have produced tax savings equal to those brought about by tax incentives. Thus, by 1966 the entire bundle of tax

3. This statement is not quite correct. Actual depreciation charges, D, include accelerated amortization of emergency facilities; $D - D^*$ therefore reflects not only the depreciation accounting changes introduced in 1954 but also accelerated amortization. Excluding amortization from D would make sense only if amortized acquisitions could be eliminated from the expenditure series used to calculate D^*, but it was not possible to obtain the data needed to make this adjustment.

incentives was equivalent to a reduction of 9·1 percentage points (from 52 to 42·9 per cent) in the corporate income tax rate. Accelerated depreciation and the investment tax credit alone amounted to a 5·2 percentage point reduction – an indication of the extent to which these policies have eroded the corporate income tax.

II Tax incentives and the user cost of capital

Suppose that a competitive firm is contemplating increasing its capital stock by one (small) unit, that a unit of capital costs q dollars, and that capital deteriorates at a rate δ per period. The firm will have to make an initial outlay of q dollars and will have to increase replacement expenditures in each future period by $q\delta$. Output in each period will be increased by the marginal product of capital, $\partial Q/\partial K$; and if each additional unit of output can be sold at a price p, gross revenue in each period will be increased by $p(\partial Q/\partial K)$. Net revenue, however, will be increased by only $p(\partial Q/\partial K)-q\delta-T_i$, where T_i is the increase in direct taxes that must be paid in period i. Suppose for the moment that there is no tax credit. Defining D_i as the increase in depreciation charges for tax purposes in period i, we have $T_i = u\{p(\partial Q/\partial K)-D_i\}$.[4] The firm should add one unit to its capital stock if the discounted value of the increases in net revenue exceeds the price of a unit of capital; that is, if

$$\sum_{i=1}^{\infty} \left\{(1-u)p\, \frac{\partial Q}{\partial K} -q\delta+uD_i\right\}(1+r)^{-i} = \left\{(1-u)\, p\, \frac{\partial Q}{\partial K} -q\delta\right\}\frac{1}{r}$$

$$+u \sum_{i=1}^{\infty} D_i(1+r)^{-i} > q, \qquad 4$$

where r is the interest rate at which the firm may borrow or lend in any amount.

Let d_i be the amount of tax depreciation permitted on an investment of one dollar i periods after the investment has been made (the ds may, of course, be zero after some point), and let $B = \sum_{i=1}^{\infty} d_i(1+r)^{-i}$, i.e. B is the discounted value of depreciation charges stemming from a current dollar of capital expenditures. Then

$$\sum_{i=1}^{\infty} D_i(1+r)^{-i} = qB+q\delta B \sum_{i=1}^{\infty} (1+r)^{-i} = qB+q\delta B\frac{1}{r}. \qquad 5$$

4. The deductability of interest payments is ignored here, primarily because of the unsolved conceptual and analytical problems it raises concerning the manner in which expenditures are financed and the appropriate measure of the cost of funds.

Hence, the firm should add one unit to its capital stock if

$$(1-u)p \frac{\partial Q}{\partial K} - q\delta + ruqB + uq\delta B > rq, \qquad\qquad 6$$

that is, if

$$p \frac{\partial Q}{\partial K} > q(r+\delta)(1-uB)/(1-u) = c. \qquad\qquad 7$$

The expression, c, on the right-hand side of the inequality is referred to as user cost; it is the implicit rental price per period of a unit of capital.[5] The firm should continue to expand its capital stock until the marginal product of capital is equal to the real price of capital, c/p.

If there were no direct tax, user cost would be $q(r+\delta)$. A direct tax with no depreciation allowance increases user cost by the factor $1/(1-u)$; a depreciation allowance reduces user cost by the factor $1-uB$, uB being the discounted value of the tax savings generated by the depreciation allowance. If firms were permitted to expense capital goods, B would be unity and the existence of the direct tax would not alter user cost.

This analysis can easily be extended to include an investment credit. If a proportion s of capital outlays can be credited against tax liabilities, and if the depreciable base of acquisitions must be reduced by a factor b if the credit is taken, then

$$c = q(r+\delta)\{1-s-u(1-b)B\}/(1-u). \qquad\qquad 8$$

The investment credit enacted in 1962 required that $b = s$; that is, the depreciable base of acquisitions had to be reduced by the amount of the credit – a provision that somewhat blunted the effect of the credit. The Revenue Act of 1964 did away with this requirement, so that beginning in 1964, $b = 0$.

Estimates of the user cost of capital in manufacturing are presented in Table 2. The GNP implicit price deflator for nonresidential fixed investment was used as an estimate of q, with a 1954 = 100 base. Jorgenson's (1963) estimate of the replacement rate for all manufacturing was adopted

5. A user cost expression similar to the one obtained here was first derived by Jorgenson (1963), but his formulation was not an appropriate one for studying depreciation policy in the United States, as I showed in a paper entitled, 'Accelerated depreciation, the investment tax credit, and investment decisions', which I delivered at the December, 1965, meetings of the Econometric Society. His user cost measure is correct only for the special case in which (a) the depreciation formula is of the declining balance form with a depreciation rate equal to δ and (b) policy-makers stipulate that the depreciable base of acquisitions is a proportion v of their cost. If policy-makers were to change v, they would not change the timing of depreciation charges, but rather the total amount of the write-off.

as an estimate of δ,[6] Moody's industrial bond yield was used as an estimate of r,[7] and general statutory corporate income tax rates were used for u. The fraction of the value of aquisitions permitted as a credit (s) was taken to be 0·029 for 1962, which was the ratio of the credit in corporate manufacturing to manufacturing investment in 1962, and 0·037 for 1963–6, which was the ratio of the credit to investment in 1963, the last year for which I had information. Two variants of B were calculated. The first employed the straight-line depreciation formula and made no allowance for the reduction in useful lives in 1962. The second variant employed the double-rate declining balance depreciation formula beginning in 1954 and in mid-1962 reduced the useful life for tax purposes from eighteen years to fifteen years, which seems to be a reasonable estimate of the reduction brought about by the new guidelines. Thus, the 1954 depreciation acceleration is characterized here as a switch from the straight-line to the double-rate declining balance depreciation formula.[8]

'Consistent straight-line user cost' in Table 2 gives estimates of what user cost would have been after 1953 had no tax incentives been enacted during the period – that is to say, it is based on the straight-line depreciation formula; the tax life of assets is held constant at eighteen years; the tax rate is held constant at 52 per cent; and no allowance is made for the tax credit. 'Actual user cost' incorporates all tax incentives enacted during the period. A word should be said about the units in which user cost is measured. Consider, for example, the 1954 consistent straight-line figure, 17·47. This indicates that the implicit rental cost in 1954 of a unit of capital selling for

6. The estimated value of δ was 0·0271 per quarter, which implies that a unit of capital loses about 85 per cent of its real value in eighteen years.
7. Choosing an appropriate measure of 'the interest rate' raises many problems regarding the definition and measurement of the cost of funds to firms. Miller and Modigliani (1966) have discussed and solved many of these problems. They have found that for the electric utility industry the AAA bond yield is far superior to a weighted average yield on bonds and equities in predicting both the level of, and magnitude of changes in, the cost of funds. Whether or not this is also true in the manufacturing sector is unknown, since research in this important area is just beginning. I have decided to proceed as if it were true. I did experiment with other assumptions regarding the cost of funds and found that the results were not very sensitive to this choice.
8. This is not an inconsequential assumption. In my dissertation I have also carried out the calculations on the assumption that the 1954 depreciation acceleration was a shift from the straight-line to the sum-of-years-digits formula. While the fit of the investment relations is the same, the sum-of-years-digits variant yields considerably higher estimates of the effects of tax policy. I feel, however, that the declining-balance variant is the relevant one for two reasons. First, it is more popular than sum-of-years-digits. Second, businessmen were slow in adopting rapid write-offs (see Ture's (1967) evidence on this), which means that declining-balance, having a lower discounted value, probably approximates actual experience more closely.

$100 was $17·47 per year. The unit of measurement is not indicated in the heading of the table because user cost is just an index number.

The last column of Table 2 presents estimates of tax rate reductions that would have yielded reductions in user cost equal to those actually brought

Table 2 Consistent straight-line user cost and actual user cost, 1947–66

Year	User cost		Equivalent tax rate reduction
	Consistent straight-line	Actual	
1947	11·60	11·60	
1948	12·98	12·98	
1949	13·17	13·17	
1950	13·62	13·62	
1951	16·01	16·01	
1952	16·83	16·83	
1953	17·76	17·76	
1954	17·47	16·84	0·049
1955	18·08	17·42	0·049
1956	20·04	19·26	0·049
1957	22·81	21·85	0·047
1958	22·94	21·99	0·048
1959	24·93	23·83	0·047
1960	25·24	24·12	0·047
1961	25·23	24·11	0·047
1962[a]	25·28	24·16	0·048
1962[b]	25·16	22·67	0·122
1963	25·22	22·54	0·134
1964	25·80	22·14	0·194
1965	26·40	22·35	0·214
1966[c]	28·64	24·12	0·202

[a] Average of first two quarters expressed at annual rates
[b] Average of last two quarters expressed at annual rates
[c] Average of first three quarters expressed at annual rates

about by tax incentives. The results are certainly striking. For example, it would have taken roughly a 20 percentage point reduction in the tax rate (from 52 to 32 per cent) to bring about as large a reduction in user cost as that produced by the entire bundle of tax incentives! It is also interesting to examine the period from 1962 through 1966 more closely to assess the relative importance of various tax incentives in reducing user cost. Precise calculations would be tedious and difficult because of the many interaction effects. Rough calculations show that the new guidelines accounted for about 63 per cent of the reductions in 1962 and 1963, the remaining 37 per cent being attributable to the investment credit. As a result of the 1964 tax rate reduction, the increase in the equivalent tax rate reduction should have been about 2 percentage points in 1964, but the actual increase was of the order of 6 percentage points, which indicates the substantial impact of the 1964 change in the tax credit provision.

III The investment function

Two specifications of the investment function were used in investigating the importance of tax incentives. The first is a capital stock adjustment model with a constant adjustment speed, i.e.

Model 1: $I_t = \beta(K_t^* - K_{t-1}) + \delta K_{t-1}$,

where I is gross investment, β is the adjustment rate, K^* is the desired capital stock, and K_{t-1} is the actual capital stock at the end of period $t-1$. The parameter δ is the replacement rate and is assumed throughout to be equal to Jorgenson's estimate mentioned above. The second specification introduces cash flow as a determinant of the adjustment speed and can be written as

Model 2: $I_t = \left\{ \beta_1 + \beta_2 \dfrac{F_{t-1}}{K_t^* - (1-\delta)K_{t-1}} \right\} \{ K_t^* - (1-\delta)K_{t-1} \}$.

The expression $K_t^* - (1-\delta)K_{t-1}$ is the amount of gross investment needed during period t to attain the stock K_t^* by the end of the period; it is what might be called the investment chore. Model 2 is based on the notion that it is the level of internal funds relative to the investment chore that in part determines the adjustment speed.

Substituting for K_t its definition in terms of past investments, namely, $K_t = \sum_{i=0}^{\infty} (1-\delta)^i I_{t-i}$, and subtracting $(1-\delta)I_{t-1}$ from both sides of the relations, we obtain

$$I_t = \beta\{K_t^* - (1-\delta)K_{t-1}^*\} + (1-\beta)I_{t-1} \qquad\qquad 9$$

and $\quad I_t = \beta_1\{K_t^* - (1-\delta)K_{t-1}^*\} + (1-\beta_1)(1-\delta)I_{t-1}$

$$+ \beta_2\{F_{t-1} - (1-\delta)F_{t-2}\}. \qquad\qquad 10$$

A cost minimization hypothesis underlies the specification of the determinants of K^*. Because of substantial lags between placement of orders and final shipments, current and future demand for output is best reflected by new orders in most manufacturing industries. Given a projection of demand, a firm will minimize the costs of producing the associated level of output by equating the marginal rate of substitution between capital and labor to the ratio of their prices. Hence, the demand for capital depends on new orders and on the ratio of the user cost of capital to the wage rate. Actual values of new orders and factor prices are likely to contain both transitory and permanent elements. It is assumed that firms base their decisions on the permanent components and that the permanent components can be approximated by a weighted average of current and past values of the variables. The weighting scheme that produced the best results for each variable was a twelve-quarter inverted-V distribution.[9]

Let X_t and c_t' denote the permanent components of new orders and relative factor prices (c/w, where w is the wage rate) for period t. Then

$$K_t^* = a_0 + a_1 X_t + a_2 c_t' \qquad\qquad\qquad \textbf{11}$$

$$\text{and} \quad K_t^* - (1-\delta)K_{t-1}^* = \delta a_0 + a_1 \Delta X_t + a_2 \Delta c_t', \qquad\qquad \textbf{12}$$

where $\Delta X_t = X_t - (1-\delta)X_{t-1}$, etc. Substituting **12** into **9** and **10**, we obtain the investment functions that were estimated:

Transformed model 1: $I_t = \beta\delta a_0 + \beta a_1 \Delta X_t + \beta a_2 \Delta c_t' + (1-\beta)I_{t-1}$,

Transformed model 2: $I_t = \beta_1 \delta a_0 + \beta_1 a_1 \Delta X_t + \beta_1 a_2 \Delta c_t'$

$$+ (1-\beta_1)(1-\delta)I_{t-1} + \beta_2 \Delta F_{t-1},$$

where $\Delta F_{t-1} = F_{t-1} - (1-\delta)F_{t-2}$. All structural parameters are identifiable from these transformed relations.

The estimated relations fitted to quarterly OBE–SEC investment data for manufacturing are presented in Table 3. Two $\bar{R}^2$s (coefficients of multiple determination corrected for lost degrees of freedom) are presented for each relation, $\bar{R}^2_I$ measuring the relations ability to explain the level of investment and $\bar{R}^2_{\Delta I}$ measuring its ability to explain changes in investment. Because quarterly investment shows a very high first-order autocorrelation, the fit obtained by regressing I_t on I_{t-1} and anything else is bound to be quite high. The statistic $\bar{R}^2_{\Delta I}$ is, therefore, very useful in evaluating the relations.

The importance of the acceleration variable is confirmed in both models. The relation containing cash flow provides a much better fit to these data, and inclusion of cash flow greatly reduces the importance of the factor–price variable. Looking at the structural parameters derived from the

9. This distribution was first suggested and successfully tested by de Leeuw (1962).

regression coefficients, we find an adjustment speed for model 1 of about 11 per cent per quarter – a rather low figure in view of the fact that a long expectations lag is already imposed on the data. Model 2 gives a more reasonable result. If, for example, cash flow were about equal to the investment chore, the adjustment rate would be about 28 per cent per quarter;

Table 3 Investment regressions and structural parameters[a] – regression coefficients and t values

Model	Constant term	ΔX	$\Delta c'$	I_{-1}	ΔF_{-1}	$\bar{\bar{R}}^2_I$	$\bar{R}^2_{\Delta I}$
1	0·2529 (2·889)	0·1014 (4·901)	−3·122 (−3·752)	0·8892 (29·22)		0·975	0·460
2	0·1125 (1·295)	0·1211 (6·258)	−1·517 (−1·770)	0·8804 (31·93)	0·1802 (3·901)	0·980	0·560

Model	Structural parameters							
	β	β_1	β_2	a_0	a_1	a_2	$E_K{*}_X$	$E_K{*}_{c'}$
1	0·1108			84·22	0·915	−28·18	0·723	−0·579
2		0·0951	0·1802	43·65	1·273	−15·95	0·897	−0·292

[a] Sixty-seven observations, 1950/1 through 1966/3

but if cash flow were very small relative to the chore, the rate would be only 10 per cent per quarter. Model 2 also provides a more reasonable estimate of E_{K*X}, the elasticity of K^* with respect to $X : 0·897$ as opposed to $0·723$ for Model 1. It should also be noted that both models give much smaller elasticities for factor prices than for output; $E_{K*c'}$ is $−0·579$ for model 1 and only $−0·292$ for model 2.

IV Tax incentives and investment expenditures

According to the model developed in this study, a reduction in the user cost of capital will produce a one-shot increase in the desired stock of capital. The magnitude of the increase depends, of course, on the substitutability of capital and labor. Net investment expenditures will be increased for a number of periods, until the new desired stock of capital is attained, and replacement investment will be permanently increased, its new stationary value being $\delta \Delta K^*$ larger than its previous stationary value, where ΔK^* is the increase in the desired stock.

Table 4 presents estimates of the increases in the desired capital stock in manufacturing brought about by tax incentives. Table 5 gives annual estimates of the increases in gross investment expenditures resulting from tax incentives. As expected, the estimates of ΔK^* from the two models differ markedly: $8·6 billion for model 1 versus $4·9 billion for model 2 over the

Table 4 Increases in the demand for capital resulting from tax policy changes (millions o 1954 dollars)

Period	ΔK^*: Model 1	ΔK^*: Model 2
1954/1–1962/2	2496	1413
1962/3–1963/4	3372	1909
1964/1–1964/4	1960	1109
1965/1–1966/3	778	440
1954/1–1966/3	8606	4871

period studied. The higher value would imply an increase in the stationary level of replacement expenditures of about $0·9 billion per year; the lower value would imply a $0·5 billion increase in replacement.

The estimates in Table 5 give some idea of the timing of expenditures generated by increases in the desired capital stock. The estimates for model

Table 5 Investment attributable to tax incentives (millions of 1954 dollars)

Year	Model 1	Model 2	Actual investment
1954	103	72	11 065
1955	438	271	11 113
1956	624	340	13 690
1957	575	296	13 870
1958	551	268	9790
1959	495	228	9972
1960	455	198	11 928
1961	420	179	11 253
1962	377	262	11 954
1963	692	422	12 673
1964	1295	704	14 848
1965	1650	882	17 663
1966[a]	1287	689	15 476
sum: 54/1–62/2	3842	1965	98 518
sum: 62/3–66/3	5120	2846	66 777

[a] First three quarters only

2 take into account the influence of tax savings on the adjustment speed, but it seems that allowance for the cash flow effect is not enough to bring the predictions of the two models closer together. Model 1 gives larger estimates of the effects of tax incentives in terms of both capital stock and investment; it suggests that 5·4 per cent of total investment expenditures from 1954 to the third quarter of 1966 was accounted for by tax incentives. Model 2 suggests that just 2·9 per cent of total investment during this period can be attributed to tax incentives.

A decisive judgment on the effectiveness of tax incentives is impossible unless one is willing to pass judgment on the relative merits of the two investment models. As was noted above, model 2 provides a superior fit to the data used here and also gives more reasonable estimates of the adjustment speed and the elasticity of capital stock with respect to output. For these reasons model 2 should be preferred to model 1, and it appears that the smaller estimates in Tables 4 and 5 are the appropriate ones for evaluating tax incentives. They suggest that the performance of tax incentives has been disappointing. Policies that produced an estimated $5·1 billion (constant 1954 dollars) in tax savings in manufacturing from 1954 through mid-1962 increased manufacturing capital expenditures by only $2·0 billion during the same period, and policies that produced an estimated $8·6 billion in tax savings from mid-1962 through the third quarter of 1966 increased expenditures by only $2·8 billion. In terms of net additions to capital stock, which is perhaps a more sensible yardstick in view of the fact that under stationary conditions tax savings from accelerated depreciation would ultimately disappear (D would approach, but would never fall below, D^*) while gross investment would continue to be enlarged by the real amount of replacement generated by the increase in the desired capital stock, $13·7 billion in tax savings produced only a $4·9 billion growth in capital stock.

References

DE LEEUW, F. (1962), 'The demand for capital goods by manufacturers: a study of quarterly time series', *Econometrica*, vol. 30, pp. 407–23.

EISNER, R., and STROTZ, R. H. (1963), 'Determinants of business investment', in Commission on Money and Credit, *Impacts of Monetary Policy*, Prentice-Hall, pp. 59–337.

GREENBERG, E. (1964), 'A stock-adjustment investment model', *Econometrica*, vol. 32, pp. 339–57.

HICKMAN, B. G. (1965), *Investment Demand and US Economic Growth*, Brookings Institution.

HOCHMAN, H. M. (1966), 'Some aggregative implications of depreciation acceleration', *Yale econ. Essays*, vol. 6.

HUNTLEY, P. (1961), 'State distribution of manufacturers' plant and equipment in place, 1954–56', unpublished dissertation, University of North Carolina.

JORGENSON, D. W. (1963), 'Capital theory and investment behavior',
  Amer. econ. Rev., vol. 53, pp. 247–59.
MILLER, M. H., and MODIGLIANI, F. (1966), 'Some estimates of the cost of
  capital to the electric utility industry, 1954–57', *Amer. econ. Rev.*, vol. 56,
  pp. 333–91.
TURE, N. B. (1967), *Accelerated Depreciation in the United States, 1954–1960*,
  National Bureau of Economic Research, Fiscal Studies no. g, Columbia University
  Press.

9 M. S. Feldstein and J. S. Flemming

Tax Policy, Corporate Savings, and Investment Behaviour in Britain[1]

M. S. Feldstein and J. S. Flemming, 'Tax policy, corporate savings and investment behaviour in Britain', *Review of Economic Studies*, vol. 38, 1971, pp. 415–34.

Much of tax policy in Britain during the past two decades has been aimed at increasing investment. Britain pioneered the use of investment allowances several years before they were adopted in the United States. In addition during much of the period, tax incentives were used to reduce dividends and encourage corporate savings in the belief that this would increase investment spending. Despite this continuing interest in the use of tax policy to stimulate capital accumulation, there has been little analysis of the direct effect of investment allowances and no analysis of the indirect effect of changes in retention behaviour.

This paper reports a study of quarterly aggregate investment in equipment and structures for the period 1954/2 to 1967/4. The analysis builds on the powerful neoclassical investment theory developed and applied by Jorgenson and his collaborators (e.g. Fromm, 1971; Hall and Jorgenson, 1967, 1969; Jorgenson, 1963, 1965; Jorgenson and Siebert, 1968, and Jorgenson and Stephenson, 1967a) and, in modified form, by Bischoff (1969, 1971), Coen (1969) and Eisner and Nadiri (1968). The formulation used here differs from that of Jorgenson in several ways which will be explained below. Differences of particular importance for studying the effect of tax policy are that: (1) the elasticity of the desired capital stock with respect to tax-induced changes in the user cost of capital is not constrained to be one or even to equal the elasticities with respect to other observed changes in the user cost, and (2) the impact of tax induced changes in retention is explicitly studied.

Section I briefly reviews the previous studies and opinions on the impact of British tax policy on investment. Section II then presents the theory of investment behaviour which forms the basis of our estimates. The third section considers the estimation problems raised by this formulation. We present and discuss the estimates in section IV and then use them (in section V) to calculate both the effects that policy changes had on investment and the effects that alternative policies would have had. The results are sum-

1. We are grateful to Ann Black and Gary Chamberlain for research assistance.

marized in a brief final section. A description of the data is presented in an appendix.

I Previous studies and opinion[2]

On the basis of qualitative survey evidence in Corner and Williams (1965) and Hart and Prusmann (1963) and an informal analysis of the aggregate national income statistics, several economists – Little (1962), Williams (1966), Musgrave and Musgrave (1968) – have concluded that the investment allowances had a stimulating effect on capital accumulation. None of these discussions offered any estimate of the magnitude of the effect on either investment spending or the long-run capital intensity of production.[3] The impact of tax induced changes in retention behaviour has received even less attention. This is particularly surprising since the effect of retained earnings on company investment has long been an unresolved issue because of the usual multicollinearity among output, output change and retained earnings; the tax change provides a way of separating shifts in the equilibrium retention ratio[4] from transitory cyclical variations in retained earnings.[5]

II The model of investment behaviour

The formulation and implications of neoclassical investment theory are now very well known (see, for example, Jorgenson, 1963, 1965). If product

2. We limit our discussion here to empirical studies, excluding theoretical discussion of the expected impact of policies; see, for example, Black (1959).
3. Agarwala and Goodson (1969) recently estimated an annual investment equation (for the short period 1958 through 1966) and calculated the effect of investment incentives. Their specification – that gross investment is a linear function of the expected rate of return and the cash flow – makes it difficult to give any economic interpretation to their result. For example, a change in rate of return would have the same absolute effect on investment regardless of the scale of output. As a result of this specification, the cash flow variable is the only one that reflects the scale of the economy; it would therefore have a positive coefficient even if internal availability of funds as such had no economic effect. Although Balopoulos (1967) included an investment allowance variable in an equation that was part of a macroeconomic model of the British economy, the specification of the equation and the definition of the allowance variable cast doubt on any interpretation of his result.
4. Feldstein (1970) showed that British tax policy was successful in influencing corporate saving but did not investigate the implications for investment.
5. Despite the absence of research on this subject, there has been no dearth of opinions. The Royal Commission on Taxation (1955) argued against the then prevailing tax incentive for retention on the grounds that it 'does not encourage companies to plough back profits so much as to retain them ...' Balogh (1958) and Streeten (1960) concurred in this view while Musgrave and Musgrave (1968) and Williams (1966) suggested that greater internal availability of funds could stimulate investment.

and factor markets (including the market for old capital goods) are perfectly competitive, if the production function has constant returns to scale and a constant elasticity of substitution between capital and labour, and if capital is completely malleable, then the optimum capital stock at time t is

$$K_t^* = \mu^\sigma \left(\frac{p_t}{c_t} \right)^\sigma Q_t, \qquad\qquad 1$$

where Q_t is output, p_t is the product price, c_t is the user cost of capital, σ is the elasticity of substitution and μ is the coefficient of capital in the production function. In the special Cobb–Douglas case adopted by Jorgenson, σ is of course 1 and μ is the production function elasticity of output with respect to capital. The user cost of capital, which is equivalent to the price at which a unit of the capital good would rent in a competitive market, is equal to:

$$c = \frac{q(r+\delta)(1-A)}{(1-u)}, \qquad\qquad 2$$

where q is the purchase price of a unit of the capital good, r is the after-tax rate of return, δ is the constant proportional rate of actual depreciation, u is the rate of tax on company profits,[6] and A is the discounted value of the tax savings due to the depreciation allowances, investment credits, etc. which follow one 'dollar' of investment. By assuming that the current tax rates and depreciation provisions will remain unchanged and that the interest rate is either a short rate or will remain unchanged, the current values of the right-hand-side variables can be used to define c_t.

The dynamic response of net investment to changes in K^* and the capital replacement based on proportional depreciation together determine the path of gross investment. More specifically, Jorgenson has used a variety of dynamic adjustment patterns of the general form

$$K_t - K_{t-1} = \sum_{j=0}^{\infty} \gamma_j (K_{t-j}^* - K_{t-j-1}^*) + e_t. \qquad\qquad 3$$

Net investment is thus a distributed lag function of past changes in desired capital stocks, with weights reflecting ordering and delivery lags.[7]

6. In studying US investment, researchers have ignored the personal income tax and identified u as the corporation tax rate. As described below, we have used a combination of personal and company tax rates.

7. For a full justification of this lag structure, see, for example, Jorgenson (1965). In estimating equation 3, Jorgenson and his colleagues used the rational distributed lag model for the weights, i.e. the generating function of the γ_js was a ratio of polynomials. In practice, relatively low-order polynomials were statistically acceptable. More recently, Hall and Jorgenson (1971) found that they could not reject further restrictions on the generating function which implied that the estimating equation could be specified without lagged dependent variables and with the coefficients of the $(K_{-j}^* - K_{i-j-1}^*)$ variable constrained by an Almon lag procedure (Almon, 1965) to satisfy low-order polynomials.

The theoretical importance of Jorgenson's approach is that it develops empirical analysis of aggregate investment behaviour from an explicit model of optimization by firms. Its great practical strength is that adopting a specific microeconomic model simplifies estimation by limiting the form of the relation and restricting the parameter values. It is important, however, to investigate whether any questionable assumptions of the underlying model are crucial for the policy conclusions implied by the estimates. For example, Eisner (1969) and Eisner and Nadiri (1968) noted that, because a Cobb–Douglas production function entails unitary price elasticity of K^* with respect to c, Hall and Jorgenson (1967, 1969) have imposed rather than estimated the long-run effect of tax policy.[8] Bischoff (1969, 1971) and Eisner and Nadiri (1968) also criticized the dynamic specification for restricting the response structure to be the same for changes in all components of K^*.[9] In addition, all of the previous work assumed that each of the components of the user cost of capital was fully allowed for by the firm in the way suggested by equations 1 through 3. For example, none of the studies examined whether the interest rate is given more or less weight relative to the value of the depreciation allowance than the formula for c implies. Similarly, the time structure of the response to all of the cost variables was always assumed to be the same.

In planning this study we wished to avoid constraining the results by the assumptions of Cobb–Douglas technology, capital malleability and a perfect capital goods market. Without the last two assumptions, the optimal investment decision is no longer myopic: the future values of output, of tax and depreciation rates, of capital and the product prices, and of the interest rate must be taken into account.[10] Because these future values are unknown at the time of the investment decision, a fully developed model of investment behaviour would incorporate a theory of choice under uncertainty. Despite the need for a more complex model, and notwithstanding the sometimes acrimonious debate that has developed about the neoclassical investment function, we believe that the primary virtues of Jorgenson's formulation can be retained for empirical analysis. Rather than introduce

8. Agarwala and Goodson (1969) also implicitly constrain the effectiveness of the tax variable by assuming a Cobb–Douglas technology.
9. If the assumption of perfectly malleable capital is replaced by the putty-clay hypothesis (i.e. that the capital: output ratio of *old* equipment cannot be changed), the response to changes in output (Q) should be faster than the response to changes in the user cost of capital. This more general dynamic model cannot be tested in a framework of which equation 3 is a special case. When slightly different models in the neoclassical spirit were studied, the slower response to changes in the user cost of capital were observed (Bischoff, 1969, 1971), Eisner and Nadiri (1968).
10. Arrow (1964) and Tobin (1967) both noted the necessity of these assumptions for the myopic rules of Jorgenson's formulation.

a series of more specific assumptions to incorporate the desired generalizations,[11] we prefer to use several rather simple extensions of equations 1 and 2 as an approximation to the more general model.

In place of the *current* values of the variables that enter K^* in the myopic formulation, we consider short distributed lags.[12] More specifically, we replace the current output variable (Q_t) of equation 1 by an expression of the form:

$$Q_t^+ = (1+g^*)^{a_*}(1+g_t)^{a_0}(1+g_{t-1})^{a_1}...(1+g_{t-m})^{a_m}Q_t, \qquad 4$$

where g_{t-i} is the growth rate for the year ending in quarter $t-i$ and g^* is the expected long-run growth rate. This implies that the output level for which the firm plans its capital stock reflects recent growth rates as well as the current output level.[13] Similarly, each of the variables affecting the user cost of capital is also allowed to be either a single value or a short distributed lag.[14] More details will be given when the estimates are presented in section IV.

A second generalization of the standard neoclassical investment model is a less restricted definition of the relative cost of capital:

$$\left(\frac{c}{p}\right)^+ = \left(\frac{q}{p}\right)^{\beta_1}(r+\delta)^{\beta_2}(1-u)^{-\beta_3}(1-A)^{\beta_4}F^\lambda. \qquad 5$$

Permitting the βs to differ from unity recognizes that, for example, firms may not respond to changes in the value of allowances (A) in the same way as they do to other components of user cost; this extra generality is particularly important in view of the tax policies that are the focus of the current study. The variable F refers to the availability of internally generated funds; if $\lambda < 0$, the firm treats retained earnings as a less expensive source of funds than borrowing or new capital issues.[15] Including F in the

11. See Bischoff (1971) for an example of how restrictive such assumptions have to be.

12. In addition, as described below, we retain an adjustment model equivalent to equation 3.

13. The constant term $(1+g^*)^{a_*}$ plays no part in the empirical analysis but permits Q_t^+ to be generally equal to or greater than Q_t even if $\sum_0^m a_i < 0$.

14. There is evidence of substantial delay in the US in adopting favourable accelerated depreciation schedules; see Bischoff (1971). In Britain, dividend policy responded to changes in differential profits taxation with a lag (Feldstein, 1970). Helliwell and Glorieux (1970) emphasize that because of delivery lags the target capital stock of the current period reflects the decisions of previous years.

15. Duesenberry (1958) provides the most thorough discussion of why managers may treat retained earnings as a cheaper source of funds. See also Meyer and Kuh (1957), Eisner and Strotz (1963), Smith (1961) and Evans (1969, chapter 5). Note that including F as part of a general model is very different from the naive 'liquidity' model examined critically by Jorgenson and Siebert (1968). Although it

user cost of capital implies an effect on the optimal capital–output ratio and not just on the timing of investment. For this reason F should represent long-run changes in the internal availability of funds and not merely cyclical variations. One of the measures of F studied below, the ratio of company saving (retained earnings plus depreciation allowances) to trend output, is likely to be too sensitive to cyclical fluctuations even when averaged over several periods. The value of F may be better represented as a function of the optimal dividend payout rate implied by the current tax structure. This also facilitates estimating the effect of changes in payout policy induced by differential profits taxation. Feldstein (1967) estimated that $(D_t^*/Y_t) = k\theta_t^\eta$ where D_t^* is the optimal dividend level, Y_t is gross profits, θ_t is the differential tax parameter (i.e. the opportunity cost of retained earnings in terms of forgone dividends),[16] η is approximately 0·9, and k is a constant. It is most convenient to measure F by $(D_t^*/Y_t)^{-1}$, the inverse of the optimal payout ratio; using the previous approximation, this is computationally equivalent to replacing F by θ and its coefficient by $-\eta\lambda$.[17]

As a further generalization, the technology was not assumed to be Cobb–Douglas. Of course, if none of the βs in equation 5 is constrained to unity, separate estimates of σ and the βs cannot be obtained from the data. Even if the βs were all constrained to equal one, the increased complexity from allowing $\sigma \neq 1$ would be a very low price to pay for the benefit of not prejudging the long-run elasticity of K^* with respect to the user cost.[18]

Finally, we introduce a multiplicative error term (V_t) in the definition of K_t^* to allow for omitted variables and for the simplicity of our functional form. The result is:

$$K_t^* = \mu^\sigma \left[\frac{p^+}{c} \right]^\sigma Q_t^+ V_t. \qquad \qquad 6$$

---

would be theoretically more satisfactory to allow F to modify r and not $r+\delta$, computational difficulties prevent this.

16. The variable θ is defined by $\theta = (1-t_y)(1+t_d-t_y-t_u)^{-1}$ where: t_u = tax rate on undistributed profits; t_d = tax rate on distributed profits; t_y = 'standard rate' of income tax.

17. This also introduces an additional constant term, $k^{-\lambda}$ in equation 5.

18. Jorgenson and Stephenson (1967) argue that a large number of cross-section studies of US production data have shown that the elasticity of substitution is not significantly different from one. However the historical priority of the Cobb–Douglas function seems inadequate reason for granting it the status of null hypothesis and therefore accepting $\sigma = 1$ even though there is substantial variation in the point estimates of σ. Moreover, there is very little evidence on the elasticity of substitution for Britain. Cross-section estimates obtained with the reduced form procedure of Arrow et al. (1961) varied between 0·640 and 1·103; direct estimates for the same observations varied between 1·5 and 1·9 (Feldstein, 1967).

Our adjustment dynamics are represented by writing equation 3 as

$$K_t = \sum_{j=0}^{\infty} w_j K_{t-j}^* + u_t, \qquad 7$$

and imposing restrictions of the generating function of the w_js.[19] Although Jorgenson could use his very restricted definition of K^* to calculate the K^* values explicitly and then estimate quite complex lag structures, we must estimate the parameters of K^* and the lag structure simultaneously. The price of our quite general specification of K^* is the need to impose a more restricted structure of the w_js than the rational distributed lag model. Nevertheless, we can employ the Pascal distribution, a rich two-parameter class capable of representing a wide variety of lag patterns. The weights are given by $w_j = C_{r+j}^r \pi^j$ where $0 < \pi < 1$ and C_{r+j}^r is the combinatorial factor; the generating function of this lag structure is given by $(1-\pi L)^{-(r+1)}$ where L is the lag operator.

Equation 7 can therefore be written:

$$K_t = (1-\pi)^{r+1}(1-\pi L)^{-(r+1)} K_t^* + \xi_t. \qquad 8$$

Multiplying both sides of the equation by $(1-\pi L)^{r+1}$ yields

$$(1-\pi L)^{r+1} K_t = (1-\pi)^{r+1} K_t^* + (1-\pi L)^{r+1} \xi_t. \qquad 9$$

The simplest case of the Pascal distribution ($r = 0$) is the familiar geometric distribution; equation 9 then becomes:

$$K_t - \pi K_{t-1} = (1-\pi) K_t^* + (\xi_t - \pi \xi_{t-1}). \qquad 10$$

Higher values of r introduce more lagged values of K_t, implying that the weights first increase and then fall;[20] in our applications we studied $r = 0$, 1 and 2.[21]

Although the Pascal distribution is less versatile than the rational distributed lag, the combination of the Pascal distribution for the w_js and individual dynamic structures for the components of K^* provide what is in important ways a more general dynamic model. Our results indicate that this tradeoff was probably worth while.

19. Rewriting equation 3 as equation 7 changes the properties of the disturbance. If the e_ts of equation 3 are serially independent, the u_ts of equation 7 are not and vice versa. Jorgenson and his collaborators originally assumed the e_ts to be serially independent but tests by Bischoff (1969) showed this to be false. If it is assumed that for $t = 0$, $K_0 = K_0^* = 0$, there is no other difference between the 'first difference' form of equation 3 and the 'level' form of equation 7.
20. For a full discussion see Solow (1960) and Malinvaud (1966, pp. 480–81).
21. The results were mutually reinforcing in indicating that higher order structures were not necessary; the reasons for this will be clear when the estimates are presented in section IV.

Since the capital stock is generated by the relation $K_t = I_t + (1-\delta)K_{t-1}$, equations 7 to 9 can be replaced by investment functions of the form:[22]

$$I_t = \sum_{j=0}^{\infty} w_i K_{t-1}^* - (1-\delta)K_{t-1} + u_t. \qquad 11$$

In the case of the geometric lag this becomes

$$I_t = (1-\pi)K_t^* - (1-\delta-\pi)K_{t-1} + v_t, \qquad 12$$

and for the Pascal lag with $r = 1$

$$I_t = (1-\pi)^2 K_t^* - (1-\delta-2\pi)K_{t-1} - \pi^2 K_{t-2} + v_t. \qquad 13$$

III Estimation problems

Consider for simplicity the geometric distribution ($r = 0$); the estimation problems and methods discussed for this case are generalized in an obvious way to the Pascal distribution with $r > 0$. Combining equations 4, 5, 6 and 12, the equation to be estimated is:

$$I_t = Q_t \left\{ B \cdot \left[\left(\frac{q}{p}\right)^{\beta 1} (r+\delta)^2 (1-u)^{-\beta_3}(1-A)^{\beta_4}\theta^{-\eta\lambda} \right]^{-\sigma} \right.$$

$$\left. \left[\prod_j (1+g_{t-j})^{a_j} \right] \cdot V_t \right\} - (1-\delta-\pi)K_{t-1} + v_t, \qquad 14$$

where $B = \mu^\sigma k^{-\sigma\lambda}(1+g^*)^{a}*(1-\pi)$ and the other variables and parameters are defined in section II. For notational convenience in considering the estimation problems, we rewrite 14 as:

$$I_t = Q_t \cdot B Z_t^a V_t - (1-\delta-\pi)K_{t-1} + v_t. \qquad 15$$

Transferring the lagged capital stock to the left-hand side and dividing both sides by Q_t yields:

$$\frac{I_t + (1-\delta-\pi)K_{t-1}}{Q_t} = B Z_t^a V_t + \frac{v_t}{Q_t}. \qquad 16$$

Assume temporarily that $1-\delta-\pi$ is a known parameter; this permits postponing discussion of the problems introduced by the presence of a lagged dependent variable.[23] The equation to be estimated is non-linear and

22. This of course implies that the replacement investment component of gross investment is a constant proportion of the lagged capital stock. A recent study (Feldstein and Foot, 1971) indicates that this common assumption may be too simple and a source of error in estimating the determinants of *net* investment behaviour.

23. The lagged dependent variable problem is seen more clearly if I_t is rewritten as $K_t - (1-\delta)K_{t-1}$.

can be linearized by a logarithmic transformation only if the additive disturbance is ignored. Ignoring v_t would be equivalent to assuming that the errors in investment behaviour can be parametricized instead as multiplicative disturbances (V_t) in the levels of the optimal capital stock. Because there is no operational way of distinguishing a disturbance in K_t^* from an error in the adjustment path to K_t^*, respecifying the model without v_t should not raise serious objections. It is, however, reassuring to know that ignoring v_t/Q_t in the estimation even though it should be in the model can be shown to introduce no large-sample bias to a first-order approximation and is likely to introduce little bias to a second-order approximation.

Taking logarithms of both sides of equation **16** and expanding the right-hand side in a second-order Taylor's series around $BZ_t^a V_t$ yields:

$$\log \frac{I_t + (1-\delta-\pi)K_{t-1}}{Q_t} = \log B + a \log Z_t + \log V_t + \frac{v_t}{Q_t BZ_t V_t}$$

$$-\frac{v_t^2}{2(Q_t BZ_t^a V_t)^2}. \qquad \textbf{17}$$

The biases in the estimates of $\log B$ and a that result from ignoring v_t in a least squares regression can be easily calculated following Theil's (1961) analysis of bias due to omitted variables. To a first order approximation (i.e. ignoring the v_t^2 term), it is clear that there is no bias if v_t has mean zero and is independent of Z_t and K_t^*. Moreover, it may be reasonable to assume that the second-order bias is small: if v_t is not homoskedastic but has a standard deviation that is proportional to $K_t^* = Q_t BZ_t^a V_t$, the composite term $v_t^2/(Q_t BZ_t V_t)^2$ has constant expected value and only the estimate of the constant term $(\log B)$ is biased by omitting the second-order term.

We now drop the assumption that $1-\delta-\pi$ is known. The non-linear (logarithmic) transformation of the composite left-hand side variable of equation **16** precludes using Liviatan's (1963) instrumental variable method to obtain consistent estimates of all the parameters including the coefficient of the lagged dependent variable. The alternative common procedure of maximum likelihood estimation by a search technique is unsuitable in the current context because of the strong assumptions that must be made about the disturbances. If the disturbances are assumed to be normally distributed and serially independent, the minimum sum of squared residuals in a one-dimensional search over values of $1-\delta-\pi$ between 0 and 1 corresponds to maximum likelihood estimates of all the parameters. Since the composite disturbances are the result of multiplication by a lag operator and subsequent logarithmic transformation, neither normality nor serial independence is plausible. Even the assumption of first- or second-order autocorrelation, which would require a two- or three-dimensional search, is likely to be unduly restrictive. The usual method of maximum likelihood estimation would therefore not be appropriate.

Fortunately, however, in all of the equations studied we have been able to identify narrow ranges that contain consistent estimates of the basic long-run investment parameters. The basis for this is the fact that if the true value of $1 - \delta - \pi$ is substituted in the left-hand side, the least squares estimates of the other parameters are consistent regardless of the serial correlation or non-normality of the disturbances. In practice, the estimates of the long-run parameters were affected very little by varying $1 - \delta - \pi$ over a grid between 0 and 1. Since one set of these estimates is consistent and all the estimates are very similar, we can identify narrow ranges within which consistent estimates lie, even though we neither know nor can estimate the value of $1 - \delta - \pi$. In presenting the estimates in Section IV, such a range is presented for each parameter.

This solution to the estimation problem implies that we are not able to obtain information about the speed with which investment responds to changes in policy instruments. However, because this study is concerned with policies designed to have a long-run impact on capital formation rather than with stabilization, this is not a serious limitation.[24]

IV The parameter estimates

The results presented in this section indicate that both investment allowances and tax policies that induce higher retention ratios have a significant impact on investment behaviour. They also show that the generalized neoclassical model of equation 14 is much more satisfactory than the constrained version of equations 2 and 3. The estimated elasticities of K^* with respect to the several components of the user cost of capital differ substantially. Constraining them to be equal yields seriously misleading policy implications.

More specifically, the elasticity of K^* with respect to the allowance variable[25] is approximately 1 while the elasticity with respect to the composite user cost of capital is only about 0·3. This does not necessarily imply that the true long-run elasticity of K^* with respect to a 'permanent'

24. The estimation problems discussed in this section could be substantially simplified if the dynamic adjustment process of equation 7 were replaced by an analogous logarithmic equation,

$$\log K_t = \Sigma \, w_j \log K^*_{-j} + \xi_t.$$

However, as Jorgenson and Stephenson (1967) have argued, this is economically very different and no longer equivalent to the adjustment process specified in equation 3. Some preliminary experiments with this formulation showed the explanatory power to be very much lower and the coefficients less sensible.
25. The allowance variable is $1 - A$ where A is the present value of tax reductions due to depreciation, allowance, etc. which follow a 'dollar' of investment.

change in the value of any variable (such as p/q or $1-u$) is lower than one. A low estimated elasticity may indicate only that the *observed* variations in (p/q), r and $(1-u)$ are unrelated to changes in the relevant expected future values, even when polynomial distributed lags are used to extrapolate recent observations. Alternatively, the differences among the elasticities of K^* with respect to the components of the user cost variable may reflect suboptimal behaviour by firms.

This helps to reconcile the apparent conflict between Jorgenson and his followers who cite cross-section evidence that the elasticity of substitution of the production function is approximately one and Eisner and others who estimate that the price elasticity of demand for capital with respect to the composite user cost is very much lower. Even if *technology* is Cobb–Douglas, the *behavioural* elasticity of K^* with respect to observed user cost may be substantially less than one. To estimate and predict the effect of changes in the policy variables, it is necessary to estimate each elasticity separately. Neither an imposed technologically determined elasticity nor an estimated elasticity with respect to composite user cost will be correct.

Because the estimates to be presented indicate no reasonable and significant response to observed changes in (p/q), $(1-u)$ and $(r+\delta)$, we begin by considering equations in which these variables are held constant (i.e. ignored). We then study the effect of introducing them alone and in combination. Tables 1 and 2 relate to the geometric lag distribution; Table 3 presents estimates for higher-order Pascal distributions that show that the lag distribution has almost no effect on the estimated parameters of the demand for capital.

Table 1 presents parameter estimates for an equation of the form:

$$I_t = B \cdot Q_t^+ \cdot (1-A)^{-\beta\sigma\theta\eta\lambda\sigma} - (1-\delta-\pi)K_{t-1} \qquad 18$$

or, more explicitly,[26]

$$\log \frac{I_t + (1-\delta-\pi)K_{t-1}}{Q_t} = \log B + \sum_{j=0}^{7} a_j \log(1+g_{t-j})$$

$$-\beta\sigma \sum_{j=0}^{7} w_{1j} \log(1-A_{t-j})$$

$$+\eta\lambda\sigma \sum_{j=0}^{7} w_{2j} \log \theta_{t-j}. \qquad 19$$

26. Each g_{t-j} is the rate of growth of output for the four quarters ending in period $t-j$. A_{t-j}, defined in the previous footnote, reflects the law prevailing in quarter $t-j$. Similarly θ_{t-j} is the effective opportunity cost of retained earnings in terms of forgone dividends in quarter $t-j$.

Table 1

Equation	Output change Σa_j	Tax incentive $\eta\gamma\sigma$	Allowance $-\beta\sigma$	Revised allowance $-\beta\sigma$	Output change a_0	a_3	Tax incentive $\eta\gamma\sigma \cdot w_{22}$	$\eta\gamma\sigma \cdot w_{24}$	Revised allowance $-\beta\sigma \cdot w_{12}$	IGF	SER	R^2
1·1	−2·84 (0·52) [−2·49, 2·92]	−0·14 (0·061) [−0·12, −0·14]	−1·74 (0·17) [−1·72, −1·74]	—	—	—	—	—	—	—	0·040 [0·039, 0·042]	0·78 [0·77, 0·79]
1·2	−1·95 (0·15) [−1·67, −2·02]	−0·15 (0·015) [−0·15, −0·16]	—	−1·39 (0·032) [−1·38, −1·42]	—	—	—	—	—	—	0·011 [0·011, 0·014]	0·98 [0·97, 0·98]
1·3	−1·71 (0·25) [−1·51, −1·79]	−0·12 (0·030) [−0·12, −0·12]	—	—	—	—	—	—	−1·28 (0·061) [−1·28, −1·31]	—	0·022 [0·022, 0·024]	0·93 [0·93, 0·93]
1·4	−1·49 (0·19) [−1·05, −1·59]	—	—	−1·29 (0·041) [−1·28, −1·29]	—	—	−0·056 (0·026) [−0·026, −0·062]	−0·046 (0·026) [−0·045, −0·052]	—	—	0·015 [0·015, 0·021]	0·97 [0·95, 0·97]
1·5	—	−0·14 (0·017) [−1·14, −0·15]	—	−1·34 (0·035) [−1·33, −1·39]	−0·95 (0·096) [−0·93, −1·05]	−0·63 (0·093) [−0·56, −0·64]	—	—	—	—	0·012 [0·012, 0·014]	0·98 [0·98, 0·98]
1·6	−2·06 (0·33) [−1·38, −2·21]	—	—	−1·17 (0·043) [−1·17, −1·18]	—	—	—	—	—	0·0038 (0·051) [−0·011, 0·0073]	0·020 [0·019, 0·022]	0·95 [0·93, 0·95]

The lag weights (a_js, w_{1j}s and w_{2j}s) are constrained to satisfy a second-order polynomial with the final weight (an 8 quarter lag) equal to zero; the w_{1j}s and w_{2j}s are assumed to sum to one.[27]

To save space, only the sums of the individual estimates are presented; i.e. $\Sigma\, a_j$, $\beta\sigma$ and $\eta\lambda\sigma$. The top line for each equation gives estimates corresponding to $\delta+\pi = 0.75$. The standard errors are given in parentheses immediately below the estimates. The square brackets indicate the minimum and maximum values of the coefficients obtained as $\delta+\pi$ was varied over six values from 0.05 to 0.95. The column headed SER gives the standard error of the regression for $\delta+\pi = 0.75$. and, in brackets, the range of SERs as $\delta+\pi$ varies over the six values. The final column presents similar information for the corrected coefficient of determination ($\bar{R}^2$). For each equation in Table 1, varying $\delta+\pi$ had almost no effect on either the long-run parameter estimates or the standard error of the regression.[28]

Equation 1.1 indicates that, for any current level of output, there is a negative elasticity of derived output capacity (Q_t^+) with respect to recent increases in output; i.e. the estimates of $\Sigma\, a_j$ range from -2.49 to -2.92. This implies that firms neither ignore nor extrapolate the very recent growth path but rather assume that deviations from the long-run trend are primarily cyclical. Since the distributed lag refers to eight quarterly observations on annual growth rates or three years of growth, $\Sigma\, \hat{a}_j = -2.84$ implies that an increased growth during the past three years has approximately no effect on Q^+; e.g. a one per cent increase in the growth rate raises Q_t by three per cent after three years but Q_t^+ rises by less than 0.5 per cent. If the higher growth rate is sustained longer, the effect through Q_t outbalances the cyclical effect through $\Sigma\, a_j$. Although the relation between historical output levels and desired output capacity is only tangential to the current study and will not be discussed further in this paper, the observed non-myopic determination of Q^+ and K^* deserves more careful study by those who develop investment equations for forecasting purposes.

The estimated elasticity with respect to the user cost of capital as affected by the allowance variable is large and highly significant. The estimates are very insensitive to $\delta+\pi$; $-\hat{\beta}\hat{\sigma}$ ranges between -1.72 and -1.74; the individual weights (w_{1j}s) generally decline over the eight lag periods. The value of $\hat{\beta}\hat{\sigma}$ is surprisingly high, possibly unrealistically so if β is assumed to

27. The equations were estimated using a modification of the Almon polynominal distributed lag procedure (Almon, 1965) developed by Robert Hall and incorporated into the Harvard version of a programme entitled Time Series Processor.
28. The internal structure of the lag distributions did change as $\delta+\pi$ was varied. The changes indicated that the time response can be estimated more accurately than the complete agnosticism with respect to $\delta+\pi$ suggests. Because the remaining uncertainty is still great and the issue of timing tangential to our primary concern, we shall not pursue this further.

be approximately one. We believe that the high value in this equation is spurious and will return to discuss this in considering equation 1.2 below.

The negative estimated elasticity with respect to the tax variable θ indicates that tax inducements for higher retention are successful in increasing capital accumulation. There are two aspects to assessing the actual magnitude of this effect: the change in investment and the change in the desired capital–output ratio. Because the elasticity of dividends with respect to θ is approximately 0·9 (Feldstein, 1970) and the retained earnings plus capital consumption allowances were approximately twice dividends,[29] the long-run effect of a 10 per cent decrease in θ would be a 9 per cent decrease in dividends and a 4·5 per cent rise in internally available funds. The estimated coefficient indicates that a 10 per cent fall in θ would raise the equilibrium capital–output ratio, and therefore the equilibrium rate of gross investment, by only 1·4 per cent. Since gross fixed investment is approximately equal to internally available funds, the comparison of 1·4 per cent and 4·5 per cent implies that about two-thirds of the effect of tax changes on retained earnings is offset by a change in the use of external funds. Despite this dilution of the effect of taxes, the historical variation in θ has implied economically important changes in capital formation. When the tax differential was ended in 1958, raising θ from 0·66 to 1·00, the desired capital–output ratio (K^*/Q^+) fell by more than six per cent. This would have both a substantial impact on investment during the adjustment period and an important long-run effect on output per man.[30,31]

Examining the observed and fitted values of investment corresponding to this equation indicated an important misspecification. For the period from the first observation in the period of fit (1954/2) through 1955/4, observed investment was always substantially higher than the fitted values; after that date there ceased to be any systematic difference. This pattern suggested a misspecification of the allowance variable. In 1954, the 'initial allowances' were generally replaced by 'investment allowances' that in effect permitted more than 100 per cent depreciation. These remained in effect until 1956/1 when the original initial allowances were reinstated. The pattern of residuals indicates that some firms failed to recognize that the investment allowance

29. Higher during the period of differential taxation.
30. The large size of this tax effect can also be seen by calculating the change in the interest rate that would alter K^*/Q^+ by six per cent. If technology is Cobb–Douglas, K^*/Q^+ rises by six per cent when $(r+\delta)$ falls by six per cent. If $r+\delta \geqq 0·16$ per cent, the net rate of interest (r) must fall by more than one per cent. The effect of the differential tax system was therefore roughly equivalent to a one per cent fall in the net rate of interest or somewhat more than a two per cent fall in the gross rate of interest.
31. It should be noted that, unlike changes in depreciation allowances, θ can be used to increase investment without any reduction in tax collections.

M. S. Feldstein and J. S. Flemming 219

was more valuable or were very slow to respond to the change. To reflect this we replaced the actual allowance values through 1956/1 with a linear interpolation between the 1952/1 value (0·27) and the 1956/1 value (0·30). The result was to end the systematic divergence between actual and fitted values of the dependent variable during the early observations and to substantially lower the standard error of the regression in each equation.

The revised allowance variable is therefore used in equation 1.2 and all subsequent equations. The output change coefficient (Σa_j) is somewhat lower but still indicates a substantial correction for cyclical variation in output. The tax coefficient $(\eta\lambda\sigma)$ is almost identical but has a very much smaller standard error. The revised allowance elasticity $(-\beta\sigma)$ ranges between $-1·38$ and $-1·42$, showing a substantial impact of allowances on investment behaviour. Although these coefficients are significantly greater than one, they do not necessarily conflict with the assumption of Cobb–Douglas technology $(\sigma = 1)$ since β may exceed 1. There are two reasons for this. First, higher allowances increased the flow of internally available funds which may have had an independent positive effect on investment. Second, the frequent changes of the allowance rate may have induced firms to try to concentrate investment expenditures on periods in which rates were high by accelerating investment when allowance rates were raised and postponing when they were expected to rise in the future. The estimates of approximately $-1·4$ may therefore reflect the timing of government policy; more frequent changes, and particularly more decreases, might have resulted in an even greater responsiveness.[32,33]

Equations 1.3 through 1.5 show that none of the conclusions based on 1.2 are altered if the distributed lags are replaced by simpler dynamic structures. In 1.3 the revised allowance variable is represented by a single observation lagged two periods; in terms of equation 15, $w_{12} = 1$ and $w_{1j} = 0$ for $j \neq 2$. The resulting estimates $(-1·28$ and $-1·31)$ are very close to the previous range, reflecting the substantial autocorrelation in the allowance series. Equation 1.4 measures the tax impact by two lagged values, θ_{t-2} and θ_{t-4}. The sum of their coefficients is somewhat less than when a full distributed lag is used but the basic quantitative implications are unchanged. Similarly, in 1.5 the output change is measured by two observations, g_t and

32. Note that this is exactly opposite to the view stated by the Royal Commission (1955) and endorsed by Williams (1966) that varying the allowance rates would reduce the effectiveness of this instrument.
33. In general, the coefficients estimate the way firms responded to the actual variation in the explanatory variables and not the way they might respond to a very different time pattern of exogenous variable changes. This is of course a quite general problem; the coefficients of a simple accelerator model would become inappropriate if the sales of a firm ceased to be highly autocorrelated and became a purely random series.

g_{t-3}, and the sum of their coefficients is slightly less than with the distributed lag. In each of these three equations, replacing one of the distributed lags leaves the other coefficient sums essentially unchanged.

Equation 1.6 replaces the tax variable by a direct measure of internally available funds: IGF is a four-quarter average of internally generated funds divided by the trend level of output. The extremely low and completely insignificant estimated elasticities may reflect this method of measuring available funds, the inadequacies of the basic data,[34] the use of output as a deflator, or the possibility of simultaneous equations bias. In any case, the estimate is in striking contrast to the significant elasticity with respect to the tax variable. If the estimate is accepted as correct, this contrast suggests that K^* is unaffected by the substantial transitory cyclical variation of IGF and responds only to long-run shifts in the retention ratio such as that caused by changes in the tax variable.[35]

The equations in Table 2 show that introducing the other components of user cost (r, q and u) and the price of output produces unsatisfactory results, especially when all the coefficients are constrained by the user cost of capital formulation to imply a single price elasticity of demand for K^*. Equation 2.1 corresponds to the 'pure' neoclassical formulation

$$\log \left\{ \frac{I_t + (1-\delta-\pi)K_{t-1}}{Q_t} \right\} = \log B + \Sigma\, a_j \log (1+g_{t-j})$$

$$-\sigma \Sigma\, w_{1j} \cdot \log \left(\frac{c}{p} \right)_{t-j}$$

in which all the variables affecting the cost of capital services are constrained to operate through a single user cost variable, $c_2 = q_t(r_t+\delta)(1-A_t)/(1-u_t)$. The equation is a generalization of the original Jorgenson formulation; the price elasticity (σ) is not constrained to 1 and recent growth of output is taken into account. The estimates of σ, ranging between $+0\cdot38$ and $+0\cdot49$, are reminiscent of the values obtained for US data with similarly formulated equations (Eisner and Nadiri, 1968; Coen, 1969). However, because this equation hides the high elasticity with respect to the allowance variable it explains investment very much less well than the equations of Table 1; the standard error of the estimate is more than six times larger than for equation 1.2.

Equation 2.2 indicates that constraining the allowance variable to be

34. The *quarterly* series of company savings involves a somewhat arbitrary allocation of dividends and earnings over the year.
35. It should be noted that the current formulation does not test whether cyclical variation in the availability of funds affects the timing of investment.

Table 2

Equation	Output changes	Tax incentive [θ]	Revised allowance [1−A]	Deflated user cost [c/p]	Price ratio [a/p]	User cost per £ of capital goods $\frac{(r+\delta)(1-A)}{(1-u)}$	Gross required return $\frac{(r+\delta)}{(1-u)}$	Net required return [r+δ]	Tax rate [1−u]	SER²	R²
2·1	−2·26 (0·75) [−2·23, −2·36]	—	—	−0·40 (0·10) [−0·38, −0·49]	—	—	—	—	—	0·071 [0·070, 0·071]	0·31 [0·29, 0·40]
2·2	−2·02 (0·53) [−1·98, −2·17]	0·28 (0·12) [0·19, 0·30]	—	−0·23 (0·16) [−0·19, −0·41]	—	—	—	—	—	0·050 [0·050, 0·054]	0·66 [0·66, 0·67]
2·3	−0·72 (0·32) [−0·69, −0·82]	0·24 (0·070) [0·14, 0·26]	—	—	−3·27 (0·34) [−3·19, −3·61]	0·33 (0·11) [0·17, 0·37]	—	—	—	0·028 [0·028, 0·033]	0·90 [0·88, 0·90]
2·4	−1·66 (0·13) [−1·51, −1·82]	−0·16 (0·021) [−0·16, −0·16]	−1·60 (0·094) [−1·60, −1·61]	—	0·77 (0·26) [0·46, 0·84]	—	—	—	—	0·011 [0·011, 0·016]	0·98 [0·97, 0·98]
2·5	−1·75 (0·18) [−1·69, −1·98]	−0·082 (0·042) [−0·052, −0·210]	−1·25 (0·08) [−1·18, −1·58]	—	—	—	0·10 (0·06) [−0·075, −0·140]	—	—	0·015 [0·014, 0·017]	0·97 [0·97, 0·97]
2·6	−1·34 (0·21) [−1·33, −1·41]	−0·23 (0·05) [−0·20, −0·38]	−1·44 (0·11) [−1·38, −1·75]	—	—	—	—	0·13 (0·10) [−0·014, −0·160]	0·24 (0·10) [0·17, 0·51]	0·012 [0·011, 0·014]	0·98 [0·98, 0·98]

a Output change is measured by two values (g_t and g_{t-8}), as in equation 1·5 instead of the 8 quarter distributed lag part of the user cost of capital causes the tax variable to enter with the wrong sign. Equation 2.3 shows that splitting $\log(c/p)$ into $\log(q/p)$ and $\log[(r+\delta)(1-A)/(1-u)]$ has implausible results: an unreasonably high negative elasticity with respect to q/p and a positive elasticity with respect to the other components of cost.

Equation 2.4 shows that the previous coefficient of (q/p) reflected the use of a composite cost of capital variable and the exclusion of the allowance variable as such. When r and u are held constant, as in 2.4, the allowance, tax and output change variables appear as they did in the equations of Table 1. The elasticity with respect to the relative price variable is positive and therefore still implausible. It seems most sensible to conclude that the observed variation of the price ratio is not closely enough related to expectations about future movements on which firms act to have any explanatory value. In the presence of substantial uncertainty, short-run relative price variations contribute too little information to have an economic impact. This variable will therefore be ignored in subsequent equations.

The required gross rate of return $[(r+\delta)/(1-u)]$ is introduced in equation 2.5 where it is completely insignificant. When the required net rate of return $(r+\delta)$ and the tax variable $(1-u)$ are separated in equation 2.6, the rate of return variable has the wrong sign (positive).[36]

Table 3 presents estimates for the more general second- and third-degree Pascal distributed lags.[37] Again the value of $\delta+\pi$ is varied over six values in the interval from 0·05 to 0·95. To conserve space, not all estimates are presented. For each value of $r+1$, the table indicates the *range* of estimates of each of the parameters. Because the estimates corresponding to low values of $\pi+\delta$ (i.e. $\pi+\delta = 0·05$ and, for $r+1 = 3$, also $\pi+\delta = 0·25$) generally differed substantially from the others, these estimates are shown separately. Wherever there is a substantial difference in the estimates, the equation corresponding to low $\pi+\delta$ values are markedly inferior in terms of explanatory power.

The basic implication of Table 3 is that using more general distributed lags does not alter the conclusions based on the geometric lags of Tables 1 and 2. Equation 3.1 corresponds to the most satisfactory of the previous specifications, equation 1.2. The new estimates are very close to those obtained with the geometric lag, although generally slightly lower in absolute

36. This coefficient may be biased because r is measured as a nominal rate rather than a real rate; for estimates of the magnitude of this bias and evidence that it could account for the incorrect sign, see Feldstein (1970a). Unfortunately, the possible importance of this bias was recognized only after the estimation for this paper was completed.
37. I.e. for $r+1$ equal to 2 and to 3 in the lag operator generating function $(1-\pi L)^{-(r+1)}$; the geometric lags considered in Tables 1 and 2 correspond to $r+1 = 1$.

Table 3

Equation	r+1	π+δ	Output change	Revised allowance [1−A]	Tax incentive [θ]	Deflated user cost [c/p]	S E R	R²
3.1	2	0.25 to 0.95	−1.62 (0.21), −1.74 (0.14)	−1.28 (0.038), −1.31 (0.057)	−0.10 (0.027), −0.12 (0.018)	—	[0.012, 0.018]	[0.96, 0.98]
		0.05	1.91 (2.05)	−1.24 (0.54)	−0.16 (0.25)		0.17	0.21
	3	0.35 to 0.95	−1.71 (0.18), −1.77 (0.15)	−1.28 (0.038), −1.30 (0.047)	−0.11 (0.022), −0.12 (0.018)	—	[0.012, 0.015]	[0.97, 0.98]
		0.25	−1.22 (0.98)	−1.32 (0.26)	−0.10 (0.12)		0.082	0.53
3.2	2	0.25 to 0.95	−1.29 (0.76), −1.58 (0.75)	—	—	−0.21 (0.086), −0.28 (0.080)	[0.078, 0.080]	[0.13, 0.13]
		0.05	2.02 (1.69)			−0.29 (0.19)	0.18	0.10
	3	0.35 to 0.95	−1.45 (0.76), −1.58 (0.75)	—	—	−0.21 (0.086), −0.22 (0.087)	[0.078, 0.080]	[0.13, 0.13]
		0.25	−1.02 (1.06)			−0.27 (0.12)	0.11	0.087
		0.05	2.69 (5.99)			0.014 (0.69)	0.63	0.02
3.3	2	0.25 to 0.95	−2.54 (0.60), −2.62 (0.61)	—	0.16 (0.13), 0.24 (0.12)	−0.28 (0.17), −0.43 (0.17)	[0.049, 0.051]	[0.67, 0.68]
		0.05	−0.48 (2.09)		−0.54 (0.42)	−1.34 (0.58)	0.17	0.23
	3	0.35 to 0.95	−2.54 (0.60), −2.61 (0.61)	—	—	−0.28 (0.17), −0.36 (0.17)	[0.049, 0.050]	[0.68, 0.68]
		0.25	−2.49 (1.14)		−0.080 (0.23)	−0.57 (0.32)	0.093	0.39
		0.05	10.53 (7.73)		1.04 (1.55)	2.52 (2.15)	0.63	0.075

value.[38] The elasticity with respect to the allowance variable is approximately -1.3 and with respect to the tax incentive variable it is -0.11. The ratio of desired capacity output to current output is negatively related to the recent growth rates. Equation 3.2 is the 'pure' neoclassical investment function slightly generalized by including recent output growth rates. The results are similar to equation 2.1 but the estimated price elasticity of demand for capital is even lower (approximately 0.22 in comparison to 0.40) and the explanatory power of the equation even worse. The specification of equation 3.3 is analogous to 2.2 and confirms that when the measure of the tax incentive to retain is introduced into the 'pure' neoclassical equation 3.2 it has the wrong sign and leaves the equation substantialy worse than the more general specification 3.1.

In summary, our results show that both the investment allowances and the tax incentive for increased retention had substantial impact on investment. The generalized neoclassical investment function is substantially better than the 'pure' neoclassical function in which all variables affecting the cost of capital services are constrained to operate through a composite user cost variable. Such constraints are misleading; the resulting estimates understate the effect of investment allowances, ignore the effect of retained earnings and overstate the effect of the other components of user cost.

V Simulations of alternative policies

This section assesses the effects on capital formation of the changing allowance (A) and tax (θ) policies since 1952. The potential impact of alternative policies is also evaluated. These simulations measure only the direct effects of the policy variables; the indirect effects through changes in aggregate output and in the market rates of interest are ignored. All of the simulations use the parameter estimates of equation 1.2. Detailed results are presented for the response corresponding to $\pi + \delta = 0.95$; this implies that the capital stock responds to a change in desired capital stock with a mean lag of approximately seventeen quarters. This speed is similar to the estimates by Hall and Jorgenson (1967) for the United States; they found mean lags of five to eight quarters for equipment and fifteen to thirty quarters for structures. Less detailed results are also presented for the more rapid response corresponding to $\pi + \delta = 0.75$. It should be remembered that, in both cases, there is an additional distributed lag of up to seven quarters in the response of the desired capital stock to changes in the underlying variables.

Three different allowance policies were considered. Policy A1 corresponds to the actual time path of all the explanatory variables: the adjusted

38. No estimate is presented for $r + 1 = 3$ and $\pi + \delta = 0.05$ because the equation had no explanatory ability.

allowance variable rises slowly in the early years, has large increases in 1959 and 1962, and decreases slightly in 1966. Policy A2 keeps the allowance variable at the 1952 value of 0·27 for the entire interval while policy A3 uses the highest value (0·41, actually reached in 1962) for the entire interval. For each simulation, the actual values of θ as well as of the non-policy variables are used while the lagged values of the capital stock are generated endogenously.

The results are presented in Table 4; to conserve space, only the value for the final quarter of each year is given. The A1 policy shows substantial rises

Table 4 Investment predicted by alternative allowance policies

Period	£ million at constant prices, quarterly rate		
	A1	A2	A3
1954/4	321	297	746
1955/4	358	313	704
1956/4	383	323	668
1957/4	373	311	611
1958/4	376	299	561
1959/4	429	264	485
1960/4	488	240	430
1961/4	513	284	473
1962/4	472	275	446
1963/4	559	250	398
1964/4	548	244	381
1965/4	643	342	508
1966/4	561	354	519
1967/4	599	425	612

in investment after the allowance variable increases of 1959 and 1962. The A2 simulation shows that the rate of investment would have been very much lower throughout the period without the changes in investment allowances. If the most generous depreciation policy (A = 0·41) had been adopted in 1953 (as in simulation A3), the rate of capital formation would have been substantially greater during the 1950s than that which actually prevailed, somewhat lower during the first half of the 1960s and approximately equal thereafter.

The simplest measure of the effect of the different allowance policies is a comparison of the capital stock growth over the entire period from 1954/4 to 1967/4. In 1958 prices, the relevant capital stock was £20 600 million in

1954/4. By 1967/4, the actual constant price capital stock was £37 880 million; this is matched almost exactly by the A1 simulation, £38 007 million. In comparison, the A2 simulation indicates a capital stock in 1967/4 of only £29 506 million while the expansionary A3 policy indicates a capital stock of £40 387 million. With no change in depreciation policy after 1953 (i.e. A2), the capital stock would have grown 49 per cent less than with the actual depreciation policy while the immediate change of policy (A3) would have increased the capital stock growth by 14 per cent.

Very similar overall results are obtained when a more rapid rate of adjustment ($\pi+\delta = 0.75$) is assumed. The final capital stocks are now: £37 965 million (A1), £28 899 million (A2) and £39 297 (A3). The paths of investment differ substantially between the $\pi+\delta = 0.95$ and the $\pi+\delta = 0.75$ simulations. In particular, the more rapid response ($\pi+\delta = 0.75$) implies implausibly high rates of investment in the early 1950s and extremely volatile gross investment series corresponding to policies A2 and A3. Although the simulation corresponding to the actual policy (A1) did not imply any implausible behaviour, the correlation between the predicted and actual gross investment series ($r = 0.70$) was lower than for the corresponding simulation for the slower response speed ($r = 0.95$).[39]

Four different tax policies affecting the retention of profits were examined. Policy T1 corresponds to the actual time path of all the explanatory variables: the θ variable varies between 0.741 and 0.680 until the end of differential profits taxation in 1958, then rises to 1.00 where it remains until the corporation tax introduced a differential that lowered θ to 0.59 in 1966. The T1 simulation is of course exactly the same as the A1 simulation. Policy T2 is the same as T1 until 1958 but then, instead of discontinuing the differential, it maintains $\theta = 0.680$ for the remaining years. The result, shown in Table 5, is a substantially higher level of investment during the 1960s (until 1967 when the effect of the actual 1966 tax change has made its impact). Policy T3 keeps the original 1953 tax differential ($\theta = 0.733$) for the entire period. The corresponding investment falls slightly below the actual level in the late 1950s in response to the actual fall in θ but is then higher during the 1960s. Capital formation is of course not as great as with policy T2. Finally, policy T4 has no differential taxation, i.e. $\theta = 1$ for the entire period. The implied investment is substantially lower than the T1 policy for the 1950s; during the 1960s (when the values of θ are the same) the investment is lower with T1 reflecting the greater previous accumulation of capital.

A comparison of the final period capital stocks is again informative. In comparison to the T1 stock of £38 007 million, not ending the differential in

39. This suggests an approach to choosing among the different response speeds but we shall not pursue this further here.

1957 (T2) implies a capital stock of £40 103 million. The constant differential at $\theta = 0.733$ (T3) produces a capital stock of £39 628 million while the constant no differential policy (T4) indicates a capital stock of £37 601 million.[40] The effect on capital formation of differential taxation can there-

Table 5 Investment predicted by alternative differential taxation policies

Period	£ million at constant prices, quarterly rate			
	T1	T2	T3	T4
1954/4	321	321	321	259
1955/4	358	358	357	301
1956/4	383	383	384	334
1957/4	373	373	373	329
1958/4	376	376	361	322
1959/4	429	424	407	369
1960/4	488	549	533	492
1961/4	513	619	604	561
1962/4	472	563	550	512
1963/4	559	645	631	591
1964/4	548	624	612	574
1965/4	643	719	707	664
1966/4	561	652	641	603
1967/4	599	559	549	517

fore be considerable: with no differential, the capital stock increased 82·5 per cent in thirteen years while with the expansionary T2 policy the increase is 94·7 per cent. It should be remembered that, unlike the allowance policies, differential taxation changes reflected in θ need not reduce tax revenues.

VI Summary

This paper has used a generalized neoclassical investment function to assess the effects of tax policy on investment in Britain during the period from 1954 through 1967. The estimates show that both the accelerated depreciation allowances and the use of differential taxation to induce the retention of corporate profits had substantial and significant impacts on investment behaviour.

The generalized neoclassical investment function relaxes the assumption

40. The capital stock accumulation with the more rapid response ($\pi + \delta = 0.75$) were quite similar: £37 965 million (T1), £39 616 million (T2), £39 062 million (T3) and £36 850 million (T4).

that the price elasticities of the desired capital stock with respect to the components of the user cost of capital are all equal. The time patterns of each price response and of the response to increased output are also not constrained to be the same. Both generalizations are shown to be important. The constrained 'pure' neoclassical investment function yields misleading results; the estimates understate the effect of investment allowances, ignore the effect of retained earnings and overstate the effect of the other components of user cost.

Simulations with the investment equation showed that the increases in depreciation allowances accounted for approximately 45 per cent of net capital accumulation in the period after 1954. Until differential profits taxation ended in 1958, it raised annual investment by some £240 million or about 15 per cent of gross investment. If differential profits taxation had not been abandoned in 1958, the capital stock would have been greater when the corporation tax reintroduced a retention incentive in 1966. In short, both types of tax policy had important effects on capital accumulation.

Appendix
Data definitions and sources

Investment (I_t) is gross fixed capital formation in manufacturing, construction, distribution and other services. *Economic Trends* (1969) presents this data seasonally adjusted in constant 1958 pounds for the period after 1956/1. For earlier quarters, the series was calculated from unadjusted data at current prices as published in *Economic Trends* (1958).

Capital stock (K_t) is calculated from the capital stock identity, $K_t = (1-\delta)K_{t-1}+I_t$. The value of δ was estimated by requiring that the capital stocks for 1954 and 1967 in 1958 prices, as reported in the 1967 *National Income and Expenditure*, be consistent with the investment series and the capital stock identity.

Output (Q_t) is constructed from the indices of industrial production for manufacturing, construction, distribution and other services as reported in *Economic Trends* (1968) for the period 1958/4 to 1967/4. For the earlier years, it was necessary to use an annual index of real GDP derived from the *National Income and Expenditure* Blue Book and interpolate to obtain quarterly figures; output in manufacturing, construction, distribution and other services accounts for about eighty per cent of GDP.

The rate of return (r_t) is a weighted combination of equity and debenture yields quoted in the *Monthly Digest of Statistics*. For debentures, the 'flat yield' on irredeemable industrial debentures was used for 1952/1 through 1962/4. From 1965/1, redemption yields on twenty-year industrial debentures are used with a correction of 0·4 percentage points based on a comparison of long-term and irredeemable government bonds. For the interval from 1963/1 to 1964/4, the redemption yield on long-term government bonds, with an adjustment of 1·1 percentage points inferred from relative levels in 1961–2, was used.

The relative price variable (p_t/q_t) is the ratio of the price index for total output to the price index for fixed assets. Annual data in the *National Income and Expenditure* Blue Book was interpolated to a quarterly basis.

The tax rate (u_t) is the rate of tax on the income of a company with the average pay-out ratio. This reflects the income, profits and corporation tax rates. The tax differential (θ_t) is the opportunity cost of retained earnings in terms of forgone dividends; see footnote 16 for a more specific definition. The tax rates are presented in the annual *Report of the Commission of Inland Revenue*.

The allowance variable (A_t) is the discounted value of the tax savings due to depreciation, investment allowances and initial allowances. Depreciation is based on the allowable diminishing balance rate of depreciation and the discount rate is a constant ten per cent. The allowance variable is a weighted average of the appropriate value for each asset class weighted by its average share in the relevant gross investment over the period.

References

AGARWALA, R., and GOODSON, G. C. (1969), 'An analysis of the effects of investment incentives on investment behaviour in the British economy', *Economica*, vol. 36, pp. 377–88.

ALMON, S. (1965), 'The distributed lag between capital appropriations and expenditures', *Econometrica*, vol. 33, pp. 178–96.

ARROW, K. J. (1964), 'Optimal capital policy, the cost of capital, and myopic decision rules', *Ann. Inst. stat. Math.*, vol. 16, nos. 1–2, Tokyo.

ARROW, K. J. *et al.* (1961), 'Capital–labor substitution and economic efficiency', *Rev. econ. Stat.*, vol. 43, pp. 225–50.

BALOGH, T. (1958), 'Differential profits tax', *Economic J.*, vol. 68, pp. 528–32.

BALAPOULOS, E. T. (1967), *Fiscal Policy Models of the British Economy*, North-Holland.

BISCHOFF, C. W. (1969), 'Hypothesis testing and the demand for capital goods', *Rev. econ. Stat.*, vol. 51, pp. 354–68.

BISCHOFF, C. W. (1971), 'The effect of alternative lag distributions', in G. Fromm (ed.), *Tax Incentives and Capital Spending*, Brookings Institution, North-Holland.

BLACK, J. (1959), 'Investment allowances, initial allowances and cheap loans as a means of encouraging investment', *Rev. econ. Stud.*, vol. 27, pp. 44–9.

COEN, R. M. (1968), 'Effects of tax policy on investment in manufacturing', *Amer. econ. Rev.*, vol. 58, pp. 200–211.

COEN, R. M. (1969), 'Tax policy and investment behavior: comment', *Amer. econ. Rev.*, vol. 59, pp. 370–79.

CORNER, D. C., and WILLIAMS, A. (1965), 'The sensitivity of business to initial and investment allowances', *Economica*, vol. 32, pp. 32–47.

DUESENBERRY, J. S. (1958), *Business Cycles and Economic Growth*, McGraw-Hill.

EISNER, R. (1969), 'Tax policy and investment behavior: comment', *Amer. econ. Rev.*, vol. 59, pp. 379–88.

EISNER, R., and NADIRI, M. I. (1968), 'Investment behavior and neoclassical theory', *Rev. econ. Stat.*, vol. 50, pp. 369–82.

EISNER, R., and STROTZ, R. H. (1963), 'Determinants of business investment', in Commission on Money and Credit, *Impacts of Monetary Policy*, Prentice-Hall, pp. 59–337.

EVANS, M. (1969), *Macroeconomic Activity*, Harper & Row.

FELDSTEIN, M. S. (1967), 'Alternative methods of estimating a CES production function for Britain', *Economica*, vol. 34, pp. 384–94.

FELDSTEIN, M. S. (1970), 'Corporate taxation and dividend behaviour', *Rev. econ. Stud.*, vol. 37, pp. 57–72.

FELDSTEIN, M. S. (1970a), 'Inflation, specification bias and the impact of interest rates', *J. pol. Econ.*, vol. 78, pp. 1325–39.

FELDSTEIN, M. S., and FOOT, D. K. (1971), 'The other half of gross investment: replacement and modernization expenditures', *Rev. econ. Stat.*, vol. 53, pp. 49–58.

FROMM, G. (ed.), (1971), *Tax Incentives and Capital Spending*, Brookings Institution, North-Holland.

HALL, R. E., and JORGENSON, D. W. (1967), 'Tax policy and investment behavior', *Amer. econ. Rev.*, vol. 57, pp. 391–414.

HALL, R. E., and JORGENSON, D. W. (1969), 'Tax policy and investment behavior: reply and further results', *Amer. econ. Rev.*, vol. 59, pp. 388–400.

HALL, R. E., and JORGENSON, D. W. (1971), 'The quantitative impact of tax policy on investment expenditures', in G. Fromm (ed.), *Tax Incentives and Capital Spending*, Brookings Institution, North-Holland.

HART, H., and PRUSMANN, D. F. (1963), 'A report of a survey of management accounting techniques in S. E. Hants Coastal Region', Mimeo.

HELLIWELL, J. F., and GLORIEUX, G. (1970), 'Forward-looking investment behaviour', *Rev. econ. Stud.*, vol. 37, pp. 499–516.

JORGENSON, D. W. (1963), 'Capital theory and investment behavior', *Amer. econ. Rev.*, vol. 53, pp. 247–59.

JORGENSON, D. W. (1965), 'Anticipations and investment behavior', in James S. Duesenberry *et al.* (eds.) *The Brookings Quarterly Econometric Model of the United States*, Rand McNally, pp. 35–94.

JORGENSON, D. W. (1966), 'Rational distributed lag functions', *Econometrica*, vol. 34, pp. 135–49.

JORGENSON, D. W., and SIEBERT, C. D. (1968), 'A comparison of alternative theories of corporate investment behavior', *Amer. econ. Rev.*, vol. 58, pp. 681–712.

JORGENSON, D. W., and STEPHENSON, J. A. (1967), 'The time structure of investment behavior in United States manufacturing, 1947–1960', *Rev. econ. Stat.*, vol. 49, pp. 16–27.

JORGENSON, D. W., and STEPHENSON, J. A. (1967a), 'Investment behavior in US manufacturing, 1947–1960', *Econometrica*, vol. 35, pp. 169–220.

LITTLE, I. M. D. (1962), 'Fiscal policy', in G. D. N. Worswick and P. H. Ady (eds.), *The British Economy in the Nineteen-Fifties*, Clarendon Press.

LIVIATAN, N. (1963), 'Consistent estimation of distributed lags', *Inter, econ. Rev.*, vol. 4, pp. 44–52.

MALINVAUD, E. (1966), *Statistical Methods in Econometrics*, Rand McNally.

MEYER, J. R., and KUH, E. (1957), *The Investment Decision: An Empirical Study*, Harvard University Press.

MUSGRAVE, R. A., and MUSGRAVE, P. B. (1968), 'Fiscal policy', in R. E. Caves *et al.*, *Britain's Economic Prospects*, Brookings Institution, pp. 21–67.

ROYAL COMMISSION (1955), *The Taxation of Profits and Income*, HMSO.

SIMS, C. (1969), 'The role of prior restrictions in distributed lag estimation', Harvard Institute of Economic Research, Discussion Paper no. 60.

SMITH, V. L. (1961), *Investment and Production*, Harvard University Press.

SOLOW, R. M. (1960), 'On a family of lag distributions', *Econometrica*, vol. 28, pp. 396–406.

STREETEN, P. (1960), 'Tax policy for investment', *Rivista di diritto Finanziario e Scienza delle Finanza*, vol. 19, pp. 117–37.

THEIL, H. (1961), *Economic Forecasts and Policy*, North-Holland.

TOBIN, J. E. (1967), 'Comment on Crockett-Friend and Jorgenson', in *Determinants of Investment Behaviour*, National Bureau of Economic Research, New York, p. 156.

WILLIAMS, A. (1966), 'Great Britain', in *Foreign Tax Policies and Economic Growth*, a Conference Report of the National Bureau of Economic Research and the Brookings Institution, Columbia University Press, pp. 397–467.

10 M. A. King

Taxation and Investment Incentives in a Vintage Investment Model[1]

M. A. King, 'Taxation and investment incentives in a vintage investment model', *Journal of Public Economics*, vol. 1, 1972, pp. 121–47.

I Introduction

In recent years the literature on the econometrics of investment behaviour has been centred on two approaches. First, there are the models employing the accelerator and capital stock adjustment principles, and, second, there is the work '*à la* Jorgenson' (e.g. Jorgenson, 1963) in which investment is determined by the optimal path of the capital stock, which in turn is derived from a Cobb–Douglas production function and the usual 'neoclassical' competitive assumptions. As an alternative to these models this paper attempts to develop an investment function from a vintage production model.

One of the principal aims of the model is to analyse the effect of investment incentives and taxation, and so careful attention is paid to the measurement of the value of the tax benefits and investment incentives. Two empirical questions are examined in this paper. First, the effect of investment incentives on fixed investment expenditure, and, secondly, whether there is any long-run shifting of taxation via its effects on investment plans.

In order to do this it was felt necessary to develop a model which differed in several respects from the two approaches mentioned above, the most important difference being the separation of the influence of relative factor prices from the expansion of output. Models based on the flexible accelerator do not take explicit account of factor prices, and thus are not amenable to a discussion of the effect of investment incentives. On the other hand, Jorgenson's model can be criticized on the grounds that there is no independent test of the influence of factor prices since the cost of capital is subsumed within the accelerator term. Coen (1969) obtained very different results using a CES production function, and Thurow

1. An earlier version of this paper was presented to the Second World Congress of the Econometric Society in September 1970, and was awarded the Stevenson Prize at the University of Cambridge. I am very grateful to the following for many helpful comments and criticisms; Tony Atkinson, Christopher Dougherty, David Livesey, Mario Nuti, Roger Tarling and the referees.

(1969), using a modified form of Jorgenson's function to allow for disequilibrium behaviour, found that the results implied implausible values for the parameters of the production function. A more generalized neoclassical model has been developed by Feldstein and Flemming (1971) who relax the assumption that the technology is Cobb–Douglas and test the influence of output changes and the cost of capital separately. In much the same spirit this paper analyses investment behaviour in the context of a vintage production model. A vintage model has been proposed by Bischoff (1971) but he assumes constant returns to scale and that a constant proportion of existing capacity is scrapped each year. This means that the age of the oldest plant in use does not appear as a variable in his model.

Thus an alternative model is developed below; the theoretical model itself is set out in section II, and in section III some of the conceptual problems involved in analysing the impact of investment incentives and taxation are discussed. The model is fitted to data for UK manufacturing industry for the period 1948–68, and the results are presented in section IV.

II The model

We shall explore the investment decision in the context of a model with oligopolistic product markets in which each firm minimizes the costs of producing an exogenously given level of output, subject to a minimum constraint on the rate of return which it expects to earn on new investment. The technology of the firm is embodied in the vintage framework of the model.

Oligopolistic product markets mean that profit maximization is ambiguous and we assume that firms minimize the cost of producing a given level of output which corresponds to the expected demand they would like to satisfy. The concept of a real or 'imagined' demand curve is replaced by a target level of output. This is not an implausible representation of the behaviour of firms operating in oligopolistic markets where, in the face of uncertainty about the policies of rivals, firms decide on a certain desired level of output for the planning period and minimize the cost of producing this level of output. For example, a firm may wish to maintain, or to reach, a fixed market share. Uncertainty about future demand and cost conditions and the knowledge that, whatever the future turns out to be, it will almost certainly not be a future of steady-state growth, forces firms to limit their time horizon. Let the average gestation period be x periods. Then we assume that firms forecast the level of 'normal' demand which they would like to be able to satisfy x periods ahead without running down or building up stocks. It is the expected level of 'normal' demand, rather than actual demand, which is relevant since firms may be quite happy to plan to meet a temporary increase in demand from stocks. Therefore, they minimize the expected cost of meeting 'normal' demand.[2] The alternatives are either to invest in new equipment or to use existing plant which, if demand is expected to increase, means bringing back into use machines of progressively older vintages. We assume that there is a reserve of retired plant which could be brought back into use if firms thought it profitable to do so, and for simplicity the cost of maintaining reserve plant is assumed to be zero. The choice between investing in new plant and using existing equipment depends on their relative costs. The costs of using new plant are composed of the wage bill and an imputed capital cost which we take to be equal to the price of a machine times a given immediate rate of profit which firms require to earn if they are to invest. This immediate rate of profit (denoted by ρ) represents the constraint on the target rate of return on new investment.[3] If the expected level of quasi-rents is constant for the first n years of the plant's life, then the expected immediate rate of profit is equal to the reciprocal of the pay-off period provided this is less than, or equal to, n years. Furthermore, faced with an uncertain future, firms use the current values of factor prices in order to compute expected future costs.[4]

Armed with these assumptions we may now develop the model formally. We assume a putty-clay technology where the *ex-ante* production function for each vintage is assumed to be of the Cobb–Douglas form:

$$y_v = AI^b\, n_v^c, \qquad\qquad\qquad 1$$

where y_v = output from machines of vintage v; I_v = gross investment at constant prices in machines of vintage v; n_v = number of men employed on machines of vintage v.

We shall impose no condition on the degree of returns to scale. The objection that the Cobb–Douglas production function assumes an implausibly high elasticity of substitution does not apply in a vintage model, where the desired 'stickiness' in substitution possibilities is achieved by the putty-clay assumption. Yet we retain the attractive features of the Cobb–Douglas form such as constant distributive shares in steady-state growth.

Let $Y(v)$ be the total output which the firm plans to supply, and $T(v)$ the age of the oldest plant which it plans to utilize to produce this

2. A decision rule of this sort, formulated as a reaction to uncertainty, does not necessarily conflict with an optimal strategy derived from maximizing the firm's utility over an infinite time horizon (see Arrow, 1964).
3. By taking ρ to be a constant we are assuming away the problems which arise if the expected rate of increase in the wage–price ratio changes over time, and firms thus require a different return on capital while the plant is new.
4. Stanback (1969) in a study of firms in the American textile industry found that in every case for which information was supplied firms behaved in this way.

output – note that T is a variable. If y_τ is the total output from machines of vintage τ, then[5]

$$Y(v) = \sum_{v-T(v)}^{v} y_\tau. \qquad 2$$

Total output is given exogenously as

$$Y(v) = \bar{Y}_v. \qquad 3$$

The total costs of producing $Y(v)$ are composed of (a) the operating costs of using old plant which are assumed to be equal to wage costs, and (b) the total costs of new plant which comprise wage costs and capital costs. According to our hypothesis capital costs of new plant are equal to the immediate required rate of profit, ρ, times the money value of investment, $p_I I_v$, i.e. the price index of investment goods multiplied by investment at constant prices.

If the money wage rate is w then total costs of production, C, are given by

$$C(v) = \rho p_I I_v + w \sum_{v-T(v)}^{v} n_\tau. \qquad 4$$

To minimize total costs subject to the constraint that total output equals the sum of outputs of all vintages in use we form the following Lagrangian:

$$L(I_v, n_v, T(v), \lambda) = \rho p_I I_v + w \sum_{v-T(v)}^{v} n_\tau + \lambda(\bar{Y}_v - \sum_{v-T(v)}^{v} y_\tau), \qquad 5$$

where λ is the Lagrange multiplier. Thus the necessary conditions for a minimum are

$$\rho p_I - \frac{b\lambda y_v}{I_v} = 0, \qquad 6$$

$$w - \frac{c\lambda y_v}{n_v} = 0, \qquad 7$$

$$wn_{v-T} - \lambda y_{v-T} = 0. \qquad 8$$

Equations 6 and 7 yield

$$\frac{I_v}{n_v} = \frac{b}{c}\frac{w}{\rho p_I}, \qquad 9$$

and equations 7 and 8 give

$$cy_v/n_v = y_{v-T}/n_{v-T}. \qquad 10$$

5. A more detailed analysis of a vintage production model in which the variables are described by a continuous distribution function, rather than a discrete density function as here, may be found in Cass and Stiglitz (1969).

Equation **9** is the usual neoclassical condition for cost minimization, namely that the ratio of marginal products equals the ratio of relative factor prices, since in our model $w/\rho p_I$ is the wage–rental ratio. Although the neoclassical condition is usually derived in cases where all the output is produced on equipment whose capital–labour ratio can be varied at will, it applies equally to the case of a putty-clay vintage model. However, the condition on the marginal products now refers to the capital intensity of new plant only.[6] The other first-order condition, which is given by equation **10**, states that the marginal product of labour on new equipment must be equal to the output per head on the oldest plant. This is because in addition to the possibility of substituting capital for labour on new plant we are free to substitute labour on new plant for labour on old plant. Thus equation **10** is the boundary or 'scrapping' condition of the model.[7]

Now let Y'_v be the level of output which the firm plans to produce on existing plant and so output in excess of Y'_v is to be met by installing new capacity. Therefore $y_v = \bar{Y}_v - Y'_v$.

Let $U_v(Y)$ be the unit operating costs at the margin, where Y is the output produced on existing plant. Thus:

$$U_v(Y'_v) = wn_{v-T(v)}/y_{v-T(v)} \,. \tag{11}$$

The form of the function U_v will depend upon the past history of investment about which we, as economists, have little information. In a vintage model this is inevitable but we do know two things about $U_v(Y)$:

1 $U_v(0) = m_v$, the unit labour costs on the most recent plant $m_v = wn_{v-\theta}/Y_{v-\theta}$ where $\theta = \max t$ for which $I_{v-\tau} = 0; 0 \leqslant \tau \leqslant t$;

---

6. It is still true that the average capital–labour ratio can be altered by changes at either the forward or backward margins.

7. The scrapping condition is usually stated in terms of the price of output, p; if we assume full-cost pricing then using equation **9** it is possible to show that $zw = cpy_v/n_v$ where z is the degree of returns to scale at the optimum point. From equation **10** this gives

$$\frac{zwn_{v-T(v)}}{y_{v-T(v)}} = p.$$

Thus the perfectly competitive scrapping condition that plant is scrapped when quasi-rents fall to zero only applies if there are constant returns to scale. We may note that if there are decreasing returns to scale on new plant cost-minimizing firms may employ machines which yield negative quasi-rents. Since profit-maximizing firms facing a downward-sloping demand curve will scrap plant before quasi-rents fall to zero then there will, in general, be no unique scrapping condition applicable to all firms.

2 The *ratio* of unit labour costs on any two vintages which have already been installed must be constant – the putty-clay assumption, thus

$\dfrac{U_v(Y_i)}{U_v(Y_j)}$ is independent of m for all $i, j < v - \theta$.

Since the function U_v depends on m then for this condition to hold $U_v(Y)$ must decompose into

$$U_v(Y) = f(m)g(Y),$$

where f is a function only of m, and g is a function only of Y and is historically determined by the profile of past vintages. Since $U(O) = m$ then by substituting into **11** and taking limits as $\theta \to O$ we have

$$\frac{wn_v}{y_v} g(Y'_v) = \frac{wn_{v-T(v)}}{y_{v-T(v)}}.$$

Thus using equation **10**

$$Y'_v = g^{-1}(\tfrac{1}{c}). \tag{12}$$

We have shown that both Y'_v and $\bar{Y}_v$ are independent of the investment decision, and therefore y_v is determined exogenously to the model of cost minimization. From **1** and **9** by taking logarithms we have

$$\log I_v = k + \frac{1}{b+c} \log y_v + \frac{c}{b+c} \log \left(\frac{w}{\rho p_1} \right), \tag{13}$$

where $k = (1/b+c)\,(c \log b/c - \log A)$.

Thus we have now specified the investment function in terms of variables which are exogenous to the investment decision model. Moreover this function is separable in the following sense; namely that the influence of relative factor prices and the expansion of output are represented by separate terms. However, it is impossible to specify exactly an investment equation in a vintage model because, as economists, we do not have the requisite information on the level and productivity of past investment in each vintage. Log y_v is a complex function of the expected increase in output, the form of the function depending upon the past history of investment about which we have little precise information. In some cases the shape of the function g will lead to replacement echoes; in others, output plans will be influenced by the market structure. The specification will depend upon the individual case and the information available. It is as well to state this rather than claim universal validity for any one specification.

III Taxation and investment incentives

The experience of the UK provides a good opportunity to study the effect of fiscal policy on investment. Direct incentives to invest have comprised both cash grants and several kinds of tax allowances. The system of company taxation has also changed several times altering the extent to which it discriminated against distributed profits. Up until 1958, companies in the UK paid, in addition to the standard rate of income tax, a rate of profits tax which was higher on that portion of profits distributed than on that retained. When the differential profits tax was abolished in 1958 this discrimination disappeared, only to reappear with the introduction of corporation tax in 1965. Bearing this in mind let us turn to the question of how to incorporate taxation and investment incentives into the model.

We shall first develop the model to allow for the effects of taxation. In Section II we derived an investment function which contained ρ, the required immediate rate of profit. In this behavioural sense ρ should be defined as the post-tax rate of profit. But in our expression for the relative costs of using new and old plant the ρ used there refers to the pre-tax rate of profit, as can be seen by interpreting equation 4 as the 'required revenue' for the firm to invest an amount I_v. The question is whether, in the face of an increase in the tax rate, firms reduce their required post-tax rate of profit and simply aim at a given pre-tax rate of return on new investment, or maintain the same desired post-tax rate of profit and alter their investment plans accordingly. To test this we introduce a variable, a, which, in the particular sense defined above, can be described as the coefficient of long-run tax shifting.[8] If we write the behavioural value of the required rate of profit as $\bar{\rho}$, then the pre-tax rate of profit which this implies is

$$\rho = \bar{\rho} + at\rho,$$

where t = tax rate on profits; a = coefficient of long-run tax shifting; $0 \leqslant a \leqslant 1$, $a = 0$ for zero shifting of the tax, $a = 1$ for full shifting of the tax.

In 13 we replace ρ by $\bar{\rho}/(1-at)$.

Thus $\log I_v = k' + \dfrac{1}{b+c} \log y_v + \dfrac{c}{b+c} \log \left(\dfrac{w}{p_1}\right) + \dfrac{c}{b+c} \log (1-at),$ **14**

where $k' = k - \dfrac{c}{b+c} \log \bar{\rho}.$

We cannot estimate linearly equation **14** as it stands because a is an unknown parameter.[9] So we use the expansion of $\log (1+x)$ to approximate

8. 'Long-run', not because of any time lags involved but because it relates to tax shifting in the context of investment and expansion.
9. Since it was desired to estimate a large number of regression equations using different specifications, alternative tax rates, and several values for the discount rate (see below), it was felt to be too expensive in computer time to use a nonlinear estimation method. Consequently the estimates of the shifting parameter obtained by using the logarithmic approximation are biased.

log $(1-at)$ by $(-at)$ since both a and t are fractions.[10] Thus **14** becomes

$$\log I_v = k' + \frac{1}{b+c} \log y_v + \frac{c}{b+c} \log \left(\frac{w}{p_1}\right) - a\left(\frac{c}{b+c}\right) t. \qquad \textbf{15}$$

In this way the model yields a method of estimating long-run tax shifting coefficients; *a priori* we would expect the coefficient of the tax rate to be negative and to lie between 0 and -1.

Tax shifting is normally thought of in a short-run sense when, assuming the capital stock to be constant, the effects of tax changes on prices and profits are examined. Although our model says nothing about short-run shifting it does provide a possible link between the concept of long-run shifting and the effect of tax changes on pricing policy. Suppose that to earn a certain immediate rate of profit on new plant, firms adopt a 'full-cost' pricing policy where the 'full-costs' are the total unit costs of using new plant. Then it can be shown quite easily,[11] that if we assume equal rates of inflation in the capital goods sector and in the particular sector concerned (for example in a study of pricing behaviour in manufacturing as a whole), then

$$\dot{p} = \dot{w} - \gamma + \frac{b}{1-b}\left(\frac{a}{1-at}\right)\Delta t, \qquad \textbf{16}$$

where $\dot{p}$ = rate of growth of prices, $\dot{w}$ = rate of growth of money wages, γ = a variable approximately equal to the trend growth rate of output per man, Δt = incremental change in tax rate.

10. $\log(1+x) = x - \dfrac{x^2}{2} + \dfrac{x^3}{3} - \dfrac{x^4}{4}$, with $-1 < x \leqslant 1$.

11. For full-cost pricing the selling price p is given by

$p = (wn_v + \rho p_I I_v)/y_v$.

If we assume the *ex-ante* production function is given by $y_v = A e^{av} I_v{}^b n_v{}^c$ then by using equation **9** and differentiating the resultant expression for p logarithmically we obtain $\dot{p} = -a + (1-b-c)\dot{n}_v + (1-b)\dot{w} + b\dot{\rho} + b\dot{\rho}_I$ where we denote the rate of growth of a variable by a dot over the variable. Assuming equal rates of inflation in the capital goods sector and the sector whose price we are looking at (i.e. $\dot{p} = \dot{p}_I$) then

$$\dot{p} = \dot{w} - \gamma + \frac{b\dot{\rho}}{1-b},$$

where $\gamma = \dfrac{a}{1-b}\left(\dfrac{1-b-c}{1-b}\right)\dot{n}_v$.

It can be seen from the *ex-ante* production function that γ is the steady-state growth rate of output per man if the labour force is growing at a rate $\ddot{n}_v$ and is therefore approximately equal to the trend rate of growth of output per head. Since $\rho = \dot{p}/(1-at)$ we have

$$\dot{p} = \dot{w} - \gamma + \frac{b}{1-b}\frac{a}{1-at}\Delta t.$$

240 Effects of Tax Policy

Equation **16** bears an obvious relationship to the kind of econometric price equation estimated by, amongst others, Neild (1963), where price increases are related to wage increases minus the trend growth rate in labour productivity. However, our price equation also includes tax rates and we may illustrate the effect of tax changes on prices by the following numerical example. Consider an increase in the tax rate of 5 percentage points from 45 per cent to 50 per cent and let $b = 1/3$. If the tax increase is fully passed on, i.e. $a = 1$, then our equation implies that prices will rise by 4·5 per cent.

Before testing the model of tax shifting given by equation **15** we must settle a conceptual problem as to which is the relevant tax rate to use in a model of investment behaviour. As was mentioned above the relative rates of tax on distributed and undistributed profits have changed several times in the post-war period, and so we may distinguish three concepts of the appropriate tax rate. First, it might be thought that if management calculates the post-tax benefits to shareholders then it will be interested in the ratio of retentions plus *net* dividends to taxable income. This concept has been used by Harcourt (1968) and by Feldstein and Flemming (1971). An alternative hypothesis is that management views the distribution of post-tax income as a choice between retained profits and gross dividends, and so it may regard the relevant tax rate as that concerning the ratio of retentions plus *gross* dividends to taxable income. This approach was adopted by Agarwala and Goodson (1969). But managements may evaluate projects with reference only to the effect on retained profits. The tax penalty on distributed profits may be regarded as something which can be passed on to the shareholder. Taxation of distributed profits is the tax burden borne by shareholders, and taxation of retentions falls on the profits available to management for fixed investment, take-overs, or other uses. In this case the relevant tax rate for evaluating investment projects is the rate on retained profits.

It is tempting to call these three tax rates, which we may denote by t_A, t_B and t_C, the 'shareholder', 'mixed', and 'managerial' rates respectively. However, there are strong theoretical grounds for believing that all firms, regardless of their motivation, will consider the tax rate t_C to be the appropriate rate to use when forming their investment plans, and regard any tax penalty on dividends as something which falls on shareholders. To see this we shall first construct a model of the tax system. The total tax liability of a company,[12] TL, is given by

$$\text{TL} = t_C (P-A) + \frac{1-\theta}{\theta} D, \qquad\qquad 17$$

12. Defined to be the total corporation or profits tax liability plus the income tax liability of the shareholders.

where $P =$ gross income; $A =$ capital allowances deductible for tax purposes; $D =$ net dividends; $t_C =$ rate of tax which would be paid if no profits were distributed;[13] $\theta =$ opportunity cost of retained earnings in terms of net dividends foregone, i.e. the amount of net dividends which shareholders could have received if one pound of retained earnings had been distributed. This is determined by the extent to which the tax system discriminates against distributed profits. If cash in the hands of the company and cash in the hands of the shareholder can be interchanged without attracting an additional tax liability then there is no discrimination, and the value of θ is one. If θ is less than one then dividends are taxed more highly than retentions, and vice versa.

Equation **17** states that the amount of tax payable by a company is equal to the amount of tax which must be paid even if nothing is distributed, plus the extra element of tax which arises as a result of paying dividends when dividends are taxed more highly than retentions. Since θ is the opportunity cost of retentions in terms of net dividends then $1-\theta/\theta$ is the extra tax paid if one unit of net dividends is distributed.

If we denote retained profits by R then the appropriation of gross income is given by the identity

$$P \equiv D+R+T. \qquad \qquad \textbf{18}$$

Combining equations **17** and **18** we have

$$D = \theta \{(1-t_C)P+t_CA-R\}. \qquad \qquad \textbf{19}$$

If we consider a neoclassical firm maximizing the present discounted value of the future stream of net dividends then the optimal growth policy for the firm is given by the solution to the problem

$$\text{Max} \int_0^\infty \theta\{(1-t_C)P+t_CA-R\}e^{-rt}\mathrm{d}t, \qquad \qquad \textbf{20}$$

13. We can derive the following expressions for the tax rates:

$$t_A = t_C+\frac{1-\theta}{\theta}\,\frac{D}{P-A},$$

$$t_B = t_A-\frac{SG}{P-A} \text{ by definition,}$$

where $S =$ shareholders' rate of income tax, $G =$ gross dividends $= \dfrac{D}{1-S}$.

$$\text{Thus } t_B = t_C+\frac{D}{P-A}\left(\frac{1-\theta}{\theta}-\frac{S}{1-S}\right)$$

$$= t_C+\frac{1-\theta-S}{\theta(1-S)}\,\frac{D}{P-A}.$$

where r equals the post-tax rate of interest. If we assume that r is independent of θ then since θ is simply a constant this problem is equivalent to

$$\text{Max} \int_0^\infty \{(1-t_C)P+t_CA-R\}e^{-rt}dt$$

and we can see that the optimal policy is independent of θ. The investment policy of the firm depends only upon t_C, the rate of tax on retained profits.[14] Thus even for a neoclassical firm there seems little *a priori* justification for considering tax rates t_A and t_B to be relevant, and this in itself would constitute a strong objection to their use in a model of investment behaviour. Nevertheless it would also seem desirable to have some empirical evidence on this matter, and so we shall test the model developed above. To estimate the model given by equation **15** we assume that the expected tax rate used by firms is the rate which is 'currently prevailing', since this is the best guide firms have as to the future. The definition of 'currently prevailing' is, in most cases, simply the current rate of tax. However there are some exceptions to this, primarily because we allow expectations about future tax rates to be influenced by announcements

Table 1 Comparative tax rate results

	β_1	β_2	β_3	β_4	β_5	$\bar{R}^2$	DW
t_A	1·482	0·599	0·056	0·311	0·554	0·893	1·68
	(1·011)	(0·242)	(0·028)	(0·364)	(0·223)		
t_B	1·511	0·681	0·057	0·413	0·512	0·879	1·60
	(1·026)	(0·301)	(0·028)	(0·501)	(0·221)		
t_C	1·524	0·784	0·059	−0·127	0·452	0·910	1·80
	(1·048)	(0·329)	(0·027)	(0·176)	(0·215)		

$\log I_t = \beta_1 + \beta_2 \log (w/p_I)_{t-1} + \beta_3(\Delta Y)_{t-1} + \beta_4 \text{ (tax rate)}_{t-1} + \beta_5 \log I_{t-1}$.
(Standard errors in brackets)

about changes in tax rates to be made in the future. Details of announcements of tax changes and the way in which they are incorporated into our series for tax rates are given in the appendix. These series were used to test equation **15** employing, in turn, the three tax rates t_A, t_B, and t_C. The results

14. For further discussion of this model and its extension to the case where the firm has a different objective function see King (1974). The above argument rests, of course, on a partial equilibrium view and in a general equilibrium model r might depend upon the tax rates on income.

are shown in Table 1, and the specification, data, and estimation procedure used are described in Section IV below.

The standard errors of the estimated coefficients of the tax rate term are rather high and this points to the need for caution in interpreting the results. Nevertheless t_C has a coefficient of the right sign and has a slightly

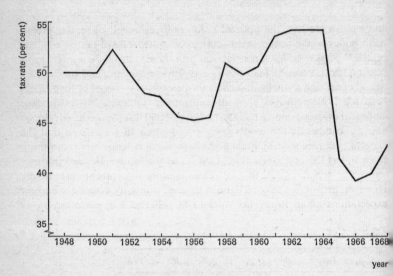

Figure 1 Tax rate on retained profits, UK, 1948–68

better explanatory power than either t_A or t_B, both of which have the wrong sign. Taken with our theoretical reasoning above we conclude from this evidence that the relevant tax rate is t_C.[15] In subsequent analysis we shall assume that this is the tax rate which firms use. This point is not insignificant because the system of company taxation employed in the UK has changed several times in the post-war period, and the three tax rates defined above have behaved in different ways. The behaviour of t_C in the

15. Support for the view that t_C is the relevant tax rate may be gleaned from comments made about the effect of the UK corporation tax in lowering the value of capital allowances. For example, 'capital allowances will now be allowable only against the corporation tax not against the 56.25 per cent combined rate' (*Economist*, 1 May 1965), and 'the reduction in the effective value of capital allowances occurs because the rate of tax on undistributed profits has been reduced from about 54 per cent to whatever the new rate of corporation tax turns out to be' (Williams, 1966). Both of these views imply that what is relevant is the tax rate on retained profits.

post-war period is illustrated in Figure 1. If our hypothesis regarding t_C is correct then some doubt is cast on the results of Feldstein and Flemming (1971) and Agarwala and Goodson (1969) who used tax rates t_A and t_B respectively.

We may use t_C to calculate the value of tax allowances given for fixed investment.[16] Such allowances have been a major feature of the UK system of investment incentives. Since the war these incentives have comprised both tax allowances and cash grants. The incentives varied according to industry, type of asset, and also to some extent regionally. Series for the present value of these investment incentives for plant and machinery in UK manufacturing industry were constructed, and are described in detail in the appendix. Five such series were calculated corresponding to different rates of discount used to evaluate the present value of future benefits – 5 per cent, 10 per cent, $18\frac{1}{3}$ per cent, 25 per cent and 'first-year benefits only'.[17, 18] The most striking feature of these series, shown in Table 2, is the magnitude of the value of investment incentives in the UK, amounting in some cases to around half the cost of the asset. Admittedly these figures include depreciation allowances but nevertheless the picture is clearly one of substantial inducements to productive investment. Investment incentives can be visualized as reducing the effective price which a firm has to pay for an asset, and so we can use this information to construct price indices for plant and machinery corresponding to the various discount rates.[19] These 'effective' price indices may be compared with the actual market price index. Such comparisons clearly show the sensitivity of the value of the incentive to the discount rate and type of incentive given. Between 1963 and 1968, a period in which the system was changed from one of tax allowances to one of cash grants, the market

16. Equation 19 gives the value of these allowances as $t_C A$.
17. These series are for the present value in year $t+1$ of the incentives given for investment expenditure made in year t. This makes it possible to compare the series calculated using different discount rates with the series for 'first-year benefits only', since the average time lag between the expenditure and the initial receipt of benefits, whether in the form of a lower tax payment or a cash investment grant, was about twelve months.
18. Each series corresponds to a given value for the discount rate, whereas in reality the actual rate used by firms may have changed over time. There is no easy way to get round this problem because to identify the discount rate with some observable market rate (e.g. the yield on debentures) would prevent us from calculating several series using different values of the discount rate, and one of the contentions of this paper is that policy conclusions as to the best method of giving investment incentives are sensitive to the discount rate assumed to be used by firms.
19. When calculating effective price indices the present value series were discounted back one more year to year t; to discount the series for 'first-year benefits only' we use an arbitrary rate of discount of 15 per cent.

price of plant and machinery rose by 16·4 per cent, the effective price index evaluated with a 5 per cent discount rate rose 32·8 per cent, exactly double, and the effective price index allowing for first-year benefits only rose by 9·7 per cent, about half the market price increase. This is illus-

Table 2 Present value of investment incentives, UK manufacturing 1948–68. New plant and machinery (as a percentage of initial cost)

Year	r = 5%	r = 10%	r = 18⅓%	r = 25%	First-year benefits
1948	42·29	37·37	32·45	29·98	17·68
1949	44·19	40·40	36·61	34·72	25·25
1950	44·82	41·41	38·00	36·30	27·28
1951	46·32	42·79	39·27	37·51	28·70
1952	40·63	35·00	29·38	26·56	12·50
1953	39·70	34·65	29·60	27·07	14·44
1954	45·13	39·42	33·72	30·88	16·63
1955	45·05	39·24	33·42	30·51	15·97
1956	38·90	34·30	29·70	27·40	15·88
1957	38·11	33·67	29·23	27·02	15·93
1958	43·46	39·08	34·70	32·51	21·57
1959	48·59	43·15	37·95	35·35	22·36
1960	51·26	45·56	39·87	37·02	22·78
1961	53·79	47·81	41·84	38·85	23·91
1962	54·96	48·91	42·87	39·84	24·73
1963	59·80	53·75	47·70	44·68	29·56
1964	59·80	53·75	47·70	44·68	29·56
1965	46·36	41·67	36·98	34·64	22·92
1966	48·26	44·49	40·73	38·84	29·43
1967	52·05	48·48	44·91	43·13	34·20
1968	53·43	49·64	45·84	43·95	34·46

trated in Figure 2. So when evaluating the relative merits of a system of cash grants and a system of tax allowances more attention should be focussed on the range of values of the discount rate used by the 'typical' or the 'dominant' firm. To test the impact of investment incentives we use the actual market price index and the various 'effective' price indices for investment goods in the model developed in section II, and compare the results.

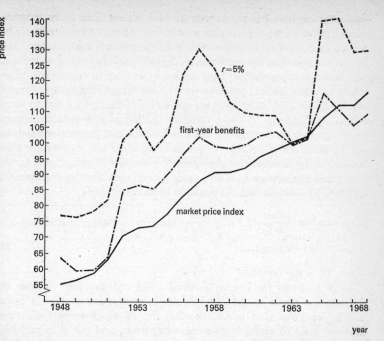

Figure 2 Price indices (1963 = 100) for investment in plant and machinery, 1948–68

IV Results

The model was fitted to UK annual data for investment in plant and machinery in manufacturing industry for the period 1948–68. The data were obtained from *National Income and Expenditure* and working sheets supplied by the UK Central Statistical Office. Two further points need to be discussed before we arrive at the final form of the equation to be estimated: (a) the specification of the output term $\log y_v$. In section II we concluded that $\log y_v$ was a complex function of the expected increase in output, but since we are here concerned with investment in total manufacturing we approximate $\log y_v$ by a linear function of the expected increase in output. In turn we express the expected change in output as a linear function of past changes in output, ΔY. Thus:

$$\log y_v = a_0 + a_1 \Delta Y.$$

For manufacturing as a whole this may not be an unreasonable assumption although for applications to individual industries and firms the particular oligopolistic mechanism at work would need to be specified more carefully.[20] (b) The lag structure; first, desired investment may be related to current or to lagged values of the independent variables. The results suggest that the response of decisions to changes in exogenous variables is not immediate. Thus desired investment in any year is determined by plans made in previous years on the basis of the values of factor prices and the other exogenous variable ruling in those years, and so when estimating equation 15 these variables are lagged one period. Second, there may be a lag between the decision to invest and the date of payment for the asset. The data refer to actual expenditure and so we must take account of the difference between desired investment at time I_t^*, and actual investment expenditure I_t. If we assume a simple geometric lag[21] then from equation 15 we have that the equation to be estimated is

$$\log I_t = \text{const.} + \frac{\lambda a_1}{b+c}.(\Delta Y)_{t-1} + \frac{\lambda c}{b+c} \log \left(\frac{w}{p_I}\right)_{t-1} - a\lambda \left(\frac{c}{b+c}\right)(\text{TR})_{t-1}$$
$$+ (1-\lambda) \log I_{t-1}, \qquad\qquad 21$$

where TR is the tax rate.

Table 3 shows the results obtained using ordinary least squares to estimate the above model. The six results correspond to the six price indices for investment goods, the first five of which employ different discount rates to evaluate investment incentives, and the sixth excludes such incentives altogether.

The first conclusion to be drawn from Table 3 comes from the point estimate of $(c/b+c)$ implied by the results. Only in those cases where the model embodies investment incentives is the estimate close to its expected theoretical value of less than unity. On the other hand if we exclude investment incentives the result is that we appear to overestimate the true coefficient of the relative factor price term because we are underestimating the rise in relative factor prices. Other models employing different specifications for the output term and higher-order lag structures yielded the same qualitative conclusion, namely that only when investment incentives are included in the price index for investment goods do we obtain point estimates which are consistent with the theoretical model.

20. For any degree of aggregation greater than that of the individual firm we need to add the further assumption that the market as a whole adopts the policy of joint cost minimization, since the model yields an investment function which is loglinear this removes the often neglected difficulty of aggregating over firms. This assumption, parallel to that of joint profit maximization, we take as describing the most satisfactory policy for a firm operating in an oligopolistic market.
21. In logarithmic form $\log I_t = \lambda \log I_t^* + (1-\lambda) \log I_{t-1}$.

Table 3

Discount rate (per cent)	β_1	β_2	β_3	β_4	β_5	$\dfrac{c}{b+c} = \dfrac{\beta_2}{1-\beta_5}$	$\alpha = \dfrac{-\beta_4}{\beta_2}$	$\bar{R}^2$	DW
5	2.485 (1.086)	0.284 (0.129)	0.059 (0.025)	−0.719 (0.341)	0.586 (0.176)	0.71	2.53	0.919	1.84
10	2.286 (1.050)	0.309 (0.141)	0.061 (0.025)	−0.596 (0.294)	0.598 (0.179)	0.77	1.93	0.923	1.85
18⅓	2.083 (1.016)	0.324 (0.149)	0.063 (0.024)	−0.478 (0.238)	0.614 (0.181)	0.84	1.47	0.926	1.87
25	1.998 (0.997)	0.339 (0.154)	0.066 (0.024)	−0.425 (0.221)	0.619 (0.182)	0.89	1.25	0.930	1.88
first year	1.504 (0.926)	0.253 (0.158)	0.072 (0.023)	−0.269 (0.198)	0.86 (0.172)	0.86	1.06	0.933	1.91
excluding incentives	1.524 (1.048)	0.784 (0.329)	0.059 (0.027)	−0.127 (0.176)	0.452 (0.215)	1.43	0.16	0.910	1.80

$\log I_t = \beta_1 + \beta_2 \log (w/P_I)_{t-1} + \beta_3 (\Delta Y)_{t-1} + \beta_4 (TR)_{t-1} + \beta_5 \log I_{t-1}$
(Standard errors in brackets)

The second conclusion is given by the estimates of a, the degree of tax shifting, and runs counter to our previous result. We stated above that a should lie between 0 and 1 and this is true only for the case where investment incentives are excluded. However, the standard errors are very high and, as noted above, using the logarithmic approximation for the tax term introduces a bias into the estimates of the shifting parameter. All the coefficients have the correct sign and although for the first three discount rates the degree of shifting is significantly different from zero,[22] none of the estimates of a is significantly different from one.[22] Thus there does seem to be some evidence of 'long-run' shifting of company taxation through its effects on investment plans. If this is accepted together with the hypothesis about 'full-cost' pricing discussed above then an increase in the rate of tax on retained profits will reduce investment and raise prices, whereas an increase in the tax rate on distributed profits would affect neither. This has obvious implications for choosing the optimum system of company taxation.

Since the model includes the lagged dependent variable as an independent variable, the Durbin–Watson statistic shown in Table 3 is not very meaningful. Thus we have used an iterative method to eliminate serial correlation in the residuals. The method, which is described in Malinvaud (1966), consists of estimating the equation by OLS and then regressing the residuals on their previous values to find the coefficient of serial dependence. This coefficient is then used to adjust the data and new parameter estimates are calculated, again by OLS. The process is repeated until the difference between successive coefficients is less than 0·01. The estimates of $(c/b+c)$ and a obtained by using this iterative procedure are shown in Table 4. The estimates are very close to those given in Table 3, and this confirms that the best results are obtained from models which include investment incentives, and that higher discount rates perform slightly better than lower rates. If investment incentives are included the estimates of the parameters b and c are consistent with either constant or increasing returns to scale.

The effect of investment incentives on the level of fixed investment may be illustrated as follows. If we take as an example a discount rate of $18\frac{1}{3}$ per cent, the results imply that an increase in the rate of nvestment grants by 5 percentage points would, at 1968 values, increase manufacturing investment in plant and machinery by £43·2 million in the long run, an increase of 4·4 per cent. Of course, an increase in the rate of investment grants by 5 percentage points (say from 25 per cent to 30 per cent) has a proportionately greater effect on investment in cases where the present value of investment incentives is high than in cases where it is

22. At the 5 per cent level.

small because the reduction in the effective price index is proportionately greater where the index is already low. In the example above the increase in investment would only have been 3·3 per cent if the initial rate of investment grants had been zero. This response is much smaller than that

Table 4 Results using iterative method

Discount rate (per cent)	$\frac{c}{b+c}$	a	$\bar{R}^2$	DW
5	0·70	2·47	0·895	1·91
10	0·76	1·89	0·897	1·91
18⅓	0·82	1·44	0·899	1·93
25	0·86	1·22	0·903	1·95
first year	0·84	1·03	0·907	1·99
excluding incentives	1·41	0·15	0·885	1·86

found in other studies. Feldstein and Flemming (1971) estimated that the impact of tax allowances on investment was about twice as great as our figures would imply, and Agarwala and Goodson (1969) suggested an effect about 25 per cent greater than our estimate.

V Conclusions

Each of the investment models so far proposed in the literature has a major weakness, and the model put forward in this paper is no exception. The determination of output and the role of monetary variables are not discussed, and the treatment of the lag structure is very crude. The aim was not to produce an econometric forecasting equation but to develop a framework which could be used to examine the influence of government policy on investment behaviour via taxation and investment incentives. In this sense our model has some advantages over other models, and quantitative estimates of the impact of these policies have been derived.

A great many *a priori* assumptions are inevitably built into any model, not only about the technology of the economy but also about the theory of the firm, and it is important to find out how sensitive the conclusions and policy recommendations are to changes in these assumptions. Jorgenson, in a survey of the literature, has written:

We conclude that there is no fundamental disagreement about the theory of the firm underlying alternative specifications of econometric models of investment behaviour. The objective of the firm is to maximize discounted profits . . . (Jorgenson, 1970).

M. A. King 251

Since much has appeared recently on 'new theories of the firm' it is disappointing that the importance of these issues has not been put to the empirical test. The model presented here cannot claim to do more than raise the problem, but it does show that such questions should not be ignored. We have shown that the choice of the relevant tax rate depends upon constructing a suitable model of the firm, and that something as mundane as the choice of discount rate has important implications for government policy (e.g. in deciding between a system of cash grants and one of tax allowances).

VI Appendix: investment incentives and taxation in the UK

To encourage productive investment, post-war governments have introduced a series of measures designed to give financial incentives for fixed investment. Apart from the normal depreciation allowances (henceforth 'annual allowances') these incentives have taken three forms:

1 *Initial allowances*: a form of accelerated depreciation whereby a larger than usual proportion of the cost of the asset can be written off in the first year;

2 *Investment allowances*: like initial allowances these are a specified percentage of the cost of the asset allowable against tax. However, the granting of the investment allowance is ignored in computing the series of annual allowances so that the aggregate of the annual allowances equals the cost of the asset, whereas under system 1 the aggregate of the annual allowances equals the cost of the asset minus the initial allowance granted;

3 *Investment grants*: cash grants to manufacturing, construction and extractive industries. The grants vary both regionally and to a limited extent according to the type of asset.

These incentives vary for different types of asset and also regionally. Since we are concerned with one asset only, new plant and machinery, this removes one source of difficulty but we have to face the problem of special rates for development areas. Between 1963 and 1966 grants of 10 per cent for new plant and machinery were made in the Development Districts, and firms in these Districts could write off capital expenditure for tax purposes at any rate they chose. These two schemes are ignored here, partly because no data have been found showing the proportion of total investment carried out in the Development Districts. In the case of the special grants this may not be too serious – the cost of the scheme was never more than about £26 million a year compared with the cost of investment grants of several hundred million pounds for the development areas – but ignoring the free depreciation scheme is probably more serious.

The one regional variation we do allow for is that for investment grants. We weight the rates of grant by the proportions of total investment eligible for such grants carried out in the respective areas, obtained from Board of Trade (1968).

Annual allowances are an attempt to allow for 'wear and tear'. For plant and machinery and vehicles the reducing-balance method is normally used, in which case the allowance is a specified percentage of the capital expenditure incurred less the total amount of any initial allowances, or annual allowances, granted in respect of that plant in previous years.

Data on the rates of incentives given in each year were obtained from *National Accounts Statistics: Sources and Methods* C S O 1956 and 1968.

We shall now attempt to combine the different incentives into a single index of the present value of such allowances. We assume a lag of one year between the time when profits are earned and the payment of tax due on these profits, and between the date of purchase of an asset and the receipt of an investment grant for such a purchase.[23] Thus we calculate the present value of these incentives in the year following the actual expenditure, because in this way we are able to compare the series for 'first-year benefits only' with those series which use different discount rates in the present value calculation.

Then remembering that an investment grant must be deducted from the cost of an asset before capital allowances are calculated we have that if:

V = present value in year $t+1$ of incentives for an investment project costing I in year t,

g = rate of investment grant,

i_v = rate of investment allowance,

i_n = rate of initial allowance,

d = rate of annual allowance,

r = rate of discount used by firms,

t = tax rate used by firms to calculate the cash value of tax allowances,

then $V = I\left[g+t(1-g)\left\{i_v+i_n+d+ \sum_{t=1}^{\infty} \frac{d(1-i_n-d)(1-d)^{t-1}}{(1+r)^t}\right\}\right]$,

thus $\frac{V}{I} = g+t(1-g)\left[i_v+i_n+d+\frac{d(1-i_n-d)}{r+d}\right]$.

In calculating the 'effective' price indices the present value was discounted back to the year t.

23. In the period considered investment grants were received with an average lag of about twelve months – see Board of Trade (1968).

'Currently prevailing' tax rates

The definition of 'currently prevailing' is, in most cases, simply the current rate of tax. However there are some exceptions to this. First, we ignore the excess profits levy which was in force between 1 January 1952 and 1 January 1954. This was clearly a temporary tax which should not have entered expectations about future tax rates.[24] Secondly, we allow expectations about future tax rates to be influenced by announcements about changes in tax rates to be made in the future. This can be illustrated by reference to the treatment of corporation tax. This tax was officially introduced in the Budget of 1966, although it was first mooted in the Budget of November 1964 and discussed more fully in the 1965 Budget. In the latter case there was some mention of various possible initial rates for the new tax; most forecasters predicted that the initial rate would be between 35 and 40 per cent and investment plans made in the last three quarters of 1965 took this into account.[25] Immediately after the Budget the *Economist* anticipated a rate of 35–40 per cent and on 4 July of that year used a rate of 37·5 per cent to illustrate the effect of corporation tax. In view of this we regard corporation tax at a rate of 37·5 per cent as affecting investment plans from April 1965 onwards. We regard the 40 per cent rate as effective from April 1966 until the end of 1967 when, following devaluation, it was announced that the rate would be raised in the next Budget from 40 to 42·5 per cent.

Details of announcements of tax changes were found by consulting the Financial Statements of the Chancellor, Dow (1964), and the Calendar of Economic Events produced by the National Institute which can be found, for the period 1955–9 in the March 1960 issue, and for subsequent years in the first issue of the *Economic Review* in each year.

In this way it was possible to construct time series for the different tax rates for the period 1948–68.[26]

24. An explanation of the scope of the excess profits levy is given on p. 93 of the *97th Report of the Commissioners of HM Inland Revenue*.
25. There were many complaints that the new tax would lower the value of investment and initial allowances. This issue is raised several times in the *Economist* in 1965. For example, in the issue for 10 April 1965 we find 'There is to be no compensation for the fact that the introduction of the corporation tax next year will devalue the effectiveness of the investment allowances.'
26. Since the tax rates t_A and t_B depend on the pay-out ratio, two different methods were used to calculate values for these rates, using (a) actual average pay-out ratios, and (b) desired pay-out ratios predicted by an econometric model of dividend behaviour described in King (1971).

References

AGARWALA, R., and GOODSON, G. C. (1969), 'An analysis of the effects of investment incentives on investment behaviour in the British economy', *Economica*, vol. 50, pp. 377–88.

ARROW, K. J. (1964), 'Optimal capital policy, the cost of capital, and myopic decision rules', *Ann. Inst. stat. Math.*, vol. 16, pp. 21–30, Tokyo.

BISCHOFF, C. W. (1971), 'The effect of alternative lag distributions', in G. Fromm (ed.), *Tax Incentives and Capital Spending*, Brookings Institution, North-Holland.

BOARD OF TRADE (1968), Investment grants: annual report.

CASS, D., and STIGLITZ, J. E. (1969), 'The implications of alternative saving and expectations hypotheses for choices of technique and patterns of growth', *J. pol. Econ.*, vol. 77, pp. 586–627.

COEN, R. M. (1969), 'Tax policy and investment behavior: comment', *Amer. econ. Rev.*, vol. 59, pp. 370–79.

DOW, J. C. R. (1964), *The Management of the British Economy 1945–60*, Cambridge University Press.

FELDSTEIN, M. S., and FLEMMING, J. S. (1971), 'Tax policy, corporate savings and investment behaviour in Britain', *Rev. econ. Stud.*, vol. 38, pp. 415–34.

HARCOURT, G. C. (1968), 'Investment-decision criteria, investment incentives and the choice of technique', *econ. J.*, vol. 78, pp. 77–95.

JORGENSON, D. W. (1963), 'Capital theory and investment behavior', *Amer. econ. Rev.*, vol. 53, pp. 247–59.

JORGENSON, D. W., HUNTER, J., and NADIRI, M. I. (1970), 'A comparison of alternative econometric models of quarterly investment behavior', *Econometrica*, vol. 38, pp. 187–212.

KING, M. A. (1971), 'Corporate taxation and dividend behaviour – a comment', *Rev. econ. Stud.*, vol. 38, pp. 377–80.

KING, M. A. (1974), 'Dividend behaviour and the theory of the firm', *Economica*, vol. 41, pp. 25–34.

MALINVAUD, E. (1966), *Statistical Methods of Econometrics*, North-Holland.

NEILD, R. R. (1963), 'Pricing and employment in the trade cycle', NIESR Occasional Paper 21, Cambridge University Press.

STANBACK, T. M. (1969), 'Tax changes and modernization in the textile industry', Fiscal Studies no. 13, National Bureau of Economic Research.

THUROW, L. C. (1969), 'A disequilibrium neoclassical investment function' *Rev. econ. Stat.*, vol. 51, pp. 431–5.

WILLIAMS, A. (1966), 'Tax policy and economic growth in post-war Britain', *Tax Policy and Economic Growth in Selected Countries*, National Bureau of Economic Reseach and the Brookings Institute.

Part Six
Further Developments

The three papers in this part provide examples of only a few of the directions in which further developments are taking place. Reading 11 extends the neoclassical framework to include both fixed and liquid capital, provides a separate test of the influence of relative prices, and attempts to account more sensibly for adjustment costs. Reading 12 is a well-known example of the increasingly common practice of treating the demand for capital goods as one of the interdependent set of demands for productive factors. Consistency constraints may then be imposed to permit more accurate parameter estimates than would be available from an investment equation estimated on its own. Reading 13 attempts to disentangle lags in the expectations processes from those in the spending process. In the course of doing this, the paper shows how the use of expectations processes with explicit horizons facilitates the use of investment anticipations data compatibly with structural information in forecasting investment expenditure.

11 R. Schramm

The Influence of Relative Prices, Production Conditions, and Adjustment Costs on Investment Behaviour[1]

R. Schramm, 'The influence of relative prices, production conditions and adjustment costs on investment behaviour', *Review of Economic Studies*, vol. 37, 1970, pp. 361–76.

I Introduction

In recent years much attention has been given to the use of neoclassical theory to provide a more meaningful basis for studies of investment behaviour. Jorgenson and others have presented numerous studies (e.g. Hall and Jorgenson, 1967; Jorgenson, 1963; Jorgenson and Stephenson, 1967) where an investment equation is derived from a constrained wealth maximization problem and then tested under various assumptions about lagged capital adjustment. Studies of this type have concluded that 'a theory of investment behaviour based on the neoclassical theory of optimal accumulation of capital provides a highly satisfactory explanation of actual investment expenditures' (Jorgenson and Stephenson, 1967, p. 216).

These studies have drawn attention to the need to derive investment models from explicit assumptions about underlying economic conditions and have popularized the user cost of capital as a convenient vehicle for incorporating a range of important economic factors. On the other hand, the interpretation of their empirical results is much more controversial. Of particular importance to this study is the criticism that these studies have failed to isolate and directly test relative price effects on investment behaviour.[2] While Jorgenson states that 'the central feature of a neoclassical theory is the response of the demand for capital to changes in relative factor prices or the ratio of factor prices to the price of output' (Jorgenson, 1963, p. 247), relative prices are never tested directly with the user cost lumped with an output measure and other factor prices neglected entirely in empirical analysis. At the same time, other studies testing relative prices directly (e.g. Eisner and Nadiri, 1968; Hickman, 1965) are devoid of the explicit theoretical basis characteristic of neoclassical

1. This paper has benefited greatly from discussions with Robert E. Lucas, Jr. and Maurice Wilkinson.
2. This criticism has best been stated in the recent study of Eisner and Nadiri (1968).

studies so that interpretation of their empirical results is much more difficult.[3]

The objective of this paper is to derive and test an investment equation from extended neoclassical conditions which allows relative price effects to be tested directly while providing a basis for interpreting the empirical results in terms of underlying assumptions about production and market conditions. Utilizing, with some extensions, the past theoretical work of Haavelmo (1960), Jorgenson (1963), Eisner and Strotz (1963) and Lucas (1967), this study derives an investment equation relating investment expenditures to long-run expected levels of output, input and investment funds prices and currently held levels of all factors of production. This model is then empirically tested under different assumptions about the specific inputs entering the production and adjustment cost functions and the method by which long-run price expectations are formulated. The choice of productive inputs to include (initially) labour and 'liquid capital', along with depreciable capital, allows testing of wage rate and labour input effects on investment which have been ignored in most studies of investment and provides an alternative theoretical basis for studying the influence of 'liquidity' effects on investment.

II A theory of optimal adjustment of factors of production

To provide a basis for the study of investment behaviour it is useful to derive a theory of optimal adjustment of all factors of production and then focus more directly on adjustments of capital stock.[4] This section presents the underlying assumptions about the production process, the nature of inputs, market and price conditions, taxation influences and producer decision behaviour and then derives the implied factor of production adjustment behaviour. Later sections apply this model to the theoretical and empirical investigation of one input change equation in this system: that of net investment in depreciable capital.

Consider a firm which produces one homogeneous output using N

3. An exception is the recent study of Bischoff (1966) who considers in some detail the production conditions underlying investment behaviour and tests user cost and output influences separately. Bischoff, however, follows a different theoretical approach from that used here in that he *assumes* that ' "desired" capacity is a roughly constant multiple . . . of "expected" output' whereas here output is treated as an endogenous variable. Furthermore, his empirical work tests depreciable capital user costs but does not include other factor costs.
4. The theoretical development follows Lucas (1967) except that we make explicit assumptions about the mathematical form of production and adjustment cost functions, treat all inputs as subject to adjustment costs rather than distinguishing capital and non-capital inputs on the basis of existence of adjustment costs, and derive input change equations in terms of discrete time periods rather than continuous time to provide a basis for later empirical analysis of quarterly data.

productive inputs. This production process and the associated input adjustment process will be represented as follows: At the beginning of each period, the firm has achieved input levels which will be combined over that period to produce output by the end of the period. All transactions for output and inputs will be assumed to occur at the end of the period. Concurrent with this period's production, the firm adjusts input flows and stocks to new levels which then become available for production of output during the next period. Thus the firm is simultaneously combining existing levels of inputs to produce output over the period and taking steps to adjust these input levels in preparation for next period's production. While the first process will be treated as determined by production relationships and the input levels at the start of each period, the second process, that of adjusting input levels over time, will be considered subject to conscious choice and critical to the achievement of the firm's long-run objectives.

This process may be represented as follows: Assume the firm produces one homogeneous output $F(X_t)$ by employing N inputs $X_t = (X_1, X_2, ..., X_N)'_t$ in a production process which is defined for non-negative values of X_t, has continuous first and second derivatives, positive first derivatives and a symmetric negative definite $N \times N$ matrix of second derivatives,

$$H = \{\partial^2 F(X_t)/\partial X_{it}\, \partial X_{jt}\}, i, \quad j = 1, 2, ..., N.$$

$F(X_t)$ will be approximated by the following quadratic function[5] satisfying the above properties:

$$F(X_t) = aX_t + X'_t A X_t, \qquad\qquad 1$$

with $a = 1 \times N$ vector of constants,

$A = N \times N$ symmetric negative definite matrix of constants.

The input vector X_t consists of M capital inputs and $N-M$ noncapital inputs ordered so that $X_t = (X_1, ..., X_M, X_{M+1}, ..., X_N)'_t$. Each capital input X_j subject to a loss of value over time not due to external price changes (e.g. depreciation of equipment, deterioration of inventory) will be assumed to require 'replacement' at a constant rate δ_j[6] so that

$$X_{jt+1} = X_{jt} - \delta_j X_{jt} + I_{jt}, \quad j = 1, 2, ..., M, \qquad\qquad 2$$

with I_{jt} representing gross changes in X_j over the period t.

5. A quadratic production function is assumed to provide linear marginal productivity conditions and a consequent linear second-order difference equation system which can be solved for implied input change behaviour relationships. An alternative approach, followed by Lucas (1967), is to not assume any particular mathematical form for the production function but to assume that deviations of the resulting dynamic model from its stationary solution can be approximated as linear.
6. Taubman and Wilkinson (1967) incorporate a variable depreciation rate affected by changes in capital utilization rates.

The existence of various costs of adjustment, or phenomena which can be represented in terms of economic adjustment costs, make the input adjustment decision more than just an automatic instantaneous adjustment of inputs to their long-run optimal levels. These costs arise in a variety of ways and can be associated with a variety of different inputs depending on such characteristics as the nature of the input, the transient properties of the production process, the time and effort involved in the 'installation' of an input, the existence of input market imperfections, etc.[7]

Let $C(\Delta X_t)$ be the sum of adjustment costs for *all* inputs with each individual input adjustment cost function defined for all levels of the input change (equalling zero for no input change), with continuous first and second derivatives, and positive second derivatives. $C(\Delta X_t)$ will be approximated by the simplified quadratic function

$$C(\Delta X_t) = \Delta X_t' \, D \Delta X_t, \qquad\qquad 3$$

with $D = N \times N$ diagonal matrix, (d_{ii}),

$i = 1, 2, ..., N$, with $d_{ii} \geqslant 0$ for all i,

$\Delta X_t = N \times 1$ vector of input changes, $X_{t+1} - X_t$.

In determining the desired levels of output and inputs we assume that the firm draws primarily on its knowledge of the production process, current and past prices in its output, input, and capital funds markets, and current and past values of important tax parameters. The price and tax information is used to formulate expected prices in the markets faced by the firm, with tax parameters entering after-tax 'user costs' or 'rental prices' of capital inputs. The producer forms price expectations, which are held with certainty and expected to remain constant over all future periods in the firm's planning horizon.[8] Long-run expected input prices held at the start of period t will be represented as $s = (s_1, s_2, ..., s_N)'$ with the M capital inputs valued at their after-tax rental prices or user costs,[9] $u = (u_1, u_2, ..., u_M)'$, and non-capital inputs valued at their after-tax input costs, $w = (w_{M+1}, ..., w_{M+N})$, so that $s = (u', w')'$. After-tax output price and cost of capital will be represented by p and r.

7. For detailed discussion of adjustment costs, see Eisner and Strotz (1963), Alchian (1959), and Hirshleifer (1962).
8. For an evaluation of the role of expected price assumptions in a model similar to that employed here, see Gould (1968). Our model can be extended to the case of constant growth rates in output and factor prices yielding the same general investment relationship.
9. The user cost definition employed here is presented in Jorgenson (1963, p. 249). Recent refinements of this concept are presented in Coen (1965) and Hall and Jorgenson (1967).

Under the above production, adjustment cost and market conditions, the producer is assumed to form long-run price expectations and to choose the time pattern for each input which maximizes the present value of the firm. This may be achieved by choosing input levels to maximize the value of all future net after-tax cash flows associated with the sale of the product and payments to input factors, discounted by the firm's after-tax cost of capital. This approach provides the implicit user costs or rental prices for capital services as a by-product of the analysis. An alternative approach providing equivalent first-order conditions for present value maximization is to begin with the implicit rental prices and assume the producer maximizes the firm's present value with all capital services rented at these rental prices. This converts the cash flow pattern associated with the purchase and use of a capital good into an equivalent period to period rental payment. In this context the present value, P, of the firm over an horizon of T periods is

$$P = \sum_{j=1}^{T} (1+r)^{-j}\{pF(X_j) - s'X_j - pC(\Delta X_j)\}, \qquad 4$$

with adjustment costs valued at the after-tax output price to reflect revenue losses due to input adjustment. Other treatments are obviously possible, including the incorporation of adjustment costs into specific input costs directly or into the production function.[10]

Differentiating equation 4 with respect to X_t, equating the N first-order conditions to zero, and solving for marginal productivity conditions, we have

$$\frac{\partial F(X_t)}{\partial X_t} = \frac{s}{p} + (1+r)\frac{\partial C(\Delta X_{t-1})}{\partial X_t} + \frac{\partial C(\Delta X_t)}{\partial X_t}. \qquad 5$$

The marginal productivity conditions reduce to the conventional conditions of profit maximization only in the case of costless input adjustment.

Substitution of the production and adjustment cost functions, equations 1 and 3, into equation 5 yields the following system of N second-order linear difference equations

$$X_{t+1} + \{D^{-1}A - (2+r)I\}X_t + (1+r)X_{t-1} = (2D)^{-1}\left(\frac{s}{p} - a'\right).$$

To derive an expression for implied input changes, ΔX_t, the above system of equations can be expressed in terms of deviations from the equilibrium solution, X^*, and then reduced to a system of first-order equations and solved. This derivation is presented in Lucas (1967, pp. 81–3), Schramm

10. See Lucas (1967a) and Gould (1968).

(1966, pp. 91–8). The following N input adjustment equation system is derived:[11]

$$\Delta X_t = B(X^* - X_t), \qquad\qquad 6$$

where B is an $N \times N$ matrix of adjustment coefficients dependent on production and adjustment cost functions and the cost of capital. Lucas (1967) proves that the matrix B is a non-singular, asymmetric (in general) matrix with positive diagonal elements and symmetry in the *signs* of off-diagonal elements. While consistent with accelerator studies which theorize that investment is positively related to a difference between the desired and actual level of capital, this formulation extends the accelerator theory to include the effects of other inputs and indicates the symmetry of interdependence of input change decisions.

Since B is not in general a diagonal matrix, equation **6** indicates that adjustment of any input will (in general) depend upon the differences between desired and actual levels of *all* inputs. In this model B will be diagonal if and only if the factors of production are independent in the production function, i.e. if A in equation **1** is a diagonal matrix. Thus if the productivity of any one input is independent of the levels of all other inputs (and vice versa) the decision to adjust that input need only consider the returns and adjustment costs associated with different levels and adjustment rates of that individual input.[12] In the context of equation **6** the estimation of an investment equation which does not include measures of the desired and existing levels of inputs other than depreciable capital implies the above restrictive production function assumption.

We have seen how production function relationships influence the extent of interdependence in the adjustment process. How is the adjustment process related to the underlying assumptions of adjustment costs associated with the rate of change of each input? Schramm (1966) shows that if adjustment costs of *all* inputs are very high (relative to the productivity of the inputs) then the adjustment matrix B will approach zero, i.e. all inputs will be adjusted very slowly to their desired levels. If adjustment costs of *all* inputs approach zero, inputs will be adjusted much more rapidly to their desired levels. In the special case of independence of inputs in the production function, B will approach the identity matrix I as adjustment costs go to zero.

11. This is the discrete time period analogue to the generalized accelerator model developed by Lucas with the exceptions noted in footnote 4. For the one input case, this is analogous to the model of Eisner and Strotz (1963).
12. Of course, it is also possible to have both independent and interdependent inputs in a production function. In this case only the elements of B and A associated with the independent inputs would be diagonalized.

In the more typical case of production interdependence of inputs and varying levels of adjustment costs associated with different inputs it is more difficult to specify the exact characteristics of the adjustment matrix B, beyond the properties outlined above. However, Schramm (1966) indicates that relative differences in input adjustment costs may generate asymmetries in the influence pattern between desired and actual input levels and input change decisions. Specifically, the analysis suggests that if input i has high adjustment costs relative to input j then the difference between desired and actual levels of i will have relatively more influence on the decision to change input j than differences between desired and actual levels of j will have on the decision to change input i. Thus if labour can be changed easily with low adjustment costs then the labour change decision becomes 'subordinate' to the decision to change capital stock with its high adjustment costs in the sense that desired and actual levels of capital stock may influence the labour change decision but the converse is not true. This result is analogous to treating some factors as variable subject to the current level of fixed factors.

The stationary solution to equation system **6** is:

$$X^* = (2A)^{-1}\left(\frac{s}{p} - a'\right)$$

$$= R\left(\frac{s}{p} + c\right), \qquad\qquad 7$$

where $X^* = N \times 1$ vector of desired input levels,
$R = N \times N$ symmetric negative definite matrix of constants,
$c = N \times 1$ vector of constants.

Combination of equations **6** and **7** results in

$$\Delta X_t = Bc + BR\left(\frac{s}{p}\right) - BX_t. \qquad\qquad 8$$

Equation **8** relates all input changes to a vector of long-run expected after-tax input costs deflated by output price and to the initial levels of all productive inputs. Combining the properties of B and R presented earlier, Lucas (1967) has shown that the matrix BR is symmetric negative definite. Thus the underlying theoretical framework provides an expression for input adjustments which emerges directly from the basic maximization problem and indicates the main (testable) properties of this input adjustment system.

The link between equation **8** and investment behaviour requires consideration of the inputs entering the production and adjustment cost functions and how long-run expected prices can be measured or price expectation formation behaviour approximated. These questions will be considered in the next two sections.

III Application of the input adjustment model to the study of investment behaviour

The empirical study of the input adjustment equation 8 and its implications for investment behaviour will (initially) treat the case of three inputs to the production process: labour, depreciable capital and 'liquid capital'. This particular classification of productive inputs provides an explicit basis for examining the interrelations between depreciable capital, labour and liquid assets of importance to our study of investment behaviour.

The production process is assumed to have the economic and analytical properties outlined in Section II with all inputs having finite costs of adjustment rising more than proportionately with the rate of input adjustment. For an increase in the firm's capital stock to be achieved quickly, a range of additional costs may have to be incurred: the higher costs of expediting the ordering, production, and shipping of the capital equipment; the possible influence of market imperfections on the price of capital goods due to increased rate of expenditure of this type good; the costs of faster 'installation' of equipment and the production inefficiencies arising as the equipment is rushed into service, etc. Changes in the flow of labour are also subject to costs related to the rate at which the flow is changed. These costs include hiring and training costs and layoff costs. These costs and others reflecting transient production inefficiencies and market imperfections will rise with the magnitude of labour force adjustment over a given period and probably more than proportionately.[13] Other evidence for the existence of adjustment costs for labour is presented by those who argue that labour has important fixed components which make rapid adjustments more difficult (i.e. more costly) than gradual adjustments.[14]

In the context of our input adjustment model we will regard liquid capital[15] as a factor of production,[16] providing productive services to the firm, related to other inputs and outputs according to the assumed properties of the production function, and subject to adjustment costs dependent on its rate of change. These adjustment costs may arise due to costs of adjusting inventory levels at different rates. Adjustment costs

13. This approximation is discussed at length in Holt *et al.* (1960).
14. See, for example, Oi (1962), and Hildebrand and Liu (1965).
15. In this study liquid capital will be treated as non-fixed capital plus financial assets and will include inventories, cash, short-term securities and receivables (net of payables), on approximately the accounting definition of working capital. For economic definitions of working capital see Hicks (1950), Keynes (1930).
16. For a recent study of the demand for money building on the assumption that money may be treated as a factor of production, see Nadiri (1968).

associated with financial assets may indirectly reflect the capital *funds* market imperfections stressed by the 'liquidity' investment theorists discussed below. This is true to the extent the process of borrowing money at an increasing marginal cost can be compared with the process of borrowing at a constant interest rate in a perfect capital funds market and then 'buying' liquid assets in markets where the marginal cost increases with the rate at which assets are bought. The magnitude of these adjustment costs, presumably lower than for labour and depreciable capital, are subjected to empirical estimation.

With three inputs, labour L_t, liquid capital, M_t and depreciable capital K_t, we have from equation **6**:

$$\begin{bmatrix} \Delta L \\ \Delta M \\ \Delta K \end{bmatrix}_t = B \begin{bmatrix} L^*-L \\ M^*-M \\ K^*-K \end{bmatrix}_t. \qquad\qquad \textbf{6}'$$

As discussed earlier, since B is a 3×3 matrix, this formulation stresses the influence of differences between desired and actual levels of *all* inputs.[17] Focusing on depreciable capital change we have:

$$\Delta K_t = \beta_1 (L^*-L)_t + \beta_2 (M^*-M)_t + \beta_3 (K^*-K)_t,$$

which highlights the effects of other input change decisions on investment behaviour and provides an explicit framework for considering labour and liquid influences on investment which have either been neglected in investment studies or tested in a different framework entirely.[18]

In the three input case, the final adjustment equation **8** relates each input change to long-run expected prices and current input levels as follows:

$$\begin{bmatrix} \Delta L \\ \Delta M \\ \Delta K \end{bmatrix} = Bc + BR \begin{bmatrix} w/p \\ u_m/p \\ u_k/p \end{bmatrix} - B \begin{bmatrix} L \\ M \\ K \end{bmatrix}_t, \qquad\qquad \textbf{8}'$$

17. For examples of this general formulation applied to specific input change decisions under different implicit assumptions about inputs entering the production process, see Chow's (1966) study of the demand for money, numerous capacity acceleration models of investment such as Eisner (1960, 1962), Grunfeld (1960), Hickman (1965) and Koyck (1954), and the labour adjustment studies of Brechling (1965).

18. This treatment of liquid capital effects provides a theoretically plausible basis for a liquidity stock influence which has not found empirical support. As Meyer and Glauber (1964, p. 93) write:

The probable explanation of these low correlations [between liquid assets and investment] is that the level of current assets held by different firms is likely to be determined by basic differences in policy orientation. As long as the stock of liquidity is near the desired policy level, the absolute value is unlikely to have much influence on investment expenditures.

where w is the wage rate, u_m the after-tax user cost of liquid capital,[19] u_k the after-tax user cost of depreciable capital, and p the output price. From the properties of equation **8**, individual input change decisions will respond inversely to changes in their own input prices (deflated by output price) and to their own current input levels. The response to other independent variables when examining the individual equations separately are not predictable. This requires closer study and testing of properties of the entire input adjustment system and will not be conducted here.[20]

From the three input equation system **8′** we see that net investment in depreciable assets is

$$\Delta K_t = f_0 \left(w/p, \, u_m/p, \, u_k/p, \, L, \, M, \, K \right)_t, \qquad\qquad 9$$

with $\partial(\Delta K_t)/\partial(u_k/p) < 0$ and $\partial(\Delta K_t)/\partial K_t < 0$.[21]

From the analysis of Section II, low adjustment costs of labour or liquid capital relative to depreciable capital would reduce the relative importance of L_t or M_t in equation **9**. That is, if labour can be adjusted at low costs its initial position becomes less important in considering other input decisions as well as labour adjustment itself. Thus it can be seen that the inputs entering the production function and their adjustment costs relative to depreciable capital determine the variables entering equation **9**. For example, if liquid capital is not treated as a factor of production then u_m/p and M would drop out of equation **9**. If it is a factor of production but with very low adjustment costs relative to depreciable capital then u_m/p would remain an influence on investment but M would lose its importance in equation **9**. The same argument can be made with respect to labour variables.

If one compares the investment equation **9**, and the implied set of investment equations for different input and adjustment cost assumptions, with neoclassical, accelerator, and liquidity type studies of investment,[22]

19. The after-tax user cost of liquid capital treats the input price of liquid capital as a weighted average of '1' (for all non-inventory components of liquid capital) and the output price (for all inventory components). The replacement rate for liquid capital is assumed to be zero.
20. For discussion and testing of complete input adjustment systems, see Schramm (1966) and the recent study of Nadiri and Rosen (1968).
21. Since B has positive diagonal elements and BR is negative definite.
22. The breakdown of investment studies into three groups is obviously an oversimplification, particularly when one considers the current efforts to include a broad range of factors in investment models subjected to empirical analysis. This breakdown is used only to suggest relative emphasis in the development of the model and interpretation of results with neoclassical reference to studies by Jorgenson and others (Hall and Jorgenson, 1967; Jorgenson, 1963; Jorgenson and Stephenson, 1967), acceleration studies such as Eisner (1960, 1962) and liquidity studies such as Meyer and Kuh (1957) and Meyer and Glauber (1964).

some similarities and differences are apparent. While the equations include the user cost of depreciable capital common to many neoclassical studies, this price variable is introduced separately, not combined with the output level which is considered an endogenous variable in the theoretical structure developed here. In addition, other relative price effects central to a neoclassical treatment of investment are included here which have been generally excluded from investment studies in the past.[23] The inclusion of several relative price variables presumably incorporates the output variable influence used in previous neoclassical and accelerator studies where output or sales levels are treated as exogenous. The inclusion of current capital stock in capacity accelerator studies is similar to the treatment in the investment models here, only this 'capacity' influence has been generalized to include all factors of production which involve costs of adjustment, so that labour and liquid capital levels may enter the investment relationship. Finally, the inclusion of liquid capital variables resembles the concern of liquidity investment theorists about the role of internal liquidity in investment behaviour. In the context of the input adjustment model developed here, however, the liquidity influence is formulated in terms of relative price changes reflecting the relative cost of different types of capital and possible substitution between the two forms of capital. The liquid capital stock influence results from costs of adjusting liquid capital within a given period of time which need not reflect differences in the internal–external sources of investment funds stressed in liquidity studies.

IV Empirical analysis of investment behaviour

This section presents the results of standard least squares regression analysis of a set of investment equations implied by equation 9 for different input and relative adjustment cost assumptions and modified to incorporate price expectations behaviour. The empirical analysis provides quantitative estimates of the relative importance of different variables influencing investment behaviour. These estimates and their associated statistical reliability represent partial tests of the theory presented in Section II although identification of the production-adjustment cost structural parameters requires empirical estimates for the coefficients of all the input adjustment equations in the system 6'.

The process by which price expectations are formed and the way this process is related to other decisions of the firm is critical to an understanding and testing of the investment behaviour represented by equation 9. It will be assumed here that firms use a weighted average of the

23. For a recent exception see Hickman (1965).

current price level and the price previously expected to prevail at this time:[24]

$$\left(\frac{s}{p}\right)^e_{t+1} = [I-a]\left(\frac{s}{p}\right)^e_t + a\left(\frac{s}{p}\right)_t,\qquad\qquad 10$$

where $(s/p)^e_{t+1}$ represents the $N\times 1$ vector of long-run expected prices (s/p) in equation 8, $(s/p)_t$ is an $N\times 1$ vector of current prices, I is an $N\times N$ identity matrix and a is an $N\times N$ diagonal matrix with diagonal elements all between zero and one. Equation 8 in terms of $(s/p)^e_{t+1}$ is

$$\Delta X_t = Bc + BR\left(\frac{s}{p}\right)^e_{t+1} - BX_t.\qquad\qquad 8''$$

Lagging equation 8'' one period and solving for $(s/p)^e_{t+1}$ we have

$$\left(\frac{s}{p}\right)^e_t = (BR)^{-1}(\Delta X_{t-1} - Bc + BX_{t-1}).$$

Substituting the above expression into equation 10 and the result into equation 8'', we have

$$\Delta X_t = EBc + EBR\left(\frac{s}{p}\right)_t + (I-B-E)\Delta X_{t-1} - EBX_{t-1},\qquad\qquad 11$$

where $E = BRa(BR)^{-1}$.

As can be seen in equation 11 the assumed price expectation behaviour introduces lagged input levels and changes into the investment model, with these lagged input variables incorporating both adjustment cost and past price influences. As price expectations depend more and more on current prices (i.e. $a\to 1$), equation 11 approaches the form of equation 8 with (s/p) representing current prices; conversely, as prices way into the past become dominant (i.e. $a\to 0$), current input change behaviour approaches a constant percentage of last period's input changes with the influence of current input levels and prices eliminated.

The introduction of lagged variables into the input adjustment equation 8 has resulted from the assumption of a particular form of price expectation formation behaviour. This approach was followed to provide an explicit rationale for the inclusion of lagged variables and to show how adjustment cost and price expectations behaviour combine to introduce

24. See, for example, Koyck (1954), Nerlove (1958), Cagan (1956), and Hammer 1964).

lagged input influences on factor adjustment. While the theoretical simplicity of this approach is appealing, more precise empirical estimation of the lag structure may require the more flexible approach of applying different lag operators directly to equation 6.

The input adjustment system of equation 11 includes a general investment equation which is equation 9 modified to include the effects of the assumed price expectation behaviour. In general, inputs in the production function determine the prices entering the investment equation, the existence of costs of adjustment determines which input variables themselves enter the investment relationship, and the reliance of price expectation behaviour on current versus past prices determines whether these input variables enter as current levels, as in equation 8, or as lagged levels and changes, as in equation 11.

The initial empirical analysis assumes that expected prices for all input costs are formulated using past price data so that equation 11 is appropriate and then examines variations in the investment equation 11, representing different inputs entering the production function and different relative adjustment costs of factors. In the case of the three possible inputs discussed in Section III, there are twenty-six possible sets of input and price variables that can enter the investment equation 11, given that an input level and change can only enter if the associated input price is included. From this set, eight investment equations implied by the most reasonable *a priori* combinations of inputs and relative adjustment costs were subjected to regression analysis, using quarterly time series data, 1949 to 1962, for all US manufacturing firms (standard industrial classification).[25] The results are presented in Table 1.

Before examining the statistical results, the choice of investment equations included should be noted. As one might expect, all investment equations tested included both a depreciable capital rental price and lagged levels and changes of net depreciable capital stock. Equations 11.5 to 11.7 include other factor prices but no other lagged input variables, treating labour and liquid capital changes as subject to low adjustment costs. Equations 11.2 and 11.4 represent labour-depreciable capital and liquid

25. Most details on capital and user cost data sources and adjustments can be found in Jorgenson and Stephenson (1967). The labour variable is man-hours from quarterly estimates of total full-time employees in manufacturing multiplied by the average number of hours per quarter spent at work by 'production' workers. Liquid capital is estimated as the sum of total cash, government securities, inventories and receivables less payables at the beginning of the quarter, deflated by output price. The index for output price is the quarterly average of a monthly wholesale index for all commodities other than farm products and foods. The wage rate is the hourly compensation in dollars, quarterly average, calculated from total compensation of all employees and total man-hours per quarter.

asset-depreciable capital two input situations, with both inputs subject to adjustment costs. The remaining equations represent other input–adjustment cost combinations with equation 11.0 representing the most general case.

Table 1 presents the regression coefficients, standard errors, coefficient of multiple correlation adjusted for degrees of freedom and Durbin–Watson statistic for the eight investment equations studied. While the Durbin–Watson statistic is biased in models which include lagged dependent variables,[26] it has been included as a rough indicator of the relative seriousness of serial correlation in different equations. A time trend has been included to represent the effects of time-related changes in production, adjustment cost and/or price expectation formation characteristics which are difficult to include in the individual functions underlying the derived investment relationships. Dummy variables correcting for seasonal variations were included in all regressions.

Our objective in viewing the empirical results of Table 1 is to isolate the investment equation which best explains the US manufacturing investment behaviour studied, and use these results to suggest the most reasonable underlying production and expected price conditions consistent with the theoretical structure developed earlier. In the process of narrowing down the empirical results we also attempt to interpret the changes in the roles of different variables as other variables are added or subtracted.

Depreciable capital price and input variables are statistically significant in almost all of the equations presented in Table 1. The user cost of depreciable capital is consistently negative (as predicted) and significant when tested in equations containing other price and input variables. Apart from equations 11.2, this price variable seems insensitive to the inclusion of a time trend. The effect on the depreciable capital price variable of including the user cost of liquid capital will be discussed below. Lagged net investment and capital stock measures are significant in almost all equations, with lagged capital stock having the anticipated negative sign. While we are primarily interested in the behaviour of variables in the more 'complete' models tested, the stability of depreciable capital coefficients across most equations in Table 1 is impressive.

The performance of labour price and input variables is more dependent upon the other variables included in the model being tested. In particular the wage rate (deflated by output price) coefficient varies considerably when liquid capital, labour, and time trend variables are added or subtracted. Since the wage rate presumably has a secondary impact on investment behaviour, the sensitivity of its coefficient to the inclusion of other variables to correct for other effects is not surprising. What re-

26. See Nerlove and Wallis (1966).

Table 1 US Manufacturing net investment equations for different productive input and adjustment cost conditions, quarterly, 1949–62

Equation	Constant	$(u_k/p)t$	$(u_m/p)t$	$(w/p)t$	ΔK_{t-1}	ΔM_{t-1}	ΔL_{t-1}	K_{t-1}	M_{t-1}	L_{t-1}	t	$R^2_{adj.}{}^a$	DW^a
11.0a	0.8317 (0.700)	-0.0872 (0.0249)	0.2081 (0.0644)	-0.7283 (0.497)	0.7596 (0.0624)	0.0197 (0.0120)	0.2370 (0.0740)	-0.0127 (0.0076)	0.0114 (0.0076)	0.1532 (0.0598)	—	0.940	1.519
b	2.499 (0.868)	-0.0664 (0.0241)	0.1307 (0.0653)	-0.398 (0.471)	0.7774 (0.0579)	0.0065 (0.0120)	0.1977 (0.0696)	-0.0282 (0.0088)	0.0025 (0.0079)	0.1901 (0.0567)	0.0222 (0.0077)	0.949	1.934
11.1a	0.3869 (0.627)	-0.0774 (0.0236)	0.2080 (0.0626)	-1.306 (0.274)	0.7539 (0.0579)	—	0.2487 (0.0728)	-0.0195 (0.0067)	—	0.2216 (0.0456)	—	0.938	1.310
b	2.558 (0.832)	-0.0638 (0.0213)	0.1281 (0.0602)	-0.9664 (0.3407)	0.7731 (0.0519)	—	0.1945 (0.0667)	-0.0309 (0.0068)	—	0.2067 (0.0408)	0.0239 (0.0068)	0.951	1.919
11.2a	-1.491 (0.302)	-0.0060 (0.0107)	—	0.2697 (0.2726)	0.7346 (0.0637)	—	0.3066 (0.0782)	-0.0137 (0.0071)	—	0.2765 (0.0470)	—	0.924	0.970
b	2.0611 (0.8302)	-0.0230 (0.0098)	—	-0.9453 (0.3539)	0.7672 (0.0538)	—	0.2128 (0.0687)	-0.0304 (0.0070)	—	0.2323 (0.0406)	0.0293 (0.0065)	0.947	1.722
11.3a	2.596 (0.537)	-0.1283 (0.0258)	0.3143 (0.0671)	-1.819 (0.436)	0.7370 (0.0561)	0.0322 (0.0121)	—	-0.0069 (0.0080)	0.0282 (0.0069)	—	—	0.921	0.892
b	4.346 (0.895)	-0.1110 (0.0256)	0.2449 (0.0701)	-2.228 (0.449)	0.7838 (0.0568)	0.0235 (0.0121)	—	-0.0194 (0.0093)	0.0220 (0.0070)	—	0.0207 (0.0087)	0.928	1.955
11.4a	2.0732 (0.610)	-0.0913 (0.0283)	0.2628 (0.0770)	—	0.871 (0.0539)	0.0257 (0.0141)	—	-0.0295 (0.0069)	0.0073 (0.0073)	—	—	0.892	0.904
b	2.399 (0.998)	-0.0862 (0.0311)	0.2466 (0.0870)	—	0.8854 (0.0658)	0.0237 (0.0150)	—	-0.0330 (0.0110)	0.0052 (0.0077)	—	0.0041 (0.0100)	0.890	0.911
11.5a	2.885 (0.6117)	-0.1220 (0.0298)	0.3788 (0.0745)	-0.5606 (0.3526)	0.8694 (0.0492)	—	—	-0.0195 (0.0088)	—	—	—	0.890	1.030
b	5.495 (0.882)	-0.0962 (0.0272)	0.2436 (0.0750)	-1.627 (0.422)	0.8992 (0.0442)	—	—	-0.0344 (0.0087)	—	—	0.0323 (0.0086)	0.914	1.520
11.6a	0.0042 (0.285)	0.0157 (0.0154)	—	0.1116 (0.404)	0.8927 (0.0606)	—	—	-0.0064 (0.0104)	—	—	—	0.832	0.708
b	5.160 (0.962)	-0.0174 (0.0135)	—	-1.740 (0.462)	0.9232 (0.0479)	—	—	-0.0341 (0.0096)	—	—	0.0458 (0.0083)	0.897	1.327
11.7a	2.533 (0.5794)	-0.1046 (0.0282)	0.3344 (0.0702)	—	0.8835 (0.0492)	—	—	-0.0299 (0.0060)	—	—	—	0.887	0.895
b	3.124 (0.721)	-0.0866 (0.0309)	0.2674 (0.0853)	—	0.9008 (0.0504)	—	—	-0.0404 (0.0098)	—	—	0.0099 (0.0073)	0.888	0.899

^{a} R^2_{adj} = Coefficient of multiple correlation adjusted for degrees of freedom; DW = Durbin–Watson Statistic. Standard errors of coefficients in parenthesis. Variables are defined in Section III quires explanation, however, is the persistence of a negative sign on the coefficient. The wage rate coefficient is consistently negative and, in most cases, significant when tested in models which include a time trend. One would generally expect that the substitution effect would lead to a positive impact on investment of an increase in wage rates. However, as discussed in Gould (1968, p. 52), an increase in the wage rate increases marginal costs and results in a decrease in output and the employment of *all* factors. In models such as those tested here, where output is not included separately as an exogenous variable, the influence of wage rate changes incorporates both substitution and scale effects. Furthermore since w/p also includes output price, decreases in p (raising w/p) decrease output and factor employment and thus operate against the substitution effect from changes in w. Thus the negative coefficient on w/p results from the dominance of scale effects, due to changes in w and p, over changes in factor proportions, due to changes in w.

In general, lagged levels and changes in labour represent statistically significant influences on investment behaviour, with the magnitudes of these coefficients reasonably stable over different equations, including those models which also include liquid capital variables. Since closer examination of the coefficients on lagged labour changes and levels indicates that the underlying influence is the current labour position alone,[27] additional results will be presented below where price expectation conditions are changed. If price expectations are formed using current prices only, then labour and liquid capital enter the investment equation as current, not lagged, variables. In any case, the significance of wage rates and labour input measures, whether current or lagged, provides support for the generalization of accelerator models to include labour as well as capital input measures and supports the contention that there are important adjustment costs associated with changes in the labour input.

Liquid capital user cost and input variables play a very interesting role in the different equations presented in Table 1. The user cost of liquid capital is consistently significant and positive in all equations it enters suggesting the importance of a 'liquidity' price effect on investment. The positive influence of u_m/p on investment can result from a substitution effect between depreciable capital and liquid capital strong enough to compensate for the scale effect included in the deflated user cost measure. However, since the user costs of the two types of capital both incorporate the same cost of capital measure, there is reason to suspect inherent problems of multi-collinearity. The changes in the depreciable capital user cost coefficient when the liquid capital user cost is added probably reflect this

27. This point was made by a referee of an earlier draft of this paper.

effect, with the cost of capital influence divided between the two co-efficients.

The lagged change in liquid capital, a measure which is probably highly correlated with the 'internal flow of funds' liquidity measures used in Meyer and Glauber (1964) and Meyer and Kuh (1957), is significant in all equations, except those where labour and liquid capital variables are both included (equations 11.0). This loss of significance of liquidity variables when labour variables are included raises questions about the interpretation of the results of Meyer and Glauber (1964) and Meyer and Kuh (1957), where liquidity variables are tested in models excluding labour influences. The lagged liquid capital stock variable does not perform very well, except in equations 11.3. Again, as with the lagged labour variables, it appears that the main underlying influence is the current level of liquid capital, with this influence only present when labour input variables are ommitted.

Additional tests (see Schramm, 1966) of equation **11** including a time trend variable curve were conducted to test the marginal contributions to explanatory power of adding sets of variables to the investment equation, the stability of different equations over time and over 'upswings' and 'downswings', and the sensitivity of the results to the empirical measure of the cost of capital and liquid capital used. Using standard F test procedures (see, for example, Johnston, 1963, pp. 129–30), the collective addition of wage rate and lagged labour variables provided significant additional explanatory power to the investment equation, while the addition of liquid capital price and input variables did not. Using the procedure described by Chow (1960), equation 11.2b was found to be stable both over time and between cyclical upswings and downswings. Equations 11.0b and 11.1b were also stable over time and equation 11.6b over different investment cycle phases. Tests using an alternative definition of the cost of capital (see Jorgenson and Stephenson, 1967) which includes measures of both debt and equity costs provided the same general results as Table 1, except that the user cost of liquid capital became non-significant. Different definitions of liquid capital, ranging from working capital to liquid assets, made little difference in the empirical results. These tests provide additional support for the importance of depreciable capital and labour price and input measures in explaining investment behaviour and cast additional doubt on the importance of liquid capital variables, especially liquid capital stock levels and changes.

In light of the empirical results of Table 1 and the additional tests reported, if one were to opt for an equation which 'best' explains the investment behaviour under study, equation 11.1b seems like a reasonable choice, subject to the reservations presented earlier about the role of the liquid capital user cost. Modifying this equation to include only the current level of the labour input, we have[28]

$$\Delta K_t = 2{\cdot}563 - 0{\cdot}0638(u_k/p)_t + 0{\cdot}1288(u_m/p)_t - 0{\cdot}9620(w/p)_t + 0{\cdot}2029L_t$$
$$\quad\;\;(0{\cdot}823)\;\;(0{\cdot}021)\qquad\quad(0{\cdot}060)\qquad\quad(0{\cdot}336)\qquad\quad(0{\cdot}034)$$

$$\quad + 0{\cdot}7787\Delta K_{t-1} - 0{\cdot}0307K_{t-1} + 0{\cdot}0237t$$
$$\quad\;\;\;(0{\cdot}039)\qquad\quad(0{\cdot}007)\qquad(0{\cdot}007)$$

$$R^2_{\text{adj.}} = 0{\cdot}952 \quad \text{DW} = 1{\cdot}926. \qquad\qquad\qquad\qquad \textbf{12}$$

In the context of the theory developed above, this equation is consistent with production conditions where depreciable capital, labour and liquid capital are inputs in the productive process, depreciable capital and labour are subject to significant costs of adjustment, and where expected depreciable capital user costs are formulated relying heavily on past prices while labour and liquid capital price expectations rely much more on current price levels. As mentioned earlier, identification of the specific structural parameters entering the underlying production and adjustment cost functions and the price expectation formation equation requires more precise specification of the model and empirical analysis of all input change equations.

V Summary and concluding remarks

This paper derives and tests directly the influence on investment behaviour of relative price and productive input variables and interprets the empirical results in terms of assumed production and adjustment cost conditions and expected price formation behaviour. Results from testing a range of different investment equations within the same general theoretical framework provide evidence of statistically significant depreciable capital user cost and wage rate relative prices and corresponding productive factor variables, depreciable capital and labour. The results provide no evidence of an important role for liquid capital variables in influencing investment, except for a possible substitution effect resulting from changes in liquid capital user costs.

In contrast to most investment studies this paper places much more importance on different relative prices as influences on investment behaviour and specifically excludes an output measure in investment equations. While it may be argued that the output or accelerator influence is operative

28. As in Table 1 seasonal dummy variables were also included. A regression of equation 11.0b with current liquid capital and labour measures resulted in M_t non-significant and L_t significant. Equation 12 without u_m/p did not perform quite as well. All coefficients remained about the same except that the coefficient on u_k/p dropped to $-0{\cdot}0227$.

through (say) depreciable capital and labour levels which imply an associated potential output level, capital and labour variables were included because of their 'capacity' influence stemming from their costs of adjustment and not to represent an accelerator influence. This approach is consistent with the structure of capacity accelerator models (Eisner, 1960, 1962; Grunfeld, 1960; Hickman, 1965; Koyck, 1954) but here relative prices replace output variables as the exogenous determinants of desired capital stock and depreciable capital and labour variables represent an expanded interpretation of current capacity.

It may also be argued that the importance of the time trend variable is due not only to systematic shifts over time in production and adjustment cost functions or price expectation behaviour, but also to changes in demand conditions not fully captured by the inclusion of an output price index. If this is the case, however, it would seem more appropriate to modify output demand conditions to include a shift variable such as national income, rather than introduce an output measure or output changes. Since this shift variable finds its way into the derived demand equation for investment goods, the combination of shift variable and factor prices determines desired capital stocks.[29] For that matter a demand shift variable may well represent the economic force in neoclassical models that output or sales variables represent in accelerator models which treat output as exogenous.

The empirical results presented here suggest that the extension of investment models to include labour price and input variables represents a more logical step than that followed in past studies where liquid capital variables have been included in the absence of labour measures (Meyer and Glauber, 1964; Meyer and Kuh, 1957). However, while certain types of 'liquidity' variables did not perform well empirically, the underlying model does not incorporate the internal–external investment funds cost difference which liquidity theorists believe to lie at the heart of the internal funds flow influence on investment behaviour. Modification of the model to incorporate these cost differences in the cost of capital or liquid capital user cost variable would be necessary to test this hypothesis directly.

29. This approach was followed in Schramm (1968).

References

ALCHIAN, A. A. (1959), 'Costs and outputs', in M. Abramovitz (ed.), *The Allocation of Economic Resources: Essays in Honor of Bernard Francis Haley*, Stanford University Press.

BISCHOFF, C. W. (1966), 'Elasticities of substitution, capital malleability, and distributed lag investment functions', presented to the San Francisco Meetings of the Econometric Society.

BRECHLING, F. (1965), 'The relationship between output and employment in British manufacturing industries', *Rev. econ. Stud.*, vol. 32, pp. 187–216.

CAGAN, P. (1956), 'The monetary dynamics of hyperinflation' in M. Friedman (ed.), *Studies in the Quantity Theory of Money*, University of Chicago Press, pp. 25–117.

CHOW, G. C. (1960), 'Tests of equality between sets of coefficients in two linear regressions', *Econometrica*, vol. 28, pp. 591–605.

CHOW, G. C. (1966), 'On the long-run and short-run demand for money', *J. pol. Econ.*, vol. 74, pp. 111–31.

COEN, R. M. (1965), 'Accelerated depreciation, the investment tax credit, and investment decisions', presented to the New York meetings of the Econometric Society.

EISNER, R. (1960), 'A distributed lag investment function', *Econometrica*, vol. 28, pp. 1–29.

EISNER, R. (1962), 'Investment plans and realizations', *Amer. econ. Rev.*, vol. 52, pp. 190–203.

EISNER, R., and NADIRI, M. I. (1968), 'Investment behavior and neo-classical theory', *Rev. econ. Stat.*, vol. 50, pp. 369–82.

EISNER, R., and STROTZ, R. H. (1963), 'Determinants of business investment', in Commission on Money and Credit, *Impacts of Monetary Policy*, Prentice-Hall, pp. 59–337.

GOULD, J. P. (1968), 'Adjustment costs in the theory of investment of the firm', *Rev. econ. Stud.*, vol. 35, pp. 47–55.

GRUNFELD, Y. (1960), 'The determinants of corporate investment', in A. C. Harberger (ed.), *The Demand for Durable Goods*, University of Chicago Press, pp. 211–66.

HAAVELMO, T. (1960), *A Study in the Theory of Investment*, University of Chicago Press.

HALL, R. E., and JORGENSON, D. W. (1967), 'Tax policy and investment behavior', *Amer. econ. Rev.*, vol. 57, pp. 391–414.

HAMMER, F. (1964), *The Demand for Physical Capital: An Application of a Wealth Model*, Prentice-Hall.

HICKMAN, B. G. (1965), *Investment Demand and US Economic Growth*, Brookings Institution, North-Holland.

HICKS, J. R. (1950), *A Contribution to the Theory of the Trade Cycle*, Oxford University Press.

HILDEBRAND, G. H., and LIU, T. C. (1965), *Manufacturing Production Functions in the United States, 1957: An Inter-industry and Interstate Comparison of Productivity*, New York State School of Industrial and Labor Relations, Cornell University Press.

HIRSHLEIFER, J. (1962), 'The firm's cost function: a successful reconstruction?' *J. Bus.*, vol. 35, pp. 235–55.

HOLT, C., MODIGLIANI, R., MUTH, J., and SIMON, H. (1960), *Planning Production, Inventories, and Work Force*, Prentice-Hall.

JOHNSTON, J. (1963), *Econometric Methods*, McGraw-Hill.

JORGENSON, D. W. (1963), 'Capital theory and investment behavior', *Amer. econ. Rev.*, vol. 53, pp. 247–59.

JORGENSON, D. W., and STEPHENSON, J. A. (1967), 'Anticipations and investment behavior in US manufacturing, 1949–1960', *Econometrica*, vol. 35, pp. 169–220.

KEYNES, J. M. (1930), *A Treatise on Money*, vol. 1, Harcourt Brace.

KOYCK, L. M. (1954), *Distributed Lags and Investment Analysis*, North-Holland.

LUCAS, R. E., JR. (1967), 'Optimal investment policy and the flexible accelerator' *Inter. econ. Rev.*, vol. 8, pp. 78–85.

LUCAS, R. E., JR. (1967a), 'Adjustment costs and the theory of supply', *J. pol. Econ.*, vol. 75, pp. 321–34.

MEYER, J. R., and GLAUBER, R. R. (1964), *Investment Decisions, Economic Forecasting, and Public Policy*, Harvard University Press.

MEYER, J. R., and KUH, E. (1957), *The Investment Decision: An Empirical Study*, Harvard University Press.

NADIRI, M. I. (1968), 'The determinants of corporate cash holdings', unpublished paper, Northwestern University, Evanston, Illinois.

NADIRI, M. I., and ROSEN, S. (1968), 'Interrelated factor demand, adjustment dynamics and relative prices', presented to the Econometric Society Summer Meetings, Boulder, Colorado.

NERLOVE, M. (1958), 'Adaptive expectations and cobweb phenomena', *Quarterly Journal of Economics*, vol. 72, pp. 227–40.

NERLOVE, M., and WALLIS, K. F. (1966), 'Use of the Durbin–Watson statistics in inappropriate situations', *Econometrica*, vol. 34, pp. 235–8.

OI, W. Y. (1962), 'Labor as a quasi-fixed factor', *J. pol. Econ.*, vol. 75, pp. 538–55.

SCHRAMM, R. (1966), 'Optimal adjustment of factors of production and the study of investment behavior', unpublished Ph.D. dissertation, Carnegie Institute of Technology, Pittsburgh.

SCHRAMM, R. (1968), 'Private manufacturing investment in France, 1950–1965', unpublished paper, Cornell University.

TAUBMAN, P., and WILKINSON, M. (1970), 'User cost, capital utilization and investment theory', *Inter. econ. Rev.*, vol. 11, pp. 209–15.

12 R. M. Coen and B. G. Hickman

Constrained Joint Estimation of Factor Demand and
Production Functions[1]

R. M. Coen and B. G. Hickman, 'Constrained joint estimation of factor demand
and production functions', *Review of Economics and Statistics*, vol. 52, 1970,
pp. 287–300.

Firms determine their demands for factors of production by finding the
combination of factor inputs that will maximize profits or minimize costs,
subject to a technological constraint – the production function. Because
the production function is common to decisions for all factors, the factor
demands must be interrelated; each factor demand function contains
parameters from the underlying production function which also appear in
other demand functions. Yet factor demand equations are commonly
estimated independently, with the consequence that production function
parameters implied by the different equation estimates may well be inconsistent. If the demand functions are to be included in a complete
model of an economy, it is certainly desirable, if not essential, that they
be consistent, i.e. that they imply a single set of parameters for the underlying production function.

The authors are currently engaged in constructing a medium-term macro-
model of the United States economy, an important subsector of which
consists of aggregative labor and investment demand functions. This
paper summarizes our efforts at estimating these two demand functions
with data extending back to the early 1920s, treating relative prices
and financial variables as exogenous. To illuminate the methodological
issue just raised, we present results for three estimation procedures: (a)
independent estimation of both relations, (b) a two-step approach in
which production function parameters implied by independent estimates
of one function are imposed in estimating the other relation, (c) joint
estimation of both functions.

By the nature of our approach, we obtain estimates of the production
function from estimates of the factor demand relations. Indirect estimation

1. This research was supported by National Science Foundation Grant No. GS1686.
The authors wish to acknowledge the assistance of Richard Freeman, Margaret
Simms, and Robert Willig on much of the computational work. A preliminary
version of the paper was read at the Winter Meetings of the Econometric Society,
28 December 1968. We are indebted to Sherwin Rosen for his constructive
suggestions, especially as concerns the clarification of our hypotheses on the
adjustment process.

of the production function in this way has also been suggested, though not carried out, by Dhrymes (1967) and Nerlove (1967). It seems to us to be preferable to several alternatives. The production function is a constraint relating desired or expected (long-run equilibrium) output to desired (long-run equilibrium) factor inputs, and these are generally not observable variables. Expected output may be related to current and past levels of output, and observed factor inputs are likely to be disequilibrium values associated with lagged adjustment to desired levels. Use of actual current output and actual current inputs to estimate the production function directly is objectionable for these reasons. The frequent practice of correcting measured capital stock for its utilization (usually by assuming that capital is unemployed to the same extent as labor) recognizes that the observed capital stock is not the equilibrium quantity to which the production function refers, but it seems an inadequate way of accounting for expectations and adjustment lags in capital stock decisions. Also, if lagged adjustment characterizes the labor input so that labor, like capital, is a partially fixed factor, then labor input (employment) should also be corrected for utilization. The procyclical behavior of labor productivity suggests that this is the case.

A second shortcoming of many direct estimates of the production function is that they ignore information contained in marginal productivity conditions. This information can usually be summarized in a so-called expansion path equation, i.e. an equation relating the ratio of desired factor inputs to the ratio of their prices. If the production function is estimated independently of the expansion path equation, the estimates will be statistically inconsistent. For this reason, among others, the expansion path is sometimes estimated first, and the information so obtained is then used in estimating the production function. (This is a particularly attractive approach in estimation of the constant-elasticity-of-substitution (CES) production function, since information from the expansion path estimates can be used to linearize the CES function.) While the estimates obtained in this way are statistically consistent, they are not necessarily efficient. Furthermore, the expansion path estimates are often based on the assumption that the factor input ratio is fully adjusted within one period to relative factor prices – a highly questionable premise, particularly with regard to capital. When lagged adjustment is allowed for, the specification of the expansion path commonly implies equal adjustment speeds for both labor and capital – again a highly questionable premise.

The production function estimated indirectly through the labor and investment demand relations will have a prominent role of its own in our complete model. It will be used to determine potential or full employment GNP, while actual GNP will be determined by effective demand. The implications of the production function estimates for the growth of potential output are to be explored in the next stage of our research.

This article is based on more extensive research reported in a longer paper (Coen and Hickman, 1969). In addition to the model presented here, the earlier paper includes estimates for models in which the production function is constrained to constant returns to scale and in which a flexible adjustment hypothesis is tested for the investment decision, with the speed of adjustment varying with cash flow. Readers interested in the comparison of the alternative models and in our reasons for preferring the present version, may obtain the longer paper on request to the authors.

Specification of the model

We assume an underlying Cobb–Douglas (CD) production function relating output to capital stock and labor in long-run equilibrium:

$$X^* = Ae^{\gamma t}(K^*)^a(L^*)^\beta, \quad a, \beta, \gamma > 0 \qquad 1$$

where X^* is expected long-run output, K^* is desired (long-run equilibrium) capital stock, L^* is desired (long-run equilibrium) labor input, and technical progress is assumed to occur exponentially at the rate γ. Since K^* is measured net of depreciation, γ may be viewed as the rate of embodied technical progress under the assumption that no disembodied progress occurs. (See Appendix B at the end of this reading.)[2]

Our next assumption is that businessmen decide on desired factor inputs by minimizing the cost of producing expected output. More accurately, we assume that the present value of all future investment and labor outlays is minimized for the expected output, as discussed in Appendix A. This leads to the familiar condition that the quantities of capital and labor be chosen so as to equate the ratio of their marginal products to the ratio of their prices. Assuming absence of monopsony in the factor markets and a CD production function, we have:

$$\frac{\frac{\partial X^*}{\partial K^*}}{\frac{\partial X^*}{\partial L^*}} = \frac{a \dfrac{X^*}{K^*}}{\beta \dfrac{X^*}{L^*}} = \frac{a}{\beta}\frac{L^*}{K^*} = \frac{Q^*}{W^*}$$

---

2. The interpretation of γ as the rate of embodied technical progress is strictly valid only for the case of constant returns to scale. Since our preferred empirical estimates imply increasing returns, the interpretation of the estimated parameter for technical progress reported below is ambiguous.

where a, β, L^* and K^* were defined in 1, W^* is the expected money wage rate, and Q^* is the expected money price of capital. To simplify notation we define $P^* = Q^*/W^*$, where P^* is the relative price of capital and labor.

Taken together, 1 and 2 imply the following functions for desired (long-run equilibrium) labor and capital inputs:

$$L^* = \left\{\left(\frac{\beta}{a}\right)^a A^{-1}\right\}^{1/(a+\beta)} \{(P_1^*)^{a/(a+\beta)}(X_1^*)^{1/a+\beta}e^{-\gamma t/(a+\beta)}\} \qquad 3$$

$$K^* = \left\{\left(\frac{a}{\beta}\right)^\beta A^{-1}\right\}^{1/(a+\beta)} \{(P_2^*)^{-\beta/a}(X_2^*)^{1/a+\beta}e^{-\gamma t/(a+\beta)}\}$$

If we now set:

$$a_0 = \left\{\left(\frac{\beta}{a}\right)^a A^{-1}\right\}^{1/(a+\beta)} ; a_1 = \frac{a}{a+\beta}; \qquad 4$$

$$a_2 = \frac{1}{a+\beta}; a_3 = \frac{\gamma}{a+\beta} \qquad 5$$

$$b_0 = \left\{\left(\frac{a}{\beta}\right)^\beta A^{-1}\right\}^{1/(a+\beta)} ; b_1 = \frac{\beta}{a+\beta}; \qquad$$

$$b_2 = \frac{1}{a+\beta}; b_3 = \frac{\gamma}{a+\beta} \qquad 6$$

we may rewrite 3 and 4 more simply as:

$$L^* = a_0(P_1^*)^{a_1}(X_1^*)^{a_2}e^{-a_3 t} \qquad 3a$$

$$K^* = b_0(P_2^*)^{-b_1}(X_2^*)^{b_2}e^{-b_3 t}. \qquad 4a$$

Notice that both the P^* and X^* variables carry distinguishing subscripts in the two equations. This is because the expected price underlying the labor decision may temporarily be based on different information than that underlying the investment decision, even though the stationary equilibrium value must be the same in both equations; and the same is true of expected output.

Price and output expectations are assumed to be formed as weighted averages of the corresponding current and lagged values:

$$P_1^* = P^{w_{11}}P_{-1}^{w_{12}}, \qquad w_{11}+w_{12} = 1; \; w_{11}, w_{12} > 0 \qquad 7$$

$$X_1^* = X^{k_{11}}X_{-1}^{k_{12}}, \qquad k_{11}+k_{12} = 1; \; k_{11}, k_{12} > 0 \qquad 7a$$

$$P_2^* = P^{w_{21}}P_{-1}^{w_{22}}, \qquad w_{21}+w_{22} = 1; \; w_{21}, w_{22} > 0 \qquad 8$$

$$X_2^* = X^{k_{21}}X_{-1}^{k_{22}}, \qquad k_{21}+k_{22} = 1; \; k_{21}, k_{22} > 0. \qquad 8a$$

These hypotheses could, of course, be extended to include additional lagged values of P and X, but this has not proved fruitful in our empirical work.

Finally, we shall make the assumption that actual values are adjusted towards desired values at a constant (geometric) rate per period:

$$\left(\frac{L}{L_{-1}}\right) = \left(\frac{L^*}{L_{-1}}\right)^{\lambda_1} u, \quad 0 < \lambda_1 \leqslant 1, \tag{9}$$

$$\left(\frac{K}{K_{-1}}\right) = \left(\frac{K^*}{K_{-1}}\right)^{\lambda_2} v, \quad 0 < \lambda_2 \leqslant 1, \tag{10}$$

where u and v are random disturbances. In the terminology adopted by one of us in a previous study of investment based on a similar model (Hickman, 1965), K/K_{-1} is the capital expansion ratio and L/L_{-1} the labor expansion ratio.

Several implications of our expectations and adjustment hypotheses should be noted at this point. First, as written, **7a** and **8a** imply that expected output can never be greater than current output except in a recession year. This implication is easily removed by multiplying the right-hand sides of the expressions by an expectations scale parameter h, where h is assumed to be greater than unity. Unfortunately, it is impossible to estimate the value of h by regression methods, because it becomes absorbed in the constant term. This makes no difference for most purposes, however, since the estimated values of L^* and K^* are invariant with respect to the value of h. If h is in fact greater than unity instead of equal to unity as we have assumed for convenience in our regression work, this merely means that we have underestimated X^* and overestimated the constant term in equations **3a** and **4a**, and it is easy to show that these biases are exactly compensating and that none of the other parameter values is affected. Moreover, since the invariance of K^* and L^* to different values of h merely means that the implicit value of the scale parameter A of the production function changes proportionately to h, the long-run production function **1** holds for any value of h.[3]

Second, our hypotheses imply that short-run decisions about labor and capital inputs are essentially independent. Thus, as already stressed, we allow for the possibility that expectations concerning factor prices and output may be formulated differently for the two decisions in the short run, although the expected values would necessarily be the same for both decisions under stationary conditions. More importantly, we assume that

3. Thus the only important drawback of the lack of identification of h is the fact that the true value of A, and hence of the level of the potential output path in long-run equilibrium, cannot be inferred from the factor demand regressions but must be established by other means.

the rate at which the actual capital stock is adjusted to the desired level is independent of the rate of labor adjustment.[4] As a corollary, we accept the implication that firms may seldom or never be operating on a short-run production function with fixed factor intensities.

This last point may be clarified most easily by making the simplifying assumptions that the net investment of the current period does not augment productive capacity until the following period because of gestation lags, that firms always expect the current level of output to be permanent, and that relative factor prices are fixed. Assume also that the initial position is one of long-term equilibrium with factor inputs fully adjusted to stationary levels of output and factor prices. Now let there be a once-for-all increase of output to a permanently higher level. Since productive capacity is fixed in the first period, even though net investment is occurring, the entire burden of increasing output falls initially on labor. According to the conventional short-run analysis, labor input would be increased immediately to a point on the new output isoquant. In subsequent periods, however, capital input would gradually increase and hence labor input would gradually fall along the isoquant until equilibrium was finally restored. Firms would not only always be on their production functions, but the initial adjustment of labor would always overshoot the final equilibrium, and the adjustment speeds of labor and capital would be interdependent.

Our model differs from the foregoing one in all three respects. It is *not* assumed that measured labor input is adjusted immediately to the level indicated by the new isoquant. Instead, a partial adjustment toward the new long-term equilibrium level of man-hours is postulated. Hence the firm must be off its production function in the short run, and the current output is necessarily being produced with less man-hour input than is indicated by the isoquant. Under the present restrictive assumptions, the interpretation must be that for a time labor may be used more intensively per man-hour or capital more intensively per constant-dollar unit, or both, than will be true in final equilibrium. Because of the variation in factor intensities, it is also unnecessary for the firms to overshoot the equilibrium man-hour input during the adjustment process. Finally, since the production function constraint is not binding in the short run, the adjustment processes for labor and capital are independent.

Lest these assumptions appear unduly restrictive or unrealistic, we should hasten to add that they may be relaxed considerably within the confines of the model. Thus, if the unobserved scale parameter for expected

4. For a contrasting approach stressing a postulated interdependence of the adjustment rates, the reader is referred to the interesting paper by Nadiri and Rosen (1969).

output, h, is in fact greater than unity, the unobserved isoquant for expected output will lie above that for current output. Then the partial adjustment of man-hours induced by the gap between the old and new equilibrium quantities may be sufficient (or more than sufficient) to permit production of the current output with no increase (or an actual reduction) in factor intensity. In that case, man-hour input could be on the production function even in the short run. (It remains true, however, that nothing in our model requires this to be so.) Similarly, if the assumption concerning productive capacity is relaxed to permit current investment to contribute immediately to current capacity, the observed capital–labor combination will be nearer to the current production isoquant and the implicit increase in factor intensities will be smaller.

In order to derive the final expressions for labor and investment demand, we substitute 3a, 7, and 7a into 9, and 4a, 8, and 8a into 10, and write the resulting equations in logarithmic form:

$$\log L - \log L_{-1} = \lambda_1 \log a_0 + \lambda_1 a_1 w_{11} \log P + \lambda_1 a_1 (1-w_{11}) \log P_{-1}$$
$$+ \lambda_1 a_2 k_{11} \log X + \lambda_1 a_2 (1-k_{11}) \log X_{-1}$$
$$- \lambda_1 a_3 t - \lambda_1 \log L_{-1} + \log u. \qquad \textbf{11}$$

$$\log K - \log K_{-1} = \lambda_2 \log b_0 - \lambda_2 b_1 w_{21} \log P - \lambda_2 b_1 (1-w_{21}) \log P_{-1}$$
$$+ \lambda_2 b_2 k_{21} \log X + \lambda_2 b_2 (1-k_{21}) \log X_{-1}$$
$$- \lambda_2 b_3 t - \lambda_2 \log K_{-1} + \log v. \qquad \textbf{12}$$

Equations 11 and 12 are the factor demand functions which we wish to estimate. The first point to notice is that capital and labor are *not* jointly dependent variables in this system. Insofar as the underlying theory is concerned, all the right-hand variables in both equations are predetermined, since output and relative factor prices are exogenous to the cost minimization decision of the individual firm. It is true that in a complete aggregative model, price and output would also be endogenous variables, but, for the purposes of this sectoral model, they are treated as exogenous. Thus we have no simultaneous equations problem as such. This does not mean, however, that 11 and 12 can be estimated independently without constraints, for two reasons.

First, it is possible that the stochastic terms in the two equations are correlated. Recall that we have specified the relations determining L^*, K^*, P^* and X^* to be nonstochastic. That is to say, we do not regard the desired inputs of capital and labor as subject to random variation, nor do we think of expected price and output as random variables. Rather, we think it more reasonable to assume that it is the process of adjusting the actual to the desired levels of factor inputs which is stochastic in nature. Now, we have no strong grounds for assuming that the disturbances to

he labor adjustment should necessarily be correlated with those affecting
he capital adjustment – the two markets differ substantially in institutional
characteristics and supply conditions – but we do not rule out the possibility of correlated disturbances to the two adjustment processes.

Second, the two equations are subject to joint *a priori* restrictions on
their parameters. To see this clearly, let us rewrite 11 and 12 in terms of
the parameters that would be directly estimated in an independent regression on each equation:

$$\log L - \log L_{-1} = c_0 + c_{11} \log P + c_{12} \log P_{-1}$$
$$+ c_{21} \log X + c_{22} \log X_{-1} - c_3\, t - c_4 \log L_{-1}. \qquad \textbf{11a}$$

$$\log K - \log K_{-1} = d_0 - d_{11} \log P - d_{12} \log P_{-1} + d_{21} \log X$$
$$+ d_{22} \log X_{-1} - d_3\, t - d_4 \log K_{-1}. \qquad \textbf{12a}$$

Notice that if 11a were estimated independently, it would be possible to
identify all the underlying parameters of equations 3a, 7, 7a, and 9, as
follows:

$\lambda_1 = c_4$ (speed of labor adjustment)

$a_1 = \dfrac{c_{11} + c_{12}}{c_4}$ (equilibrium price elasticity of desired labor input)

$a_2 = \dfrac{c_{21} + c_{22}}{c_4}$ (equilibrium output elasticity of desired labor input)

$a_3 = \dfrac{c_3}{c_4}$ (exponential rate of downtrend of labor requirements per
unit of output due to technical progress)

$a_0 = \text{antilog } \dfrac{c_0}{c_4}$ (scale factor in desired labor function)

$\left.\begin{array}{l} w_{11} = \dfrac{c_{11}}{c_{11} + c_{12}} \\[2mm] w_{12} = (1 - w_{11}) \\[1mm] \quad\ = \dfrac{c_{12}}{c_{11} + c_{12}} \end{array}\right\}$ (price expectation weights for equilibrium labor decision)

$\left.\begin{array}{l} k_{11} = \dfrac{c_{21}}{c_{11} + c_{12}} \\[2mm] k_{12} = (1 - k_{11}) \\[1mm] \quad\ = \dfrac{c_{22}}{c_{21} + c_{22}} \end{array}\right\}$ (output expectation weights for equilibrium labor decision).

$\qquad\qquad\qquad\qquad\qquad\qquad\qquad\qquad\qquad\qquad\qquad \textbf{13}$

Similarly, if 12a were independently estimated, all the underlying
parameters of 4a, 8, 8a, and 10 would be identified:

$\lambda_2 = d_4$ (speed of capital adjustment)

$b_1 = \dfrac{d_{11} + d_{12}}{d_4}$ (equilibrium price elasticity of desired capital input)

R. M. Coen and B. G. Hickman 287

$$b_2 = \frac{d_{21} + d_{22}}{d_4} \quad \text{(equilibrium output elasticity of desired capital input)}$$

$$b_3 = \frac{d_3}{d_4} \quad \text{(exponential rate of downtrend of capital requirements per unit of output due to technical progress)}$$

$$b_0 = \text{antilog } \frac{d_0}{d_4} \quad \text{(scale factor in desired capital function)}$$

$$\left.\begin{aligned} w_{21} &= \frac{d_{11}}{d_{11} + d_{12}} \\ w_{22} &= (1 - w_{21}) \\ &= \frac{d_{12}}{d_{11} + d_{12}} \end{aligned}\right\} \text{(price expectation weights for equilibrium capital decision)}$$

$$\left.\begin{aligned} k_{21} &= \frac{d_{21}}{d_{21} + d_{22}} \\ k_{22} &= (1 - k_{21}) \\ &= \frac{d_{22}}{d_{21} + d_{22}} \end{aligned}\right\} \text{(output expectation weights for equilibrium capital decision)}.$$

1

The difficulty with the foregoing procedure, of course, is that the system of factor demand equations is over-identified in terms of the parameters of the underlying production function. The adjustment speeds and expectation weights are independent of the production function and hence may differ in the two factor demand functions, but this is not true of the parameters inherited in common from the production function. Comparison of the parameter sets defined in 5 and 6 shows that the following restrictions must hold between the parameters in equations 3a and 4a:

$$a_2 = b_2$$
$$a_3 = b_3$$
$$a_1 + b_1 = 1$$
$$\frac{a_0 a_1}{1 - a_1} = b_0.$$

1

Restrictions 15 in turn imply the following restrictions between the parameters of 11a and 12a:

$$\frac{c_{21} + c_{22}}{c_4} = \frac{d_{21} + d_{22}}{d_4}$$

$$\frac{c_3}{c_4} = \frac{d_3}{d_4}$$

$$\frac{c_{11} + c_{12}}{c_4} + \frac{d_{11} + d_{12}}{d_4} = 1$$

$$\log \frac{c_{11} + c_{12}}{c_4 - c_{11} - c_{12}} = \frac{d_0}{d_4} - \frac{c_0}{c_4}.$$

Unless the foregoing restrictions are imposed in the estimating procedure, it will be impossible to identify a unique set of underlying parameters from the production function. Unfortunately the nonlinear nature of the restrictions **16** rules out the use of an otherwise relatively simple joint estimation technique. Equations **11a** and **12a** are linear in the logarithms of the variables, and if the restrictions were also linear, it would be possible to use the technique of joint generalized least squares subject to linear constraints on the coefficients of different equations. Instead, we make use of the full-information maximum likelihood method for joint estimation of equations **11** and **12** subject to the restrictions across equations given in **15**.[5] The final estimating forms are:

$$
\begin{aligned}
\log L - \log L_{-1} = {} & \lambda_1 \log a_0 + \lambda_1 a_1 w_{11} \log P \\
& + \lambda_1 a_1 (1 - w_{11}) \log P_{-1} + \lambda_1 a_2 k_{11} \log X \\
& + \lambda_1 a_2 (1 - k_{11}) \log X_{-1} - \lambda_1 a_3 t \\
& - \lambda_1 \log L_{-1} + \log u.
\end{aligned}
\qquad \textbf{11}
$$

$$
\begin{aligned}
\log K - \log K_{-1} = {} & \lambda_2 \log \left(\frac{a_0 a_1}{1 - a_1} \right) - \lambda_2 (1 - a_1) w_{21} \log P \\
& - \lambda_2 (1 - a_1)(1 - w_{21}) \log P_{-1} + \lambda_2 a_2 k_{21} \log X \\
& + \lambda_2 a_2 (1 - k_{21}) \log X_{-1} - \lambda_2 a_3 t - \lambda_2 \log L_{-1} \\
& + \log v.
\end{aligned}
\qquad \textbf{12b}
$$

The unknown parameters are ten in number, a_0, a_1, a_2, a_3, w_{11}, w_{21}, k_{11}, k_{21}, λ_1, λ_2. Given estimates of the as, the parameters of the production function are calculated as follows (compare **3** with **3a**);

$$
\alpha = \frac{a_1}{a_2},
$$

$$
\beta = \frac{1 - a_1}{a_2}
$$

$$
\gamma = \frac{a_3}{a_2}
$$

$$
A = \left\{ a_0^{-1} \left(\frac{1 - a_1}{a_1} \right)^{a_1} \right\}^{1/a_2}.
\qquad \textbf{17}
$$

Given α, β, γ, A and the expectational weights w_{ij} and k_{ij}, all the information is available to compute X^*, L^* and K^* from equations **1**, **3** and **4**.

In addition to the joint estimation technique just described, we also

5. For this purpose we employ the excellent computer program developed by Eisenpress of IBM for the IBM S/360, 'Non-linear Regression Equations and Systems, Estimation and Prediction'. The method is fully described in Eisenpress and Greenstadt (1966).

R. M. Coen and B. G. Hickman 289

experiment with a two-step procedure for honoring the restrictions between the parameters of the labor and investment functions. We first estimate the labor demand function **11a** by linear least squares and identify the underlying parameters of **11** by use of relationships **13**. It is then a simple matter to impose the estimated values of a_0, a_1, a_2 and a_3 on the investment function **12b**. The remaining parameters in **12b** – the expectation weights and adjustment speed – may then be estimated by linear least squares.

As will be shown below, the two-step procedure offers considerable flexibility for experimentation on alternative weighting patterns, owing to the simplicity and economy of linear least squares estimation. There are two offsetting disadvantages that should be noted, however. First, efficient estimates of the parameters will not be obtained by the method unless the disturbance terms in the two-factor demand functions are independent or at least uncorrelated, and we have already noted that this may not be the case. Second, the procedure is arbitrary in the sense that it could be reversed – first estimating the coefficients of the investment demand function and then imposing the common parameter values on the labor function – doubtless giving rise to a different set of estimated parameters. This problem will be discussed further below.

Estimation of the model

The model is fitted to annual observations for the period 1924–40 and 1949–65. Output (X) is measured by real gross private non-residential product, capital (K) by the real net stock of nonresidential structures and producers' durable equipment, and labor (L) by private man-hours. The price of capital (Q) is measured by its implicit rental rate, adjusted for taxation, and the price of labor (W) by the money wage. The derivation of the rental rate on capital is discussed in Appendix A, and further details on the data are given in Appendix B.

The best independent estimates obtained for the labor demand function are shown in Table 1. The labor function was selected from a group of twelve variants on the basic model. These differed according to the number of lagged output and price terms included, and also as to whether or not a shift in the level of the function, in the rate of technical change, or in both was assumed between the pre-war and post-war periods. The equation finally chosen is one in which a shift in level is included, but in which the trend term is continuous over the entire period and in which only the current values of output and relative prices enter.

Heavy reliance was placed on *a priori* constraints in making the final selection. The variants including lagged output and price variables had higher coefficients of determination, even after correction for degrees of freedom, but they were rejected because of numerous wrong signs on the estimated coefficients (the signs of a, β, γ, λ_1, λ_2, and the price and output expectation weights are all known a priori).

Table 1 Estimates of the parameters of the labor demand function, independent regression

Estimated parameters, equation 11a

Parameter	Estimate	Standard error
c_{01} (= $\lambda_1 \log a_{01}$)	0·9824	(0·2155)
c_{02} (= $\lambda_1 \log a_{02}$)	0·0538	(0·0237)
c_{11} (= $\lambda_1 a_1 w_{11}$)	0·1457	(0·0756)
c_{21} (= $\lambda_1 a_2 k_{11}$)	0·5871	(0·0504)
$-c_3$ (= $-\lambda_1 a_3$)	−0·0122	(0·0012)
$-c_4$ (= $-\lambda_1$)	−0·7767	(0·0638)
R^2	0·9054	
$\bar{R}^2$	0·8885	
S_u	0·0167	
DW	2·1148	

Implicit parameters

Equation 11 (labor demand)		Equation 1 (production function)	
λ_1	0·7767	a	0·2482
a_{01}	3·542	β	1·0748
a_{02}	1·072	$a+\beta$	1·3230
a_1	0·1876	γ	0·0208
a_2	0·7559	A_{01}	0·2699
a_3	0·0157	A_{02}	0·2463
w_{11}	1·0		
w_{12}	0·0		
k_{11}	1·0		
k_{12}	0·0		

A_{02} is derived from the product ($a_{01} a_{02}$) and refers to the post-war level of the production function, whereas A_{01} refers to the pre-war level

The variant including a shift parameter between the pre-war and post-war epochs had a slightly higher $\bar{R}^2$ and a more significant coefficient on price. These considerations were reinforced by the fact that the man-hours series has a conceptual discontinuity between the pre-war and post-war periods, as discussed in Appendix B.

The reasons for finally rejecting the variant with different exponential trends, and hence different estimated rates of technical change, in the pre war and post-war periods were more complicated. As compared with th regression finally selected, the labor function with an additional tren term had a superior fit and a sharper estimate of the price coefficient. I implied a substantially higher rate of technical progress post-war tha pre-war, but we could see no reason to reject that implication on *a prior* grounds. While preferring the simpler hypothesis (of a single rate o technical change throughout the period) on the principle of Occam' Razor, everything else the same, everything else was *not* the same insofa as the statistical criteria were concerned, for they favored the mor complicated hypothesis. We therefore decided to carry the variant wit different trends along with the other one to the next stage of the analysis Had it performed better at that stage (when the underlying productio function parameters as estimated from the labor demand function wer imposed on the investment demand function) it would have been chose over the simpler alternative, but this did not prove to be the case.[6]

The economic implications of the preferred labor demand function ar as follows. Adjustment of labor input to a change in output or relativ price occurs rapidly, both because a change leads to an immediate an complete revision of expectations (only current output and price ar involved in the formation of the expected values), and because the rate a which a gap between desired and actual man-hours is filled is high ($\lambda_1 = 0.78$). Insofar as the implicit production function parameters are con cerned, they imply a substantial degree of increasing returns to scal ($a + \beta = 1.32$), with a capital exponent of 0.25 and a labor exponent o 1.07. The estimated rate of technical progress is 2.1 per cent per annum.

If we turn now to the independent estimate of the investment deman function (Table 2) we find decidedly peculiar results. The investmen function fits better than its labor counterpart, and it also has the correc signs on all variables. In most other respects it is a poor equation, how ever. It implies a very slow adjustment speed ($\lambda_2 = 0.10$), sharply de creasing returns to scale ($a + \beta = 0.47$), and an extremely low labo exponent ($\beta = 0.16$). All these deficiencies appear to be traceable to th

6. A particular characteristic of our capital stock series may be responsible for the poor results obtained for the imposed form investment regression with two rates o technical progress. In constructing the capital stock series, we adopted a constant average depreciation rate for the entire period 1924–1965 (see Appendix B). If the rate of embodied progress is indeed higher in the post-war economy, the post-war depreciation rate should also be higher. Before deciding on a final set of factor demand and production functions for our macro-model, we plan to test whether an alternative capital stock series constructed from different pre-war and post-war depreciation rates will yield superior results for the imposed form investment regression with two rates of progress.

fact that the regression coefficients for current and lagged relative prices are very small and quite insignificant.

In view of the low values of the Durbin–Watson statistics for the investment regression, an attempt was made to improve the estimates by a first-

Table 2 Estimates of the parameters of the investment demand function, independent regression

Estimated parameters, equation 12a

Parameter	Estimate	Standard error
$d_0 \ (= \lambda_2 \log b_0)$	−0·6193	(0·0815)
$-d_{11} \ (= -\lambda_2 b_1 w_{21})$	−0·0195	(0·0417)
$-d_{12} \ (= \lambda_2 b_1 w_{22})$	−0·0157	(0·0429)
$d_{21} \ (= \lambda_2 b_2 k_{21})$	0·1857	(0·0299)
$d_{22} \ (= \lambda_2 b_2 k_{22})$	0·0371	(0·0312)
$-d_3 \ (= -\lambda_2 b_3)$	−0·0045	(0·0008)
$-d_4 \ (= -\lambda_2)$	−0·1044	(0·0182)
R^2	0·9575	
$\bar{R}^2$	0·9481	
S_v	0·0071	
DW	1·3303	

Implicit parameters

Equation 12 (net investment demand)		Equation 1 (production function)	
λ_2	0·1004	a	0·3106
b_0	0·0027	β	0·1580
b_1	0·3372	$a + \beta$	0·4686
b_2	2·1341	γ	0·0202
b_3	0·0431	A	17·93
w_{21}	0·5540		
w_{22}	0·4460		
k_{21}	0·8335		
k_{22}	0·1665		

order autoregressive transformation to reduce autocorrelation in the residuals, but this effort did not result in meaningful estimates of a and β, although it did increase the estimated adjustment speed moderately. We conclude that an independent estimate of the investment demand function leads to unacceptable results, whereas this is not true of the corresponding labor function.

R. M. Coen and B. G. Hickman 293

The imposed form investment function

The next investment function to be considered was estimated by imposing the implicit production function parameters from the labor demand function of Table 1. That is to say, the estimates of the a_i from the labor function were imposed in equation 12b and the remaining parameters were then determined in the process of fitting the equation to the data on investment. The new parameters to be determined were the capital-stock adjustment speed λ_2 and the expectational weights w_{2i} and k_{2i}. Because of large standard errors, however, the results from a free determination of

Table 3 Estimates of the parameters of the net investment demand function, equation 12b, imposed form with parameters from labor demand function.

Parameter	Estimate
Estimated parameters	
λ_2	0·1614
	(0·0219)
R^2	0·6240
$\bar{R}^2$	0·6240
S_v	0·0104
DW	1·6873
Imposed parameters	
w_{21}	0·0
w_{22}	1·0
k_{21}	0·8
k_{22}	0·2
a	0·2482
β	1·0748
$a+\beta$	1·3230
γ	0·0208
A	0·2699

the weights were inconclusive and are not reported. Instead, we report the outcome of a screening procedure in which alternative weighting patterns were imposed on the price and output terms, leaving only the adjustment speed to be determined directly by the regression.

In the screening procedure, we tried seven combinations of w_{21} and w_{22} – 1·0 and 0, 0·8 and 0·2, 0·6 and 0·4, 0·5 and 0·5, 0·4 and 0·6, 0·2 and 0·8, 0 and 1·0 – and similarly for the k_{2t}. This gave us forty-nine different combinations of $\log P_2^*$ and $\log X_2^*$ to try in as many equations for each model. The final equation for each model was selected from among the forty-nine contenders according to the criterion of best fit as measured by highest $\bar{R}^2$ (lowest residual variance).

The imposed form regression finally chosen is of satisfactory statistical quality (Table 3). The original version of this regression had a Durbin–Watson statistic of 0·3284, but the estimates in Table 3 are from a first-order autoregressive transformation which considerably raised the Durbin–Watson value. It should also be noted that the value of $\bar{R}^2$, while lower than those frequently encountered in time-series studies, is really rather good when viewed in proper context. We could have reported a much higher $\bar{R}^2$ merely by adding $\log K_{-1}$ to both sides of equation **12b** and running the regression with $\log K$ as the dependent variable. This linear recombination of **12b** would have yielded identical estimates of the unknown parameters and an identical residual variance to that obtained from the form used, but the $\bar{R}^2$ would have been higher because the residual variance would have been compared with the variance of a dependent variable ($\log K$) which was greater than the variance of the dependent variable actually used ($\log K - \log K_{-1}$). We deliberately chose the latter formulation because the former would have yielded such good fits for all the regressions (in view of the high correlation between $\log K$ and $\log K_{-1}$) that it would have been difficult to discriminate between them in the screening process.

Joint estimates of the complete system

An initial attempt to estimate freely all ten unknown parameters for the system comprised of equations **11** and **12b** foundered when some of the estimated expectations weights violated the *a priori* constraint that they be positive quantities. We therefore decided to impose the expectations weights on the two equations and to estimate the remaining parameters jointly. It was not possible, however, to adopt the procedure used before, of screening on forty-nine combinations of the expectations weights, since that would have been prohibitively expensive, given the high cost of full-information maximum-likelihood estimation. We chose instead to impose weight patterns consistent with those which produced the best results in the imposed form regression of Table 3.

Table 4 contains the joint estimates. Just as in the case of the imposed form investment regressions it was found that superior results were obtained from a first-order autoregressive transformation of the investment function, and the joint estimates in Table 4 are for a transformed investment function and an untransformed labor function.[7]

Comparison of alternative estimates

Upon comparing Tables 1, 3 and 4, we find that the parameters of the labor and investment functions obtained by the two-step procedure are virtually the same as those resulting from joint nonlinear estimation. Moreover, as shown in detail elsewhere (Coen and Hickman, 1969), the two-stage equations predict better over the sample period than their jointly estimated counterparts, although the margin is small. In view of the complexity and expense of joint nonlinear estimation, these findings suggest that the two-stage procedure may be preferable for an estimation problem like ours, especially since it permits great flexibility and economy in screening alternative weighting schemes. This is not to deny that the two procedures may yield rather different parameter estimates in some cases, but this is not an argument favoring either estimation method.[8] Finally, the reader is reminded that independent single-equation estimation of the investment function was notably unsuccessful and produced implausible results. Insofar as estimation procedures are concerned, the great improvement came in the recognition of the joint constraints placed on the factor demand functions by the production function, irrespective of whether this was done by joint estimation or the two-stage method.

Economic implications of the model

Since the first statistical variant of the model – estimated by the two-step procedure – has a slight edge in fit, we base our discussion of economic implications on the parameter estimates from Tables 1 and 3. These implications would be virtually the same, of course, if discussed in terms of the jointly estimated parameters of Table 4.

The implicit production function is Cobb–Douglas by specification. The implicit (long-run equilibrium) parameters are a capital elasticity of

7. The usual theoretical rationale for a first-order autoregressive transformation in a single-equation linear model does not apply strictly to our case of joint nonlinear estimation with interdependent error terms and parameter constraints. The transformation of the investment equation nevertheless considerably improved the joint estimates by randomizing the residuals of the net investment function. Interestingly enough, the investment transformation also improved the residual pattern of the jointly estimated labor function.

8. In a similar undertaking Bodkin and Klein (1967) compared two-step and simultaneous estimates of a model combining a production function and an expansion path equation. The parameter estimates were quite similar for the Cobb–Douglas case, although substantial differences were obtained for a CES specification.

0.25, a labor elasticity of 1.07, increasing returns to scale of 1.32, and a rate of technical progress of 2.1 per cent per annum. It may be noted that evidence of increasing returns to scale of the same order of magnitude has

Table 4 Joint estimates of the parameters of the labor and investment demand functions, equations 11 and 12b

Parameter	Estimate	Standard error
Estimated parameters		
a_{01}	3.3466	(0.4627)
a_{02}	1.0234	(0.5466)
a_1	0.1800	(0.0108)
a_2	0.7647	(0.0277)
a_3	0.0156	(0.0008)
λ_1	0.7475	(0.0473)
λ_2	0.1613	(0.0218)
S_u	0.0142	
S_v	0.0103	
r_{uv}	0.5167	
$\bar{R}_1^2$	0.9029	
$\bar{R}_2^2$	0.5453	
$(DW)_1$	2.6067	
$(DW)_2$	1.7433	
Imposed parameters		
w_{11}	1.0	
k_{11}	1.0	
w_{21}	0.0	
k_{21}	0.8	
Implicit parameters		
a	0.2354	
β	1.0723	
$a+\beta$	1.3077	
γ	0.0204	
A_{01}	0.2944	
A_{02}	0.2821	

A_{02} is derived from the product (a_{01} a_{02}) and refers to the post-war level of the production function, whereas A_{01} refers to the pre-war level

also been found in studies of similar aggregative data by Walters (1963), Diwan (1966), and Bodkin and Klein (1967).

The long-run equilibrium elasticities of labor and capital inputs, as specified in equations **3a** and **4a**, are as follows: the output elasticity for both labor and capital inputs is 0·76, whereas the relative price elasticities are 0·19 for labor and −0·81 for capital, where the latter elasticities measure the responses to a change in the rental price of capital relative to the money wage. The estimated rate of decline of desired capital and labor requirements per unit of expected output is 1·6 per cent per year.

The short-run responses of capital and labor inputs to a change in output or relative prices depend on the adjustment speeds and the expectation weights in the factor demand functions. The estimated annual rate of labor adjustment is 0·78, whereas net investment (strictly, the net capital expansion ratio) has an estimated adjustment rate of 0·16. Thus labor adjusts much more rapidly than capital to a difference between the desired and actual magnitudes. The time profile of either response also depends, however, on the response of expected output and price to actual output and price. In the labor function, expected output and price depend only on current output and price, so that the response of desired labor input to a change in either variable is immediate. In the investment function, however, expected price responds to actual price only after a year has passed, so that no investment is induced during the first year following a price change. In contrast, expected output responds strongly to actual output during the first year, although some of the response is delayed to the second year.

Table 5 Distributed lags of capital and labor on output and relative prices[a] (in per cent of total long-run responses)

Year	Capital		Labor
	Annual response to a once-for-all change in:		Annual response to a once-for-all change in:
	Output	Relative prices	Output or relative prices
1	13·0	0	77·6
2	14·0	16·1	17·3
3	11·8	13·5	3·8
4	9·9	11·3	0·9
5	8·3	9·5	0·3
Summation	57·0	50·4	99·9

[a] The method of calculating these lags is described in Hickman (1965, p. 38)

The time forms of the investment and labor responses to a once-for-all change of one per cent in either output or price are readily calculated from the coefficients of equations **11** and **12 b**. They are shown in Table 5 for a period of five years.

The response of capital to a change in output or relative factor prices is rather slow, so that only half or slightly more of the total adjustment takes place within five years. The humped pattern of the investment response to output is consistent with the findings of many previous studies (Coen, 1971; de Leeuw, 1962; Eisner, 1963; Hickman, 1965; Jorgenson, 1963; Nadiri and Rosen, 1969). The reaction of investment to a price change is delayed a full year and then declines gradually thereafter. In contrast, the labor response to either an output or price change takes place rapidly and follows a simple geometric lag, with 99 per cent of the total response completed within three years.

It should be stressed that some of these findings concerning short- and long-run elasticities are quite sensitive to the particular specifications of the model herein reported. Additional work on this model and some of the alternatives discussed in Coen and Hickman (1969) may lead us to different conclusions in the future. For example, we have not had time to examine the implications of the different models for the behavior of potential output – a topic on which we plan another paper in the near future. What is really in question is a triplet rather than a pair of functional relationships, and it would be unwise to ignore the properties of the implicit production function when choosing among alternative factor demand models. Moreover, as mentioned earlier, we plan to test the assumption of differing pre-war and post-war rates of technical progress on new capital stock data. Finally, factor demand functions derived from CES specification of the production function should be investigated to determine whether our data support the assumption of a unitary elasticity of substitution. In the meantime, we believe that the results in this paper have demonstrated the feasibility of our general approach to the constrained joint estimation of factor demand and production functions.

Appendix A

Derivation of the implicit rental price of capital

The rental price of capital is the cost per unit of capital per period which a firm incurs for having capital goods available for production during the period. If the firm were actually to rent its plant and equipment, it would pay this amount to the lessor in a competitive market. If it owns its plant and equipment, it pays this amount implicitly, that is to say, in its internal accounting it should charge itself this price per unit of capital on hand. Because ownership of capital goods is more common, we will usually refer to the price as an implicit rental price.

We derive the rental price by examining the optimal behavior of a firm that wishes to maximize its net worth. Given an infinite planning horizon, the firm's net worth at time 0 is

$$W_0 = \int\limits_0^\infty (pX_t - WL_t - qI_t - T_t)e^{-rt}dt \qquad \text{A1}$$

where p = price of output, X = output, W = wage rate, L = labor input, q = price of capital good (i.e. market price of a machine or building), I = gross investment, T = direct taxes, r = discount rate; and the firm wishes to maximize W_0 subject to (a) a production function

$$X_t = X_t(L_t, K_{t-1}), \qquad \text{A2}$$

where K_t is the stock of capital on hand at the end of period t, and (b) a relation indicating how current and past gross investments contribute to the current capital stock,

$$K_t = I_t + (1-\delta)K_{t-1} = I_t + (1-\delta)I_{t-1} + (1-\delta)^2 I_{t-2} + ..., \qquad \text{A3}$$

where δ may be viewed either as the real depreciation and obsolescence rate or as the replacement rate. The prices contained in A1 are, of course, expected prices, and we assume that the firm behaves as though its current expectations will hold for the infinite future. We also assume that the discount rate r, which will be discussed in more detail below, is viewed at the decision-making date as a constant over the entire planning horizon.

In defining T, we assume a direct tax at a rate u on total revenue, less wages and depreciation for tax purposes, and a tax credit for gross investment at a rate s; thus,

$$T_t = u(pX_t - WL_t - D_t) - sqI_t, \qquad \text{A4}$$

where D is depreciation for tax purposes. We assume further that depreciation policy stipulates that a fraction d_i of gross investment expenditure in a particular year may be claimed as depreciation for tax purposes in the ith year after the expenditures were made and that a proportion m of the tax credit must be deducted from the depreciable base of assets on which the credit is claimed. Then

$$D_t = \int\limits_0^\infty d_i(1-ms)qI_{t-i}\, di. \qquad \text{A5}$$

To complete the formulation of the net worth maximization problem we would have to specify the type of market in which the firm sells its product, for this would determine the product demand curve relating P and X. We know, however, that for any given P and X, the firm should select paths for the factor inputs that minimize the discounted value of outlays for factors and taxes, i.e. that minimize

$$C_0 = \int\limits_0^\infty (WL_t + qI_t + T_t)e^{-rt}\,dt. \qquad \text{A6}$$

Rather than limit our analysis to a particular and somewhat arbitrary choice for the market form, we adopt minimization of C_0 as our behavioral premise. We do assume that the firm behaves as though it faced perfectly elastic supply curves for factors of production.

First-order conditions for a minimum of **A6** subject to **A2** (with the X_t fixed for all t), **A3**, **A4**, and **A5** give

$$\frac{\partial X_t/\partial L_t}{\partial X_t/\partial K_t} = \frac{W}{q(e^r - 1 + \delta)\{1 - s - u(1 - ms)B\}/(1-u)}$$

$$= \frac{W}{Q} \qquad \text{A7}$$

for $t = 0, 1, \ldots$, where B is the discounted value of the stream of depreciation charges for tax purposes generated by a dollar of current investment, i.e.

$$B = \int\limits_0^\infty d_i e^{-ri}\,di.$$

These familiar conditions state that the marginal rate of substitution of the factors should be equated to the ratio of their prices, where the price of capital is the implicit rental price Q. The rental price is the product of $q(e^r - 1 + \delta)$, which is the rental rate in the absence of direct taxation, times an adjustment factor that captures the influence of various aspects of tax and depreciation policy.

Specification of the discount rate r raises some difficult problems. Conceptually, r is the rate at which the firm can borrow and lend funds. If for any reason, borrowing and lending rates differ, or if there is more than one borrowing rate, the firm's decision problem is considerably more complicated than the one just formulated and solved. A potential borrowing rate differential is created by the United States tax structure which allows firms to deduct interest payments from income. If debt were the only means of external finance, deductability of interest payments would be incorporated in the measure of Q by defining r as the after-tax market rate on bonds, i.e. $(1-u)r_m$, where r_m is the market rate. (The opportunity cost of internal funds would also be $(1-u)r_m$.) If equity finance is also possible, then in a competitive capital market in which risk is absent the rate that the firm must pay to obtain equity capital, say r_e, must be equal to $(1-u)r_m$. Thus, defining $r = (1-u)r_m$ in the measurement of Q would again be the proper way of incorporating the deductability of interest payments. However, if capital markets are not competitive, or if equities are viewed by investors as more risky than bonds, then $r_e \neq (1-u)r_m$. The firm's borrowing rate and tax payments in any period will depend on the type of financing it undertakes, and the financial mix will itself depend on the tax rate, among other things. Thus, while we are aware of the possible shortcomings of the practice, we have nevertheless adopted an after-tax market rate on bonds as the discount rate.

For earlier discussions of the concept and measurement of the implicit rental price of capital, the reader is referred to Bischoff (1971), Coen (1968, 1971), Hall and Jorgenson (1967), Jorgenson (1963).

Appendix B
Data used in the regression equation

The data are annual time series for 1922–40 and 1947–65. The period of fit was 1924–40 and 1949–65 but the earlier observations were needed to take account of lagged values for some of the variables. For most series, the data for 1929 and later years are from official sources, but the estimates for 1922–8 are extrapolations prepared by the authors from several primary sources. Deflated variables are in 1958 dollars.

1 *Output* (X): We have unofficially christened our output concept 'Gross private nonresidential product'. It is equal to real GNP minus real output originating in general government and real housing rent (including imputed rent on owner-occupied dwelling units).

2 *Capital stock* (K): This series is generated by use of the identity:

$$K_t = K_{t-1}+I_t-\delta K_{t-1},$$

where I_t is real gross nonresidential fixed investment expenditure as measured in the GNP accounts (nonresidential structures plus producers' durable equipment), δ is the depreciation rate and K_t is capital stock measured net of depreciation and at the end of period t. We view the measurement of capital net of depreciation as a method of vintage weighting to allow for embodied technical progress. That is to say, if the depreciation rate δ includes an allowance for obsolescence as well as for physical deterioration as ours does, then measuring capital in depreciated units is equivalent to measuring it in Solow-type productivity units, except that a trend term for the rate of embodied technical progress must be included in the production function in the former case, as explained in Hickman (1965, pp. 39–41).

$$\delta = 2d = 2 \cdot \frac{\displaystyle\sum_{t=26}^{66} \frac{D_t}{K_{t-1}^g} \cdot K_{t-1}^g}{\displaystyle\sum_{t=26}^{66} K_{t-1}^g} = 2 \cdot \frac{\displaystyle\sum_{t=26}^{66} D_t}{\displaystyle\sum_{t=25}^{65} K_t^g}.$$

Our estimate of δ is based on the OBE capital stock data. It was computed from the preceding formula.

In this formula, d is the estimated straight-line depreciation rate, computed as a weighted average over 1926–66 of the annual depreciation rates implicit in the OBE data on depreciation D and gross capital stock K^g for all nonresidential structures and equipment combined. We took the weighted average in order to abstract from changes over time in the aggregate depreciation rate due to shifts in the composition of assets among the various types of structures and equipment included in the OBE data. In accord with the usual practice, we assumed that the declining-balance rate δ to be applied to net capital stock was twice the straight-line rate.

Given the estimate of δ, the K series was computed from the aggregated gross investment data underlying the OBE capital stock estimates.

3   *Man-hours* (L): This series covers the private economy only. It is the product of private civilian employment (labor force concept) and hours of work per employed person per year in the private economy. The series on employment is discontinuous, since it refers to persons fourteen years and older in 1922–40, and sixteen years or over in 1947–65.

4   *Wage rate* (W): This variable is not measured by a wage index of the usual sort. Rather, it is the wage rate implicit in our estimates of private labor income and private man-hours. Private labor income is defined as the sum of private employee compensation (exclusive of that paid by sole proprietors and partnerships) and an imputed labor share originating in proprietors and partnerships. The latter imputation is based on the assumption that the division of income originating in proprietorships and partnerships between labor and nonlabor shares is the same as the distribution of labor and nonlabor income in the corporate sector.

5   *Implicit rental price of capital* (Q): The series used in constructing the implicit rental price of capital are described below, following the notation of Appendix A:
(a) The price of capital goods, q, is the deflator for gross nonresidential fixed investment;

(b) The bond yield, r_m, is Moody's average yield on corporate bonds;

(c) The tax rate, u, is a weighted average of effective income tax rates (federal, state, and local) on corporate profits and noncorporate profits, the weights being the proportions of corporate and noncorporate profits in total profits before tax and before inventory valuation adjustment (I VA). The effective tax rate on noncorporate profits was assumed to be the effective income tax rate on all personal income. Both the corporate and noncorporate effective tax rates were smoothed to eliminate what appeared to be purely cyclical variation;

(d) The depreciation rate, δ, is the same as that used in constructing the capital stock series;

(e) The investment tax credit rate, s, which applies only to the years 1962–5, was set equal to the effective credit rate, i.e. the ratio of the total credits claimed by sole proprietorships, partnerships, and corporations to gross nonresidential fixed investment in each year. Data for 1965 were not available, however, so the effective rate for 1964 was assumed to hold for 1965 also;

(f) The proportion of the investment credit that must be deducted from the depreciable base of assets, m, which applies only to the years 1962–5, was by law equal to unity for 1962–63 and zero thereafter;

(g) The discounted value of tax depreciation charges generated by a dollar of investment, B, was constructed to reflect major changes in depreciation policy over the period studied. Depreciation policy has dealt with both the formula used in writing off assets and the useful life of assets for tax purposes. The straight-line formula was the most widely used until 1954, and we have incorporated it in estimating B up to that date. Beginning in 1954, B is a weighted average of discounted values given by the straight-line, double-rate declining-balance, and sum-of-years-digits formulas with the weights reflecting the actual use of the various methods by business firms after 1953, as indicated in the statistics presented by Ture (1967).

Our estimated useful life for tax purposes changes over time to reflect five different eras in depreciation policy: 1922–33, during which depreciation charges were not scrutinized by Internal Revenue officials and useful lives were generally much shorter than actual service lives; 1934–48, a period of administrative tightening of depreciation rules, in which useful lives were gradually increased toward those suggested in the Treasury's *Bulletin F*; 1949–53, during which *Bulletin F* lives appear to have been enforced; 1954–61, a period of administrative liberalization which tended to reduce useful lives; 1962–65, in which suggested lives for machinery and equipment were reduced 30–40 per cent below those in *Bulletin F* (see Revenue Procedure 62–21). OBE data on straight-line depreciation and gross capital stock in historical dollars based on *Bulletin F* service lives were used to obtain an estimate of the useful life for the third era, and this life was adjusted upward or downward for the other eras in the light of whatever scattered information could be found.

References

BISCHOFF, C. W. (1971), 'The effect of alternative lag distributions', in G. Fromm (ed.), *Tax Incentives and Capital Spending*, Brookings Institution, North-Holland.

BODKIN, R. G., and KLEIN, L. R. (1967), 'Nonlinear estimation of aggregate production functions', *Rev. econ. Stat.*, vol. 49, pp. 28–44.

COEN, R. M. (1968), 'Effects of tax policy on investment in manufacturing', *Amer. econ. Rev.*, vol. 58, pp. 200–211.

COEN, R. M. (1971), 'The effect of cash flow on the speed of adjustment', in G. Fromm (ed.), *Tax Incentives and Capital Spending*, Brookings Institution, North-Holland.

COEN, R. M., and HICKMAN, B. G. (1969), *Aggregative Demand Functions for Capital and Labor in the US Economy*, Research Memorandum no. 74, Research Center in Economic Growth, Stanford University.

DE LEEUW, F. (1962), 'The demand for capital goods by manufacturers: a study of quarterly time series', *Econometrica*, vol. 30, pp. 407–23.

DHRYMES, P. J. (1967), 'Adjustment dynamics and the estimation of the CES class of production functions', *Inter. econ. Rev.*, vol. 8, pp. 209–17.

DIWAN, R. K. (1966), 'Alternative specifications of economies of scale', *Economica*, vol. 33, pp. 442–53.

EISENPRESS, H., and GREENSTADT, J. (1966), 'The estimation of nonlinear econometric systems', *Econometrica*, vol. 34, pp. 851–61.

EISNER, R. (1963), 'Investment: fact and fancy', *Amer. econ. Rev.*, vol. 53, pp. 237–46.

HALL, R. E., and JORGENSON, D. W. (1967), 'Tax policy and investment behavior', *Amer. econ. Rev.*, vol. 57, pp. 391–414.

HICKMAN, B. G. (1965), *Investment Demand and US Economic Growth*, Brookings Institution.

JORGENSON, D. W. (1963), 'Capital theory and investment behavior', *Amer. econ. Rev.*, vol. 53, pp. 247–59.

NADIRI, M. I., and ROSEN, S. (1969), 'Interrelated factor demand functions', *Amer. econ. Rev.*, vol. 59, pp. 457–71.

NERLOVE, M. (1967), 'Notes on the production and derived demand relations included in macroeconometric models', *Inter. econ. Rev.*, vol. 8, pp. 223–42.

TURE, N. B. (1967), *Accelerated Depreciation in the United States, 1954–1960*, National Bureau of Economic Research, Fiscal Studies no. 9, Columbia University Press.

WALTERS, A. A. (1963), 'A note on economies of scale', *Rev. econ. Stat.*, vol. 45, pp. 425–27.

13 J. F. Helliwell and G. Glorieux

Forward-Looking Investment Behaviour[1]

J. F. Helliwell and G. Glorieux, 'Forward-looking investment behaviour', *Review of Economic Studies*, vol. 37, 1970, pp. 499–516.

I Introduction

Most econometric models of capital expenditures have current expenditures as a function of discrepancies between actual and desired capital stock in one or several previous time periods. The models usually represent an uneasy compromise between explicit descriptions of optimal behaviour and *ad hoc* simplifications intended to make the model operational.

Optimizing assumptions are frequently used to derive a 'desired' capital stock for a given level of output and prices of capital goods, output, and finance (e.g. Jorgenson, 1965). On the other hand, there has been little quantitative analysis that has taken anything like corresponding care in the specification of the way in which expectations are formed about the future prices and quantities, and of the factor which influences the time distribution of investment outlays.[2]

Our chief concern in this paper is to develop a model which attempts to deal with the latter two problems. We continue to assume, as was done in the models (Evans and Helliwell, 1969) preceding our present work, that our quarterly data period is too short to allow us to disentangle the effects of the changes in technology and relative prices which have determined the longer-run changes in the capital–output ratio. Thus we continue to assume that we can use prices and supply constraints to explain at most the cyclical shifts of the desired capital–output ratio, and use a modified trend-through-troughs procedure to determine the longer-term movements in the optimal ratio.

In our present efforts to deal with the interaction between the lags in the expectations process and those in the spending process, we are bedevilled by lack of data, and by the large number of plausible hypotheses to be

1. This research was carried out in the Research Department of the Bank of Canada as one of a number of studies underlying a series of aggregate econometric models. At the time the paper was written, Helliwell was a part-time econometric consultant and Glorieux was a full-time member of the Research Department. No responsibility for the views expressed should be attributed to their employers.
2. Notable contributions to the related qualitative theory have been made by Eisner and Strotz (1963), Gould (1968), and Lucas (1967).

tested, but we consider the alterations we are proposing to be important enough to be worth testing even under the most unfavourable conditions. We have been troubled by the extent to which models of investment behaviour supposedly based on optimal behaviour make current investment expenditures depend directly on present and past observed capital shortages and surpluses. We prefer to think that, since firms are aware that there are necessary lags between investment decisions and actual outlays, investment planners make investment expenditures in the current period so as to avoid the appearance of capital shortages or surpluses in the future.[3] Nothing can be done about the present and past shortages; we build our model on the assumption that decision-makers can see bygones as bygones, and make their decisions entirely with respect to expected future capita requirements. As will be seen, a model based on this view of optimal behaviour leads to a different form of investment equation.[4]

Aside from whatever gains it may or may not provide in theoretical appeal or forecasting power, our procedure of making explicit the forward-looking nature of investment behaviour has an important additional advantage. Since our model makes explicit the process by which future expectations are based on past observations, it provides a framework to assess changes in plans over time, and hence a way of systematically combining forecasts obtained from an investment equation with those made directly by business firms. Thus we are able to obtain 'realization functions' which are directly derived from our model of investment behaviour. We naturally hope that the tightness of the links between the two will enable us to combine our aggregate investment equations with the forecasts made by business firms and thereby to obtain more accurate forecasts than could be obtained from either used alone.

3. It is possible to interpret a number of existing investment equations as forward-looking by assuming that planners' expectations about output in all future periods have unit elasticity with respect to current output. It is also necessary to assume that planners ignore the existence of projects under construction when they are deciding what new investment to undertake.

4. It will be seen that it is hard to regard the behaviour implied by our model as optimal by any rigorous standard, for our convention of regarding work put in place (investment outlays) as part of the capital stock means that it will be impossible to hit a highly variable desired capital stock exactly if additions to the capital stock can only be accomplished by investment expenditures over a succession of periods. We have developed an alternative framework which excludes investment expenditures from the capital stock until all expenditures on the related projects are completed, but the resulting equations are even more complicated and hard to fit than the ones we are using. At any rate, our expectations process operates so as to alter the desired capital stock in adjacent periods by fairly smoothly changing amounts, so that the theoretically possible unpleasant results of our assumptions do not cause much difficulty in our applications.

J. F. Helliwell and G. Glorieux 307

II The theoretical model

The formation of expectations

In our first efforts, we shall concentrate on how expectations are formed about aggregate desired capital stock in future periods. Putting aside, for the time being, the influence of financial variables and supply constraints on the desired capital–output ratio, the desired capital stock in any future period is equal to the (extrapolated) desired capital–output ratio times the expected value of output.

In general, we suppose that expectations about future output are based on past values, and that the expectations process contains extrapolative, regressive, and trend growth elements. We are not the first to suggest combining regressive and extrapolative elements in the formation of expectations (see Duesenberry, 1958, p. 318; de Leeuw, 1965, p. 500; Modigliani and Sutch, 1966), but the earlier work was not expressly designed to deal with variables with substantial trends. Our output variable, Y, has a marked trend. If we wish to define a regressive expectations process which is not biased, it is necessary to adjust past values of Y for changes over time in its trend value. Similarly, if we wish to define an extrapolative element with a mean value of zero (over the duration of the series) then each component should be equal to $Y_t-(1+g)Y_{t-1}$, where g is the trend rate of growth of Y. Naturally, it is difficult to make these adjustments if one has reason to suspect that the growth process does not have a constant trend element. In general, the expected trend growth rate g has to be treated as one of the estimated parameters of the expectations process. If $Y^*_{t,t-1}$ is the expectation about Y for the period t, as seen from the end of period $t-1$, then the regressive element of Y is:

$$Y^*_{REGt,t-1} = \gamma_1(1+g)Y_{t-1}+\gamma_2(1+g)^2 Y_{t-2}\dots \qquad 1$$

Adding the extrapolative element, we get:

$$Y^*_{t,t-1} = Y^*_{REGt,t-1}+b[\lambda_1\{Y_{t-1}-(1+g)Y_{t-2}\}$$
$$+\lambda_2\{Y_{t-2}-(1+g)Y_{t-3}\}\dots], \qquad 2$$

$$Y^*_{t,t-1} = \{\gamma_1+\gamma_1 g+b\lambda_1\}Y_{t-1}+\{\gamma_2(1+g)^2-b\lambda_1(1+g)+b\lambda_2\}Y_{t-2}$$
$$+\{\gamma_3(1+g)^3-b\lambda_2(1+g)+b\lambda_3\}Y_{t-3}\dots, \qquad 3$$

where we assume

$$\sum_{i=1}^{\infty} \gamma_i = 1, \ \sum_{i=1}^{\infty} \lambda_i = 1.$$

If expectations are entirely extrapolative, then $\gamma_1 = 1$ and $b > 0$. If they are entirely regressive, then $b = 0$ and $\gamma_1 < 1$.

If the theory is to be complete, it must indicate how expectations are formed, at the end of the period $t-1$, about output in period $t+n$. Let

$$\{\gamma_1(1+g)+b\lambda_1\} = \beta_1, \ \{\gamma_2(1+g)^2+b(\lambda_2-(1+g)\lambda_1)\} = \beta_2, \text{ etc.}$$

Then $\quad Y_{t,t-1}^* = \sum_{i=1}^{\infty} \beta_i Y_{t-i}.$

We will assume that expectations about output in period $t+k$ are formed recursively; thus

$$Y_{t+k,t-1}^* = \sum_{i=1}^{k} \beta_i Y_{t+k-i,t-1}^* + \sum_{i=k+1}^{\infty} \beta_i Y_{t+k-i}, \quad k = 0, \dots, n. \qquad 4$$

Equation 4 represents a system of $n+1$ simultaneous equations in $n+1$ unknowns which can be written in the following form:

$$
\begin{bmatrix}
1 & 0 \dots\dots\dots\dots 0 \\
-\beta_1 & 1 \\
& \cdot \\
-\beta_2 & -\beta_1 \quad \cdot \\
\vdots & \qquad \cdot \quad 1 \quad 0 \\
& \qquad\quad \cdot \\
-\beta_{..} \dots\dots\dots\dots -\beta_1 \quad 1
\end{bmatrix}
\begin{bmatrix}
Y_{t,t-1}^* \\
\vdots \\
\vdots \\
\vdots \\
\vdots \\
Y_{t+n,t-1}^*
\end{bmatrix}
=
\begin{bmatrix}
\beta_1 & \beta_2 \dots\dots \beta_m \\
\beta_2 & \beta_3 \dots \beta_m 0 \\
& \qquad 0 \\
& \qquad 0 \\
\vdots \\
\beta_{n+1} \dots\dots \beta_m \quad 0
\end{bmatrix}
\begin{bmatrix}
Y_{t-1} \\
\vdots \\
\vdots \\
\vdots \\
\\
\\
Y_{t-m}
\end{bmatrix}
$$
5

The matrix pre-multiplying the vector of expected Y is $n+1$ by $n+1$ where n is the number of future periods (in addition to the current period) about which expectations are formed. The matrix pre-multiplying the vector of past Y is $n+1$ by m, where m is equal to the number of past values of Y required as a basis for current expectations. Solving the set of equations for the column vector of expectations $\{Y^*\}$, and using Φ to represent the $n+1$ by m reduced-form coefficient matrix, we have

$$\{Y^*\} = \Phi\{Y_L\}, \qquad 6$$

where $\{Y_L\}$ is an m by 1 column vector of lagged values of observed Y. We can combine this expression for Y^* with a vector of desired capital–output ratios to obtain a vector of desired capital stock. We use $KMEY^*$ and $KNRY^*$ to represent the desired capital–output ratios for machinery and equipment (ME) and non-residential construction (NRC), respectively.

KME^* and KNR^* are the corresponding desired capital stocks. The desired stocks in period t may be written as

$$KME_t^* = KMEY_t^* \Phi_1\{Y_L\} \qquad\qquad 7$$

$$KNR_t^* = KNRY_t^* \Phi_1\{Y_L\} \qquad\qquad 8$$

where Φ_1 is the first row of the Φ matrix, and $\{Y_L\}$ is, as before, the column vector of lagged values of observed Y. Using M to represent an $n+1$ by $n+1$ diagonal matrix of the $KMEY^*$ for periods t to $t+n$, and N for the corresponding matrix of the $KNRY^*$, we can obtain compact expressions for the desired capital stocks within the entire n-period investment horizon:

$$\{KME^*\} = M\Phi\{Y_L\}, \qquad\qquad 9$$

$$\{KNR^*\} = N\Phi\{Y_L\}. \qquad\qquad 10$$

Combining expectations with expenditure lags

Our procedure has given us expressions for the desired capital stock in each future time period. In order to obtain an investment equation we need to combine this framework with an expenditure lag distribution. In the present context, it is more appropriate to call the latter a lead rather than a lag distribution, for we wish to use it to tell us how long in advance a project must be started if it is to be finished in time to avoid what otherwise would be a shortage of capital in some future period.

Suppose that it takes j periods of expenditures to put machinery and equipment in place. The existence of some such time profile spread over several quarters may be justified by reference either to individual investment projects or to aggregate relationships between appropriations and investment expenditures.[5] If the desired capital stock at a point in time exceeds what would normally be there in the way of depreciated capital left over from the previous period, then investment expenditures must be undertaken in the preceding j periods if production is to be arranged optimally. The investment in any particular period is therefore related to

5. Case studies of investment decisions in large firms, reported by Helliwell (1968, ch. 3), indicate that the 'investment appropriation' is the best evidence of a decision to undertake an investment project, and that actual expenditures on particular projects usually are undertaken as quickly as possible after the appropriation receives approval. Almon (1965) and Hart (1965) have fitted lag distributions linking appropriations and expenditure data. There are no corresponding appropriations data for Canada, a fact which raises problems for our empirical work.

the expected capital requirements in each of the succeeding j periods. Thus, if IME is investment expenditures on machinery and equipment:

$$IME_t = \sum_{i=0}^{j-1} W_{j-i}\{KME^*_{t+i} - (1-\rho)KME_{t+i-1}\}, \qquad \textbf{11}$$

where the W_i are weights $\left(\sum_{i=0}^{j-1} W_i = 1\right)$ indicating the time profile of investment outlays required to fill a particular capital shortage, and ρ is the periodic rate of depreciation plus obsolescence of KME.

The first step is to obtain a solution for the investment model in terms of predetermined variables. The distinction between KME^* and KME really starts to plague us at this point. KME^* is predetermined, but KME is not. The problem exists only for the j periods required to complete investment projects, since beyond that time $KME = KME^*$. Within the j periods from t to $t+j-1$, however, we are faced with a set of $2j$ simultaneous equations which must be solved to obtain the reduced form investment equations. The reason that, in general, $KME \neq KME^*$ for periods between t and $t+j-1$ is that a change in K^* for some period, say $t+h$, between t and $t+j-1$, will not allow time for the necessary adjustments to the capital stock by the time $t+h$ rolls around. One possibility would be to assume that nothing would be done to make up *ex ante* capital shortages at $t+h$, as long as $h<j-1$. What we shall assume is that some additional (or less) investment will be done, the total change in investment between now and $t+h$ being a fraction of that indicated by the change in KME^*_{t+h}. The size of the fraction of the shortage that would be provided depends not only on how large h is in relation to j, but also on the shape of the W_i distribution. Our assumption, if it is to be reasonable, requires that it be better to undertake some fraction of the indicated expenditures, over the (necessarily) shorter period, than to either ignore altogether the change in capital requirements signalled by the change in KME^*_{t+h} or to undertake a crash programme designed to meet in full the indicated capital shortage. As long as any compromise is struck between ignoring altogether the change in KME^*_{t+h} or filling it completely so that $KME_{t+h} = KME^*_{t+h}$ even when $h < j-1$, it will be necessary to solve a set of $2j$ simultaneous equations, one each in KME and IME, for each of the j construction periods. Each of the equations for IME is like the one shown above, while the equations for KME are capital stock identities of the usual form:

$$KME_t = (1-\rho)KME_{t-1} + IME_t. \qquad \textbf{12}$$

If j is very large, each reduced form equation for *IME* becomes pretty complicated. As long as j is more than 1, the equations for *IME* depend, in general, on the values of *KME** for several periods as well as on the depreciation rate ρ and the pattern of weights W_i. Considering, as a fairly simple example, the case where $j = 3$, we can see the general pattern of the solution.

In matrix form, the equations are as follows:

$$
\begin{bmatrix}
1 & 0 & 0 & W_2(1-\rho) & W_1(1-\rho) & 0 \\
0 & 1 & 0 & W_3(1-\rho) & W_2(1-\rho) & W_1(1-\rho) \\
0 & 0 & 1 & 0 & W_3(1-\rho) & W_2(1-\rho) \\
1 & 0 & 0 & -1 & 0 & 0 \\
0 & 1 & 0 & (1-\rho) & -1 & 0 \\
0 & 0 & 1 & 0 & (1-\rho) & -1
\end{bmatrix}
\begin{bmatrix}
IME_t \\
IME_{t+1} \\
IME_{t+2} \\
KME_t \\
KME_{t+1} \\
KME_{t+2}
\end{bmatrix}
$$

$$
=
\begin{bmatrix}
-W_3(1-\rho) & W_3 & W_2 & W_1 & 0 & 0 \\
0 & 0 & W_3 & W_2 & W_1 & 0 \\
0 & 0 & 0 & W_3 & W_2-(1-\rho)W_1 & W_1 \\
-(1-\rho) & 0 & 0 & 0 & 0 & 0 \\
0 & 0 & 0 & 0 & 0 & 0 \\
0 & 0 & 0 & 0 & 0 & 0
\end{bmatrix}
\begin{bmatrix}
KME_{t-1} \\
KME_t^* \\
KME_{t+1}^* \\
KME_{t+2}^* \\
KME_{t+3}^* \\
KME_{t+4}^*
\end{bmatrix} . \quad \textbf{13}
$$

If we use Γ to represent the right-hand side square matrix pre-multiplied by the inverse of the left-hand side square matrix, we have:

$$\{IME, KME\} = \Gamma\{KME_{t-1}, KME^*\}. \qquad \textbf{14}$$

When the model is generalized to make the construction time j rather than 3 periods, no fundamental changes are required. The left-hand column vector has $2j$ elements, since there is one equation each for *IME* and *KME* in each of the j periods. Γ is a square matrix of order $2j$, while the column vector by which it is post-multiplied contains KME_{t-1} and $2j-1$ values of *KME**, starting with KME_t^* and going on to KME_{t+2j-2}^*. Thus the equation for *IME* in period t is:

$$IME_t = \Gamma_1\{KME_{t-1}, KME_t^*, ..., KME_{t+2j-2}^*\}, \qquad \textbf{15}$$

where Γ_1 is the first row of the Γ matrix.

Now we are ready to combine the model of the expectations process (as summarized by equation 9) with our assumptions about investment lead times. The expectations horizon n must be defined to include $2j-1$ periods, including the current period. Thus the Φ matrix in equation 9 is $2j-1$ by m, and the reduced form equation for IME_t, in terms of lagged

Y, the present capital stock, and the parameters of the expectations and expenditure processes is:

$$IME_t = \Gamma_1\{KME_{t-1}, M\Phi\{Y_L\}\}. \qquad\qquad 16$$

This model, which is the one which we are testing empirically, assumes initially that the W_t distribution of expenditures is fixed primarily by technological and institutional factors rather than by variables currently endogenous to a macro-model. At a later stage in our experiments we introduce variables which our earlier work showed to influence the timing of investment expenditures, but we are not prepared to argue that the resulting functional forms necessarily represent the correct functional dependence of the W_t on economic factors.

Combining investment equations with investment forecasts by firms

The investment equation represented by equation **16** uses only lagged values of Y, and hence assumes that output in the current quarter is not reported soon enough to have any material impact on the expectations determining capital expenditures in the current period.[6] Equation **16** thus uses expectations formed about Y for period t and beyond using only information, available in period t, referring to $t-1$ and previous periods.

We wish also to have an investment forecast equation based on the same model of expectations and expenditures. These are already available, for $j-1$ future periods, from the investment model recorded in equation **15**, since the equations for IME_{t+1}, IME_{t+2}, etc. are based only on information from $t-1$ and earlier periods. In order to show how these forecast equations alter over time as new information appears, it is necessary to use a double subscript notation, the first subscript referring to the period in which the investment is to take place, and the second referring to the last period for which information is available. Using this notation, equation **16** for actual investment in period t is written:

$$IME_{t,t-1} = \Gamma_1\{KME_{t-1}, M\Phi\{Y_{t-1}, ..., Y_{t-m}\}\}, \qquad 17$$

and the forecast equation for investment in period $t+1$ is:

$$IME_{t+1,t-1} = \Gamma_2\{KME_{t-1}, M\Phi\{Y_{t-1}, ..., Y_{t-m}\}\}. \qquad 18$$

In order to get an expression for the forecast equation for period t, we have to lag equation **18** one period:

$$IME_{t,t-2} = \Gamma_2\{KME_{t-2}, M\Phi\{Y_{t-2}, ..., Y_{t-m-1}\}\}. \qquad 19$$

6. Evidence from earlier work by ourselves and others indicates that the current quarter's output has little or no influence on current period expenditures. See Wilson (1967) and Evans and Helliwell (1969). This 'information lag' may be traced either to lags in the reporting of current output and sales or to delays by decision-makers in taking account of the new information as it appears.

Equation **19** determines the investment forecast for quarter t, as made at a time when the actual information from $t-2$ and previous periods was available to influence expectations.

A 'realizations function'[7] attempts to relate the difference between actual and forecast expenditures to some combination of economic variables. In the absence of an explicit expectations model, it is very difficult to specify realizations functions, since it is impossible to specify the extent to which current changes in economic variables had already been built into the expectations of decision-makers at the time the initial forecast was made. Within our explicit expectations framework, however, the specification of a realizations function is very simple. Since equation **17** is the equation for actual investment in period t, and equation **19** is the forecast made during the previous period, the realizations function is simply the difference between the two. When we wish to use our quarterly investment and forecast equations to develop a realizations equation for forecasts made on an annual basis (as we shall do in the next section), the algebra becomes slightly more complicated, but the basic principle still holds.

It remains only to consider how we ought to combine our structural model with businessmen's forecasts in order to use both sorts of information in a consistent manner. We propose to fit our forecast equation **19** (or, rather, the corresponding annual equation) to the investment forecasts made by firms, in the fall of each year, of their *IME* and *INRC* expenditures during the following calendar year. We will also fit equation **17** to the national accounts figures for actual expenditures. If there is any systematic relationship between the residuals of the two equations, then there is relevant information in the forecasts by firms in addition to that already taken into account by the investment equation.

We shall take account of the survey information by two alternative methods. The first uses a genuine forecasting model, employing only information available at the time the survey is made (i.e. that required to calculate investment according to equation **19**). The second is an adaptation of the realizations function approach, and thus makes use of equation **17**, equation **19**, and the survey information.

III Empirical results

When applying our framework to Canadian quarterly and annual data, we have tried to relate our current work as closely as possible to the earlier experiments underlying the investment equations used in the quarterly econometric model of the Canadian economy, *RDX*1 (Helliwell *et al.*, 1969). This involves some constraints on our choice of financial variables, but

7. Previous empirical applications of realizations functions to aggregate investment forecast and actual expenditures have been undertaken by Eisner (1965) and others.

allows us to assess more clearly the consequences of alternative patterns of weights in the expectations process, and the interactions between the expenditure weights W_i and the parameters of the expectations process.

Even with our pattern of experiments constrained so as to relate more closely to our earlier work, we were forced to fit our model using only a sample of the possible sets of assumptions about the various parameters governing the expectations and expenditure processes. We tried to select the sets of assumptions so as to test a fairly wide range of possibilities, aware of the dangers that our experiments might miss the best specification either because we were searching far from the correct region in the parameter space or because we were searching in the right region using too coarse a grid. In the light of our results, it is likely that we have done more to avoid the latter danger than the former. On this point, the reader must make his own judgment, and be warned that our conclusion reflects optimism that more satisfactory results are somewhere to be found.

Our experiments were in two stages. In the first stage we fitted our model separately to gross quarterly investment expenditures of $INRC$ and IME, attempting to find appropriate values for the W_i weights and the expectations parameters. In the second stage of our experiments, we used the most likely sets of parameter values as a basis for constructing estimates of annual forecast and annual actual expenditures, and hence to fit an annual realizations function. Then we proceeded, as recommended in Section II, to construct an equation for actual expenditures which combines the structure of the straightforward investment equation with some fraction of the contemporaneous residuals from the forecast equation. Our report will deal with the two stages separately.

Fitting quarterly investment equations

For IME and $INRC$, separately, we experimented with three patterns of W_i weights, three different exponential distributions for the λ_i and the γ_i, and four different values for b. We treated the desired capital–output ratios $KMEY$ and $KNRY$ as exogenous to the model. Their values were obtained by applying the trend-through-troughs procedure used by Evans and Helliwell (1969) to the revised figures 1953–67 for real domestic product less agriculture (Y). To avoid the complicated interactions between the expectations parameters and the seasonality in Y, we used the index in seasonally adjusted form when deriving our series for K^*. The actual capital stock series used have also been accumulated from seasonally adjusted expenditures. The fitting period for our equations was $1Q53$–$4Q65$, the same as that used for the $RDX1$ equations. Our aim was to obtain equations which could be compared reasonably favourably with the $RDX1$ equations over the 1953–65 estimation period, yet might perform better (at least in the case of *IME*) than the *RDX*1 equations when used to derive forecasts for 1966–68.

The object of the first stage of our research was to develop two models for aggregate investment. The first model excludes all financial variables, while the second includes them. Each of the models has one equation for *IME* and another for *INRC*. In each model we shall force the expectations process for *Y* to be the same in both equations.

As for the expectations parameters, we restricted ourselves to exponentially decaying patterns for the λ_i and γ_i, truncating both distributions after several periods and adjusting the weights to make them sum to 1. If we define $e = \lambda_{i+1}/\lambda_i$ and $r = \gamma_{i+1}/\gamma_i$ then we used 0·3, 0·6, and 0·9 as alternative values for e and r. The parameter b, which establishes the relative weights attached to the regressive and extrapolative elements in the formation of expectations, was given the values 0, 0·5, 1·0, and 1·5, the larger values indicating greater weight attached to the extrapolative element. Within the constraint set by our choice of exponentially declining weights for the λ_i and γ_i, our sample of parameters gives us a complete, if somewhat coarse, grid over all possible combinations of parameters of the expectations process. It is quite possible, of course, that either the λ_i or the γ_i, or both, rise before they start declining, in which case our experiments will not have turned up the best set of expectations parameters. But we had to set some limits to our search process. After experimenting with three different lengths for the expectations process, we found that more accurate expectations are formed if the expectations process is truncated at twelve rather than ten or seven quarters. Thus all our reported equations are based on expectations processes using twelve previous values of *Y*.

Our procedure has been to make a set of assumptions about the basic parameters of the model, calculate two seasonally adjusted investment series according to equation 17, one each for *IME* and *INRC*, and then to regress each seasonally unadjusted quarterly investment series on the calculated series, making appropriate allowances for seasonality. After experimentation, we found that the allowances for seasonality used in Evans and Helliwell (1969) seemed appropriate also for our present model. Thus our *IME* equations have four linear quarterly dummy variables and four entering multiplicatively with the calculated investment series. The *INRC* equations have four trended quarterly dummy variables and only a single variable representing the calculated investment series.

We cannot present all our results in this paper, for the four values of b, three patterns each for the γ_i and λ_i, and three W_i distributions, require ninety equations for *IME* and another ninety for *INRC*. Figure 1 shows a sample of some of the better-fitting expectations mechanisms as well as the W_t distributions used for *IME* and *INRC*. *A priori*, there is every reason to suspect that the expectations process for Y which produces the best fitting *IME* regression will be different from that which gives the best-fitting *INRC* regression, if only because of sampling differences. Since we ran our first-stage experiments for *IME* and *INRC* separately, it was only after the experiments were run that we imposed the constraint that the expectations process for Y had to be the same in the *IME* equation as in the *INRC* equation. We did so by preparing tables showing the standard error of estimate for equations based on different patterns of expectations. Table 1 shows the results for *IME* and for *INRC* using the best W_t distribution for each. The W_t distribution for *IME* is the eight-quarter distribution which Almon (1965) found linking appropriations and outlays for total investment in US manufacturing.[8] The W_t weights for *INRC* (following a pattern which we call *RPLLAG*) are spread over nine quarters, as shown in Figure 1. Shorter W_t distributions for either *INRC* or *IME* fit less well than these for all of the sets of expectations parameters used.[9] Thus, since expectations are based on twelve past values of Y, and there are eight quarters in the W_t distribution for machinery and equipment, the Φ matrix for *IME* is 15 by 12 while Γ is 16×16. For *INRC*, the Φ matrix is 17×12 and the Γ matrix 18×18. We can thus generate quarterly *IME* forecasts for the current and seven subsequent quarters, and *INRC* forecasts for a total of nine quarters, using only information available now.

Returning to Table 1, we can assess the plausibility – given the 1953–65 sample of data – of various sets of expectations parameters in the model without any financial variables. Fortunately, the *IME* and the *INRC* data give fairly compatible estimates of the most likely set of parameters. In both cases, 1·5 is the most likely value for b. For *IME* the most likely values of the slopes of the exponential decline of the regressive and extrapolative elements were 0·9 and 0·6 for e and r respectively. For *INRC*, however, the most likely values for e and r were 0·3 and 0·9, although the results are really quite equivocal, as can be seen from the remarkably similar values for *SEE* in Table 1.

8. We might have expected a shorter distribution to fit better, for Almon's weights refer to *IME* plus *INRC*, and building takes longer to put in place. On the other hand, Almon's weights apply to manufacturing, while our equations relate to total business investment including considerable expenditures on hydro-electric facilities and other non-manufacturing projects with long gestation periods.
9. The W_t weights used in our present work should be distinguished from those used in Evans and Helliwell (1969). In the present context, the W_t relate only to lags between appropriations and expenditures, while in Evans and Helliwell (1969) the W_t weights were a convolution of expectations and expenditure lag distributions. The *RPLLAG* distribution for *INRC* is equal to *PLLAG* of Evans and Helliwell (1969) reduced in length by removing the two zeros at the beginning.

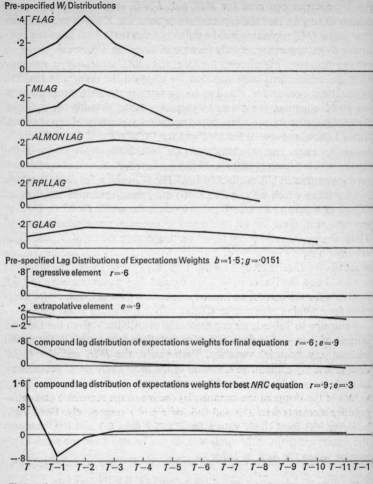

Pre-specified W_i Distributions

FLAG

MLAG

ALMON LAG

RPLLAG

GLAG

Pre-specified Lag Distributions of Expectations Weights $b = 1.5; g = .0151$

regressive element $r = .6$

extrapolative element $e = .9$

compound lag distribution of expectations weights for final equations $r = .6; e = .9$

compound lag distribution of expectations weights for best *NRC* equation $r = .9; e = .3$

T $T-1$ $T-2$ $T-3$ $T-4$ $T-5$ $T-6$ $T-7$ $T-8$ $T-9$ $T-10$ $T-11$ $T-1$

Figure 1

When moving from these independent estimates to a single 'best' set of expectations parameters, we chose that set which minimized the sums of the standard errors of estimate (*SEE*) of *IME* and *INRC*. Since for $b = 1.5$ the *IME* equations differed quite sharply in *SEE* depending on the values assigned to e and r, the final choice of e and r were 0.9 and 0.6, the values which produced the best-fitting *IME* equation. These values yielded *SEE* = 92.7, compared to 91.6 for the *INRC* equation with $e = 0.3$

Table 1 Results of gross investment equations without financial variables

		INRC			IME		
		$r = 0.9$	$r = 0.6$	$r = 0.3$	$r = 0.9$	$r = 0.6$	$r = 0.3$
$b = 0.0$		92·4	92·9	93·9	75·0	61·7	60·0
$b = 0.5$	$e = 0.9$	92·3	92·8	93·8	73·7	59·2	57·7
	$e = 0.6$	92·5	93·1	94·6	76·7	61·1	60·5
	$e = 0.3$	92·4	93·0	94·5	78·1	62·2	61·3
$b = 1.0$	$e = 0.9$	92·2	92·7	93·8	72·2	56·9	56·2
	$e = 0.6$	92·7	93·6	95·5	79·1	66·7	62·8
	$e = 0.3$	92·3	93·2	95·9	82·5	63·4	66·1
$b = 1.5$	$e = 0.9$	92·1	92·7[a]	93·9	70·5	54·9[b]	55·6
	$e = 0.6$	93·0	94·3	96·6	82·8	60·9	67·9
	$e = 0.3$	91·6	94·1	97·8	92·0	67·5	77·6

$$INRC = 0.0934\hat{I} - 1.90TQ1 + 3.39TQ2 + 8.23TQ3 + 5.47TQ4 + 500.65$$
$$\qquad (2.65) \quad (1.56) \quad (2.83) \quad (7.02) \quad (4.76) \quad (19.64)$$
$$SEE = 92.7 \qquad \bar{R}^2 = 0.653 \qquad DW = 0.658$$

$$IME = 0.464\hat{I}Q1 + 0.478\hat{I}Q2 + 0.451\hat{I}Q3 + 0.627\hat{I}Q4 + 292.0Q1$$
$$\qquad (5.30) \qquad (5.83) \qquad (5.68) \qquad (8.19) \qquad (4.93)$$
$$+ 440.9Q2 + 327.3Q3 + 189.6Q4$$
$$\quad (7.78) \quad (5.86) \quad (3.46)$$
$$SEE = 54.9 \qquad \bar{R}^2 = 0.814 \qquad DW = 0.448$$

The estimating form of the equations is shown at the bottom of the table, along with the coefficients and test statistics from the chosen equations. The figures in the body of the table are the standard errors of estimate, in millions o 1957 dollars, of the indicated equations

All equations have expectations defined using twelve previous values of Y. The W_i distributions are Almon for IME and RPLLAG for INRC. The growth rate of Y has been estimated in a separate regression and has the value $g = 0.0151$

$= 0.9$. The coefficients and test statistics for the IME and INRC equations with $e = 0.9$, $r = 0.6$ are shown at the bottom of Table 1.

Our experiments with financial variables are still at a fairly early stage. We have tried the variables which performed well in the RDX1 equations and also a few plausible alternatives. For IME, the cash flow ratio (CFR) was once again the only financial variable which we found to play a significant role (ruling out those interest rate variables with 'significant' coefficients of the wrong sign). The implications of the present model are materially different from those of the RDX1 equation, however, since in the earlier model CFR entered strongly in a current linear form, while it performs best in our present IME equation when given the inverse of the

Almon lag structure[10] and then multiplied by the quarterly calculated investment figures. It was interesting to find that the shape of the likelihood surface, or at least as much of it as was revealed by our experiments, was almost exactly the same with and without the cash flow variable. Thus the expectations pattern that was best in the first model is also best with the cash flow ratio applied with lag weights equal to the inverse of the Almon-distribution (*CFRA*). The only difference is that the standard error of estimate is about $10 million lower, regardless of which set of parameter values is used as the basis for comparison. Only one equation, the best, need therefore be written out. It uses, as before, $b = 1.5$, $e = 0.9$, $r = 0.6$;

$1Q53–4Q65$ *OLS*

$$IME = 0.451\hat{I}(CFRA)(Q1) + 0.584\hat{I}(CFRA)(Q2) + 0.446\hat{I}(CFRA)(Q3)$$
$$(7.05) \qquad\qquad (7.98) \qquad\qquad (7.63)$$
$$+ 0.592\hat{I}(CFRA)(Q4) + 302.2Q1 + 440.5Q2 + 333.4Q3 + 212.4Q4;$$
$$(10.60) \qquad\qquad (6.98) \quad (10.56) \quad (8.13) \quad (5.25)$$
$$SEE = 43.4, \bar{R}^2 = 0.884, DW = 0.701.$$

We then performed a first-order autoregressive transformation of all the data, using $\rho = 0.65$, as estimated by the DW statistic in the above equation, and re-estimated, obtaining a useful reduction in the *SEE* and the following parameter estimates:

$1Q53–4Q65$ *AUTO*

$$IME = 0.551\hat{I}(CFRA)(Q1) + 0.548\hat{I}(CFRA)(Q2) + 0.485\hat{I}(CFRA)(Q3)$$
$$(8.64) \qquad\qquad (8.68) \qquad\qquad (7.83)$$
$$+ 0.611\hat{I}(CFRA)(Q_4) + 240.9Q1 + 401.4Q2 + 308.5Q3 + 200.4Q4;$$
$$(10.22) \qquad\qquad (5.29) \quad (8.95) \quad (6.90) \quad (4.52)$$
$$SEE = 32.8, \bar{R}^2 = 0.900, DW = 1.79.$$

To simplify comparisons in a forecasting context, we used the *OLS* equations in the experiments reported in the next section.

The fact that *CFRA* enters multiplicatively with $\hat{I}$ in the *IME* equation suggests that cash flow plays a restraining role at the time regular investment projects are initiated. This differs somewhat from the role of *CFR* in the corresponding *RDX*1 equation, since, in that model, cash flow had a direct influence only on current expenditures. In the *RDX*1 *INRC* equation, *CFR* was thought to play an expectational role, altering the value of

10. Current investment expenditures are the sum of expenditures on projects started in the present period and in a number of past periods. If all investment projects were started j periods in advance of the indicated capital shortage, then a variable which acts as a constraint at the point of decision should influence actual expenditure with a lag distribution equal to the inverse of the W_t distribution.

the desired capital stock. In order to define an analogous role for *CFR* in our present model, we chose an expectational process for *CFR* and then made desired capital stock in a particular future period equal to expected *CFR* in period $t+1$ times the desired capital–output ratio times expected output. Thus at any point in time, all future values of expected output are multiplied by the same values for expected *CFR*. The argument in favour of this specification is that expected *CFR* is an index of confidence which applies equally to inflate or deflate the expected values of output in all future periods. For simplicity, we assumed that the best expectational process for $Y(b = 1·5, e = 0·9, r = 0·6)$ also applies to *CFR*, except that for *CFR* the growth parameter g equals zero, since *CFR* is a ratio to trend (see Appendix).

We applied this formulation to *INRC*, and then found that we could achieve a better-fitting equation by also including a separate linear variable *CFRR*, defined as *CFR* lagged by the inverse *RPLLAG* weights. The rationale for the inclusion of this latter variable is the same as that for the *IME* structure. We suppose that, in addition to its role as an indicator of confidence, *CFR* plays a constraint role at the time regular investment projects are initiated. The pattern of results is similar to that shown for *INRC* in Table 1, in that the standard errors do not give very clear advice about which is the best set of expectation parameters. The lowest *SEE* (52·6) is for $b = 1·5, e = 0·3, r = 0·9$, just as in the model without financial variables. The model we must choose in order to share the same expectations process for Y in both *IME* and *INRC* equations, is $b = 1·5$, $e = 0·9, r = 0·6$, which has the following estimated structure:

$$INRC = 0·0244\hat{I} - 0·94TQ1 + 3·30TQ2 + 7·78TQ3 + 5·12TQ4 - 293·1$$
$$\quad (3·03) \quad (1·33) \quad (4·79) \quad (11·09) \quad (7·66) \quad (2·70)$$
$$\quad + 797·7 \, CFRR;$$
$$\quad (7·08)$$
$$SEE = 53·7, \bar{R}^2 = 0·884, \text{DW} = 1·51,$$

where $\hat{I}$ is the calculated investment series described in the preceding text.

We did not regard the indicated autocorrelation of residuals in the *INRC* equation as serious enough to make autoregressive transformation and re-estimation worthwhile.

Compared to the *RDX*1 equations, our new equation for *INRC* is clearly inferior to our *IME* equation. It may be that movements in aggregate non-residential construction spending are so sluggish that a model as complicated as ours is a waste of time. At least for the 1953–65 data period, our *INRC* equation is certainly not as good as that used in *RDX*1. The equation for machinery and equipment investment, on the other hand, seems to produce a much higher payoff for our explicit model of expectations. The primary test, however, lies in the forecasting, particularly in the presumed advantage that our present model has in being able to coordinate structural equations with information obtained from the survey of investment intentions.

The model in a forecasting context

In this section we show how our model can be used to make genuine forecasts, ones that do not require any information about the values of either endogenous or exogenous variables during the forecast period. The problem will be discussed in the context of annual forecasts made during the last quarter of the preceding year, since in Canada there are comparable annual surveys (e.g. Canada, Department of Trade and Commerce, 1952) of the investment intentions of business firms. We shall also fit realizations functions which make use of information accumulating during the forecast year.

The usual way of computing an annual forecast from a quarterly investment equation is to add up the predicted values from the quarterly equations. This is usually done by assuming that the values of variables (like Y) outside the investment sector are known for the year but that actual values of investment in the earlier quarters of the year are not known when the forecasts of the later quarters are being made. Thus it is not possible to use knowledge about the autoregressive structure of the errors in order to improve forecasts in the later quarters in the year. Using the terminology of our present model, such a calculated annual value for IME, called $IMEC$, can be defined as follows:

$$IMEC = I\hat{M}E_{t+1,t} + I\hat{M}E_{t+2,t+1} + I\hat{M}E_{t+3,t+2} + I\hat{M}E_{t+4,t+3} \qquad 20$$

where t is the fourth quarter of the year preceding the forecast year.

In general, we would expect that such annual calculated values should be closer to the actual values than would be forecasts which did not make use of actual values of Y generated during the forecast year. Our model can be used to calculate annual forecasts which depend only on information available at the end of the third quarter of the year preceding the forecast year. Such a calculated value is really our model's best estimate of what an aggregate of typical firms would give as a response to a survey conducted in the fourth quarter of the year preceding the forecast year. Naturally, our calculated value will only be a good estimate of what the survey actually turns up if firms do form their expectations in a way something like that assumed by our equations. We refer to our constructed survey figure for IME as $IMESC$, and it is defined as:

$$IMESC = I\hat{M}E_{t+1,t-1} + I\hat{M}E_{t+2,t-1} + I\hat{M}E_{t+3,t-1} + I\hat{M}E_{t+4,t-1}. \qquad 21$$

We have calculated *IMEC* and *IMESC* for our 1953–65 fitting period, and the corresponding series for *INRC*, and have made several annual regressions whose results are shown in Table 2. We would expect that a regression of actual annual investment outlays on *IMEC* and *IMESC* would show the former series to be a better predictor, since it makes use of some actual values, rather than expectations, of *Y* during the forecast year. We might also expect that a regression of the survey figures (*IMES*) on the calculated forecast series *IMESC* would fit more closely than a regression of actual *IME* on *IMESC*, because both *IMES* and *IMESC* are constructed in ignorance of anything that actually happens during the forecast year, while actual *IME* presumably does depend on some actual values of *Y* during the forecast year. If we are lucky, we may also find that a regression of *IME* on our calculated forecast series *IMESC* will fit more closely than a regression of *IME* on the survey series *IMES*.

The results in Table 2 show the foregoing wishful supposition to be true in general, with some interesting exceptions. For *IME* all the suppositions are borne out, except that the calculated forecast series does not forecast as well as the annual intentions survey. For *INRC*, the tables are turned somewhat, as the regression of *INRC* on the calculated forecast series (*INRCSC*) is not only much better than the survey, but is also marginally better than the regression of actual on the calculated actual *INRCC*. However, it remains true, as surmised, that the calculated forecast series is even better as a predictor of the survey *INRCS* than of actual investment *INRC*.

Thus we find, amongst other things, that during the fitting period our forecasting model does better than the investment survey for *INRC* and slightly worse for *IME*. The same is not true beyond the fitting period, however, for our model fails, just as did the *RDX*1 equations, to predict the 1966–7 boom in machinery and equipment expenditures. This boom was such as to drive the actual capital–output ratio for machinery and equipment far above the 'desired' levels assumed by our model. The investment survey, on the other hand, was unusually accurate during these years.

However, we need not stop with a simple comparison of our forecasts with those of the intentions survey, for it may be possible to combine the model with the intentions information to produce better forecasts at different points in time. We have done this for two points in time; the last quarter before the forecast year and the last quarter of the forecast year. In neither case does the method require any information about actual investment during the year, but in the latter case (standing in the fourth quarter of the forecast year) we assume that the values of *Y* for the first three quarters are known.

The 'combined model' for the genuine annual forecast is based on a

Table 2 Annual investment and forecast equations, 1953–65

INRC Non-residential construction	IME Machinery and equipment

Regression of actual on calculated actual

$INRC = 19.0 + 0.992\ INRCC$ $IME = 15.2 + 0.944\ IMEC$
    (0.1) (13.8)   (0.1) (9.7)
   $SEE = 101.1,\ \bar{R}^2 = 0.941,$ $SEE = 144.3,\ \bar{R}^2 = 0.886,$
           DW = 1.95   DW = 0.895

Regression of actual on calculated forecast

$INRC = 5.1 + 0.999\ INRCSC$ $IME = -11.9 + 1.005\ IMESC$
    (0.0) (14.3)   (0.0) (4.9)
   $SEE = 98.0,\ \bar{R}^2 = 0.944,$ $SEE = 251.6,\ \bar{R}^2 = 0.653,$
          DW = 2.04   DW = 1.47

Regression of survey[a] on calculated forecast

$INRCS = 266.2 + 0.925\ INRCSC$ $IMES = -86.3 + 0.983\ IMESC$
    (1.5) (13.4)   (0.3) (8.4)
   $SEE = 96.7,\ \bar{R}^2 = 0.937,$ $SEE = 142.3,\ \bar{R}^2 = 0.853,$
         DW = 1.42   DW = 1.84

Regression of actual on survey

$INRC = -123.0 + 1.019\ INRCS$ $IME = -33.8 + 1.066\ IMES$
    (0.4) (9.7)   (0.1) (8.2)
   $SEE = 140.2,\ \bar{R}^2 = 0.886,$ $SEE = 167.9,\ \bar{R}^2 = 0.846,$
         DW = 1.78   DW = 1.80

Combined forecast model using calculated forecast and survey information

$INRC = 2.0 + 0.998\ INRCSC$ $IME = 104.7 - 0.324\ IMESC$
    (0.0) (3.2)   (0.3) (−0.9)
      $+0.012\ INRCS$ $+1.352\ IMES$
      (0.0)   (3.8)
   $SEE = 102.8,\ \bar{R}^2 = 0.939,$ $SEE = 170.1,\ \bar{R}^2 = 0.842,$
         DW = 2.05   DW = 1.87

Forecast errors:
   66 = 8.5%, 67 = 4.6%,   66 = −3.5%, 67 = −3.6%,
     68 = 5.3%   68 = −14.59%

Realizations model using calculated forecast, calculated actual, and survey information

$INRC = -191.2 + 1.044\ INRCS$ $IME = 54.9 + 1.031\ IMES$
    (0.8) (10.7)   (0.0) (12.7)
      $+0.908\ (INRCC-INRCSC)$ $+0.547\ (IMEC-IMESC)$
      (1.8)   (4.3)
   $SEE = 128.3,\ \bar{R}^2 = 0.904,$ $SEE = 103.8,\ \bar{R}^2 = 0.941,$
         DW = 1.94   DW = 2.02

Forecast errors:
   66 = 3.2%, 67 = −1.8%,   66 = 3.2%, 67 = 10.5%,
     68 = −3.9%   68 = 3.2%

[a] To allow comparison with the constant dollar investment expenditures, the current dollar investment survey figures have been deflated using the appropriate national accounts deflators for the fourth quarter of the year preceding the forecast year

linear regression of actual expenditures (*IME*) on the calculated forecast (*IMESC*) and the investment intentions survey (*IMES*). The combined model for the fourth quarter of the forecast year is what is usually called a 'realizations function' (see Eisner, 1965) estimated in a slightly different form. The usual method is to express the difference between the actual and the survey as a function of events affecting the actual expenditures but not known or not fully taken into account at the time the survey is made. In terms of our model, the relevant linear realizations equation for *IME* in this form would be:

$$IME - IMES = a + b(IMEC - IMESC). \qquad 22$$

If we wish to allow for a proportionate (rather than absolute) bias in the investment survey, we can transfer *IMES* to the other side and estimate the realizations function in the form:

$$IME = a + bIMES + c(IMEC - IMESC). \qquad 23$$

The term in brackets is the difference between the model's best guess of *IME* as seen from the fourth quarter of the forecast year (*IMEC*) and as seen from the fourth quarter of the year preceding the forecast year (*IMESC*).

Table 2 shows the estimated parameters for the 'combined model' and the realizations functions **23** for both *IME* and *INRC*. Below each equation are the percentage annual forecast errors for 1966 to 1968. As we would expect, the realizations functions for *IME* are more accurate than the combined forecast equations, both inside and outside the fitting period. We expect this to be so because the forecast model was only using information available before the forecast year while the realizations model takes account of subsequent events. For *IME* the combined model does not fit any better than the survey, and does not forecast 1966–8 as well. The realizations model fits the data period much better than either, but still does not perform as well as the survey 1966–8. The realizations equation has an average annual percentage error of 5·6 per cent, compared to 4·1 per cent for the current dollar investment survey.[11]

For *INRC* the forecast model (based on *INRCSC*) fits the data period so much better than either the survey or the equation based on *INRCC* that the combined forecast model attaches no importance to the new information represented by the survey. Even the realizations function does

11. The 'actual' figures for 1968 were still on a preliminary basis, and thus did not provide an accurate test of the relative predictive power of the model and the survey. Subsequent revisions to the national accounts reduced 1968 *IME* substantially, thus improving the accuracy of the calculated forecasts relative to the survey.

not fit the data as well as the calculated forecast model, but it does perform best of all our models outside the fitting period, producing estimates for 1966–68 with a mean annual percentage error of slightly less than 3 per cent, compared to an average percentage error of 2·1 per cent for the survey.

We have no satisfactory explanation for the result that the *IME* equation fits better than the *INRC* equation inside the sample period but does not forecast as well beyond this fitting period. This may indicate that changes in technology, price expectations or some other excluded variable have a more marked effect on machinery and equipment than on building expenditures, but we have no direct evidence to hand.

Overall, our forecasting experiments seem to us to indicate considerable promise for the model. The big advantage of the explicit expectations mechanism we employ is that it is easy to prepare forecasts for any future period or periods, and also to combine an explicit model with any extraneous information that is available on a regular basis. Even though our present application of the model is fairly crude, involving explicit expectations about only *Y*, it seems to have reasonable explanatory power, especially when coupled with information from the survey of investment intentions. We believe that a more comprehensive treatment of financial variables will improve the performance of the model, and make it much more useful for simulation purposes. In addition, we suspect that the inclusion of price expectations will help our equations, especially that for *IME*, to deal with the troublesome 1966–8 period, but so far we have not found a satisfactory testable form for our suspicions.

Appendix

Key to the variables

Dependent variables – first stage: quarterly equations

IME	Gross investment in machinery and equipment. Millions of 1957 dollars. Seasonally unadjusted.
INRC	Gross investment in non-residential construction. Millions of 1957 dollars. Seasonally unadjusted.

Independent variables – first stage: quarterly equations

CFR	Cash flow ratio. Cash flow is the sum of corporate retained earnings and depreciation allowances deflated by the ratio of current to constant dollar business capital spending. *CFR* is the ratio of actual deflated cash flow to its linear trend value.
CFRA	Weighted moving average of *CFR*.

CFRR	Weighted moving average of *CFR*.
$IME_{t,\,t-1}$	Synthetic series for actual investment in machinery and equipment, based on information available at the end of quarter $t-1$. Millions of 1957 dollars. Seasonally adjusted.
$IME_{t+1,\,t-1}$	Synthetic series for anticipated investment in machinery and equipment, based on information available at the end of quarter $t-1$. Millions of 1957 dollars. Seasonally adjusted.
$INRC_{t,\,t-1}$	Synthetic quarterly series for actual investment in non-residential construction, based on information available at the end of quarter $t-1$. Millions of 1957 dollars. Seasonally adjusted.
$INRC_{t+1,\,t-1}$	Synthetic quarterly series for anticipated investment in non-residential construction, based on information available at the end of quarter $t-1$. Millions of 1957 dollars. Seasonally adjusted.
KME*	Desired level of stock of machinery and equipment. Millions of 1957 dollars. Seasonally adjusted.
KNR*	Desired level of stock of non-residential construction. Millions of 1957 dollars. Seasonally adjusted.
KME_{t-1}	Net stock of machinery and equipment at the end of quarter $t-1$. Accumulated from seasonally adjusted investment on a base figure for stock using a quarterly depreciation rate of 5 per cent. Millions of 1957 dollars.
KNR_{t-1}	Net stock of non-residential construction at the end of quarter $t-1$. Accumulated from seasonally adjusted investment on a base figure for stock using a quarterly depreciation rate of 1 per cent. Millions of 1957 dollars.
Y	Real domestic product less agriculture. Millions of 1957 dollars. Seasonally adjusted.
ALMON, FLAG, GLAG, MLAG, RPLLAG	Labels of patterns of lead distribution W_i tested and illustrated in Figure 1.
b	Proportion of the extrapolative element in the formation of expectations on *Y*.
g	Constant quarterly rate of growth of *Y*.

γ_i, r	Regressive element in the formation of expectations on Y:
	$$r = \frac{\gamma_{i+1}}{\gamma_i}; \ \Sigma \gamma_i = 1.$$
λ_i, e	Extrapolative element in the formation of expectations on Y:
	$$e = \frac{\lambda_{i+1}}{\lambda_i}; \ \Sigma \lambda_i = 1.$$
ρ	Constant proportional quarterly depreciation rate of the capital stock.

Dependent variables – second stage: annual equations

| IME | Gross investment in machinery and equipment. Millions of 1957 dollars. |
| INRC | Gross investment in non-residential construction. Millions of 1957 dollars. |

Independent variables – second stage: annual equations

IMEC	Synthetic series for actual investment in machinery and equipment. Sum of quarterly estimates calculated in the first stage equation. Millions of 1957 dollars.
IMES	Investment intentions of business firms for machinery and equipment as of the last quarter preceding the forecast year. Deflated by the appropriate National Accounts deflator in the last quarter preceding the forecast year. Millions of 1957 dollars.
IMESC	Synthetic series for intended investment in machinery and equipment. Calculated by solving equation **13**, using the coefficients estimated in the first-stage equations.
INRCC	Synthetic series for actual investment in non-residential construction. Sum of quarterly estimates calculated in the first-stage equation. Millions of 1957 dollars.
INRCS	Investment intentions of business firms for non-residential construction as of the last quarter preceding the forecast year. Deflated by the appropriate National Accounts deflator in the last quarter preceding the forecast year. Millions of 1957 dollars.

INRCSC	Synthetic series for intended investments in non-residential construction. Calculated by solving equation 13, using the coefficients estimated in the first-stage equations.

References

ALMON, S. (1965), 'The distributed lag between capital appropriations and expenditures', *Econometrica*, vol. 33, pp. 178–96.

CANADA, DEPARTMENT OF TRADE AND COMMERCE (1952) (annual), *Public and Private Investment in Canada Outlook*, prepared jointly by the Dominion Bureau of Statistics and the Department of Trade and Commerce, Queen's Printer.

DE LEEUW, F. (1965), 'A model of financial behaviour', in J. S. Duesenberry *et al.* (eds.), *The Brookings Quarterly Econometric Model of the United States*, Rand McNally, pp. 465–32.

DUESENBERRY, J. S. (1958), *Business Cycles and Economic Growth*, McGraw-Hill.

EISNER, R. (1965), 'Realization of investment anticipations', in J. S. Duesenberry *et al.* (eds.), *The Brookings Quarterly Econometric Model of the United States*, Rand McNally, pp. 95–108.

EISNER, R., and STROTZ, R. H. (1963), 'Determinants of business investment', in Commission on Money and Credit, *Impacts of Monetary Policy*, Prentice-Hall, pp. 59–337.

EVANS, R. G., and HELLIWELL, J. F. (1969), *Quarterly Business Capital Expenditures*, Bank of Canada Staff Research Studies, no. 1, Ottawa, p. 82.

GOULD, J. P. (1968), 'Adjustment costs in the theory of investment of the firm', *Rev. econ. Stud.*, vol. 35, pp. 47–55.

HART, A. G. (1965), 'Capital appropriations and the accelerator', *Rev. econ. Stat.*, vol. 47, pp. 123–36.

HELLIWELL, J. F. (1968), *Public Policies and Private Investment*, Clarendon Press.

HELLIWELL, J. F., OFFICER, L. H., SHAPIRO, H. T., and STEWART, I. A. (1969), *The Structure of RDX1*, Bank of Canada Staff Research Studies, no. 3, Ottawa.

JORGENSON, D. W. (1965), 'Anticipations and investment behavior', in J. S. Duesenberry *et al.* (eds.), *The Brookings Quarterly Econometric Model of the United States*, Rand McNally, pp. 35–92.

LUCAS, R. E. (1967), 'Optimal investment policy and the flexible accelerator', *Inter. econ. Rev.*, vol. 8, pp. 78–85.

MODIGLIANI, F., and SUTCH, R. (1966), 'Innovations in interest rate policy', *Amer. econ. Rev.*, vol. 56, pp. 178–97.

WILSON, T. A. (1967), *Capital Investment and the Cost of Capital: A Dynamic Analysis*, Studies of the Royal Commission on Taxation, no. 30, Queen's Printer, p. 127.

Further Reading

The list of suggestions for further reading is in alphabetical order. Some discussion may be useful in relating the titles in this list to the material in the rest of the volume.

To supplement the survey of issues in Part One, there are two survey articles among the suggestions for further reading. The long paper by Eisner and Strotz contains an extensive survey of empirical studies prior to 1960, as well as a difficult but insightful treatment of the theory of adjustment costs. The survey by Jorgenson is especially useful as a retrospective view of the important work by himself and several collaborators. The brief survey by Klein provides a broader and more recent perspective.

The chapter by Locke Anderson in the conference proceedings edited by Fromm provides an eclectic view of investment more recent than Reading 2.

The paper by Rothschild is a fairly difficult recent theoretical contribution to the subject of adjustment costs.

Relating to Part Four, the most important paper is that by Jorgenson and Stephenson containing spirited commentary on Eisner and Nadiri's criticisms in Reading 5. The Eisner and Nadiri reply is also in the list. Jorgenson's survey article probably contains the best statement of his final assessment of the various tests of his version of a neoclassical framework. The paper by Rowley also involves tests of the Cobb–Douglas production function against alternatives.

Hall and Jorgenson's 1967 *American Economic Review* article and their chapter in the Fromm volume have been influential in the study of effects of tax policy on investment. Interested readers should also refer to the related comments and reply in the *American Economic Review* in 1969. The volume edited by Fromm contains a number of useful papers assessing the role of US tax policy in influencing investment expenditure.

In the realm of further developments, the reading list contains Berndt and Christensen's application of a more general logarithmic production function, Nadiri and Rosen's study of interdependent factor demands, and Feldstein and Foot's preliminary study of the determinants of replacement investment.

Those with appetites for a longer reading list may wish to obtain further references from the survey of issues in Part One.

E. R. Berndt and L. R. Christensen, 'The translog function and the substitution of equipment, structures and labor in US manufacturing 1929–68', *J. Econometrics*, vol. 1, 1973, pp. 81–114.

R. Eisner and M. I. Nadiri, 'Neoclassical theory of investment behaviour: a comment', *Rev. econ. Stat.*, vol. 52, 1970, pp. 216–22.

R. Eisner and R. H. Strotz, 'Determinants of business investment', in Commission on Money and Credit, *Impacts of Monetary Policy*, Prentice–Hall, 1963, pp. 59–337.

M. S. Feldstein and D. K. Foot, 'The other half of gross investment: replacement and modernization expenditures', *Rev. econ. Stat.*, vol. 53, 1971, pp. 49–58.

G. Fromm (ed.), *Tax Incentives and Capital Spending*, Brookings Institution, North-Holland, 1971.

R. E. Hall and D. W. Jorgenson, 'Tax policy and investment behavior', *Amer. econ. Rev.*, vol. 57, 1967, pp. 391–414. (See also the comments and reply in vol. 59 of the *Amer. econ. Rev.*).

D. W. Jorgenson, 'Econometric studies of investment behavior: a survey', *J. econ. Lit.*, vol. 9, 1971, pp. 1111–47.

D. W. Jorgenson and J. A. Stephenson, 'Issues in the development of the neoclassical theory of investment behavior', *Rev. econ. Stat.*, vol. 51, 1969, pp. 346–53.

L. R. Klein, 'Issues in econometric studies of investment behavior', *J. econ. Lit.*, vol. 12, 1974, pp. 43–9.

M. I. Nadiri and S. Rosen, 'Interrelated factor demand functions', *Amer. econ. Rev.*, vol. 59, 1969, pp. 457–71.

M. Rothschild, 'On the cost of adjustment', *Q. J. Econ.*, vol. 75, 1971, pp. 605–22.

J. C. R. Rowley, 'Investment functions: which production function?' *Amer. econ. Rev.*, vol. 60, 1970, pp. 1008–12.

Acknowledgements

Acknowledgements are due to the following for permission to reproduce the Readings in this volume:

1 J. F. Helliwell
2 *Econometrica*
3 University of Chicago Press
4 *Review of Economic Studies*
5 *Review of Economics and Statistics*
6 *Review of Economics and Statistics*
7 Brookings Institution
8 American Economics Association
9 *Review of Economic Studies*
10 North-Holland Publishing Company
11 *Review of Economic Studies*
12 *Review of Economics and Statistics*
13 *Review of Economic Studies*

Acknowledgements are also due to many of the authors of the reprinted papers for suggesting improvements to the introductory survey of issues. John Fountain and Robyn Packard provided helpful editorial assistance at an early stage. Richard Harris and Estelle Murray compiled the indexes.

Indexes

Author Index

Abramovitz, M., *93, 277*
Ady, P. H., *231*
Agarwala, R., 207n., 209n., *230*, 241, 245, 251, *255*
Alchian, A., 80n., *93*, 262n., *277*
Almon, S., 35, 42, *48*, 177n., *191*, 208n., 218n., *230*, 310n., 317n., *329*
Ando, A., 25, *48*
Anderson, W. H. L., 18, *48*, 331
Andrews, W. H., 15, *52*
Arrow, K. J., 16, 17, *48*, 103n., *106*, 163n., *191*, 209n., 211n., *230*, 235n., *255*

Balogh, T., 207n., *230*
Balopoulos, E. T., 207n., *230*
Baumol, W. J., 15, *49*
Beale, E. M. L., 141, *155*
Berndt, E. R., *10*, 331
Bischoff, C. W., 17, 19, 22, 23, 26, 32, 45, *49*, 107, 127n., *131*, 133–56, 147, 152n., *155*, 157, 159–92, 206 , 209, 210n., 212n., *230* 234, *255*, 260n., *277*, 302, *305*
Black, J., 207n., *230*
Board of Trade, *255*
Bodkin, R. G., 296n., 297, *305*
Bonini, C. P., 78n., *94*
Brechling, F., 43 , *49*, 53, 267n., *278*
Brown, M., 17, *49*

Cagan, P., 42, *49*, 270n., *278*
Cani, J. S. de, 17, *49*
Cass, D., 236n., *255*
Caves, R .E., *232*
Chenery, H. B., 38, *48*, *49*, 57n., 58n., 73, *74*, 110, *191*
Chow, G. C., 169n., *191*, 267n., *275*, *278*
Christ, C., *50*, *106*
Christensen, L. R., *10* , *331*
Clark, J. M., *74*, 90n., *93*
Clark, P. G., 57n. , 58n., 62, 73
Coen, R. M., 16, 21, 22, 30, 31, 32, 40, 43 , *49*, 134n., 148n., 152, *155*, 157, 193–205, 206 , 221, *230*, 233, *255*, 262n., *278*, 280–305, 282, 296, 299, 302, *305*
Cohen, K. J., 44, *52*
Corner, D. C., 207, *230*
Cyert, R. M., 15, *49*

De Leeuw, F., 34, 37, 42 , 43, *49*, 57–74, 189n., *191*, 201n., *204*, 299, *305*, 308, *329*
Diewert, W. E., *10*
Diwan, R. K., 297, *305*
Douglas, P. H., 17, *49*
Dow, J. C. R., *255*
Driehuis, W., *10*
Dhrymes, P. J., 21, *49*, 112n., *131*, 281, *305*
Duesenberry, J. S., *49*, *51*, *52*, 58n., *74*, *132*, *155*, *191*, 192, 210n., *231*, 308, *329*

Eisenpress, H., 289n., *305*
Eisner, R., 13, 21, 32, 41, 43 , 44, *49*, 57n., 58n., 66, 73, *74*, 80n. , *93*, 95n., 96, 101, 105, *106*, 109–32, *132*, 133–56 *passim*, *155*, 186, 187, *191*, 194n., *204*, 206, 209, 210n., 216, 221, *231*, 259, 260, 262n., 264n., 267n., 268n., *277*, *278*, 299, *305*, 306n. , 314n., 325, *329*, 331
Encarnación, J., 15, *49*
Evans, M. K., 134n., 137n., 148n., *155*, 186, 187, *192*, 210, *231*
Evans, R. G., 17, *49*, 306, 313n., 315, 317n., *329*

Feige, E. L., 42, *50*
Feldstein, M. S., *10*, 17, 23, 24, 25, 41, 42, 45 , *50*, 206–32, 207n., 210n., 211n., 213n., 219, 223n., *231*, 234, 241, 245, 251, *255*, 331, *332*
Ferber, R., *51*, 53, *132*
Fisher, F. M., 27, *50*, 172n., *192*
Flemming, J. S., 23, 25, 42, 45, *50*, 206–32, 234, 241, 245, 251, *255*

Subject Index

More about Penguins and Pelicans

Penguinews, which appears every month, contains details of all the new books issued by Penguins as they are published. From time to time it is supplemented by *Penguins in Print*, which is a complete list of all titles available. (There are some five thousand of these.)

A specimen copy of *Penguinews* will be sent to you free on request. For a year's issues (including the complete lists) please send 50p if you live in the British Isles, or 75p if you live elsewhere. Just write to Dept EP, Penguin Books Ltd, Harmondsworth, Middlesex, enclosing a cheque or postal order, and your name will be added to the mailing list.

In the U.S.A.: For a complete list of books available from Penguin in the United States write to Dept CS, Penguin Books Inc., 7110 Ambassador Road, Baltimore, Maryland 21207.

In Canada: For a complete list of books available from Penguin in Canada write to Penguin Books Canada Ltd, 41 Steelcase Road West, Markham, Ontario.

Introducing Economics

A. A. Sampson, P. D. Kitchen, G. P. Marshall,
B. J. McCormick and R. Sedgwick

Introducing Economics was written as a result of the authors'
dissatisfaction with existing introductory textbooks, and is
intended for those coming to economics for the first time,
whether in school, college or university.

The reluctance of economists to make value judgements has
become increasingly apparent during this century; concentration
on the 'positive' as opposed to the 'normative' side of the
subject has resulted in a refusal by many to acknowledge the
social consequences of the policies they advocate. In looking
more closely at the workings of the State, and in highlighting the
problems of income distribution, poverty and inequality, this
book has attempted to reinstate economics as a moral science.
Marxist analysis is made an explicit part of the study.

Institutions and non-market analysis have been largely ignored
in many of the traditional textbooks, but are included in this
book as an integral part of the economic theory, since 'some
economies and about nine-tenths of the human drama have been
enacted in non-market economies'. Contemporary economic
theory is viewed in its historical context, demonstrating the way
in which theory has emerged from historical problems; it is then
tested against real-world examples. Mathematical techniques and
mathematical exposition are applied to the basic approach, in the
belief that further advances in economics can be greatly assisted
by the use of mathematics.

Each chapter contains a summary and questions which aim to
measure and extend the student's understanding. The material for
this text was tested with students at colleges, institutions and
schools over a three-year period.

Economics of Retailing

Edited by K. A. Tucker and B. S. Yamey

Everyone knows about retailing but, in much economic theory
and analysis, the treatment of it is as if producers sold directly to
consumers - retailers are scarcely present. This volume of
Readings presents the major aspects of the economics of these
missing intermediaries.

In Part One are short extracts from J. S. Mill, A. Marshall and
others on pricing policies and the behaviour of retail prices.
Competition and concentration in retailing are the central topics
of Part Two, while Part Three considers cost functions in
retailing as well as cost structures and differences among
different sizes of firms. The articles in Part Four examine
competition, factor prices, technology and consumer preferences
as constraints on the individual retailer. The last part investigates
various pricing arrangements such as resale price maintenance and
includes a well-known piece on retail trading in Nigeria.